# Managing Employment Relations

6th edition

John Gennard, Graham Judge, Tony Bennett and Richard Saundry

The Chartered Institute of Personnel and Development is the leading publisher of books and reports for personnel and training professionals, students, and all those concerned with the effective management and development of people at work. For details of all our titles, please contact the publishing department:

*tel:* 020 8612 6204

*email:* publish@cipd.co.uk

The catalogue of all CIPD titles can be viewed on the CIPD website:

www.cipd.co.uk/bookstore

An e-book version is also available for purchase from:

www.ebooks.cipd.co.uk

# Managing Employment Relations

## 6th edition

John Gennard, Graham Judge, Tony Bennett and Richard Saundry

**Chartered Institute of Personnel and Development**

Published by the Chartered Institute of Personnel and Development
151 The Broadway, London SW19 1JQ

This edition first published 2016

© Chartered Institute of Personnel and Development, 2016

Designed and typeset by Exeter Premedia Services, India

Printed in Great Britain by Ashford Colour Press Ltd, Gosport, Hampshire

British Library Cataloguing in Publication Data

A catalogue of this publication is available from the British Library

ISBN 9781843983781
eBook ISBN 9781843984351

The views expressed in this publication are the authors' own and may not necessarily reflect those of the CIPD.

The CIPD has made every effort to trace and acknowledge copyright holders. If any source has been overlooked, CIPD Enterprises would be pleased to redress this in future editions.

# CIPD

Chartered Institute of Personnel and Development

151 The Broadway, London SW19 1JQ
Tel: 020 8612 6200
Email: cipd@cipd.co.uk
Website: www.cipd.co.uk
Incorporated by Royal Charter. Registered Charity No. 1079797

# Contents

# Figures and tables

# Author biographies

The late **John Gennard** was Professor of Human Resource Management at the University of Strathclyde.

**Graham Judge** is a Freelance Consultant and Writer specialising in Change Management and Employee Relations.

**Tony Bennet** is currently a Freelance Consultant, Writer and Researcher on HRM.

**Richard Saundry** is Professor of HRM and Employment Relations at Plymouth University.

# Acknowledgments

We would like to thank Keri Dickens, who was extremely helpful and patient when timetables and deadlines ran a little over what had been agreed. We would particularly like to thank Michelle and Rosey and the rest of our families: without their support this book would never have been written.

# Tribute

**John Gennard**

I was first introduced to John in the late 80s when he was heavily involved in the training of lay union officials for the National Graphical Association, one of the 'print' unions, and I was the HR director for a large printing company. His passion for the subject area of 'employee relations' was immediately obvious and he was very keen that the 'lay officials' he was training should be exposed to a management perspective. Consequently, he asked me if I would attend one of the training sessions and speak to the students. This was the beginning of what was to become a very close working relationship that lasted for over 20 years until John's death on 2 February 2011.

By 1990, John had been appointed as the Institute of Personnel and Development's Chief Examiner for Employee Relations and he kindly invited me to become a member of his team of exam markers. In discussing our stance on the standards necessary to achieve a pass mark, John was always very clear about what should be expected of students aspiring to achieve CIPD qualification: they should be very clear on the theoretical principles underpinning employment relationships, but they should be capable of articulating clear practical solutions to the questions they had to answer in the examination papers.

In the mid-90s, the IPD was going through a process of revising the professional examination structure, and invited each of the chief examiners to put forward proposals for a new text to support their subject area. Having agreed to produce a new textbook, John asked me if I would be willing to be his co-author, and we began work on the first edition in 1996. In considering the approach that the book should take, we decided that the principles that underpinned our approach to exam marking should be the basis for the text. Those principles, a balance between the theory and the practical, have been enshrined in every edition we produced from 1996 onwards.

Whilst John was the academic, and I was the practising HR professional, our work was not divided along these lines. John may have been an academic, but he was also a very experienced practitioner who was much in demand as a 'conciliator' in industrial disputes. From my perspective this merely served to strengthen our working relationship.

Working with him was an absolute pleasure, and because our thoughts and approach to the subject were complementary, there were never any serious differences of opinion about either the marking standards we set for the examinations or about the tone and content of the book.

It is because ours was such a close collaboration that I made the decision to hand over the reins for this edition to our two new colleagues, Richard Saundry and Tony Bennett. While staying true to the principles John and I espoused, they have produced an enhanced book that I know John would have been extremely proud to have been associated with, and I would like to dedicate this edition to his memory.

Graham Judge

September 2015

# Walkthrough of textbook features and online resources

## LEARNING OUTCOMES

At the beginning of each chapter a bulleted set of chapter objectives summarises what you expect to learn from the chapter, helping you to track your progress.

## CASE STUDIES

A range of case studies from different countries illustrate how key ideas and theories are operating in practice around the globe, with accompanying questions or activities.

## REFLECTIVE ACTVITY

In each chapter, a number of questions and activities will get you to reflect on what you have just read and encourage you to explore important concepts and issues in greater depth.

## KEY LEARNING POINTS

At the end of each chapter, a bulleted list of the key learning points summarises the chapter and pulls out the most important points for you to remember.

**?**

REVIEW QUESTIONS

1   To what extent do you agree that employers hold the balance of power within the employment relationship?

2   Considering your own job – to what extent do you share the interests of your employer? Which interests are different and how does this shape your attitude to work?

3   Find and consider the way in which a particular industrial dispute is considered in the following newspapers: the *Daily Mail*, the *Guardian* and the *Morning Star* – what perspectives of the employment relationship do you think these stories display?

4   What role do you think gender plays in the way that employment relations are perceived and managed in your organisation?

## REVIEW QUESTIONS

Review questions at the end of each chapter will test your understanding of the chapter and highlight any areas of development before you move on to the next chapter.

EXPLORE FURTHER

BUDD, J. and BHAVE, D. (2008) Values, ideologies and frames of reference in industrial relations. In BLYTON, P. *et al* (eds). *SAGE handbook of industrial relations.* London: SAGE. pp92–113.

CULLINANE, N. and DUNDON, T. (2006) The psychological contract: a critical review. *International journal of management reviews.* Vol 8, No 2. pp113–129.

DUNLOP, J. T. (1958) *Industrial relations systems.* New York: Holt.

EDWARDS, P. (2003) The employment relationship and the field of industrial relations. In EDWARDS, P. (ed). *Industrial relations.* 2nd ed. Oxford: Blackwell, pp1–36.

FOX, A. (1974) *Beyond contract: work, power and trust relations.* London: Faber.

## EXPLORE FURTHER

Explore further boxes contain suggestions for further reading and useful websites, encouraging you to delve further into areas of particular interest.

## ONLINE RESOURCES FOR TUTORS

- PowerPoint slides – design your programme around these ready-made lectures.
- Lecturer's guide – including guidance on the activities and questions in the text.
- Additional case studies – these can be used as a classroom activity, for personal reflection and individual learning, or as the basis for assignments.

## ONLINE RESOURCES FOR STUDENTS

- Annotated web-links – click through to a wealth of up to date information online
- Regular updates – access the very latest in employment relations

## EBOOK BUNDLING

CIPD have partnered with Shelfie to offer print and eBook bundling. Shelfie has built a free eBook bundling app for iOS and Android that allows you to get a discounted eBook if you own the print edition.

Visit www.bitlit.com/how-it-works/

# CHAPTER 1

# Introduction

## OVERVIEW

### LEARNING OUTCOMES

The key themes that underpin this book are that:

- an employment relations system consists of actors, their institutions, and government agencies, and is set within its own economic, legal, social and technological environmental context
- changes in this corporate environment impact on the balance of bargaining power between the employers and employees and on the employment relations policies adopted as a result by an organisation
- Europe and European institutions, and increasingly global pressures, influence the employment relationship, and that there is a need for practitioners to be aware of, and understand, these influences
- there is a need to understand and appreciate the relevance of employment relations within both unionised and non-union environments
- if employers are to engage their employees and improve organisational performance, management approaches to employment relations need to reflect and promote fairness, equity and trust
- negotiation, communication, consultation, listening, persuasion and presentation are all key employment relations skills
- line managers in particular need support in developing people management skills
- there is a growing imperative to devise coherent strategies and practices for managing workplace conflict.

In the last three decades, employment relations has undergone significant change. Union membership has declined rapidly, collective bargaining has contracted and there has been a significant and seemingly permanent reduction in the incidence of strikes and other forms of industrial action. At the same time, the development of human resource management has put an emphasis on communication, employee engagement and business performance. In this context, students sometimes question the relevance of employment relations for the contemporary HR practitioner. To this end, in this opening chapter we set out the case for acquiring the knowledge, skills and insight that underpin employment relations.

## 1.1 THE RELEVANCE OF EMPLOYMENT RELATIONS

First, employment relations is not only relevant to the management of people in unionised organisations. On the contrary, its fundamental objective is to understand and, therefore, more effectively manage the employment relationship between employer and employee, irrespective of whether or not that individual belongs to a trade union. Furthermore, despite the increasingly individualised nature of employment relations, collective relationships still exist in all organisations which require appropriate channels of voice through, for example, collective bargaining, employee councils or joint consultative committees. Similarly, in both unionised and non-unionised environments, employee grievances have to be resolved, disciplinary matters processed, procedures devised, implemented, operated, reviewed and monitored.

Second, the study of employment relations provides practitioners with insights that are largely missing in other management disciplines. A core objective of this book is to broaden our readers' understanding of the management of power and conflict in the workplace. The interests of different parties within any organisation do not always align. This book is designed to help you to identify the causes of conflict and to develop responses and strategies to the benefit of both the organisation and its employees. For instance, a fundamental employment relations concept is the relative balance of bargaining power between the buyers and sellers of labour services. If certain knowledge and skills are scarce in the labour market, or unions are strong in a particular sector, employees are more likely to be able to negotiate improved terms and conditions. Conversely, if labour is cheap and easily replaceable, or unions are less strong or absent from a workplace, the employer is more likely to be able to set the agenda for any discussion on the terms and conditions of employment for its workforce.

Third, the context within which organisations operate is central to the study and practice of employment relations. Bargaining power is shaped by the external environment and therefore changes in product and labour markets, government economic policy or employment legislation fundamentally shift the terms on which employers and employees interact. Good examples are the changes in representational rights in grievance and disciplinary procedures and the statutory recognition procedures contained in the Employment Relations Act (1999), which provided an opportunity for trade unions to gain a foothold in organisations that were hostile to their involvement. In contrast, the financial crash and subsequent recession of 2008 radically reduced the bargaining power of labour, and growing employment insecurity meant that workers accepted deteriorating terms and conditions in order to stay in work. At the time of writing, the Employment Bill (2015) proposes new restrictions on the ability of trade unions to take industrial action, which will strengthen the hand of managers when negotiating with trade unions. We investigate the merits and limitations of such laws later in the book, but, crucially, the professional employment relations manager has to be capable of offering advice on how their organisation might deal with such situations that stem from decisions over which they have no direct control. This book is designed to help in this regard.

Fourth, changes in the corporate environment help to explain the dynamic nature of employment relations. In the late 1960s and early 1970s, in the context of rising prices, low unemployment and with the pay of most employees decided by collective bargaining, trade union membership grew steadily, strike action was more frequent, and higher wage increases were obtained by employees from their employers. Today, trade union membership has fallen, strike action is relatively rare and most employers are able to decide unilaterally on the rules and regulations that govern employment and, courtesy of low inflation, wage increases are much smaller. Employment relations professionals require an understanding of the impact of such changes so that they can develop an effective and realistic employment relations strategy.

Fifth, in conducting their employee relations activities, professional managers should behave in a fair and reasonable manner and seek to persuade their management colleagues to behave similarly. This means acting with just cause and conducting all stages of employment relations procedures in a way that is compatible with the standards of natural justice. For example, as we explain in Chapter 12, when handling a disciplinary matter, it is crucial that: the employee concerned is aware of the detail of allegation against them; they are given the opportunity to respond to this; they are provided with the opportunity to be accompanied to a disciplinary hearing; and they can appeal against any decision that is made. However, practitioners must also appreciate why such 'good practice' is essential to protecting and advancing the interests of the organisation – namely, the avoidance of costly and damaging litigation but also, and perhaps more importantly, establishing a degree of workplace justice which can in turn secure the trust and engagement of employees. In short, good employment relations practice also helps to underpin high levels of productivity and performance.

Finally, it is crucial to acknowledge that the effective management of change and innovation in employment relations policies and practices is essential in a modern economy. This involves being able to analyse the suitability of new processes and practices, and anticipating any problems with implementation, and, in particular the wider implications for relationships with key stakeholders. However, this also requires employment relations professionals to be able to identify the different negotiating situations in which managers may find themselves, appreciate the different stages through which negotiation may proceed, and be familiar with the skills required.

More broadly, a fundamental objective of this book is to equip our readers with the key knowledge, skills and insight to successfully satisfy the requirements of the CIPD professional standards. We understand that many students who study employment relations have very little prior knowledge or understanding of the subject and have often graduated in other disciplines or perhaps come to study through their managerial experience. For this reason, we try to provide the necessary basic knowledge to understand employment relations and also the perspectives to allow for a more critical and nuanced analysis of the subject.

## ? REFLECTIVE ACTIVITY 1.1

What are your initial thoughts on the study and practice of employment relations? Which areas have you had experience of already in your professional work? Which areas appear challenging and why? What strategy might you adopt to overcome these challenges in your study and practice?

## 1.2 THE CIPD HR PROFESSION MAP

In the last two decades or more there has been a shift in the focus of the HR profession. It is now increasingly charged with improving the performance of the organisation by building sustainable organisational capability – not just delivering on the day-to-day people management role, although that remains important. In light of this trend, the CIPD decided that a radical re-visioning was necessary to equip the profession for the challenge ahead. So, in 2008, it commissioned one of the most comprehensive surveys of the HR community yet undertaken. Around 4,500 people answered detailed questions about their job, their professional needs and their aspirations. The results showed that:

- increasing numbers of HR people go beyond their traditional role and are now required to understand what drives business performance and to bring into focus the employee capabilities their organisations will need in the future
- whereas 50% of participants saw themselves as HR generalists, 50% saw themselves as specialists – for example, in the areas of reward, learning and development and

employment relations – but also in roles such as that of 'business partner'. They wanted to go narrower and deeper in their basic and subsequent training

- 30% had an international dimension to their job
- 29% were studying. This included recent entrants studying to become CIPD-qualified but also people doing MBAs and other master's degree programmes. The survey demonstrated that members of the HR community were looking for more structured learning and accreditation as they progressed in their careers.

The key messages from the survey were:

1   There is a greater need for HR practitioners to know the organisation inside out. They are increasingly required to demonstrate an understanding of business strategy and an ability to apply that understanding while working in partnership with senior people to contribute to organisational performance.

2   The profession has become broader in reach, with greater depth in its expertise and a greater number of critical specialisms.

3   HR professionals rely on a combination of technical knowledge (what you need to know), practical application (what you need to do) and behaviours (how you need to do it). The research showed clearly that what defines HR professionals is practical application.

A major feature of this book is that it is based on a critical analysis and understanding of the key concepts and context of employment relations, in order for students to subsequently be able to successfully apply that knowledge in a practical way in the workplace. This approach is grounded in the recognition that the key challenge facing HR professionals is to move from a primary focus on supporting line managers to ensuring that the organisation has the sustainable capability it needs to deliver its aims both today and in the future.

The CIPD HR Profession Map has been informed by an extensive and ongoing programme of consultation with senior HR professionals and their leaders in business, the public services and management education. The clear message is that in order to deliver 'sustainable capability', HR practitioners need to:

- know their organisation and understand the drivers of sustainable business performance and the barriers to achieving it
- know the main ways in which HR expertise can make an impact and contribute beyond the confines of the traditional role
- have the behavioural skills to turn knowledge into effective action.

The current version (2014) of *The CIPD Profession Map: Our Professional Standards* can be found on the CIPD website. It charts the profession across three main dimensions – functional specialisms, levels of competence and key behaviours. The map contains ten different HR specialisms, which are referred to as the *professional areas*. These are:

- strategy, insights and solutions
- leading and managing the function
- organisation design
- resourcing and talent planning
- organisational development
- learning and talent development
- performance and reward
- employment relations
- employee engagement
- information and service delivery.

Each specialist area has four bands of competence moving from what might reasonably be expected of an entry-level practitioner (Band 1) through to what is essential expertise for a board-level HR director (Band 4). Examples of an activity at four levels of competence might be:

- Band 4 (HR director) – Leads processes to identify, articulate and reinforce the organisation's core values and behavioural expectations, and influences leadership at all levels to behave in a manner that is consistent with them.
- Band 3 – Develops ongoing communications and management plans to ensure that employees and other stakeholders understand and respect the organisation's values and behavioural expectations and act in accordance with them.
- Band 2 – Ensures that the values and behavioural expectations permeate through the organisation's processes, policies, intranet and other literature.
- Band 1 (entry-level) – Advises staff and managers about the organisation's values and behavioural expectations.

For example, in *Employment relations*, practitioners in their first job are required to develop their understanding of the organisation's goals in employment relations and how activity in this area contributes to delivering them. They are expected to feed ideas and observations to senior colleagues, to look for ways to support line managers more effectively, and to evaluate the impact of their work.

In addition to the ten professional areas and four levels of professional competence, the HR Profession Map sets out eight behaviours corresponding to what HR practitioners need in order to be effective. These behaviours are divided into three clusters:

*Insights and influence*

- Curious
- Decisive thinker
- Skilled influencer

*Operational excellence*

- Driven to deliver
- Collaborative
- Personally credible

*Stewardship*

- Courage to challenge
- Role model

Let us take the example of 'Courage to challenge'. In broad terms, someone exhibiting this behaviour 'shows courage and confidence to speak up and challenge others, even when confronted with resistance or unfamiliar circumstances'. This behaviour will then be used and demonstrated in different ways depending on the seniority of the role – or in Map terms, the Band. For instance, one component of 'Courage to challenge' develops in this way:

- Band 4 (HR director) – Acts as a 'mirror' to colleagues' challenging actions which are inconsistent with expressed values, beliefs and promises.
- Band 3 – Holds own position determinedly and with courage when it is the right thing to do, even when those in power have divergent views.
- Band 2 – Observes, listens, questions and challenges to ensure full discussion.
- Band 1 (entry-level) – Uses questions to explore and understand others' viewpoints, taking these into account.

An individual with the CIPD Associate Membership qualification should be capable of adding value to their organisation. They cannot do this on their own – they need to collaborate with others both within and outside the organisation. These outcomes are not necessarily what an academic would emphasise in a master's degree programme. Here, students would be expected to be aware of the plurality of perspectives on employment relations issues and themes, and be able to critically evaluate competing theories and perspectives. Skills development to solve employment relations problems would have much less emphasis. In this version of the book, we have sought to integrate the rigour of critical analysis of competing theories and concepts of employment relations but, crucially, also the tangible application of that knowledge in the day-to-day practice of the discipline.

 **REFLECTIVE ACTIVITY 1.2**

Reflecting on the requirements to attain the professional standards, through our discussion so far and by visiting the CIPD website, how might you begin to plan the achievement of the employment relations elements of the Profession Map? In what way will you utilise the book to this end?

## 1.3 THE INFLUENTIAL MANAGER

It is clear from the discussion so far that if HR practitioners, at any level of seniority, are to be proactive and to have influence in an organisation, they must demonstrate certain abilities (see Figure 1.1). First, they require a successful record of professional competence in the HRM field, which is recognised by their managerial colleagues both within and outside the HR function. Second, they must demonstrate an understanding of the HR function as a whole and how its separate components integrate. Third, they must understand the interests of the organisation. Fourth, they must develop a network of contacts with managers, both within and outside the HR function, in their own organisation and with managers in other organisations, including employers' associations and professional bodies such as the Chartered Institute of Personnel and Development (CIPD) and the British Institute of Management (BIM). Fifth, they also need to build fruitful relationships with their superiors and to possess excellent interpersonal skills, particularly with respect to communications and team-building. Each of these five abilities is a necessary condition for an effective and influential personnel/HRM professional practitioner – and each is insufficient on its own.

Figure 1.1 The abilities required of an HR practitioner

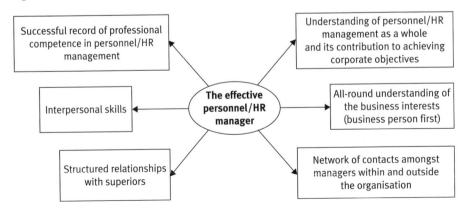

All people managers, regardless of their seniority, need to understand the nature of business in the organisation in which they manage in terms of its mission, objectives, strategies and policies. In the private sector, effective and influential HR practitioners will understand the 'bottom line' for the business and be able to contribute constructively, at the appropriate level of decision-making, to discussions on how the business might be developed and expanded. In the public sector, the effective and influential HR practitioner will understand how employment relations are linked to the quality of service delivery, efficiency and value for money.

The effective HR practitioner can also explain how the various components of resourcing, development, reward and relations contribute to the achievement of the objectives of the HR function. This means that he or she must fully understand how the strategies and policies of the components of the HR function link together to achieve the goals of the function.

The discussion in the book also centres on the growing trend in many organisations to devolve responsibility for HR across management teams. Devolution often means that the services of an HR practitioner with a specialism will not always be required. However, the activities of the employment relations function must nevertheless be delivered to the management team. Generalist HR practitioners with employment relations skills are essential to any management team. This book therefore aims to provide the generalist HR practitioner – and crucially any other managers who have to manage people – with the appropriate employment relations knowledge and skills necessary to successfully solve people management problems.

## 1.4 THE STRUCTURE OF THE BOOK

To summarise our discussion so far, the CIPD employment relations specialism centres on understanding, analysing and critically evaluating:

- different theories and perspectives on employment relations
- the impact of local, national and global contexts in shaping employment relations
- the roles and functions of the different parties in the control and management of the employment relationship
- the strategic integration of employment relations processes and how they impact on key people management policy, practice and organisational outcomes such as employee engagement and employee performance
- the strategic importance of involving employees in decision-making through employee voice mechanisms such as communications, consultation and collective negotiation
- the need to develop and deliver coherent policies, practices and procedures for effectively managing all elements of conflict in the workplace.

To facilitate the acquisition of the key knowledge and skills set out in the Profession Map, and to reflect the emergence of new issues and arguments in the field of employment relations, the structure of the book has been substantially revised for this sixth edition.

Following this introductory chapter, the book is set out in three interlinked sections. In section 1, encompassing Chapters 2 to 5, we aim to equip the reader with knowledge and understanding of the main concepts and models of employment relations needed to critically analyse the themes and debates developed in the book and, crucially, to be able then to apply that understanding in practical situations. This section also covers in detail the context, or environment, in which employment relations are played out in the modern workplace and the challenges this presents for all HR practitioners. The discussion considers the impact, for instance, of changes of government on employment policy and practice in the UK, the impact of employment legislation on organisations and also the environmental impact on business of EU membership and the continuing growth in globalisation.

Section 2 commences with Chapter 6 and a review of the role of strategy. As we have noted in relation to the Profession Map, much weight is accorded to the notion of employee engagement, in order to gain the commitment of the workforce. It is a key element of employment relations strategy and practice and is considered in depth in Chapter 7. The discussion in this section highlights the centrality of effective leadership, which is explored in Chapter 8 in relation to the role of the line manager, which, given the devolution of people management, is increasingly important in shaping employment relations. Similarly, the theory and practice of employee voice underpins effective workforce engagement. Therefore in Chapter 9 we critically review the development of employee representation in UK workplaces before examining the nature and impact of processes designed to facilitate employee involvement and participation in Chapter 10. Section 2 closes with a model that incorporates all the key concepts covered in the first two sections and acts as a bridge to the discussions in the final section.

Chapter 11 offers a conceptual framework for understanding the notion of workplace conflict and also contextualising the debates that take place in the subsequent chapters. This final section of the book reflects the growing recognition by both practitioners and writers of the need for the HR professional, and indeed all managers, to strategically address, through policy and practice, the causes and consequences of conflict in the workplace. To this end, Chapters 11 to 15 cover in detail each of the key areas of conflict management: discipline and performance management, responding to employee grievances, managing redundancies and, a more contemporary development, workplace mediation.

In this way, this text is designed to fully support the CIPD-accredited employment relations specialist module by also covering the skills required by an employment relations professional practitioner in handling employee complaints against management behaviour (commonly referred to as grievances), in handling disciplinary proceedings, in managing a redundancy situation and in managing health and safety. It additionally covers the management skills, knowledge and understanding required in devising, reviewing and monitoring procedural arrangements, and negotiation (collective and individual). Given the fundamental importance of equality and diversity to all aspects of organisational life and, therefore, the study and practice of employment relations, this key element of managing people is integrated into all chapters as appropriate. The book closes with a concluding chapter, which revisits in summary the key themes and issues raised in the previous discussions and reflects also on the future nature of employment relations, the opportunities and challenges this may present to organisations and, specifically, the HR practitioner and line manager.

*We hope you enjoy reading this book. If you can acquire and develop a deep understanding and appreciation of its contents, you will have an excellent chance of reaching the CIPD practitioner Professional Standards in Employment Relations.*

**Tony Bennett, Richard Saundry and Graham Judge**

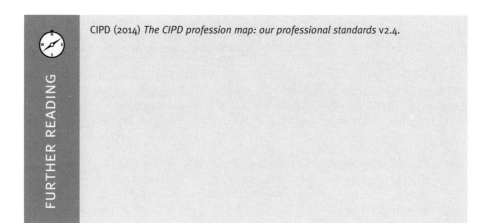

**FURTHER READING**

CIPD (2014) *The CIPD profession map: our professional standards* v2.4.

# CHAPTER 2

# The Concepts and Processes of Employment Relations

## OVERVIEW

This chapter is in three parts. First we explain and define employment relations, which we argue is fundamentally concerned with the way that employers, employees, government and other third parties use a range of rules and processes to negotiate and regulate behaviour at the level of workplace and the work community. We then outline the roles played by the key employment relations actors and their interests and also examine the main theoretical perspectives that have been developed to explain and understand employment relations. We explore systems theory and the main frames of reference before going on to discuss more radical approaches such as labour process theory and feminist perspectives of employment relations. Finally, we identify and examine the core processes used to regulate the employment relationship.

## LEARNING OUTCOMES

When you have completed this chapter, you should be able to:

- understand and analyse the nature of the employment relationship
- describe the key actors (the participants) in employment relations and critically evaluate the roles that they play and their interests
- critically assess competing theoretical approaches to employment relations
- understand the main processes available to employers and employees through which the employment relationship is regulated and conflict is mediated and accommodated
- assess different perspectives of the role and implications of employment relations processes.

## 2.1 INTRODUCTION

Forty years ago, the conventional approach to employment relations centred on the collective regulation of labour through bargaining between trade unions and employers. This was underpinned by a legal and policy framework developed by government, which also intervened in its role as employer to influence the negotiation of pay and conditions. The relationship between employers and individual employees was seen as secondary. However, the institutions of employment relations have been progressively eroded to the point at which, in 2011, the *Workplace Employment Relations Study* reported that more than three-quarters of workplaces in Britain had no union members at all and, in private manufacturing, unions were recognised in fewer than 10% of workplaces (van Wanrooy *et al*, 2013).

The driving force behind the erosion of collective employment relations has been a marked change in the political and economic context. As we explore in Chapters 3 and 4, the election of the Conservative Government under Margaret Thatcher, its commitment to free market economics and hostility to organised labour was a seminal moment in British employment relations. However, a global process of deindustrialisation was already well under way by the end of the 1970s, with the consequent decline of industries, which epitomised collective institutional approaches to employment relations. Furthermore, the growing dominance of the service sector, economic globalisation and rapid technological change have had a profound impact on the composition of the labour market, the nature of product market competition and the demand for knowledge and skills.

In this very different environment, the balance of workplace bargaining power and the focus of employment relations has shifted towards a greater emphasis on the relationship between the individual employee and the employer. The day-to-day preoccupation of employment relations is no longer the negotiation of wages and other terms and conditions through trade unions but the management of performance and attempts to secure employee engagement. Employment relations specialists are less concerned with collective industrial action than with individual expressions of conflict (Dix *et al*, 2009).

Nonetheless, despite these significant changes, the basic purpose of employment relations remains the same: to establish rules, agreements and processes to regulate the employment relationship. Moreover, it is concerned with how to gain, in a number of different situations, employees' commitment to the achievement of an organisation's goals and objectives, and also to successfully manage and negotiate organisational change.

## 2.2 WHAT IS EMPLOYMENT RELATIONS?

To answer this question, we first have to understand the nature of the employment relationship. In some ways, this can be seen as a simple economic transaction, an exchange of labour for pay. However, it is much more complex than, for example, buying a house or a car. First, the terms of the transaction and the relationship are shaped by the bargaining power of the parties and, in most cases, this is unequal, with the employer enjoying the more powerful position. This is because the employer can replace the employee much more easily than the employee can find work. The employer does not have to employ the worker, but the worker needs to be employed (and to be paid) in order to provide themselves and their family with a reasonable standard of living. Second, and partly as a result of this, there is an authority relationship between employer and employee. By agreeing to work for the employer, the employee undertakes to 'obey' any reasonable instructions that they are given. Third, the employment contract is open-ended and indeterminate. While the employer can buy the employees' capacity to work, how that work is performed cannot be set out in sufficient detail in a contract of employment. It is this gap in the contract of employment that employment relations has to fill.

Therefore, employment relations is concerned with developing, applying and negotiating processes and rules through which the employment relationship is conducted and regulated. It is also about trying to develop and maintain trust and confidence between employers and employees. A central element is determining the wages that employees will be paid. Of course, when an employee accepts a job they also accept the wage that is offered or negotiated at the time. However, as the job progresses and the situation and contexts change, that wage (or the other elements of the employment package) may not be adequate to maintain commitment, effort and performance. For example, as we discuss later in this book, key antecedents of employee engagement are trust and perceptions of procedural and distributional justice (Purcell, 2012; Saks, 2006). In short, if people feel they are being rewarded and recognised fairly, they are likely to be committed to the organisation. In this way there is an ongoing negotiation and renegotiation of what Behrend (1957) termed the 'wage-effort bargain'.

However, as Watson (1995) argues, this overemphasises the material rewards of work and the 'factory shop-floor situation'. Instead, he suggests that there is an 'implicit contract' between employers and employees, which reflects the broad range of issues that shape the nature of the employment relationship. These include autonomy, control, security, satisfaction, status and power and the balance of these issues will affect employees' attitudes to both work and employment. In recent years, the notion of the 'psychological contract' has become increasingly fashionable and influential. While in its original form the psychological contract refers to the mutual expectations of employer and employee (see for example Schein, 1978), more contemporary iterations (see for example Rousseau, 1995) have tended to focus on the obligations of the individual employee and neglected reciprocal obligations on the part of the employer (Guest, 2004). Moreover, as Cullinane and Dundon (2006) point out, it provides a singularly individualised account of the employment relationship, which is relegated to an exercise in the securing of organisational engagement. They argue that the employment relationship is not only unequal but is formed and reformed within a complex and dynamic set of social, economic and institutional relationships, and it is to this that we now turn.

## 2.3 ACTORS AND INTERESTS IN EMPLOYMENT RELATIONS

The nature and quality of employment relations is ultimately defined by the interaction between three main 'actors': employers, employees (and their representatives) and the State.

### 2.3.1 EMPLOYERS AND MANAGERS

More than 80% of employees (24.4 million) work in the private sector and of these more than 14 million work in small and medium-sized enterprises (SMEs), which employ 250 workers or fewer. In fact, 99% of private businesses are SMEs. Many of these are owned and managed by either an individual or family and have no shareholders. Employment relations in SMEs tend to be highly personal and informal, and only a small number of SMEs will have a specialist HR function, often relying on consultants, lawyers, employers' associations or Acas for HR and employment relations advice (Forth et al, 2006).

In SMEs there is often no, or little, separation between the employer and the manager. In contrast, many larger private companies are owned by shareholders but controlled by a professional cadre of managers with the support of a specialist HR function. Some commentators have argued that managers' and shareholders' interests may diverge and certainly the way that employment relations are managed may be dictated by the demands of shareholders – for example, shareholder demands for higher profitability may lead to attempts to reduce costs through restricting pay or downsizing. However, research has generally shown that views of managers and owners are similar (Zeitlin, 1989). Larger companies may also establish productive capacity or service provision in other countries or be part of a company owned and controlled outside the UK. As we discuss in Chapter 5, this can significantly shape the nature of employment relations.

About 1 million workers are also employed by not-for-profit organisations, which are usually small and have social rather than economic objectives. They do, however, include some large organisations such as Oxfam, the Save the Children Fund, the British Heart Foundation, local housing associations and the Red Cross. The voluntary sector also contains worker or producer co-operatives where the enterprise is owned and controlled by its members.

The largest single employer in the UK is the Government, with 5.7 million public sector employees. The majority of public sector workers are employed in the NHS (1.6 million), education (1.5 million) and local government (1.1 million). In these areas, employment relations are conducted at arms' length from government, with relatively autonomous and complex managerial structures. The emphasis on the delivery of public services rather than profit maximisation could be argued to shape the orientation of management and employment relations. In addition, the Government has traditionally used its position as an employer to set a 'good example' for others. Partly as a consequence of these factors, public sector employment has tended to be characterised by job stability, long tenure, high levels of union involvement and relatively good pay and conditions. Moreover, public sector workplaces are more likely to have specialist employment relations managers (van Wanrooy *et al*, 2013). This is also reflected in managerial attitudes. For example, public sector managers are more receptive to trade unions than their private sector counterparts (Bach *et al*, 2009).

However, over the last three decades, the differences between the orientations of private and public sector employers has changed significantly, as the Government has demanded what it sees as better 'value for money' and the public sector has been exposed to competitive pressures through the privatisation and marketisation of public services (Bach *et al*, 2009). In recent years, under the Coalition Government elected in 2010 and the new Conservative Government elected in 2015, there has been a major shift from public to private sector employment and a more hostile approach to the activities of public sector trade unions. This is examined in greater detail in the next chapter.

The interests of employers are also represented by employers' associations. In the private sector, the most well known of these are the CBI (Confederation of British Industry), FSB (Federation of Small Business), BCC (British Chambers of Commerce) and the EEF (Engineering Employers' Federation). In the public sector, similar bodies include the LGA (Local Government Association) and NHS Confederation. Although employers' associations, particularly in the public sector, play some role in national-level collective bargaining, their main functions are to represent their members through campaigning and lobbying the policy decision-making bodies of the UK Government and the European Union. In addition, employers' associations increasingly provide their members with specific advice and guidance services on employment relations issues.

---

**?    REFLECTIVE ACTIVITY 2.1**

What do the contents of the CBI website (www.cbi.gov.uk) and its Twitter feed (@CBItweets) suggest about its perspective on employment relations and its main priorities?

---

### 2.3.2 EMPLOYEES, REPRESENTATIVES AND UNIONS

Some employees attempt to strengthen and enhance their interests by presenting a collective face to the employer, notably in relation to their terms and conditions. The main way they do this is through trade unions. We explore the history and development of the function of trade unions in much greater detail in Chapter 9; however, there are essentially three different types of unions. First, occupation-based unions – for example, BALPA (airline pilots) and ASLEF (train drivers) – focus on recruiting employees who perform certain jobs. Second, 'industrial' unions confine their recruitment to all grades of employees employed in a particular industry. Third, General unions, such as the GMB, organise any workers regardless of skill across the boundaries within and between industries. Similarly, the largest UK union, Unite – formed in 2007 by the merger between AMICUS and the Transport and General Workers' Union – organises professional, craft and lesser-skilled employees in manufacturing, financial services, the public sector, transport and construction centres. The Trades Union Congress (TUC), established in 1868, acts as the collective voice of the UK trade union movement to government and international trade union bodies (such as ETUC and the International Confederation of Trade Unions), as well as attempting to influence the behaviour of its affiliated unions.

Unions are generally structured into local branches. These may be located within regions, certain professions or workplaces and elected branch officials will tend to deal with workplace-level issues. Branches are supported by regional offices, which will normally be led by elected officials but will also contain full-time employed regional officers or organisers. These officers may be called on to deal with more serious issues or to respond to issues that have wider implications. The union's leadership will be located at the national headquarters, which deals with national bargaining and broader policy issues.

Traditionally, most union representation tended to revolve around collective bargaining and negotiation with the employer or employers' associations over terms and conditions. But increasingly, as collective bargaining has declined, a significant part of union work is representing individual members in conflict with their employer. This can involve informal discussions, representation at disciplinary, grievance or absence meetings and in some cases supporting members through employment tribunal action. These issues are discussed in greater detail in Chapter 9.

> ### ? REFLECTIVE ACTIVITY 2.2
>
> What do you think are the main reasons why people join trade unions? Do you think these reasons are as relevant today as when the TUC was formed in 1868?

In 2014, there were just 6.4 million union members in the UK, approximately one-quarter of the workforce. This represents a significant reduction from the peak of more than 13 million in 1979 (BIS, 2015). Furthermore, unions bargain over their members' wages and conditions in only 13% of all workplaces and just 6% in the private sector (van Wanrooy et al, 2013). However, trade unions still play an influential role within employment relations. Almost all (91%) public sector workplaces are unionised, as are half of all workplaces with 50 employees or more. Although trade union membership has declined significantly in recent years, there has not been a corresponding growth in non-union forms of representation. As we discuss in Chapter 9, despite some high-profile examples like the business improvement group system in Marks & Spencer PLC, non-union representatives can be found in just 7% of workplaces. Furthermore, non-union representatives play a very different role and are much less likely to be involved with negotiation of terms and conditions, and the representation of workers in disciplinary and grievance hearings (van Wanrooy et al, 2013).

### 2.3.3 THE STATE

As we noted above, the State plays a substantial role in shaping the way that employment relations are conducted, through its role as an employer. However, it also has an important influence in two main respects. First, through legislation, it provides a regulatory framework within which employment relations is conducted. It is also responsible for the machinery through which these laws are enforced; the system of employment tribunals and the wider judicial system, including the Court of Appeal and the Supreme Court. Second, as we explore in the next chapter, the Government has a significant impact on employment relations through its management of the economy and the consequent effects on economic growth, unemployment, interest rates and inflation.

## State as Legislator

For many readers, and particularly HR practitioners, employment legislation has a major influence on their working lives. However, our existing legal framework is a relatively recent development. As we discuss in detail in Chapter 4, up until the 1960s, the Government did little to intervene directly in employment relations, instead pursuing a 'voluntarist' approach whereby employers were largely left to manage their workplaces relatively free of regulation and trade unions were the main source of protection for workers.

However, over the last half century, this has gradually changed. It could be argued that there have been three critical developments that define the role of the Government as a legislator. First, the 1970s saw the development of a framework of individual employment rights, which included the right to claim unfair dismissal, equal pay and protection against sex and race discrimination. The system of employment tribunals that we have today was developed and in 1975 Acas was established. Second, between 1979 and 1993, successive Conservative governments introduced seven separate pieces of legislation designed to regulate and restrict industrial action by trade unions. This included making secret postal ballots mandatory for lawful industrial action and the outlawing of strike action taken by one group of workers in support of another (secondary action). Finally, following its election in 1997, the new Labour Government signed the Social Chapter of the 1992 Maastricht Treaty on European Union, which led to EU employment legislation being transposed into UK law and a significant extension of the existing framework of employment protection.

The framework of employment legislation and policy is also supported by a number of state agencies that have a statutory role in employment relations, whether that role is in respect of individual or of collective issues. In the UK, there are three major agencies of this kind: the Advisory, Conciliation and Arbitration Service (Acas), the Central Arbitration Committee (CAC) and the Certification Office for Trade Unions and Employers' Associations.

Acas was established in 1975 in order to foster good employment relations practice and, at the time, to promote collective bargaining, although this element of its remit was removed by the Conservative Government in 1993. Acas provides advice to employers, employees and trade unions on employment relations issues and offers a range of training services. It is responsible for the development of a series of Codes of Practice and guidance, the most well known of which is the Code of Practice on Disciplinary and Grievance Procedures. Perhaps most importantly, Acas offers mediation, arbitration and conciliation in both individual and collective disputes (see Chapter 11 for further details). Acas is independent of direct government intervention, although its sponsoring ministry is the Department for Business, Innovation and Skills (BIS). It is governed by an independent council responsible for setting its strategic direction, policies and priorities. It consists of a chairperson and 11 other members drawn from trade unions, employers' bodies, small business organisations and academia.

## ACAS – PROMOTING BEST PRACTICE AND GOOD EMPLOYMENT RELATIONS

The main duties of Acas are to:

● promote good practice through the issuing of Codes of Practice on discipline and grievance procedures, on the disclosure of information to trade unions for collective bargaining purposes, and on time off for trade union duties and activities

- provide information and advice and guidance on a wide range of employment relations matters through its helpline, which can be contacted by anyone and is free, confidential and impartial
- conciliate in complaints to employment tribunals. It has a statutory duty to act as conciliator in a wide range of individual employment rights complaints including alleged unfair dismissal, alleged discrimination and equal pay claims
- conciliate and mediate in the case of collective disputes
- resolve employment disputes by facilitating arbitration by which the parties to a dispute agree of their own volition that a jointly agreed arbitrator consider the dispute and make a decision to resolve it.

The Central Arbitration Committee (CAC) is a permanent independent body with statutory powers whose role is to resolve disputes in England, Scotland and Wales under legislation relating to recognition and derecognition of trade unions, disclosure of information for collective bargaining, information and consultation of employees and European Works Councils and European Companies and Co-operative Society and cross-border mergers. The CAC's powers to arrange for voluntary arbitration in trade disputes have not been used for some years.

The CAC consists of a chairperson, 11 deputy chairpersons, 28 members experienced as representatives of employers and 26 members as representatives of workers. All members of the Committee are appointed by the Department for Business, Innovation and Skills after consultation with Acas. CAC decisions are made by panels of three committee members appointed by the chairperson and consisting of either the chairperson or a deputy chairperson, one member whose experience is representative of employers and one member whose experience is representative of workers.

The post of Certification Officer was established in 1975. Its main responsibilities are to maintain records of independent trade unions, staff associations and employers' associations. This is important as only trade unions that are independent from employer influence and domination enjoy specific rights and responsibilities under UK employment law. The Certification Officer also deals with complaints by trade union members over a range of issues including financial matters, member registrations, the conduct of internal elections and the management of union political funds.

### Government as Economic Manager

The development of economic policy and how this has shaped employment relations over time is a major theme of the following chapter. However, for our purposes, it is important to set out the role the Government plays. The economic goals of government tend to be relatively uniform, generally due to the fact that they are central to whether they are re-elected at the subsequent General Election. Therefore, most governments will aim to maximise economic growth, employment and prosperity, or at least the prosperity of those groups who will deliver electoral success. The main tools available to government relate to fiscal policy – put crudely, how the Government decides to raise tax revenues, how it spends those revenues, and the extent to which it relies on borrowing additional funds to finance further expenditure. Monetary policy in the UK is directed by the Bank of England, which has a remit to control inflation, which it does through interest rates and controlling the supply of money within the economic system. While the Bank of England is nominally independent, there is little doubt that government policy and direction have a significant influence on its strategy and operations.

The key differences between the main political parties are the ways in which those goals are achieved. At the current time, there is a clear divide between the two main parties, Labour and Conservative; the Labour Party would attempt to achieve economic growth through a greater emphasis on investment (both public and private) in transport, housing, education and health. The reduction of income inequality would also be a key policy priority for any Labour administration and it is likely that additional investment would be financed by a more redistributive approach to taxation, for example maintaining higher tax rates for high earners. The focus of the Conservative Government is on minimising both the tax burden (especially on business) and also public expenditure in a belief that this will stimulate private business activity, which will in turn lead to high levels of employment. For Conservatives, the prosperity of those at the lower end of the income 'ladder' are best served by providing a framework within which private enterprises can flourish and create wealth.

These different economic philosophies have significant implications for employment relations. For example, Labour's greater emphasis on spending to maintain public services will support employment in parts of the economy with higher levels of unionisation. In addition, Labour policy, in recent years, has focused on the importance of workplace partnership between employers and unions in underpinning high productivity and economic performance. In contrast, Conservative policy to 'rebalance' the economy towards private sector employment will indirectly weaken trade union organisation and influence. Furthermore, the belief that trade unions represent an obstacle to the free market will continue to underpin attempts to constrain and restrict union activities.

## 2.3.4 INTERESTS – CONFLICT, CO-OPERATION AND CONTRADICTION

Table 2.1 sets out the interests of the three main actors in employment relations. This list is not exhaustive but seeks to provide some insight into the relationship between the interests of employers, employees and government.

Table 2.1 Interests in employment relations

| Employee | Employer | The State |
|---|---|---|
| Employment | Profit maximisation | Power |
| Income | Shareholder value | Economic growth |
| Fairness | Stakeholder interests | Ideology |
| Voice | Quality and service | Continuity |
| Job satisfaction | Employee engagement | |
| Occupational identity | Creation of employment | |
| Autonomy | Control | |

Adapted from Budd and Bhave, 2008

### Employee Interests

In the labour market, employees are generally looking for the best possible available employment conditions. At one level, income and employment are needed to survive and pay for the basic necessities of life; however, some individuals will be driven to maximise income, both to improve their living standards and also to provide a degree of recognition of their value or contribution to the organisation. Therefore, notions of fairness and equity become important for many workers – this may be based on comparability with colleagues within the organisation or across the sector, or simply based on an individual's perceptions of whether she or he is being fairly rewarded.

Employees may also be looking for job satisfaction and in some cases this can compensate for lower levels of financial remuneration. Indeed, Maslow's (1943) hierarchy of needs, while much criticised, focuses attention on the role of intrinsic rewards over extrinsic rewards of pay. This could include a sense of solidarity and friendship with work colleagues or the opportunity to exert employee voice and have a say in the decisions that shape the nature and conditions of work. Similarly, workers may value a degree of autonomy and the freedom and discretion to exert control over their own labour process. Finally, we may get significant utility from our identity at work as a teacher, engineer, nurse or doctor. Of course, it is important to note that the views of employees will vary widely; for example, some may be driven by a desire for pay while others will value their occupational identity above other issues. Moreover, the balance of these different interests is dynamic and will be shaped by the changing external context. For example, in times of recession, employees may prioritise employment security above other issues and be prepared to sacrifice higher levels of pay or a degree of control and autonomy over their work.

### ?   REFLECTIVE ACTIVITY 2.3

What is your monetary and non-monetary package of employment conditions? Which elements of this are the most important to you? Why?

### Employer Interests

The interests of the employer will vary depending on the nature of the organisation – in private enterprises, the key objective will be to maximise profitability. This will be accentuated in companies whose shares are publicly traded (for example the London Stock Exchange) and who therefore are answerable to the short-term demands of shareholders who are looking for increased stock prices and dividends. In private enterprises that are family-owned, the focus on profitability may be balanced against other objectives, such as preserving employment, reputation in the local community and the longevity of the organisation. While publicly owned and not-for-profit organisations may not have a profit motive and may be driven by concerns over service delivery, like their counterparts in the private sector, cost minimisation will be a central objective.

Therefore, it could be argued that employers' and employees' interests are incompatible and that conflict is inherent within the employment relationship. However, as Edwards (2003) has argued, employers must try to balance the need to exert control over employees with securing their co-operation. In short, work rules may ensure that workers adhere to certain organisational norms and expectations, but if the employer wants to maximise organisational performance they must also secure the commitment of employees. Intensifying work and adopting a hire-and-fire approach may minimise costs, but whether this is sustainable in the long term is more questionable. The precise balance between control and co-operation is likely to be shaped by a number of different factors.

First, the nature of the job – if the job is relatively unskilled and employees are seen as replaceable, employers may take the view that job satisfaction and commitment to the organisation is not necessary and is less important than keeping costs as low as possible. Second, the nature of the labour process and, in particular, the degree of autonomy afforded to employees, will shape the approach of the employer. As the following case study demonstrates – where tasks are repetitive, automated and measurable – control, for example through the application of rules, is likely to be much more direct than where job roles are less well defined and there is an emphasis on creativity.

## A TALE OF TWO WORKPLACES

Research conducted by Richard Saundry and Gemma Wibberley (2012) into the way that the online fashion retailer Shop Direct Group (SDG) manages workplace conflict highlighted the link between the nature of the labour process and the different approaches adopted by management. SDG, at the time, operated a number of call centres and warehouses that generally dealt with the retail elements of its operation. It also had a large headquarters, which housed its administration and management, and also its creative teams involved with design and buying. Head office staff generally enjoyed a significant amount of discretion both in terms of how they completed their tasks and the management of working time. Work there was seen to be more creative and staff

tended to be more highly paid. Therefore, work was not tightly controlled as it was felt that this would hamper performance. Consequently, working hours and performance were not closely monitored and strict application of procedure was seen as inconsistent with creating a creative culture.

The approach was very different within the contact centre and warehousing environments. Here, work was routinised, pay was relatively low and key performance indicators were examined by managers on an ongoing basis. A trade union representative interviewed by the researchers explained that managers could 'press a button and for the eight hours [an individual worked] ... that'll show every key stroke you've done, every number you've dialled... everything...'

Third, the nature of the labour market shapes the balance between control and co-operation – if the labour market is tight and skills are scarce, the employer will be forced to find ways of increasing engagement – through improving terms and conditions or allowing greater degrees of autonomy. Where there is an available supply of labour, employers may be able to adopt a much closer focus on cost reduction.

## ? REFLECTIVE ACTIVITY 2.4

Consider a group of employees in your organisation. What package of monetary and non-monetary employment conditions does your organisation offer to attract that group to come to work for it, and to continue to work for it? Why that package?

### The Interests of the State

So far in this chapter we have tended to use the terms 'Government' and 'State' interchangeably. However, when we are examining the interests of the State, we need to be more precise. The Government essentially refers to the ruling political party that forms the 'Government', sets out a political programme, and enacts legislation and other levers of economic, social and foreign policy during its term of office. In addition to the Government, however, the State is made up of a variety of institutions which may be shaped by, but are in theory, independent of government – these include the civil service, the judiciary and the armed forces.

The Government of the day has a clear interest in employment relations as it exists to manage the economy but is also focused on winning and retaining political power. Of course, these issues are closely related – economic policies that successfully secure economic growth and rising living standards are likely to lead to positive political results. In broad terms, it is widely accepted that economic competence is a key factor in voting behaviour at general elections. Indeed, in the 2015 General Election, the economy remained the most important issue for voters, although compared with recent years the relative importance of health and immigration have grown.

This has two main implications for employment relations: first, the Government will adopt economic policies that will inevitably shape the nature of employment relations. Second, the Government may adopt certain stances towards its own employees or towards trade unions that are designed to indicate that it supports business. In general, since the election of the Conservative Government in 1979, on a platform of reducing union power, successive governments have sought to persuade the public that they are 'pro-business'. In the case of Conservative administrations, this has meant introducing legislation designed to restrict union power, while Labour governments have distanced themselves from the historic ties between the Labour Party and trade unions.

While governments come and go, the apparatus of the State continues to function – again there are a range of different interests that can be identified. As we note below, some would argue that the State in the form of the civil service and judiciary provides a degree of neutrality, where the State effectively acts to balance the competing interest within the labour market (Budd and Bhave, 2008). It has also been argued that the make-up of the British judiciary also reflects the senior echelons of government and business. Professor Sir Geoffrey Lionel Bindman QC, who specialises in human rights law, wrote in 2012 that 'only five of the 54 most senior judges are women and in the Supreme Court only one out of 12. None of the 54 is black. And the majority are privately and Oxbridge educated.' Therefore, it has been argued that the State and particularly the judiciary tend to act in a way that reinforces managerial authority and preserves the 'status quo'. For example, Richard Hyman, writing in 1975, argued that many judges 'express in their judgments a strong ideological bias against collective action by workers'.

## 2.4 KEY CONCEPTS AND PERSPECTIVES

How we interpret, explain and understand the processes through which the main employment relations actors interact depends on our conceptual approach. In what follows, we examine the main theoretical perspectives that have been developed to help us make sense of the complexities of employment relations.

Table 2.2 Theoretical approaches to employment relations

| Systems theory | Marxist approaches | Frames of reference |
|---|---|---|
| Web of rules (output)<br>↓<br>Actors<br>(employers/employees/<br>state agencies)<br>↓<br>Environmental context<br>(technology/markets/<br>power distribution)<br>↓<br>Ideology | Antagonistic class relations between labour and capital<br><br>Radical conflict of interest between labour and capital underlines what happens in employment relations<br><br>An increasing power struggle is an essential feature of employment relations | *Unitarist*<br>Workers and managers united by common interests and values: enterprise is harmonious<br>*Pluralist*<br>Recognising differing interests in the employment relationship: conflict channelled through institutions<br>*Radical*<br>Gross disparity of power between the employer and the individual employee (property-less) |

## 2.4.1 SYSTEMS THEORY

The first concerted attempt to formulate a theoretical framework of employment relations was John Dunlop's *industrial relations system* (1958). With reference to Parsons' theory of social systems, Dunlop defined the industrial relations system as an analytical subsystem of industrial societies and located it on the same logical plane as an economic system. Dunlop's work had the advantage of positioning the core components of an industrial relations system and made the rules and norms of the workplace the centrepiece of analysis, as opposed to the then accepted orthodoxy of industrial conflict or collective bargaining.

Dunlop saw the industrial relations system as a web of rules. He identified the basic components of an industrial relations system as: three groups of actors (managers, workers and their respective organisations, and governmental institutions dealing with industrial relations), three different environmental contexts (technology, markets, and economic and power distribution) and an ideology that consists of the common beliefs of the actors and that binds the industrial relations system together. In Dunlop's model, the dependent variable is rules that govern industrial relations behaviour at various levels (international, national, sector, etc), whereas the interaction between the actors, contexts and ideology is the independent variable.

However, Dunlop's approach has been subject to a number of criticisms:

1   It is simply a statement of how the rules of the workplace are made and cannot be presented as a general theory of industrial relations. It is solely 'a general framework to organise a description of the interaction between the actors, the environmental context and the ideologies' (Meltz, 1991: 14). It merely collapses to an identification of the key elements and components that have to be given weight when analysing an industrial relations system.

2   Little attention is given to the employment relationship in the model, which is a central variable in any employment relations system. Dunlop regarded industrial relations more expansively to include all relations between workers, management and governmental agencies and in which the central concern is the 'web of rules'.

3   There is no account (let alone an analysis) of the processes by which the rules of the industrial relations system are determined, and only fleeting attention is given to the role of the State in this regard (Marsden, 1982).

4   The centrality of conflict to the employment relationship is underplayed (Muller-Jenstch, 2004). Instead, the essential focus of the systems model is stability as the central purpose of the industrial relations system rather than industrial disputes or wage-settling through collective bargaining (Hyman, 1975).

## 2.4.2 MARXIST AND RADICAL APPROACHES

In contrast to the systems approach, many observers claim that conflict is a fundamental aspect of the employment relationship. This draws on the ideas of Karl Marx, who argued that the capitalist system of production was inherently exploitative, with the owners of capital maximising profit by essentially appropriating part of the value created by workers. Therefore, within capitalist employment relations, the interests of capital and labour are diametrically opposed. In short, workers will seek to increase wages and improve conditions, but this eats into profit and so will be opposed by employers – with the consequence being industrial conflict. Furthermore, the employment relationship is characterised by an asymmetry of power; while workers must work in order to obtain a decent standard of living, an employer can simply replace one worker with someone who is unemployed, drawn from what Marx referred to as the 'reserve army of labour'. This power imbalance allows employers to maintain authority and control over workers and also minimise labour costs.

## The Political Economy of Industrial Relations

Perhaps the best known and most influential Marxist analysis of employment relations is set out by Richard Hyman in his book *Industrial Relations: A Marxist Introduction*, first published in 1975. He argued that to define industrial relations in terms of a web of rules was far too narrow and that employment relations are concerned with the maintenance of stability and the regulation and control of industrial conflict. He argued that systems theory ignored the processes through which disagreement and disputes between employers and employees are generated and the roles played by existing structures of ownership and control. Therefore, 'order' and 'regulation' were only one side of employment relations, and instability and disorder must be given equal weight. This led Hyman to conclude that the study of industrial relations was not that of job regulation but rather 'the study of processes of control over work relations'. Moreover, he claimed that those processes could be theoretically explained only with reference to class structure and the nature of the political, social and ideological power relations generated by the capitalist system of production.

The political economy of industrial relations developed by Hyman has formed the basis for a number of theoretical contributions. Perhaps the most widely used in contemporary employment relations research is John Kelly's work (1998). In his book, *Rethinking Industrial Relations*, he developed our understanding of patterns of industrial conflict by linking 'mobilisation' theory (Tilly, 1978) to an analysis of economic long-wave trade cycles. He argued that exploitation and domination by employers within capitalism inevitably leads to perceptions of injustice among workers and consequently shared collective grievances. However, whether such grievances are 'mobilised' into resistance, for example in the form of strike action, depends on a number of factors: interests, organisation, mobilisation, opportunity, and counter-mobilisation. Whether grievances are defined collectively and the ability of unions to organise is partly a function of the economic context, and Kelly claims that each turning point between upswing and downswing is associated with an upsurge of mobilisation expressed by increased strike activity. Under such conditions, workers are likely to see their living standards eroded by rising inflation and be subject to managerial attempts to reduce costs, providing issues around which collective grievances can be clearly framed. At the same time, union organisation is more likely to be robust given high levels of employment. Nonetheless, converting this sense of grievance into concrete action requires leaders who are able to spread the feeling of injustice and to elevate the collective identity of workers. This is made easier when unemployment is relatively low and consequently workers feel secure and are in a stronger bargaining position. However, employers do not sit back and let this happen. They counter-mobilise against trade unions with the support of the capitalist State.

---

CASE STUDY 2.2

### MOBILISATION THEORY – THE CASE OF THE RMT

In recent years, trade unions have generally become more quiescent in the face of rapid membership decline, the erosion of workplace organisations and an increasingly hostile political and legislative environment. In this context, levels of industrial action have fallen steadily. One exception to this has been the rail transport industry – the largest union, the RMT (Rail, Maritime and Transport Union) has used industrial action and the threat of industrial action over a wide range of issues including pay, health and safety, pensions, job losses and the impact of privatisation (Darlington, 2009). This can be analysed using mobilisation theory as a theoretical lens.

First, rail unions have tended to have high levels of union density and fairly healthy demand for the service they offer, giving rail workers a fairly high degree of bargaining power. However, growing competition and a drive by employers to increase efficiency has led to changes to terms and conditions, and attempts to restrict pay increases. This has provided a number of shared grievances around which collective resistance can be organised. Critically, a key role was also played by the General Secretary of the largest rail union, the RMT, the late Bob Crow, supported by a network of active and militant local representatives.

Crow was elected in 2002 and, while heavily criticised by many politicians and the media, he was undoubtedly a charismatic leader. Not only was he able to command significant support for industrial action on a number of occasions, but the membership of the RMT increased rapidly during his time in the job. As Ralph Darlington (2009) has argued, this can be explained by the effectiveness of the RMT in winning demonstrable gains for its members. The response of local and national government to industrial action in the rail industry is also a good example of counter-mobilisation, with the Mayor of London at the time, Boris Johnson, calling for legislation to further restrict industrial action and this subsequently being introduced by the newly elected Conservative Government in the form of the 2015 Trade Union Bill.

### The Labour Process Debate

Another strand of theory underpinned by a Marxist approach to work and employment is the debate on the character of the labour process. The focus of the discussion is the so-called transformation problem, which Marx had already defined as the transformation of (bought) labour power into performed work or, expressed more simply, the problem of managerial control of labour. The labour process debate stems from the work of Harry Braverman in his book *Labour and Monopoly Capital*, published in 1974, in which he argued that the key task of capitalist management is the continual control of the labour process in order to extract a maximum of surplus value by transforming labour power into work performance.

Central to Braverman's theories is that management (capital) controls technology and uses it as a management tool to increase capitalist power and exploitation. In short, technology, machinery and equipment are used by management to systematically deprive workers of their control over the job. Workers become deskilled, management acquires greater and greater control, and labour becomes more homogenous. Given the dynamics of exploitation and control, relationships between capital (management) and labour (workers) in the workplace are of 'structured antagonism' (Edwards, 1986). At the same time, management (capital), in order to constantly revolutionise the work process, requires some level of co-operation from the workforce. The result is a continuum of worker responses ranging from resistance to accommodation, compliance and consent.

### Feminist Perspectives on Employment Relations

An important contribution to the conceptual debate over employment relations has come from feminist scholars who have criticised research for ignoring the gendered nature of employment relations, despite the feminisation of the UK labour market (Wajcman, 2000). In particular, it is argued that the key employment relations actors, such as trade unions, the State and employing organisations, are portrayed as gender neutral when the opposite is the case (Wajcman, 2000: 184).

We discuss above radical approaches that highlight asymmetrical power relations, however feminist scholars also argue that power inequalities based on gender shape employment relations processes and outcomes. Moreover, the key actors of employment relations have traditionally acted to reinforce gender divisions in work and employment. For example, trade unions were still negotiating separate pay scales for men and women doing the same work right up to the introduction of the Equal Pay Act in 1970, while progress on closing the gender pay gap and countering occupational segregation has been tortuously slow. Moreover, as Kirton and Healy (2013) have argued, despite the fact that women now form a majority of trade union members, there are significant barriers preventing this being fully reflected in the leadership of trade unions.

Employment relations research has also tended to focus on masculine settings and environments where trade unions have traditionally been strong, despite the fact that these represent a small and decreasing part of the labour market. Areas in which women are more likely to work are much less likely to be explored by researchers and so their importance and significance tends to be underplayed. This is beginning to change; however, Wajcman argues that existing theorisation of the employment relationship still separates work from the household despite the fact that the sexual division of labour underpins the way that work is organised. Therefore, gender should be an integral part of the analysis of employment relations.

## 2.5 FRAMES OF REFERENCE

Perhaps the most widely used theoretical framework is Alan Fox's idea (Fox, 1974) that employment relations can be conceptualised in terms of three frames of reference: pluralist, radical and unitary. It is important to note that these are not 'models' or 'management styles' but different perspectives through which employment relations can be understood and explained. The pluralist perspective recognises the differing interests in the employment relationship, therefore conflict is an inevitable part of organisational life. However, it assumes that conflict can be managed and resolved through the 'institutions' such as trade unions, collective bargaining and dispute resolution procedures. Importantly, the State is seen as playing a neutral role, facilitating bargaining, negotiation and good employment relations.

Pluralists see the organisation as a coalition of interest groups; however, they fundamentally accept the legitimacy of managerial authority to promote the long-term needs of the organisation as a whole by paying due concern to all the interests affected – employees, shareholders, customers, the community and the national interest. This involves management holding the 'right' balance between the divergent claims of all these participant interests. Trade unions are also seen as an essential way of correcting the unequal power balance in the employment relationship, allowing negotiation to take place on more equal terms. Pluralists do not claim anything approaching perfection for this system. They accept that in some situations imbalances in the relative bargaining power between employers and employees (unions), or between management and a particular group of employees, may be such that for one side or the other, justice (the outcome) is distinctly rough. Such situations, however, are not so numerous or unfair as generally to discredit the system, either from the employees' point of view or from that of management.

In many ways, the pluralist perspective was the dominant paradigm of post-war employment relations and built on the belief that the best way to manage employment relations was through a recognition of difference and structures through which those differences can be resolved – therefore governments of all political persuasions supported the idea of collective bargaining and encouraged the use of systematic procedural approaches to discipline and grievance.

The starting point for those holding the radical frame of reference is the largely unequal distribution of power between the employer and the individual employee. Lacking property or command over resources, the employee is seen as totally dependent on being offered employment by the owners or controllers of property, and so the dependent relationship between the employer and the employee is a power relationship. From this position of weakness, employees have little ability to assert their needs and aspirations against those of the employer. Employees are simply viewed as a commodity.

From a radical perspective conflict is also inevitable but, unlike pluralists, radicals would argue that the institutions of employment relations simply mask the reality of the capitalist employment relationship, disguising the inequalities of power and exploitation. Even trade unions represent a myth that their presence restores the balance of power in the employment relationship. The only way that trade unions can change this is by moving away from an agenda that focuses solely on collective bargaining and terms and conditions, and instead encourage worker resistance to challenge the basis of capitalist employment relations. This also involves confronting the State, which is portrayed as acting to support the interests of capital by, for example, introducing legislation to suppress resistance and enhance managerial control over the labour process.

Unitarism, by contrast, views the enterprise as a harmonious whole, with workers and managers united by common interests and values. Unitarists propagate a concept of an enterprise (organisation) in which management is the only legitimate source of authority, control and leadership. The enterprise is viewed as a united team pulling together for the common good. Conflict is seen to be the result of irrational behaviour and of 'troublemakers' having infiltrated the organisation. These external influences are to be resisted and removed from the enterprise. A trade union is seen, by unitarists, as a purely self-seeking force trying to assert itself in an otherwise integrated and unified organisation.

In some respects, a key feature of contemporary employment relations has been the growing dominance of the unitarist perspective. There is substantial evidence that the vast majority of managers have a largely unitaristic perspective of employment relations. While such views have traditionally been commonplace in smaller and family-owned businesses, they are now widely reflected in larger, and sometimes unionised, organisations. For example, in WERS2011, eight out of every ten managers responded that they would rather consult directly with employees than through trade unions (van Wanrooy et al, 2013). It has also been argued that human resource management is largely founded on unitarism (Guest, 1987; Bratton and Gold, 2015). There is little doubt that the perspectives that have underpinned government policy over the last fifty years have undergone a substantial shift away from pluralism towards unitarism – while the Thatcher Government elected in 1979 adopted a very clear unitaristic philosophy in which trade unions were seen as militant agitators and collective bargaining an obstacle to the free market, it could be argued that this has also been reflected in the policy orientations of subsequent Labour and Conservative administrations (Howell, 2000).

## 2.6 EMPLOYMENT RELATIONS PROCESSES

The main employment relations actors outlined above use various employment relations processes (mechanisms) to make rules that regulate and control behaviour in the workplace and work community. The most important of these processes are:

- collective bargaining
- unilateral employer action
- employee involvement and participation
- employee engagement
- third-party intervention
- industrial sanctions.

### 2.6.1 COLLECTIVE BARGAINING

Collective bargaining is not only an employment relations process for jointly determining employment rules but also a system of industrial governance whereby unions and employers jointly reach decisions concerning the employment relationship. Most commonly, it involves employers negotiating with trade unions to set pay and conditions on behalf of the workers for whom they are recognised. In practice, this often means that if a union is recognised to bargain on behalf of a group of workers, any agreement, such as a pay increase, will be applied to workers of that type, whether they are union members or not.

Companies that do not recognise unions may also take into account collectively bargained pay rates in their industry or in comparator firms when deciding on their own employees' employment conditions if they are to remain competitive in the labour market. Many non-union companies also seek to avoid unionisation by paying better than the union-negotiated pay rates and other employment conditions for their industry. Therefore, collective bargaining activity influences terms and conditions across the economy.

From a pluralist perspective, collective bargaining is a vital way of accommodating different interests and resolving conflict through negotiation. In addition, it could be argued that the employee 'voice' provided by collective bargaining underpins trust and fairness. One of the key benefits to employers of collective bargaining is to reduce the transaction costs of negotiating terms and conditions. In large workplaces, individual negotiation would be impractical, time-consuming and costly, therefore collective bargaining is a relatively efficient way of determining pay and other terms of employment. However, for some employers with a unitarist perspective, bargaining with trade unions is seen as an obstacle to change and a barrier to flexibility. In this context, the scale and scope of collective bargaining has contracted rapidly in the last four decades, mirroring the broader decline in trade union organisation. The percentage of employees with pay determined through collective bargaining fell from around 70% in the 1970s to 23% in 2011 (van Wanrooy *et al*, 2013). In addition, there has been a significant reduction in the extent to which collective bargaining takes place at national level, with bargaining at the level of the employer or even the workplace much more common. Within the public sector, in which trade unions remain influential, less than half (44%) of employees are covered by collective bargaining, partly as a result of the increased use of pay review bodies to set pay in the NHS, schools and prisons. Moreover, even where collective bargaining still takes place, its scope has narrowed. According to WERS2011, the proportion of unionised workplaces in which pay, hours and holidays were normally negotiated fell from 32% in 2004 to 25% in 2011. The reduction was particularly steep in the private sector, from 27% to 18% (van Wanrooy *et al*, 2013).

### 2.6.2 UNILATERAL ACTION

Given the decline of collective bargaining and the high cost of negotiating with individual employees, most terms and conditions are set unilaterally by the employer. Even in highly unionised organisations (for example, local authorities and NHS trusts) there have been examples of the unilateral imposition of changes by management on issues such as wage increases, the taking of holidays, overtime opportunities and changes in job descriptions. In some organisations there may be consultation through staff forums, but ultimately if employees are dissatisfied with their pay and conditions, they are faced with few alternatives apart from to look for a better deal elsewhere. For managers, this has short-term efficiency benefits and underlines their right to manage. However, it also runs the risk of eroding employee engagement and increasing employee turnover as employees look for alternative routes to improve their working conditions.

### 2.6.3 EMPLOYEE INVOLVEMENT AND PARTICIPATION

Given the progressive silencing of employee voice through collective bargaining, employee involvement processes have arguably taken on an added significance. Employee involvement (which is examined in greater detail in Chapter 10) is a broad term that covers a range of processes designed to enable employees to voice their views to the employer and, in some cases, to participate in, or contribute to, management decision-making. Employee involvement processes include direct communication forms – such as regular workforce meetings between senior management and the workforce and team briefings – through which management disseminates key information and messages to their staff. Other direct processes of involvement provide employees with some input into decision-making processes, for example through their role in problem-solving groups that discuss aspects of performance (for example, quality). Managers may also consult with their staff over various matters, inviting their views on proposed changes or innovations.

Interestingly, the use of direct communication appears to be increasing; in 2011, four out of every five workplaces have workplace meetings with all staff (an increase from 75% in 2004), while two-thirds used team briefings (compared with 60% in 2004) (van Wanrooy et al., 2013). Employers were also more likely to disclose financial information to their staff. However, there was a decrease in use of problem-solving groups, which provide a degree of influence in the decision-making process.

Consultation can also take place through a representative forum (such as a Works Council) or some other form of joint consultation machinery. In joint consultation, management seeks the views of employee representatives prior to making a decision. Although joint consultation may involve discussion of mutual problems, it leaves management to make the final decision. There is no commitment to act on the employees' views. Issues dealt with by joint consultation vary from social matters – such as the provision of canteen or sports facilities – to issues such as the scheduling of production. Employers also have a statutory duty to consult over certain issues such as redundancy and transfer of undertakings (see Chapter 14 for more detail).

As with collective bargaining, the scale of joint consultative arrangements appears to be reducing. In 2004, 38% of workplaces had a functioning joint consultative committee at the workplace, but by 2011, this had fallen to 25%. This fall was not restricted to the private sector and, while joint consultative committees (JCCs) remain in the majority of public sector workplaces, the proportion reduced from 71% in 2004 to 64% in 2011. Taken together with our discussion of collective bargaining above, this illustrates the growing problem of a representation gap in British workplaces, with only 35% having any structure for the representation of employees' views (van Wanrooy et al, 2013).

Given the discussion, it is therefore not surprising that only one-third of employees rate their managers as good or very good at allowing views of employees and representatives to influence decisions (van Wanrooy et al, 2013). This would seem to reflect a shift away from pluralist approaches in which employment relations are jointly regulated towards an emphasis on the provision of information. This in turn is underpinned by unitaristic assumptions that conflict and discontent can be simply avoided through effective communication.

### 2.6.4 EMPLOYEE ENGAGEMENT

What might be seen as a crisis of employee voice within British workplaces is arguably reflected in the focus among employment relations professionals on employee engagement. However, there is much debate about the nature of engagement and whether it is an attitude, a set of behaviours or an outcome. An employee might feel pride and loyalty (attitude) and/or be a great advocate for the company to customers or go the extra mile to finish a piece of work (behaviour). Outcomes may include lower accident rates, higher productivity, more innovation, lower labour turnover and reduced absence rates.

Advocates of engagement argue it is a workplace approach designed to ensure that employees are committed to their organisation's goals and values, are motivated to contribute to organisational success, and are able, at the same time, to enhance their own sense of well-being. Engaged organisations are said to have strong and authentic values with clear evidence of trust and fairness based on mutual respect, where two-way promises and commitments – between employers and staff – are understood and fulfilled. Employee engagement strategies are said to enable people to be the best they can at work, recognising that this can only happen if they feel respected, involved, heard, well-led and valued by those they work for and with. Employee engagement is analysed in more detail in Chapter 7.

---

### ? REFLECTIVE ACTIVITY 2.5

What are the main processes used to regulate employment conditions in your organisation? Why are these the main processes used rather than others?

---

#### 2.6.5 THIRD PARTY INTERVENTION

In situations where the actors in the employment relations system are unable to resolve their differences over the making of employment rules and/or over the interpretation and application of existing rules, they may agree voluntarily to seek the assistance of an independent third party. In the UK, third party intervention can take one of three forms: conciliation, mediation or arbitration. These processes are examined in detail in Chapters 11 and 15.

In relation to collective disputes, the parties generally turn to Acas for help in seeking to resolve the issues between them. In conciliation of collective disputes, the Acas conciliator acts as a link between the disputing parties by passing on information that the parties will not, for whatever reason, pass directly to each other, until either a basis for agreement is identified or both parties conclude that there is no basis for an agreed voluntary settlement to their problem. The arbitration process removes from employers and employees control over the settlement of their differences. The arbitrator hears both sides' cases and decides the matter by making an award. Both parties, having voluntarily agreed to arbitration, are morally bound, but not legally obliged, to accept the arbitrator's award.

When the dispute is between two individuals or an individual and the employer, workplace mediation is sometimes used as a way of repairing the relationship. This normally takes place before employment has been terminated and involves trained mediators engaged from Acas, private mediation providers or from an organisation's own staff. The mediator plays an impartial role and the process is confidential and voluntary. Importantly, parties are not accompanied by trade union representatives or any other individual. The mediator will listen to each person individually and then, in a joint meeting, will help them to discuss the issues between them, identify common ground and hopefully develop a mutually agreed resolution. However, in cases in which the relationship has already broken down and an individual is considering making a claim to an employment tribunal, Acas will seek to conciliate. In fact, prior to lodging an employment tribunal application all claimants must first notify who will offer both parties conciliation – again this process is entirely voluntary. Only when this process has been exhausted can an employee make a claim against their employer.

The use of third-party intervention reflects the changing nature of employment relations. The use of collective conciliation, mediation and arbitration has fallen. On average, in the three years after its establishment, Acas dealt with more than 3,000 requests for collective conciliation. In contrast, in the last three years (2008–11), the average was 858 (Acas, 2014; Podro and Suff, 2009). At the same time, there is some evidence of growth in the use of workplace mediation on individual issues with requests to Acas doubling between 2004/05 and 2010/11 (Acas 2005, 2011). Furthermore, Acas dealt with more than 60,000 conciliation cases between April and December 2014.

Conflict resolution processes, such as mediation and conciliation, are a classic pluralist response to workplace conflict and consequent employment disputes. Through the intervention of third parties, such as Acas, disputants are given an opportunity to voice their concerns and are then helped to identify areas of common ground so that a mutually acceptable settlement can be reached. However, a radical critique would suggest that this is simply a way of helping employers to reassert their control over the labour process and restoring order to the employment relationship.

### 2.6.6 INDUSTRIAL SANCTIONS

If the processes of employment relations break down, either employers or employees can impose industrial sanctions. The main sanction open to employers, given the structure of UK employment law, is either locking out some, or all, of the workforce, closing down the organisation or relocating operations to another site. While these sanctions are rarely used in practice, the threat, particularly of closure or job loss, is extremely potent, as we explore in more depth in Chapter 5. Indeed, the threat by multinational employers to relocate production has played a significant part in shifting the balance of workplace power towards the employer and forcing trade unions and their members to accept changes in working conditions.

At an individual level, the employer can simply terminate the employment relationship. While employees enjoy protection against unfair dismissal, this only applies after two years' continuous service and employees must also overcome the potential obstacles of employment tribunal fees and legal costs to bring a claim. Furthermore, only a small minority of claims succeed (Morris, 2012), and even if they do, compensation is limited to a year's salary unless the employee earns more than £78,335. These considerations inevitably shape the ways in which employees and employers respond to employment disputes.

Of course, employees can also attempt to impose industrial sanctions. Traditionally, this has been done collectively through industrial action organised by trade unions. In this way, employees can maximise the potential weight of the sanction and so their bargaining power. The main industrial sanctions that employees can impose on employers are:

- overtime ban
- working-to-rule
- selective stoppage, that is, a one-day stoppage
- all-out strike.

The threat of the imposition of industrial sanctions can be important in bringing about a settlement of the differences between the employers and the employees. The threat that one player might impose industrial sanctions on the other, with their ensuing costs, may be as important as if sanctions were imposed. It is the threat effect that can oblige players to adjust their position and negotiate a peaceful settlement. Both parties will be reluctant to go ahead and impose industrial sanctions because of their associated costs. However, their existence means that the employment relations players have to take them into account and adjust their behaviour accordingly.

We examine the changing shape of workplace conflict in some detail in Chapter 11, but there is little doubt that the use of industrial action to influence employment relations outcomes has become much less prevalent. Between 1965 and 1979 there were, on average, well over 2,000 strikes every year, but in 2013 there were just 114. When strikes do occur they tend to take place in the public sector and involve a relatively large number of workers. However, unions are more likely to use one- and two-day stoppages as a way of minimising the impact on their members. The reasons for these changes are clearly linked to the declining influence of trade unions in general, a more hostile legal environment, and in the private sector, the globalisation of production. In short, the potential sanction of employers relocating operations or downsizing has increasingly carried greater weight than the potential costs incurred through industrial action.

## 2.7 SUMMARY

This chapter has shown that employment relations is essentially concerned with how the employment relationship is regulated. This is not straightforward because the exchange of labour for pay is not a simple transaction. Critically, the two parties do not come together on equal terms – there are instead asymmetrical power relations. In some cases individual employees may enjoy a relatively high level of bargaining power; however, employers are normally in a more powerful position due to their ability to hire replacement workers and their ownership of the equipment, premises and often intellectual property that employees need in order to be able to do their job. Furthermore, the employment relationship is open-ended – while the employer can secure labour, securing commitment, knowledge and ability is much more difficult and very hard to specify in a contract. Therefore, employment relations fill the gap in the contract of employment through rules and processes of negotiation, mediation and accommodation.

However, the main parties to employment relations have a range of interests and it is how these interests are played out that is the focus of theory. Until relatively recently, the dominant perspective in employment relations has been pluralism, which accepts that there are differing interests but that these interests can be accommodated, and conflict managed and avoided through a range of processes and structures. This approach has been criticised by radical commentators who focus on the inequalities inherent within the employment relationship. From this perspective the pluralist processes of conflict resolution, including the role played by the State, are simply ways through which employers cement their control over the labour process and preserve the status quo, whether this is in terms of gender, economic power or social status.

In terms of the practice of employment relations, it is the unitarist perspective that appears to be in the ascendancy. This discounts conflict as an aberration or a function of miscommunication or militant agitation. It also assumes that employers and employees enjoy common interests – a view that appears to be increasingly held by managers and one that is reflected in contemporary debates over HRM, partnership and employee engagement, and the decline of collective employment relations. However, while these remain the key themes of contemporary employment relations, more recent developments in the wake of the financial crash of 2008 have again shone a light on the inequalities within the employment relationship.

1   The employment relationship has a number of distinct characteristics: the parties do not enter the relationship on equal terms; there is an authority relationship between employer and employee – it is incomplete and open ended.

2   Employment relations are primarily concerned with regulating this relationship through rules, processes and institutions. These include collective bargaining, employee involvement and participation, and third party processes, such as mediation and conciliation.

3   Dunlop saw the industrial relations system as a web of rules. He identified the basic components of an industrial relations system as: the actors (employers, employees and the State), the environmental context, and an ideology that consists of the common beliefs of the actors and that binds the industrial relations system together.

4   The systems approach, however, says little about the social processes through which rules are created and negotiated, and ignores the role of conflict within the employment relationship.

5   Pluralist perspectives of the employment relationship accept that conflict is inevitable; however, it can be managed and regulated through the development of workplace institutions and processes of negotiation and mediation. The State is seen to play a neutral facilitating role.

6   Radical perspectives focus on the inequality inherent within capitalist employment relations. Conflict is inherent, but employment relations processes simply reinforce managerial control over labour. This is underpinned by the institutions of the State.

7   Unitarist perspectives see conflict as a result of either misunderstanding or militant agitation. It assumes that employees and employers have shared interests and goals – accordingly the collective institutions of employment relations have little value.

8   Employment relations practised in the post-war period was dominated by pluralist approaches with an emphasis on supporting processes of negotiation and mediation. In the last three decades, managerial perspectives have become increasingly unitarist, which is reflected in the development of HRM and the increased emphasis on employee engagement.

**?**

**REVIEW QUESTIONS**

1   To what extent do you agree that employers hold the balance of power within the employment relationship?

2   Considering your own job – to what extent do you share the interests of your employer? Which interests are different and how does this shape your attitude to work?

3   Find and consider the way in which a particular industrial dispute is considered in the following newspapers: the *Daily Mail*, the *Guardian* and the *Morning Star* – what perspectives of the employment relationship do you think these stories display?

4   What role do you think gender plays in the way that employment relations are perceived and managed in your organisation?

5   Looking at the employment relations policies of the Conservative, Labour and Liberal Democrat Parties, to what extent are they underpinned by a unitarist perspective?

6   What are the limitations of the theoretical perspectives outlined in this chapter? Are theoretical approaches from other disciplines useful in exploring employment relations?

**EXPLORE FURTHER**

BUDD, J. and BHAVE, D. (2008) Values, ideologies and frames of reference in industrial relations. In BLYTON, P. *et al* (eds). *SAGE handbook of industrial relations*. London: SAGE. pp92–113.

CULLINANE, N. and DUNDON, T. (2006) The psychological contract: a critical review. *International journal of management reviews*. Vol 8, No 2. pp113–129.

DUNLOP, J. T. (1958) *Industrial relations systems*. New York: Holt.

EDWARDS, P. (2003) The employment relationship and the field of industrial relations. In EDWARDS, P. (ed). *Industrial relations*. 2nd ed. Oxford: Blackwell, pp1–36.

FOX, A. (1974) *Beyond contract: work, power and trust relations*. London: Faber.

GUEST, D. (1987) Human resource management and industrial relations. *Journal of management studies*. Vol 24, No 5. pp503–21.

HYMAN, R. (1975) *Industrial relations: a Marxist introduction*. Basingstoke: Macmillan.

KAUFMAN, R. (ed) (2004) *Theoretical perspectives on work and employment relationships*. Ithaca: Cornell University Press.

KELLY, J. (1998) *Rethinking industrial relations: mobilization, collectivism and long waves*. London: Routledge.

**Website links**

www.acas.org.uk is the official website of the Advisory, Conciliation and Arbitration Service.

www.bis.gov.uk is the website of the Department for Business, Innovation and Skills, and outlines the main provisions of employment legislation.

www.cac.gov.uk is the website of the Central Arbitration Committee.

www.cbi.org.uk is the website of the CBI, the central employers' organisation in the UK.

www.cipd.co.uk is the official website of the Chartered Institute of Personnel and Development.

www.tuc.org is the official website of the Trades Union Congress.

# CHAPTER 3

# The Context of Employment Relations

## OVERVIEW

The purpose of this chapter is to examine the factors external to the organisation – economic, political (legal) and technological – that shape the way in which employment relations are conducted. We explore how the State plays an important part in determining the corporate environment in its role as an economic manager and a lawmaker. In addition, the State is a direct 'player' in the employment relations system through its role as an employer. Next, we explore the influence of changing social attitudes towards work, gender and trade unions, with particular reference to the findings of the British Social Attitudes Survey. This is followed by an examination of the role played by changing technology in shaping employment relations. Finally, we provide an analysis of contemporary developments in the UK labour market, drawing special attention to the growth in the proportion of women workers, the increased diversity in contractual types, perceived changes in job security and increased flexibility.

## LEARNING OUTCOMES

When you have completed this chapter, you should be able to:

- describe how the UK Government in its role as economic manager influences employment relations
- understand the principal economic approaches used by the UK Government since World War II
- explain and evaluate the impact of changes in the labour market on employment relations
- provide an analysis of how the corporate environment affects the relative balance of bargaining power
- critically analyse the impact of new technology on the working environment.

## 3.1 INTRODUCTION

The business and organisational environment in which employment relations professionals operate is constantly changing. Over the last four decades we have seen a radical shift in the nature of the labour market, with a rapid increase in the number of women in work, a growth in part-time and temporary forms of working, the growing domination of employment in services and concerns over job security and income inequality. These changes have been driven by deindustrialisation in developed economies, the globalisation of production and competition and, in the UK, a sustained shift away from corporatist approaches to economic management to neo-liberal approaches based on privatisation and marketisation. The scale and pace of these changes presents practitioners with considerable and complex challenges, which we explore in the rest of this chapter.

## 3.2 THE CHANGING POLITICAL AND ECONOMIC ENVIRONMENT

As we saw in Chapter 2, the role played by the State in employment relations can be interpreted in different ways. For radicals, the State always acts to support capital, whether in restricting the ability of trade unions to take industrial action or in opening up public services to private sector investment. In contrast, a pluralist perspective characterises the Government as a neutral referee providing a framework in which employers and employees can accommodate their differing interests. However, irrespective of the extent to which governments intervene directly in employment relations, through legislation or their role as an employer, their management of their economy ultimately determines the relative bargaining power of labour and capital, and consequently shapes the nature and climate of employment relations.

### ?    REFLECTIVE ACTIVITY 3.1

What are the main economic, legal/political and technological factors that have impacted on your organisation in the last five years? How have these affected the balance of power between the employer and employees?

### 3.2.1 GOVERNMENT INTERVENTION AND FULL EMPLOYMENT

For nearly 30 years after World War II, successive UK governments, regardless of their political complexion, were committed to a policy of full employment. During this period, economic management was heavily influenced by Keynesian economics, the basic principles of which were:

- the general level of employment in an economy is determined by the level of spending power in the economy
- the overall spending power in the economy depends upon the amount of consumption and investment undertaken by individual households and employing organisations as well as UK government expenditure on matters including health, education, social security and defence
- full employment is achieved by the Government regulating overall spending power in the economy by its fiscal (tax), monetary (interest rates), exchange rates (value of the pound relative to other currencies) and public expenditure policies
- if unemployment rises due to a lack of overall spending power in the economy, the Government should inject spending power by reducing taxes on private and corporate incomes, property, expenditure (VAT, excise duties), by lowering interest rates, and/or by increasing its own expenditure.

Essentially, Keynes argued that government could generate demand in the economy, and therefore employment, through public investment and spending. He believed that the response to a recession should not be a reduction in government spending but greater investment in infrastructure, schools and other public assets. Following World War II, application of the Keynesian model of economic management led to economic growth, increased public provision (in such areas as housing, education and the National Health Service) and personal prosperity for the majority of households. From the perspective of trade unions, full employment provided them with increased bargaining power – not only did union membership and density grow but labour shortages and high levels of demand meant that the threat of industrial action carried significant weight.

However, notwithstanding the increase in the overall standard of living during this period, the British economy underperformed compared with its major competitors. This relative economic underperformance had a negative impact on the climate of employment relations in British workplaces. By the latter part of the 1960s the effect of high wage settlements, poor management and defensive union attitudes caused many commentators to take the view that this deterioration in productivity and competitiveness was a direct consequence of poor workplace industrial relations (Nolan and Walsh, 1995). The immediate response of the then Labour Government was threefold: first it sought to limit wage increases in an attempt to choke off inflation; second, it set up a Royal Commission in 1965 (the Donovan Commission), to investigate the UK's system of industrial relations; and third, it sought to introduce restrictions on the ability of trade unions to take industrial action.

For followers of Keynesian economics, if creating full employment gave rise to inflation, the implementation of a productivity, prices and incomes policy was necessary. Because wage costs account for such a significant proportion of employers' total costs, rising wage levels lead to increases in the rate of inflation, workers therefore demand high pay rises in order to maintain living standards, creating an inflation spiral. One way of combatting inflation is to introduce an 'incomes policy', whereby wage increases are linked to productivity and prices. However, a major problem with this approach was that government only had direct power to enforce pay limits in public sector workplaces, while private sector employers were able to find routes around the restrictions. Consequently, the living standards of public sector workers began to fall and the Government faced strike action from unions in defiance of pay restraint.

Concerns over high levels of industrial action also led the Government to establish the Royal Commission on Trade Unions and Employers' Associations in 1965 under the chairmanship of Lord Donovan. The publication of the Donovan Report (in 1968) was perhaps one of the most significant moments in the history of British employment relations and its recommendations are still reflected in the system which we work today. Essentially, Donovan concluded that the root cause of high levels of strike action was the fragmented and informal nature of workplace bargaining. Wages and conditions were often determined at site and plant level, which meant that groups of workers in the same industry were employed under different conditions and this lack of comparability was a significant source of conflict. There were also very few workplace institutions and procedures through which conflict and disputes could be resolved. Therefore, issues that might involve an individual employee or a small group of workers were subject to collective bargaining and could trigger large-scale industrial action.

Donovan's solution to this problem was to 'institutionalise' conflict by encouraging the development of national structures of collective bargaining with specific provisions for conciliation and arbitration in the case of disputes. In addition, the Commission recommended the introduction of a distinct set of employment rights and, in particular, the right to claim unfair dismissal alongside the development of a system of industrial tribunals to provide workers with a speedy and accessible route to justice. In this way, Donovan sought to remove individual disputes from the ambit of collective bargaining and provide a system for adjudicating and resolving such issues that negated the use of industrial action. In many respects, the establishment of Acas in 1975 epitomised this pluralist response to the 'problem' of industrial conflict. Acas was charged with encouraging the development of collective bargaining structures as well as acting as an arbitrator and conciliator where such bargaining broke down. At the same time, the first Acas Code of Practice on Disciplinary Practice and Procedures, introduced in 1977, set out guidance on how employers, employees and trade unions should deal with disciplinary matters. This code, while not legally binding, defined good practice and was used by industrial tribunals as a guide as to what could be expected of a reasonable employer. Crucially, it provided a route through which such issues could be fairly decided, without recourse to industrial action.

Finally, the Labour Government under the leadership of Harold Wilson attempted to introduce legislation to regulate strike activity. Initial proposals were made in a White Paper entitled 'In Place of Strife', published in 1969. Its main measures included a requirement for ballots before strike action could be called and a 28-day cooling-off period in respect of unofficial or unconstitutional action. It also followed the recommendations of Donovan in proposing the introduction of a right to claim unfair dismissal and new arrangements in relation to union recognition (Tyler, 2006). However, trade union opposition meant that these proposals were quickly dropped, only for some of the main measures to be included in the 1971 Industrial Relations Act by the Conservative Government led by Edward Heath. The fate of this legislation and also the Heath Government provides a stark illustration of the influence of trade unions and also the weakness of management at the time. The Industrial Relations Act failed essentially due to the fact that employers were not prepared to enforce it, fearing that to do so would simply see a further deterioration in employment relations.

While for many employers, and also politicians, the actions of trade unions were seen as irresponsible and led by 'militant' and unrepresentative union leaders, it could also be argued that the approaches taken by trade unions were at least in part a response to deep-rooted structural problems within the UK economy. Weak management performance during the period was also a contributory factor but, more importantly, the UK was plagued by problems of low investment in innovation, research and skills. It is also important to note that the economic conditions of the late 1960s and 1970s stimulated the growth of trade union membership as workers looked to powerful unions to maintain 'real' wage levels.

## ? REFLECTIVE ACTIVITY 3.2

Explain the main elements of the Keynesian approach to macroeconomic management. What would the implications be for employment relations if Keynesian economic policies were introduced by a future government in the UK?

### 3.2.2 THATCHERISM AND THE SUPREMACY OF THE MARKET

In the winter of 1978/79, in the face of inflation rates of around 8%, low-paid public sector employees took strike action to gain pay increases in excess of a 5% pay limit set by the then Labour Government. This led to widespread disruption of public services and formed the backdrop to the General Election that took place in May 1979. The Conservative Party, led by Margaret Thatcher, campaigned on the promise of better management of the economy, lower income taxes, less government expenditure and curtailing union power – all of which they claimed would help the UK economy regain competitiveness. They committed themselves to introducing legislation designed to restrict union influence. This was not simply based on an emotional aversion to trade unionism, but on a fundamental belief that unions represented an obstacle to the working of the free market. Trade unions, it was argued, priced workers out of a job, causing unemployment by increasing wages above the market clearing level through collective bargaining. The Thatcher Government argued that removing trade union influence would allow labour markets to operate freely and wages to fall to the level at which employers were able and prepared to employ workers. Similarly, regulation of the labour market was also seen to act as a barrier to employment, efficiency and competitiveness.

This was related to a broader monetarist economic philosophy, which held that the key to reducing unemployment and controlling inflation was to enhance the ability of the economy to increase the supply of goods and services to the market more efficiently by:

- creating an environment conducive to private enterprise
- creating incentives for individuals to work
- creating incentives for firms to invest, produce goods and services, and employ workers
- liberalising product markets
- privatising publicly-owned enterprises
- reducing taxation
- deregulating labour markets.

Conservative governments from 1979 demolished the prevailing post-war consensus in areas such as the welfare state, UK government intervention in industry, tripartite discussions between government, employers and unions, and maintaining full employment. Instead, they made clear their intention of letting the market decide. As outlined above, monetarist policies were introduced as a means of reducing inflation, which meant sharp increases in interest rates, higher indirect taxes (especially VAT), and deep cuts in public expenditure. The result was a large and rapid increase in unemployment, especially in the country's manufacturing industries such as shipbuilding, car manufacture and steel. Furthermore, many of these traditional industries, which had been owned and controlled by the State and heavily subsidised, were privatised on the basis that being exposed to the rigour of market forces would force management, employees and trade unions to become more efficient in order to survive.

At the same time, the size of the welfare safety net was progressively reduced. While the Government argued that this was designed to increase incentives to work, it also reduced the bargaining power of those already employed and their capacity to challenge managerial authority by deepening the risks associated with unemployment. In addition, and as we explain in Chapter 4, it was made easier to hire and fire staff by increasing the qualifying period before employees could claim unfair dismissal to two years. Furthermore, Wages Councils, which maintained a system of minimum wages in occupations which were unprotected by unions and bargaining, such as hairdressing, were abolished in 1986.

The Conservatives also made it clear that they were no longer prepared to promote the Government's traditional role as a 'model employer' or, at least, the model that they envisaged was very different from the pluralist ideal encapsulated in the Donovan reforms. The UK Government became less favourably disposed to collective bargaining and instead argued that employees should be rewarded as individuals. The Government ceased to encourage people to become members of trade unions or to take part in collective bargaining. An important step in this regard was the establishment of pay review bodies for nurses and midwives in 1983, and for school teachers in 1991, taking groups of highly unionised public sector workers out of collective bargaining. Furthermore, the duty of Acas to promote collective bargaining was removed in 1993.

Not surprisingly, these measures were met with significant opposition from trade unions and the early years of the Thatcher Government were characterised by the high levels of industrial conflict that the Conservatives had pledged to combat. However, these reforms, together with the introduction of legislation to restrict the ability of trade unions to mount effective industrial action (which we examine in greater detail in the next chapter), swung the balance of power firmly in the direction of management, who were left in no doubt that the Government would support any reassertion of their prerogative. This was encapsulated in two major industrial disputes, the Miners' Strike of 1984/85 and, two years later, the strike by print-workers against the decision of *News International* to move its production of newspapers such as *The Sun* to Wapping in East London, imposing the introduction of new technology and effectively derecognising the print and journalists' unions. Both disputes involved strong trade unions opposing measures which would result in significant job losses. However, the Government not only made its support for the actions of management clear, but in the case of the Miners' Strike actively prepared for a confrontation, intervened to prevent a possible settlement and deployed the resources of the State to break the dispute (Brown, 2004; Beckett and Henke, 2009). The eventual defeat of the unions in these disputes was significant in three ways. First, it demonstrated that the State would go to significant lengths to support managerial authority. Second, it was a huge blow to the morale of unions and their members. Finally, it reduced the influence and therefore the effectiveness of trade unions in the eyes of potential new union members.

> **?    REFLECTIVE ACTIVITY 3.3**
>
> In what ways do you think Thatcherism changed society? What implications does this have for the management of employment relations today?

### 3.2.3 NEW LABOUR – FAIRNESS NOT FAVOURS?

The Labour Government elected in 1997 accepted key elements of the Thatcherite programme, such as their commitment to the free market, privatisation and legislation to restrict industrial action. In particular, it made it clear that it was not going to provide 'favours' to trade unions and instead adopted a very clear pro-business message. Nonetheless, it took the view that 'fairness' at work was a key driver of improved performance and competitive advantage. This provided the rationale for the introduction of the national minimum wage, the signing of the Social Chapter of the EU Treaty, the extension of a framework of improved individual employment rights and a new union recognition procedure. Successive Labour governments between 1997 and 2010 also presided over increased spending on the NHS and on education, in some respects reminiscent of classic Keynesian approaches to boost demand through public investment. As a consequence, employment in the public sector increased by approximately 850,000.

However, in some areas, there was a continuation of the economic and employment relations policies developed under previous Conservative administrations. Despite demands from trade unions and others within the party, New Labour failed to reverse any of the privatisations enacted by previous governments, for example, the sell-off of British Rail, which was completed in 1997. Furthermore, it encouraged the increased marketisation of public services and the increased role of private providers in the NHS. In particular, it expanded the private finance initiative (PFI) as a way of raising money for public expenditure from the private sector. While the Government argued that private sector investment was vital in improving infrastructure and services, public service unions argued that it resulted in significant costs to the taxpayer and privatisation 'through the back door'. Also, despite the introduction of the right to recognition under certain circumstances, noted previously, it presided over the continued decline of collective bargaining and followed the lead of previous Conservative governments in diluting bargaining within the public sector, extending the pay review body for nurses and midwives to the rest of NHS staff (apart from doctors, dentists and senior managers) and introducing a new pay review body for prison officers in 2001 (Bach, 2010).

In addition, Labour governments during this period continued the approach to the financial services sector that had been adopted by previous Conservative governments – relying on the City of London to drive economic growth, it followed a light-touch approach to regulation in establishing the Financial Services Authority. The subsequent banking crisis of 2008 and the Government bailout of the UK banking system not only triggered recession but placed increased scrutiny on the level of public expenditure. As a consequence, the recent political agenda has been dominated by the goal of reducing or removing the deficit – the gap between government income and expenditure.

### 3.2.4 COALITION, CONSERVATIVES AND DEFICIT REDUCTION

Following the 2010 General Election, a coalition government was formed between the Conservative Party, which had the largest number of seats in Parliament, and the Liberal Democrats. Its five years in power were defined by the continuing economic implications of the 2008 financial crash and a policy emphasis on austerity. The core theme of government policy was the reduction of public expenditure. Overall, over the life of the Government, departmental spending was cut in real terms by around 8%; however, as certain areas were protected from cuts, such as the NHS and education, the reduction in 'unprotected' departments, such as local government, were swingeing, with total real terms cuts amounting to 21% (Institute for Fiscal Studies, 2015).

This commitment to austerity and deficit reduction has a number of important implications for employment relations. First, there has been a significant shift from public to private sector employment. As Figure 3.1 shows, while private sector employment increased from 23 million to 26 million between 2010 and 2015, public sector employment fell from 6.4 million to 5.3 million. While this was an identified policy goal of the Coalition Government, it also represented a move away from relatively highly unionised and collectively regulated employment.

Figure 3.1 Public and private sector employment, 2010–15

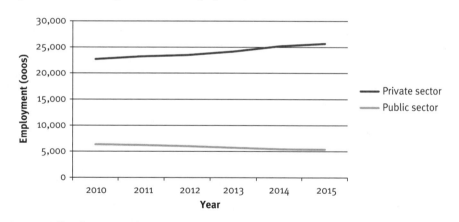

Source: Office for National Statistics

Second, pressure on public expenditure has seen government intervention to limit pay increases in the public sector. Most public sector workers had pay frozen or limited during the five years of coalition government. For example, school teachers received a 2% rise across the whole period. In the 2015 budget, Chancellor George Osborne placed a further four-year cap on public sector pay increases of just 1% per year. Moreover, the Coalition and Conservative governments have moved further to break up public sector pay structures by, for example, attempting to end the common practice of pay increments based on service, which have been an established part of collectively agreed pay structures. Some commentators point out that public sector pay remains above that in the private sector. However, this gap is closing and, as well as being a potential source of industrial conflict in the coming years, it has been argued that pay restraint could lead to problems in recruiting key public sector workers (Cribb *et al*, 2014).

Third, the pressure on the public sector to cut costs and find greater efficiencies is likely to have a significant impact on the way that employment relations are conducted. For example, research conducted by one of the authors in 2014 and 2015 found evidence that more robust attitudes to the management of performance and absence were an increasing source of workplace conflict as staff are faced with a significant intensification of work and far-reaching organisational change (Saundry *et al*, 2016).

A central theme of coalition government policy between 2010 and 2015 was to reduce what it saw as the regulatory burden being placed on business. In particular, there was a focus on the system of dispute resolution and the cost of defending employment tribunal applications (BIS, 2011). This is examined in much greater detail later in this book; however, a range of measures were introduced to reduce the risks of employment litigation. This included the introduction of employment tribunal fees, an increase in the qualifying period for claiming unfair dismissal from one to two years, and new regulations on settlement agreements, providing safeguards to employers in their efforts to negotiate the exit of employees from their organisation. For employers, these changes were a necessary deterrent to weak and speculative claims (see for example CBI, 2013); however, others argued that this was supported by little hard evidence and the new regime was simply a barrier to justice (Ewing and Hendy, 2012; Hepple, 2013).

Liberal Democrat members of the coalition repeatedly argued that their presence restrained Conservative ministers from adopting more extreme policies, particularly in the field of employment relations. Certainly the early signs following the election of a majority Conservative Government in 2015 would appear to confirm this. The Trade Union Bill 2015 has proposed a range of measures, including requiring a threshold whereby 50% of eligible members must vote in an industrial action ballot for the result to stand. In certain public services, unions will also have to win the support of 40% of eligible voters. In addition, the Bill provides powers for government ministers to limit the time off that trade union representatives in the public sector receive to carry out their duties and further restrictions on industrial picketing. Finally, by insisting that union members must opt in to pay into their union's political fund, the Bill seeks to choke off union funding for the Labour Party. While the CBI has welcomed these proposals, trade unions have argued that they effectively outlaw strike action in the UK. We discuss these issues in greater depth in Chapters 4 and 9; however, there is little doubt that this is an attempt by government to further limit the bargaining power and influence of trade unions.

 REFLECTIVE ACTIVITY 3.4

How would you describe the attitude of the current government to trade unions? Why do you think it holds this view and do you think that it is justified?

### 3.2.5 GLOBALISATION

The policy developments outlined in the previous section have taken place within an international economic environment increasingly dominated by multinational companies and the expansion of the global marketplace. Processes of globalisation have led to the rapid development of new markets in developing economies and a significant increase in the mobility of capital and labour, which has allowed corporations to locate production in order to take advantage of lower labour costs, specific skills, natural resources and proximity to emerging markets. In particular, corporations can locate different elements of their operations in different countries to maximise profit and return on investment. For example, this may mean an organisation benefiting from high skills by basing its research and development in the UK and taking advantage of low labour costs and loose employment regulation by locating production in a developing economy.

We explore this issue in detail in Chapter 5. However, the globalisation of production and consumption has had, and is likely to have, a fundamental impact on the nature of employment relations in the UK. Supporters of globalisation would argue that for both consumer and employee it has built bridges, created a greater sense of global community, and provided employment and opportunity for millions, and that this stimulus for change has created actions and events that have, on the whole, had major positive benefits. In contrast, opponents would counter that multinationals have invested in less developed economies in order to take advantage of cheap labour and increase profits.

Competition (which usually underpins the urge to globalise) breeds insecurity. Employees have a tendency to feel unsafe when they know that their employer is competing in the global marketplace. At any time, a new process, product or service can undermine the very basis of their jobs and the threat that production, and therefore employment, can be 'offshored' has undermined the bargaining power of employees and trade unions, and left employers in a very strong position to introduce changes to terms, conditions and working practices in order to compete in international markets.

Increasingly, economic activity is interconnected and therefore the bargaining power of employees and employers is dependent on external developments over which they have no control. Although the UK is not a member of the European single currency, economic difficulties within the Eurozone will have an impact on the demand for British goods in European markets. Similarly, in 2015, the effects of slowing economic growth and demand in China, now the second largest economy of the world, have had major implications for the UK economy.

## THE END OF THE BRITISH STEEL INDUSTRY?

The Chinese steel industry makes up around one-half of global production; however, with declining markets at home, in 2015, Chinese producers flooded international markets with cut-price steel. This put significant pressure on the British steel industry, which has reduced in size substantially in recent years due to international competition, and cannot operate profitably at current international prices. As a direct result, the SSI steel plant at Redcar in the north-east of England was closed in October 2015 with the loss of 2,200 jobs. Within days of the announcement, further job losses were announced in local transport services and coal suppliers that had serviced the coke ovens and blast furnaces at Redcar.

The example of SSI (see box above) is a stark reminder that employment relations in the UK does not operate in a vacuum and employment relations professionals need to be able to anticipate and analyse the potential consequences of global economic conditions.

## 3.3 THE SOCIAL CONTEXT OF EMPLOYMENT RELATIONS

The radical changes in the political and economic environment discussed so far in the chapter have been accompanied by changing social attitudes, which inevitably shape the way that we view work and employment. In the UK, our social attitudes have been tracked since 1983 by the British Social Attitudes Survey. The most recent report, published in 2013, pointed to two key changes: first, there has been a decline in collectivism measured by a reduction in attachment to collective institutions. We discuss the decline in trade union membership in Chapter 5; however, perceptions of union influence shrank rapidly between 1983 and 1997, as Figure 3.2 shows. In 1983 around one-third of people thought that unions had a great deal of influence, but by the time New Labour had been elected this had fallen to just 3%.

Figure 3.2 How much influence do trade unions have?

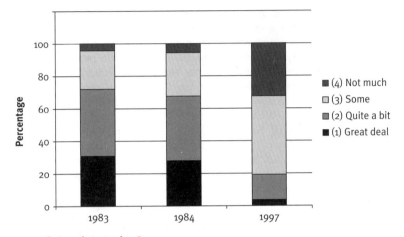

Source: British Social Attitudes Survey

There has also been a significant reduction in the proportion of people who see themselves as belonging to a political party or a particular religion. Whereas 8% of people did not identify with any party in 1983, this increased to 18% in 2013. Second, social attitudes to women and work have changed significantly. As Figure 3.3 shows, between 1984 and 1994 the view that married women worked to be able to afford 'extras' (to supplement their husband's income), a belief that underpinned historic employment discrimination, became much less commonly held.

Figure 3.3 Do married women work only to earn for 'extras'?

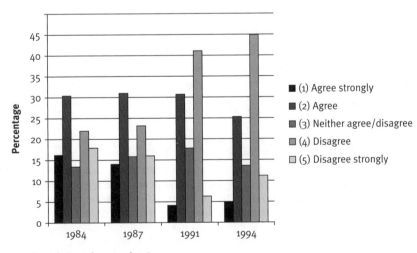

Source: British Social Attitudes Survey

Between 1983 and 1994, support for sex discrimination legislation increased from 78% to 84%. Furthermore, positive views in relation to working mothers have become more widespread. Fifty-nine per cent of people agreed in 1989 that 'working mothers could establish a warm relationship with their children', but by 2012 this had increased to 78%. Therefore, attitudes in relation to women and the labour market became increasingly progressive.

However, we must also be cautious about overstating either the scale or impact of these trends. Data from the BSA, while charting the decline of trade unions and other collective institutions, also shows that public perceptions of unions have generally become more positive over time, with around a quarter of the population believing that trade unions have too little power and more than half feeling that they have about the right amount of power. In addition, improving attitudes to women at work have not addressed some of the fundamental inequalities embedded in the labour market. According to the Fawcett Society (2015), the gender pay gap in 2014 was 19%. Although this represented a significant reduction from 28% in 1997, women are still more likely to work in part-time jobs than men and are more likely to be segregated into feminised sectors, which tend to be less well paid than male-dominated occupations.

Therefore, while the social context plays an important role in shaping employment relations, it is important not to underestimate the resilience of existing structures and institutions, which reflect, among other things, existing divisions in terms of class, gender and race. For example, irrespective of changing attitudes in society, occupational segregation remains a major barrier to achieving equal pay.

## 3.4 THE CHANGING TECHNOLOGICAL CONTEXT

Every organisation operates within certain technological constraints, which impact on its size and structure. In turn, the size and structure of an organisation will undoubtedly have an influence on its culture. Because culture affects relationships between people, it can be seen that technology and technological development are important factors in employment relations.

It is important that employment relations professionals understand the term 'technology'. If it merely implies some form of process or engineering, does it have any relevance outside of manufacturing? Technology is more than an engineering process. From the perspective of an organisation it is about the application of skills and knowledge. It is, therefore, both relevant and necessary to understand it.

In the context of employment relations, it is possible to identify three perspectives from which to view the impact of new technology. One is that new technology, because of its impact on traditional skills, acts as both a de-skilling agent and a creator of unemployment. Second, it can be argued that technology allows managers and employers to increase their control over the labour process by using technology to closely monitor the activities and performance of their employees. Third, new technology can be seen as a positive force in creating new opportunities for employees who have the chance to learn new skills and can eliminate unpleasant or repetitive tasks.

The way in which these factors combine to impact on employment relations is not straightforward. We noted in Chapter 2 that Harry Braverman had argued that technology played a central role in de-skilling workers and allowing managers to gain greater control of the workforce. There is little doubt that in many areas of manufacturing increased automation has both cut jobs and also reduced the autonomy and discretion of workers. New technology, in this sense, undermines the power and influence of labour. However, for those workers who remain, conditions are often better.

For example, in 1970, the UK car manufacturing industry employed around 850,000 workers and produced just over 2 million cars. It was highly unionised and also strike prone, with more than 500 stoppages in that year. In 2014, production was just a little lower at 1.6 million cars, but the industry employed just 138,000 workers and, while it remains highly unionised, there were just 12 industrial stoppages in 2014 involving just over 2,000 workers (Rhodes and Sear, 2015; Office for National Statistics, 2015). Undoubtedly, part of the reason for this change was automation, and it could be argued that improved working environments have contributed to more harmonious employment relations. At the same time, the impact of new technology on jobs and employment security, together with the globalisation of competition, critically undermined the bargaining power of car workers. Therefore, the partnership working that we see today in the UK car industry is at least in part a product of the relative weakness of organised labour.

It has also been argued that technological change has heralded the rise of the 'knowledge worker' whereby organisations have a greater requirement for workers with high levels of skills, who in turn can enjoy greater autonomy and discretion over their work. However, while it is possible to point to the growth of specific hi-tech sectors and organisations that rely on workers with very highly developed skill sets, the overall picture is one of relatively little change (Williams and Adam-Smith, 2009). While the shift from manufacturing to service industries has seen a growth in non-manual occupations, work in, for example, call centres is routinised, standardised and offers workers little discretion or autonomy (Taylor and Bain, 1999).

It is also important to acknowledge that technology is not just something that employers can utilise to increase productivity, replace labour or increase their control over the labour process. One of the most significant recent technological developments has been the growth of online social networks such as Facebook, Twitter and Instagram. Although the use of social media is a significant part of many occupations and is actively encouraged by some employers, it has provided managers and HR practitioners with a number of significant challenges (see Broughton et al, 2011, for a review). Employees may use social media for personal reasons during working hours, reducing productivity. In addition, the misuse of social media platforms to denigrate employers and/or their colleagues is becoming an increasingly common reason for disciplinary action in UK workplaces. This reflects the way in which social media is blurring the lines between social and work life, and also potentially reshaping personal and work relations, as individuals discuss work issues in the public gaze and managers and their subordinates become 'Facebook friends'. Recent research (Saundry et al, 2016) found that social media provided a 'venue' in which conflict could escalate outside the control of the employer; whereas in the past a disagreement at work would either be forgotten by the next day or could be addressed and resolved by managers, the argument can be carried on through social media so that by the following morning the issue is not only more serious but has potentially spread across a group of colleagues.

The discussion above suggests that the impact of technology is complex and must be considered in conjunction with wider changes to workplace relations. A commonly held view about the impact of technological change is that it creates problems, particularly where trade unions are represented in the workplace, and is often resisted. When change is on the agenda, both trade unions and employees generally will have fears over job losses, de-skilling and increased management control. Of course, the skill of the employment relations professional lies in understanding these concerns and seeking ways of mitigating them, but it is also important to recognise the way that technology can have a broader impact on the conduct of employment relations.

What changes in technology do you expect to affect your organisation, or the sector in which you operate, in the next five years? What is their likely impact on employment relations behaviour?

## 3.5 THE TRANSFORMATION OF THE UK LABOUR MARKET

One of the main consequences of the changing political and economic context has been a radical transformation of the UK labour market. Perhaps the most notable feature has been the shift from employment in manufacturing to employment in the service industry. It is important to note that this is not a new phenomenon and, while it accelerated as a result of the election and subsequent policies of the Thatcher Government, this process of deindustrialisation had begun in the early 1960s and affected all developed economies.

Figure 3.4 Percentage of working people employed in each industry group, 1911–2011

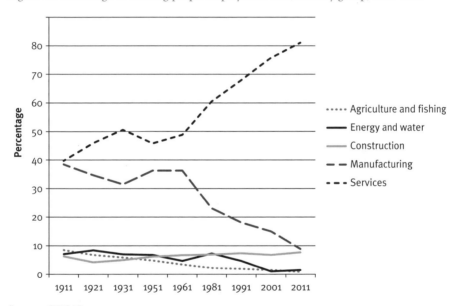

Source: ONS/Census

As Figure 3.4 clearly shows, this transformation has been part of a long-term trend. In 1911, there was parity between manufacturing and service employment, but the gulf began to widen from 1960 and, by 1981, just two years after the election of the Thatcher Government, service employment accounted for six out of every ten jobs. This trend has continued to the point where, in 2011, manufacturing represented less than 10% of the total workforce, with 81% of workers employed in services. This in turn has contributed to a reduction of manual jobs traditionally carried out by men and an increase in the percentage of women in employment, from 53% in 1971 to 67% in 2013. At the same time, the proportion of men in work has fallen from 92% to 76%.

Moreover, there has been a change in the nature of employment with an increased diversity of employment types. Some commentators have argued that the relative growth in jobs in the service sector in comparison with the manufacturing sector has led to an increase in 'McJobs' – part-time, badly paid and with low status – which has contributed to the decline in trade union membership and influence. It is argued that the lack of security offered by this type of employment has made people less inclined to join trade unions because they are afraid to challenge their employer. The decline in traditional union strongholds, such as mining and shipbuilding, has had an effect, but as with most things in employment relations, the reality tends to be more complex.

In fact, 15 years of economic growth between 1993 and 2008 had positive impacts on the labour market, increasing employment stability and security, and restraining job intensification that had been a feature of the 1990s (van Wanrooy *et al*, 2013). But WERS2011 found evidence that the recession which started in 2008 had led to renewed fears over employment security, particularly in the public sector, as government sought to reduce expenditure. In addition, there was renewed growth in the use of part-time working and temporary contracts, and a significant increase in the use of atypical contracts (such as so-called zero-hours contracts) in the private sector (van Wanrooy *et al*, 2013).

## ZERO-HOURS CONTRACTS

A recent phenomenon of the labour market has been the increased use of zero-hours contracts. These can be defined as arrangements where the employee is not guaranteed a fixed number of hours – essentially they are 'on call' and can be asked and are expected to work at short notice and will only be paid for the hours that they work. In the past, similar arrangements were used in industries in which the demand for labour was highly variable, such as dock work. However, they have become increasingly used in jobs in which variability of demand is much more limited. For employers, a major benefit is that such contracts are unlikely to accrue employment rights, and if there is a dip in demand labour costs can easily be reduced. According to the Office for National Statistics, between April and June 2015, 744,000 people were employed on a zero-hours contract in their 'main job'. This represented 2.4% of the workforce, an increase from 2% in the same period in 2014. On average, those on such contracts worked 25 hours a week and most were women, students and either under 25 or over 65. Approximately 40% of businesses in accommodation and food services, and 25% of those in education, made some use of such contracts.

However, it is important to put the use of 'non-standard' employment contracts in perspective. Table 3.1 sets out OECD data which shows that temporary employment makes up only a small proportion of overall employment in the UK. In 2014, this stood at less than 7% and, while there has been some growth since the recession of 2008, this figure has remained relatively stable.

Table 3.1 Incidence of permanent and temporary employment – UK, 2000–2014

|  | Share of permanent employment | | Share of temporary employment | |
|---|---|---|---|---|
|  | Total workforce | 15–24 yrs | Total workforce | 15–24 yrs |
|  | % | % | % | % |
| 2000 | 93 | 85.8 | 7 | 14.2 |
| 2001 | 93.3 | 86 | 6.8 | 14 |
| 2002 | 93.6 | 87.1 | 6.4 | 12.9 |
| 2003 | 93.9 | 87.5 | 6.1 | 12.5 |

| | Share of permanent employment | | Share of temporary employment | |
|---|---|---|---|---|
| | Total workforce | 15–24 yrs | Total workforce | 15–24 yrs |
| | % | % | % | % |
| 2004 | 94 | 87.2 | 6 | 12.8 |
| 2005 | 94.2 | 87.7 | 5.8 | 12.3 |
| 2006 | 94.2 | 87.2 | 5.8 | 12.8 |
| 2007 | 94.2 | 86.7 | 5.9 | 13.3 |
| 2008 | 94.6 | 88 | 5.4 | 12 |
| 2009 | 94.4 | 88.1 | 5.6 | 11.9 |
| 2010 | 93.9 | 86.2 | 6.1 | 13.8 |
| 2011 | 93.8 | 86.4 | 6.2 | 13.6 |
| 2012 | 93.7 | 85 | 6.3 | 15 |
| 2013 | 93.8 | 85.3 | 6.2 | 14.7 |
| 2014 | 93.6 | 84.8 | 6.4 | 15.2 |

Source: OECD

Interestingly, the use of temporary employment is much more prevalent among younger workers, reaching 15% in 2014. Furthermore, again we can see a steady increase that coincides with the onset of the recession. Table 3.2 provides data from the Workplace Employment Relations Survey 2011. Perhaps surprisingly, the use of part-time workers, temporary contracts and agency workers is much more common in the public sector. However, the areas of growth appear to be the use of temporary contracts in the private sector while there has been a substantial increase, albeit from a low base, in the use of both homeworking and zero-hours contracts since 2004.

Table 3.2 Incidence of use of non-standard employment by workplace, 2004–11

| | Private Sector | | Public Sector | |
|---|---|---|---|---|
| | 2004 | 2011 | 2004 | 2011 |
| | % | % | % | % |
| Part-time work | 76 | 77 | 92 | 89 |
| Temporary contracts | 17 | 21 | 53 | 51 |
| Freelancers | 11 | 15 | 10 | 10 |
| Agency workers | 10 | 10 | 23 | 19 |
| Homeworkers | 7 | 11 | 2 | 8 |
| Zero hours | 4 | 8 | 4 | 8 |

Source: WERS2011 (van Wanrooy et al, 2013).

Whatever the statistics, there is no doubt that the ability of managers to adjust the size of their workforces in line with requirements and demand – usually referred to as numerical flexibility – appears to be relatively widespread. The implications of these changes are quite complex. Guy Standing (2011), for example, has argued that globalisation, among other things, has led to the creation of what he has termed the 'precariat' – a new class of workers made up of migrant labour, young people, those on temporary and short-term contracts and workers displaced from traditional full-time, skilled industrial occupations. These workers not only face job insecurity, but a lack of autonomy and occupational identity.

At the same time, there has been growing concern that the UK has become an 'hourglass economy' characterised by a labour market which is polarised between highly paid and highly skilled jobs at one end and low-paid, low-skill jobs at the other – with a significant decline in semi-skilled manufacturing and administrative jobs 'in the middle'. This, it has been argued, will potentially fuel wage inequality (Holmes and Mayhew, 2012). CIPD research conducted by the ESRC Centre on Skills, Knowledge and Organisational Performance (SKOPE) and published in 2014 (CIPD, 2014) found that about a third of British workers were overqualified for their jobs. This has been caused in part by government policy that encourages competition on the basis of low-cost, low-skill production and a lack of investment in training and skills. For example, the report found large numbers of graduates who were forced to settle for low-paid and low-skilled work, mainly in the service sector. The UK has the second highest level of overqualification and low-skilled jobs in the OECD. This not only threatens to lead to income inequality but is also seen as one reason for the UK's poor productivity record compared with other developed economies. Of course, not all flexibility is necessarily bad for employees and in recent years there has been a substantial increase in the availability of flexible working arrangements, including homeworking, term-time-only working, flexitime and job-sharing, at least among continuing workplaces. Furthermore, this has been helped by government measures to improve work–life balance.

Issues around the jobs and workplaces of the future need to be carefully considered, and the employment relations specialist must be a key player in this debate. That requires them to constantly be aware of new research, government policy and economic developments. Commentators typically assert that the forces of globalisation and technology are challenging current patterns of working, but find little else on which to agree. At the extremes, pessimists conjure a haunting spectre of mass unemployment, growing insecurity and widening social divisions, while optimists claim that the emerging 'new' economy will liberate many employees from the dull, dreary and degrading jobs that stifled working lives in the past. Both scenarios remain ungrounded in any systematic theory or evidence, and a pervasive weakness is the absence in such accounts of an adequate historical perspective. Nevertheless, the debate over the future of work will continue, and – given the effects of one of the deepest recessions we have yet experienced – the prospects for work and employment are of major importance, not just to policymakers at the macro level, but also to organisational practitioners.

## 3.6 CONTEXT AND THE BALANCE OF BARGAINING POWER

The Government's economic and legal policies have major implications for the conduct and outcome of employment relations. If economic policies are directed towards the creation of full employment and the maximising of economic growth, this weakens the relative bargaining power of the employer but strengthens that of the employee. A high level of demand for goods and services in the economy as a whole generates demand for labour to produce/provide those goods and services. If the demand for labour services increases relative to their supply (that is, to the extent that shortages develop), the 'price' employers will have to pay to secure those services will also increase.

If, on the other hand, Government economic policies give the highest priority to reducing inflation by lowering household and corporate spending, and reducing public expenditure, the demand (spending power) in the economy will fall and, as a consequence, so will the demand for labour. The result will be labour 'surpluses', giving rise to redundancies and increased unemployment. The effect of the supply of labour exceeding demand is downward pressure on the 'price' of labour services. And, if labour prices are inflexible downwards, less labour will be employed than previously (that is, there will be a rise in unemployment) at the same price. In such situations, the relative balance of bargaining power of employers will be strengthened and that of the employees weakened.

If the Government introduces legislation favourable to employers' interests, the bargaining power of employers relative to employees is strengthened. This is what Conservative governments did during the period 1980–97, by introducing a series of labour law reforms. If a government introduces legislation favourable to the interests of employees and trade unions, the bargaining power of employees relative to employers is strengthened. For example, some employers feared that the introduction of the statutory recognition procedures contained in the Employment Relations Act (1999) and other legislation introduced by the Labour Government elected in 1997 would swing the balance of power towards trade unions. This also coincided with a period of economic growth and high employment. However, while the pace of union decline slowed in this period, union influence did not return to its previous levels. In part this may be due to the fact that while the Labour Government provided a more favourable context for trade unions, it left much of the legislation introduced in the previous 17 years in place. Perhaps more importantly, other contextual changes, in particular the globalisation of competition and production, provided employers with significant leverage in their dealings with trade unions.

The implementation of new technology also impacts on bargaining power. For example, developments in communications have helped to produce global markets that have increased product market competition. This can lead to downward pressure on the 'price' of labour services and a shift in bargaining power towards the employer. The reverse can also be true. By creating new jobs, requiring new skills and making some industries more capital-intensive, organisations may become increasingly reliant on key skills and production processes may become much more susceptible to disruption.

Finally, changes to the structure of the UK labour market have generally undermined the bargaining power of labour. While it is important not to exaggerate the growth of 'atypical' employment, the rapid increase in the use of zero-hours contracts weakens the ability of workers to voice concerns or challenge managerial authority as they will be less likely to be offered 'hours' in the future. At the same time, the shift of employment away from highly unionised sectors of the economy and the recent reductions in the number of public sector jobs can only further erode trade union organisation and influence.

## ? REFLECTIVE ACTIVITY 3.6

Can you identify where the relative balance of bargaining power lies in your organisation? Is this balance static, or is there the potential for any significant shift in power? How has the context within which your organisation operates contributed to this?

## 3.7 SUMMARY

This chapter has examined the role of the UK Government as an economic manager. The use of monetarist macro-economic policy in the early 1980s and the increased emphasis on the 'free market' led to the promotion of deregulation, privatisation and marketisation, which undermined collective approaches to the management and regulation of employment relations. This has been accentuated by the globalisation of economic activity and the ability of multinational corporations to relocate (or threaten to relocate) productive resources to less developed economies to take advantage of lower labour costs and weaker regulation. The 2008 recession and the dominance of economic policies of austerity would appear to further erode areas in which trade union organisation is relatively strong and skew the balance of workplace bargaining power towards the employer.

In addition, the concept of the Government as a 'model employer' has changed over time. In the immediate post-war years there was encouragement of collective bargaining and an attempt to ensure comparability of pay between the public and private sectors. From 1979, the emphasis was on a more individual approach to the employment relationship, with a clear discouragement of national pay bargaining. This has continued despite the election of three successive Labour governments between 1997 and 2010. The election of a Conservative majority administration in 2015 is likely to see further legislation to restrict trade union activity.

Alongside the changing political and economic context, we have also seen broader changes to social attitudes and rapid technological change, which will also have profound implications for our attitudes to work and the way in which employment relations are managed in the future. The growing diversity of labour markets means that work–life balance issues and particular demands for greater equality are likely to become increasingly prominent. At the same time, the increased use of zero-hours contracts and other atypical forms of employment raise important questions of employment security, inequality and organisational performance. Furthermore, the pervasive influence of social media in reducing the barriers between work and personal life, and its increased organisational use, creates challenges for employment relations professionals.

## KEY LEARNING POINTS

1   Changes in economic management and reforms to labour law have undermined the organisation and influence of trade unions in the UK, and have (in general) reduced the bargaining power of labour.

2   The role of the State in employment relations has fundamentally changed, and it no longer adopts a pluralist approach through the support of collective bargaining and collective employment relations institutions.

3   The continuing globalisation of markets will be a major influence on organisational change and thus employment relations. The threat of employers moving production to less developed economies further reduces the bargaining power of labour.

4   Social attitudes can have an important impact on employment relations – in the UK there is a decline in attachment to collective institutions, which could be reflected in the difficulties faced by trade unions in recruiting new members. At the same time, attitudes to working women have become much more progressive. Consequently, issues such as the gender pay gap have become increasingly important.

5   Technological innovation will continue to influence the workplace, and will therefore impact on employment relations practices. While this has brought an improvement in working conditions in some industries, technology has also led to an intensification of work and extended employer control over the labour process.

6   The UK labour market has been transformed over the last four decades. There has been a continuing growth in service-sector employment and a significant rise in the number and proportion of women employed. Recent increases in the use of 'zero-hours' contracts and the shift from public to private sector employment threatens to reduce employment security and further reduce the bargaining power of labour.

REVIEW QUESTIONS

1   What are the main consequences of the current UK Government's economic strategy?

2   To what extent could the position of trade unions be affected by future general elections in the UK?

3   How have changing social attitudes in the UK over the last 40 years shaped the way in which employment relations are conducted? What impact do you think this could have in the next two decades?

4   What impact will the increased use of social media (both inside and outside work) have on employment relations, and what challenges does this pose for the management of employment relations?

5   Where does the relative balance of bargaining power lie in your organisation? Do you see this balance as static and, if so, why? Or, if there is potential for a significant shift in power, explain how and why this might occur.

EXPLORE FURTHER

BROUGHTON, A., HIGGINS, T. and HICKS, B. (2011) *Workplaces and social networking – the implications for employment relations*. Acas research papers, No 11/11. London: Acas.

BROWN, W. (2004) Industrial relations and the economy. In: FLOUD, R. and JOHNSON, P. (eds) *The Cambridge economic history of modern Britain volume 3: structural change and growth, 1939–2000*. Cambridge: Cambridge University Press. pp399–423.

CIPD (2014) Industrial strategy and the future of skills policy – the high road to sustainable growth. *Research insights*. London: CIPD.

THE FAWCETT SOCIETY (2105) The gender pay gap. Available at:www.fawcettsociety.org.uk/our-work/campaigns/gender-pay-gap/ [Accessed 04 October 2015].

GENNARD, J. (2009) The financial crisis and employee relations. *Employee relations*. Vol 31, No 5. pp451–454.

HEPPLE, B. (2013) Back to the future: employment law under the coalition government. *Industrial law journal*. Vol 42, No 3. pp203–223.

HOLMES, C. and MAYHEW, K. (2012)*The changing shape of the UK job market and its implications for the bottom half of earners*. London: Resolution Foundation.

VAN WANROOY, B., BEWLEY, H., BRYSON, A. *et al* (2013) *Employment relations in the shadow of the recession*. Basingstoke: Palgrave MacMillan.

**Websites**

www.natcen.ac.uk/our-research/research/british-social-attitudes/ is the website that contains findings from the British Social Attitudes Survey.

www.ons.gov.uk/ons/index.html is the website for the Office for National Statistics, which contains raw labour market data and a range of publications related to employment and employment relations statistics.

# CHAPTER 4

# Employment Relations and the Law

## OVERVIEW

The chapter begins by outlining the process by which UK legislation is approved and then goes on to consider the fundamental basis of employment relations, the *contract of employment*, which defines and regulates the relationship between the employer and the employee. The chapter traces the nature and development of state intervention, and in particular the shift from 'voluntarism' towards more active government involvement in creating a framework of individual employment rights and regulating industrial action. Next, the chapter examines the functions of the law in employment relations, drawing on the work of Otto Kahn-Freund, who outlined three functions of the law in regulating employment rights: auxiliary, regulatory and restrictive. It then explores key legal issues that confront employment relations and HR professionals in their daily work, and on which they are routinely asked for advice. Therefore, the chapter outlines the law related to unfair dismissal, redundancy and equality, with a particular focus on the employment tribunal system. The nature and jurisdiction of employment tribunals, including the application process, the hearing and the decision are all examined in some detail. The final part of the chapter discusses criticisms of the system of individual employment rights and asks whether a more proactive approach to regulation is required.

## LEARNING OUTCOMES

When you have completed this chapter, you should be able to:

- understand and describe the legislative process
- explain the legal basis of the contract of employment and analyse issues related to employment status
- understand the main functions of the law and critically evaluate the development of the legal framework underpinning UK employment relations
- understand and critically assess the key principles of employment legislation relating to discrimination
- describe the employment tribunal process and critically analyse tribunal reform.

## 4.1 INTRODUCTION

For most managers and HR professionals, the law has become a prime consideration in the way in which they respond to employment relations issues. This is a relatively recent development and up to the late 1960s, employment relations in the UK was characterised by 'voluntarism' in which the role of the state was to provide a basic legal framework that supported 'free' collective bargaining between employers and trade unions, and 'plugged gaps' in collective regulation (Dickens and Hall, 2010). However, since the publication of the report of the Donovan Commission in 1968, and the introduction of the right to claim unfair dismissal, the extent and influence of employment law has steadily grown to the point that it imposes itself on every facet of the employment relationship. In this context, it is important that the employment relations professional does not view the law as simply a process of compliance. While an awareness of the legal implications of managerial decisions is crucial, positive employment relations will not be achieved by the rigid and restrictive application of the law, but by approaches that are underpinned by fairness and trust.

Nonetheless, because of its scale and complexity, employment law can often overwhelm even the most experienced of practitioners, and for this reason its range and impact need to be clearly understood. It is not our intention to provide a detailed explanation of every piece of legislation. Textbooks, such as Lewis and Sargeant's (2015) *Essentials of Employment Law*, Kathy Daniels' (2016) *Introduction to Employment Law: Fundamentals for HR and Business Students*, and online facilities, such as the CIPD Employment Law Service, can do that in a much more effective way. Our purpose is to examine the legislation in the context of employment relations and to explain how relationships can be influenced by the way in which individual employers apply legislative rules and standards.

## 4.2 THE LEGISLATIVE PROCESS

Employment law in the UK principally derives either from legislation passed or sanctioned by the UK Parliament, or that established through the European Commission and Parliament (the influence of European legislation is examined in greater detail in Chapter 5). Lewis and Sargeant (2015) provide a detailed explanation of 'the sources and institutions of employment law', but generally, the process by which the legislation is enacted is as follows. The Government of the day might issue what has traditionally been called a 'Green Paper' followed by a 'White Paper' followed by a 'Bill', which, after the parliamentary process has been exhausted, becomes an 'Act of Parliament'. The first two stages are not obligatory and governments can bypass them if they so wish.

The Green Paper is a consultative document and is used by the Government to obtain the views of interested parties to proposed legislation. It also provides an important opportunity for employers' organisations, trade unions and bodies, such as the CIPD, to influence the detail of legal changes. Recent examples on which the Government has entered into consultation include shared parental leave, zero-hours contracts and charging fees in the Employment Tribunal and the Employment Appeals Tribunal.

Once the consultation is complete, the Government will usually issue a White Paper setting out its policy intentions. This again provides an opportunity for a further round of lobbying and public debate where interested parties seek to petition MPs and government to recognise their specific interests in terms of the implications of the law being enacted. A Bill is then introduced into Parliament and, assuming it survives the scrutiny of both the House of Commons and the House of Lords, and is given Royal Assent, the agreed Bill becomes an Act – for example, the Employment Rights Act (1996). In addition, Acts of Parliament can give government ministers powers to make detailed orders, rules and regulations without Parliament having to pass a new Act. These are known as Statutory Instruments (SIs) and are used to provide detail and make minor changes that would be too complex to include in primary legislation. For example, although the primary legislation providing for the National Minimum Wage is contained in the National Minimum Wage Act 1998, changes to the level of the minimum wage are enacted by Statutory Instrument.

**?    REFLECTIVE ACTIVITY 4.1**

Compare the Trade Union Bill, tabled in 2015, with the eventual legislation. Can you identify any changes that were made during its passage through Parliament? If yes, why do you think the legislation was revised?

Sometimes the distinction between legislation driven by domestic political issues and that derived from the European Union is not easily identified (Bercusson, 1996). It is also the case that legislators will often merge these two influences in an attempt to maximise the use of parliamentary time. For example, the Employment Relations Act (1999) contains provisions – on part-time workers and parental – leave that derived from the European process as well as provisions derived from the UK political process, that is, trade union recognition and the right to be accompanied at disciplinary and grievance hearings. For HR and personnel practitioners, a classic example of how the source of legislation can become confused can again be demonstrated by the National Minimum Wage Act (1998). The proposal for a minimum wage was a clear manifesto commitment of the Labour Party prior to the 1997 General Election and was, in part, a product of its close relationship with the trade union movement. Once they were elected, it became one of their priorities for legislation, and yet many practitioners remain convinced that the minimum wage was introduced because of an EU Directive.

## 4.3 THE CONTRACT OF EMPLOYMENT

The most important and major influence in employment law is the contract of employment. It is vital that the employment relations professional understands its impact. This is because it defines and regulates the relationship between the employer and the employee. However, the contract cannot possibly anticipate every situation and contingency that may develop in the relationship between an employer and employee. Therefore, it has to be supplemented by the informal processes and formal procedures that constitute employment relations.

This is in part illustrated by the definition of the contract of employment. Section 230(2) of the Employment Rights Act 1996 provides that a *'contract of employment'* means *'a contract of service or apprenticeship, whether express or implied and (if it is express) whether oral or in writing'*. As this suggests, a contract of employment does not need to be written down but can be entered into on the basis of informal verbal agreement or understanding. The danger with such an arrangement, however, is that the lack of detail and clarity can easily lead to misunderstanding and conflict between the parties.

For this reason, it is always advisable to set down as much of the contract of employment as possible in writing. Under section 1 of the Employment Rights Act 1996, employers are required to give employees a written statement of their main terms and conditions of employment within two months of starting work. This has to contain certain information. It can also be made up of more than one document. If this does happen, one of the documents (called the 'principal statement') must include a number of specific details, which are set out in the box on page 58.

**The written statement of terms and conditions of employment**

Principal statement:

- Start date and, if a previous job counts towards a period of continuous employment, the date the period started
- Level of pay and when employee will be paid
- Hours of work, including provision for Sunday, night and overtime working
- Holiday entitlement, including whether this includes public holidays
- Location of work and whether they might have to relocate
- Name of the employer and employee
- Job title or a description of work

In addition to the principal statement, employees must also be given in writing details of:

- Length of contract and end date if fixed-term/temporary
- Notice periods
- Details of any collective agreements that may apply
- Pensions
- Who to go to if the employee has a grievance and how to complain about how a grievance is handled
- How to complain about a disciplinary or dismissal decision

The written statement must also say where the following can be found:

- Sick pay and procedures
- Disciplinary and dismissal procedures
- Grievance procedures

Importantly, the statement is not a contract of employment in itself but is evidence of what the parties have agreed. This is because the contract of employment can also include other terms. First, where pay and conditions are subject to collective bargaining, the terms of collective agreements will generally be incorporated into the contract. Second, rules that are determined and applied by the employer can form part of the contract. Third, where a particular rule or practice has not been written down or expressly agreed but is widely accepted and has been followed for a considerable time, it can form part of the contract – this is known as 'custom and practice'.

## CUSTOM AND PRACTICE?

**Park Cakes Ltd v Shumba and others [2013] EWCA**

For a term to be implied in a contract of employment through custom and practice, it is generally agreed that it should be: fair, well established over a period of time, known to employees, and also clear and unambiguous.

In this case, which was heard by the Court of Appeal in 2013, a number of employees argued that although it was not included in their written statement of terms and conditions, an enhanced redundancy package had been implied into their contracts of employment as a result of custom and practice.

The employees demonstrated that there had been a group-wide policy of normally paying the package and that it was also included in the company's HR manual as terms were available on request from the HR department.

The tribunal originally rejected the claim because the policy had not been 'followed without exception' previously. The employees' appeal to the EAT was successful and this decision was upheld by the Court of Appeal. It concluded that whether a term was implied should be judged not in terms of what the employer intended but whether the employer's conduct suggested it to the employee. For example, in this case, having the policy available on request conveyed the message to staff that the employer was bound to pay the enhanced terms.

---

Fourth, some pieces of legislation either imply or impose terms into all contracts of employment. For example, section 1 of the Equal Pay Act 1970 states that:

> 'If the terms of a contract under which a woman is employed at an establishment in Great Britain do not include (directly or by reference to a collective agreement or otherwise) an equality clause they shall be deemed to include one.'

Other legislation that shapes contracts in this way includes: the National Minimum Wage Act 1998, the Working Time Regulations and awards made by the Central Arbitration Committee.

Finally, a series of terms are also implied into the contract of employment by common law – these 'implied terms' are duties that have been established by the courts through case law. For example, employers have a duty to pay wages, provide work, take reasonable care of the employee and provide references. Employees also have duties to the employer to obey lawful and reasonable orders, act with fidelity, and to exercise reasonable skill and care. The implied term that most affects the day-to-day operation of employment relations is that of 'mutual trust and confidence'. This applies to both employers and employees, and is central to the consideration of unfair dismissal. We will examine this in greater detail later; however, employee actions that undermine 'trust and confidence' will normally be seen as constituting gross misconduct and so potentially justifying summary dismissal. At the same time, actions taken by employers that breach the duty to maintain mutual trust and confidence may constitute constructive dismissal, whereby employees feel they have no other option but to resign.

?     REFLECTIVE ACTIVITY 4.2

How would you explain to a line manager the importance of issuing employees with a written statement of their terms and conditions of employment?

## 4.4 EMPLOYEE STATUS

Understanding the legal basis of the contract of employment is also vital, as its existence defines employee status. Section 230(1) of the Employment Rights Act (1996) defines an 'employee' as an 'individual who has entered into or works under (or, where the employment has ceased, worked under) a contract of employment'. In recent years the ways in which individuals are contracted to organisations have becoming increasingly diverse. In particular we have witnessed the growth of agency work, freelance working, fixed-term and zero-hours contracts. However, in law, the key distinction is between 'employee' and 'independent contractor', with only the former entitled to the full protection afforded by current employment legislation and, in particular, the right to claim unfair dismissal. In many cases it will be absolutely clear that a person is an employee, but there are a wide variety of relationships that exhibit characteristics of both employment and self-employment, and it is in relation to these relationships that the difficulties lie.

Whether or not an individual is working under a contract of employment is extremely complex and is largely determined through case law. There have been many attempts by the courts to provide a simple and easily understandable definition, but in *Montgomery* v *Johnson Underwood Limited*, the Court of Appeal confirmed that in determining whether a contract of employment exists the 1968 case of *Ready Mixed Concrete (South East) Limited* v *Minister of Pensions and National Insurance* offers the best guidance. In the *Ready Mixed Concrete* case it was held that a contract of employment exists if three conditions are fulfilled. The first condition is that there exists a 'mutuality of obligation' between the parties. If an individual agrees to provide his or her own work (ie personal service) and skill for the employer when the employer requires him or her to do so, and the employer in return agrees to provide work for the individual and pay a wage or other remuneration for that work, then there will exist a mutuality of obligation. The second condition is that the individual is *under the control* of the employing company. Some of the relevant factors to be considered when determining whether an individual is under the control of the employing company are whether the individual:

- is under a duty to obey orders
- has control over his or her hours
- is subject to the company's disciplinary procedure
- is supervised as to the mode of working
- provides his or her own equipment
- has to comply with the company's rules on the taking of holidays
- works regular hours
- can delegate his or her duties
- can work for others at the same time as working for the particular company
- is integrated into the employer's business (ie is he or she responsible for issuing management instructions, and does he or she have the power to discipline the company's workers?).

Finally, tribunals will assess whether the other provisions of the contract are consistent with it being a contract of service. Relevant factors include who has responsibility for tax and National Insurance and whether the individual is in receipt of sick pay/holiday pay. Notwithstanding that these factors may be present, the first two conditions (mutuality of obligation and control) are the 'irreducible minimum' required for a contract of employment. In recent years, the growth in the use of zero-hours contracts has highlighted these issues. In principle, if someone is employed on a zero-hours contract there is no guarantee of work and therefore no mutuality of obligation. However, whatever the contract stipulates, tribunals will look at the reality of the relationship between the organisation and the worker, as the case of *Pulse Healthcare* v *Carewatch Care* demonstrates. The details of this are outlined in Case Study 4.2:

---

**CASE STUDY 4.2**

### ZERO-HOURS CONTRACTS AND EMPLOYMENT STATUS

*Pulse Healthcare* v *Carewatch Care (2012) UKEAT/0123/12/BA*

Five care workers were employed by Carewatch under zero-hours contracts and supplied to a primary care trust to provide round-the-clock care for a severely disabled individual. Under the contracts, Carewatch was under no obligation to provide work and the carers were free to work elsewhere. However, the employees worked fixed hours on a regular basis. The contracts made repeated mention of employment and contained clauses related to annual leave, sickness, pension and the provision of uniforms.

However, the Employment Appeal Tribunal (EAT) found that the written contract did not reflect the reality of the situation – while contracts indicated 'zero hours', the care workers worked as part of a team that provided a care package for a client for an agreed number of hours per week. Although they could question working certain shifts when rosters were produced, they worked on regular shifts of 24 or 36 hours per week. They were also not allowed to use a substitute worker to perform their duties. Therefore, the EAT concluded that they worked on global contracts of employment and were 'employees'.

---

Once these tests have been satisfied and it is clear that an individual is employed under a contract of employment, he or she effectively has the following full rights under current employment legislation:

- Protection from unfair dismissal
- Statutory redundancy payment
- Maternity leave and statutory maternity pay
- Statutory sick pay
- Parental and urgent family leave
- A minimum period of notice
- A written statement of particulars of employment.

However, if an individual does not meet the tests outlined above but nonetheless still carries out 'personal services' for another party under a contract, they may be defined as a 'worker' under section 203(3) of the Employment Rights Act (1996).

The great majority of agency workers, homeworkers, casuals and freelancers are likely to be workers. Someone who falls within the definition of a 'worker' will enjoy rights, like employees, to the National Minimum Wage, holiday pay, protection against unlawful discrimination, and the right not to be treated less favourably if they work part-time. They are also covered by the Working Time Regulations and legislation relating to health and safety at work and whistle-blowing. However, they do not have the right to claim unfair dismissal.

> ### ? REFLECTIVE ACTIVITY 4.3
>
> What are the main characteristics that suggest that an individual is an employee, working under a contract of employment? In your organisation, is there anyone who you think would be considered an employee under the law but who is not treated as such by the employer?

## 4.5 THE FUNCTION OF THE LAW

So far in this chapter we have examined the contract of employment and the rights that this confers. However, in the context of employment relations, we need to consider the law in a much broader framework. Otto Kahn-Freund in his classic book *Labour and the Law* (1972) stated that the *'principal purpose of labour law [was] to regulate, to support, and to restrain the power of management and the power of organised labour'*. He outlined three functions of the law in regulating employment relations that would achieve this purpose. These were:

- The *restrictive function*, where the law establishes the 'rules of the game' when employers and employees are in the process of making agreements. This type of legislation effectively lays down the circumstances in which employers and trade unions can impose industrial sanctions on each other without the parties having redress to the legal system.
- The *auxiliary function*, where the law is designed to promote certain behaviours (for example, collective bargaining) towards certain ends.
- The *regulatory function*, where the law regulates management's behaviour towards its employees and trade union officers' behaviour towards their members. This is the area of individual employment rights and the rights of individual trade union members.

In this chapter, we will be linking these three functions to key pieces of employment law in order to demonstrate how the legislative framework develops over time.

### 4.5.1 THE RESTRICTIVE FUNCTION OF THE LAW

Throughout most of the 1950s and 1960s there was tacit support, from both the main political parties and through the legislative process, for the principle of collective bargaining. In the absence of a comprehensive legislative framework, employment was essentially regulated through negotiation between employers and trade unions. However, from the late 1960s, high levels of industrial conflict led many people to question this principle. Many employers argued that the scale and scope of collective bargaining, together with strong trade unions, restricted increased labour costs and hampered competition and efficiency. For the Conservative Government, elected in 1979, trade unions and their ability to maintain and increase wages through collective bargaining represented a major impediment to the operation of the free market. In particular, trade unions enjoyed immunity from actions for civil damages. Consequently, trade unions could use a variety of strategies to call, and to implement, effective industrial action.

They could call, without a legal liability arising, for industrial action in connection with any kind of industrial dispute, no matter how remote those taking the action were from the original dispute. They were also able to call on workers not directly involved in the dispute to take sympathy or 'secondary action'. Secondary action is that taken against an employer with whom the trade union has no dispute but who might, for example, be a key customer of an employer with whom they currently do have an industrial dispute. By taking this type of industrial action the union hopes the secondary employer will put pressure on the employer involved in the main dispute to settle the dispute on terms more favourable than presently on offer.

However, after the election of the Conservative Government in 1979, legislation came at regular intervals, and between 1980 and 1993 there were seven Acts of Parliament designed to restrict trade union activity and behaviour. Critically, for strike action to be lawful, and so retain legal immunities for trade unions, it had to be supported by a postal ballot. While the Government (of the time) argued that this would democratise decisions over industrial action, it also hoped that this would have a moderating influence. In practice, participation in ballots substantially decreased. At the same time, the balloting process itself was made increasingly complex – unions were required to give employers notice of any ballot and details of the groups of members that would be voting. In addition, the ballot paper had to fulfil a number of strict criteria including the incorporation of a 'health warning' cautioning voters that subsequent industrial action could be a breach of their employment contracts. If industrial action was subsequently called, unions were again required to give employers a specified notice. Any failure to meet these requirements could provide employers with an opportunity to seek an injunction to prevent industrial action taking place. In addition, industrial action in support of another group of workers in dispute with their employer was made unlawful and lawful industrial action picketing was limited to a worker's workplace and to a maximum of six pickets. As a consequence, strike action became a less potent threat, inevitably undermining the bargaining power of organised labour.

---

## RESTRICTING THE ROLE OF TRADE UNIONS – LEGISLATION BETWEEN 1980 AND 1993

*The Employment Act (1980)* removed the unions' immunity if their members engaged in picketing premises other than their own place of work.

*The Employment Act (1982)* narrowed the definition of a trade dispute, outlawed the practice of pressuring employers not to include non-union firms on tender lists, and enabled employers to sue trade unions for an injunction or damages where they were responsible for unlawful industrial action.

*The Trade Union Act (1984)* introduced pre-strike ballots.

*The Employment Act (1988)* amongst other things effectively outlawed the closed shop.

*The Employment Act (1990)* removed unions' immunity if they organised any type of secondary action in support of an individual dismissed for taking unlawful action.

*The Trade Union and Labour Relations (Consolidation) Act (1992)* brought together in one piece of legislation much of the law relating to collective provision.

*The Trade Union Reform and Employment Rights Act (1993)* made some amendments to existing requirements, most particularly in relation to ballots for industrial action.

**?**    REFLECTIVE ACTIVITY 4.4

Do you think that legislation to restrict or regulate industrial action is necessary? Does current legislation go too far or are further measures needed?

A political consensus has developed around these measures. Requiring unions to hold a ballot of their members prior to taking industrial action has become part of the employment relations landscape and has not been questioned by any of the major political parties. However, the election of a new majority Conservative Government in 2015 has again put the restriction of trade union activity firmly on the political agenda. The most recent development is the Trade Union Bill, which seeks to further constrain the ability of trade unions to organise industrial action, limit facility time for trade union representatives and make it more difficult for trade unions to make political donations. The central proposal is to insist that at least 50% of eligible members have to vote in a ballot for it to be used as a lawful basis for industrial action. In essential public services, at least 40% of the total constituency must also vote in favour. Proponents of such measures argue that under the current system industrial action can be called when only 20% or 30% of members have actively voted in favour. Against this, trade unions point out that current legislation restricts them from using electronic and other forms of voting that may boost participation and also that minimum voting thresholds are not applied in political life.

## TRADE UNION BILL 2015 – MAKING INDUSTRIAL ACTION IMPOSSIBLE?

- In order for industrial action to retain immunity it must be supported by a majority of those voting and the turnout must be at least 50% of those entitled to vote. There is an additional requirement that 40% of all relevant members vote in favour where the workers involved either provide or are ancillary to the provision of an important public service. This would include teachers, all hospital workers, and firefighters.
- Unions must provide additional information on the ballot paper to make clear the issues involved in the dispute and which issues remain unresolved, the precise type of industrial action being considered and an indication of the date of the action. Furthermore, the mandate for a ballot will automatically expire four months after the ballot. This is designed to prevent ballots being used for a prolonged series of one-day strikes.
- Unions must provide information regarding any industrial action and any political expenditure in trade unions' annual returns to the Certification Officer, who will also have wide-ranging powers to make enquiries 'as he sees fit' into complaints made by members and to investigate issues in relation to financial affairs or breaches of duties in relation to the register of members even where no complaint has been made. The Certification Officer will also be given new powers to impose financial penalties on trade unions for a failure to meet these and other reporting obligations.
- The period of notice that unions must give before industrial action can commence will be extended from seven to fourteen days.
- Union members will have to opt in in order to pay into the political fund of a trade union.
- All public sector employers must publish details of trade union facility time in order to 'promote transparency and public scrutiny of facility time; and to encourage those employers to moderate the amount of money spent on facility time in light of that scrutiny'. Government ministers will also have the power to place a cap on the amount of facility time that a union representative might receive.

### 4.5.2 THE AUXILIARY FUNCTION OF THE LAW

Prior to the more restrictive approach epitomised by successive Conservative governments between 1979 and 1996, the auxiliary function of employment law predominated. From the end of World War II and throughout most of the 1950s and 1960s, there was tacit support, from both the main political parties and through the legislative process, for the principle of collective bargaining. In essence, however, the Government simply provided a basic framework to support free collective bargaining and limited any further intervention to areas in which there was little collective regulation, for example through the establishment of Wages Councils, which set minimum wages in industries such as agriculture and hairdressing. Although high levels of industrial action in the late 1960s and throughout the 1970s prompted greater government intervention, the law was still used to underpin and promote collective bargaining. For example, the Employment Protection Act 1975 introduced a statutory union recognition procedure, established the CAC and also established Acas as a statutory body. The election of the Conservative Government in 1979 signalled the decline of the law as an auxiliary mechanism for supporting collective industrial relations. For example, the 1980 Employment Act repealed the recognition procedure introduced by the 1975 Act.

The election of the Labour Government in 1997 saw a limited return to the auxiliary function of the law. Perhaps most notably, the Employment Relations Act (1999) set out a new procedure for statutory recognition. In addition, a right to accompaniment by either a trade union representative or a work colleague at discipline and grievance hearings was introduced for all employees irrespective of trade union recognition. These measures arguably represented an acceptance of the importance of the positive role that could be played by trade unions within employment relations and also provided unions with a foothold to maintain and extend workplace presence. Reflecting the growing importance of European law, 1999 also saw the incorporation of the European Works Councils (EWCs) Directive into UK law. Perhaps more importantly, in 2002 the EU Information and Consultation Directive led to the introduction of the ICE Regulations in 2004. These provided employees with a general statutory right to be informed and consulted by their employers on a range of key business, employment and restructuring issues. However, as we see in the next chapter, the impact of the ICE Regulations has been relatively limited (Hall *et al*, 2010).

### 4.5.3 THE REGULATORY FUNCTION OF THE LAW

The regulatory function of the law has provided the foundation for a series of statutory rights for individual employees. These began to emerge in the early 1960s. Parliament justified providing such rights on the grounds that private arrangements (for example, by collective agreement) had failed to provide an adequate minimum acceptable level of protection for individual employees against certain behaviour by their employers. Interestingly, trade unions were initially opposed to such initiatives as the Redundancy Payments Act because they believed it undermined their own role. Nonetheless, the introduction of individual rights at work also sent a clear message to employers that they must act with just cause and be 'fair and reasonable' in the treatment of their employees.

A floor of legal rights was created, which has since been expanded and developed, by successive UK governments and the courts. These minimum levels can be enhanced by private agreements – for example, via collective bargaining or simply by employers who wish to offer a more attractive employment package. Many organisations now offer maternity pay and leave that goes beyond the statutory minimum, for instance, because they need to attract women back to work after the birth of a child. But this is a matter of policy for individual organisations. What is important for the employment relations professional is to understand the range and importance of these individual rights.

## 4.6 DISCRIMINATION

Discrimination law continues to be one of the most dynamic and complex areas of employment law. Many employers place significant emphasis on the avoidance of litigation related to discrimination due to the fact that there is no limit on potential compensation and high-profile cases may lead to damaging publicity. However, high levels of compensation in discrimination are relatively unusual. Consequently, it is perhaps more important to see the eradication of discrimination, harassment and inequality as a fundamental part of developing a culture of fairness and trust, and a climate of good employment relations. The law on discrimination in employment is set out in the Equality Act 2010, which drew together the disparate pieces of legislation in this area. The Act provides protection in relation to a number of protected characteristics.

---

### PROTECTED CHARACTERISTICS UNDER THE EQUALITY ACT 2010

**Age** – workers of all ages are protected.

**Disability** – under the Equality Act, a worker is disabled if they have a physical or mental impairment that has a substantial and long-term adverse effect (lasted or likely to last for at least 12 months) on their ability to carry out normal day-to-day activities such as shopping, eating, washing and walking.

**Gender reassignment** – protection is provided to transsexual workers who have started, are going to start or have completed a process to change their gender.

**Marriage and civil partnership** – workers who are married or in a civil partnership are protected against discrimination, but single people are not protected.

**Pregnancy and maternity** – women are protected against discrimination on the grounds of pregnancy and maternity during the period of their pregnancy and any statutory maternity leave.

**Race** – this includes colour, nationality and ethnic or national origins.

**Religion and belief** – the Act protects workers against discrimination on grounds of their religion or belief, or lack of religion or belief. A religion must have a clear structure and belief system. A 'belief' must be genuinely held and a weighty and substantial aspect of human life and behaviour. It must not conflict with the fundamental rights of others.

**Sex** – both men and women are protected under the Act.

**Sexual orientation** – the Act protects bisexual, gay, heterosexual and lesbian people, and also those who are discriminated against because of perceptions about their sexual orientation.

---

The requirement not to discriminate applies before and during the employment relationship (and to a limited extent after employment), and therefore covers recruitment, performance review and appraisal, training, compensation packages, promotion and dismissal.

One complex issue relating to discrimination law is the extent to which different protected characteristics might be inconsistent with each other. This was underlined in two recent cases involving employees who were dismissed after refusing to undertake certain duties on the grounds that this was counter to their religious belief. Gary McFarlane, a marriage counsellor, was sacked after objecting to giving sex therapy advice to gay couples, and registrar Lillian Ladele was disciplined after she refused to conduct same-sex civil partnership ceremonies. Both individuals brought claims for discrimination on grounds of religion and belief against their employers but were unsuccessful. Essentially, these cases established that where employees hold religious beliefs, employers are entitled to require them to comply with equality policies – in short this is seen as a proportionate way of achieving the legitimate aim of providing a non-discriminatory service.

However, these cases also illustrated the potential impact of the Human Rights Act and the European Convention on Human Rights in employment cases. The Convention for the Protection of Human Rights and Fundamental Freedoms (the Convention) was signed by the UK in 1950, but it was only transposed into UK legislation through the Human Rights Act (1998) in 2000. Courts and employment tribunals are obliged to construe domestic legislation compatibly with the European Convention on Human Rights (ECHR) so far as it is possible to do so and public bodies must also act compatibly with its provisions. Both McFarlane and Ladele argued that the actions taken against them were in breach of both the UK discrimination law and their rights under Article 9 to freedom of thought, conscience and religion. When their claims were rejected by the UK courts, they unsuccessfully appealed to the European Court of Human Rights in Strasbourg. Another case heard at the same time, taken by Nadia Eweida, a former British Airways employee, was successful. Here the ECHR found that the attempts by British Airways to prevent Eweida from wearing a crucifix in contravention with the organisation's dress code did not strike a fair balance between religious belief and the need to project their corporate image. This demonstrates the importance of organisations taking care in designing policies in light of the beliefs of their employees.

## 4.6.1 DIRECT AND INDIRECT DISCRIMINATION

Under the Equality Act there are three main types of discrimination. *Direct discrimination* occurs when an individual is treated less favourably because of their sex, race or other protected characteristic. For example, if someone is dismissed or not recruited because they are a woman, that would be direct discrimination. In addition, if someone is treated less favourably because someone either perceives them to have a protected characteristic or because of their association with someone with a protected characteristic, this will also be direct discrimination.

---

**CASE STUDY 4.3**

### DISCRIMINATION BY ASSOCIATION AND PERCEPTION

**Weathersfield Ltd v Sargent**

Mrs Sargent started work for a vehicle hire firm but was told by her employer, 'If you get a telephone call from any coloureds or Asians you can usually tell them by the sound of their voice. You have to tell them that there are no vehicles available.' She checked with a director who confirmed that this was company policy. Sargent resigned and successfully claimed constructive dismissal and racial discrimination.

**English v Thomas Sanderson Blinds Ltd**

English had worked for Sanderson Blinds and argued that during his employment he had been subject to endless 'homophobic banter' mainly on the basis that he had attended a boys' boarding school and that he lived in Brighton. However, the alleged harassers knew that English was not gay. Eventually, he resigned and claimed unfair constructive dismissal and discrimination on grounds of sexual orientation. The Court of Appeal ruled in his favour and argued that it was irrelevant whether Mr English was gay or not, the actions still constituted harassment on grounds of sexual orientation.

---

In most cases, the only defence against direct discrimination is to show that no discrimination took place unless an employer can show that the only way to comply with other legislation is to discriminate or that a protected characteristic is a 'genuine occupational' requirement for the role. For example, in some caring professions, it may be justified to require employees to be of a particular gender. Also, an employer who runs an Italian restaurant could insist on only hiring a chef who is Italian.

*Indirect discrimination* occurs if an employer applies 'a provision, criterion or practice which is discriminatory in relation to a relevant protected characteristic'. Here, a claimant would need to show that a substantially higher proportion of a group with a particular protected characteristic would not be able to comply with a specific rule or condition. For example, in 2004, Jessica Starmer, a pilot who worked for British Airways, asked to be able to work 50% of her normal hours due to the irregular nature of pilots' hours and her need to care for her children. This was refused and she was subsequently informed that BA had introduced a rule that pilots who worked part-time had to work 75% of full-time hours. She argued that such a provision disproportionately and adversely impacted on women, who would be more likely to have childcare and other caring responsibilities. This argument was accepted by the Employment Tribunal and upheld by the Employment Appeal Tribunal (EAT).

However, employers can defend a claim of indirect discrimination by arguing that it is 'a proportionate means of achieving a legitimate aim'. For example, a council trying to recruit a youth worker to work predominantly within a particular community may ask for applicants with a certain level of fluency in a particular language.

### 4.6.2 HARASSMENT AND VICTIMISATION

The third form of discrimination is harassment, which is defined as:

> 'unwanted conduct related to a relevant protected characteristic, which has the purpose or effect of violating an individual's dignity or creating an intimidating, hostile, degrading, humiliating or offensive environment for that individual.'

This means that employees can complain about offensive behaviour even if it is not directly aimed at them. It is also worth noting that employers may also be liable if their staff are subjected to harassment from customers or clients. However, harassment will not be shown to have occurred just because the behaviour complained of offends the claimant – the tribunal will need to be satisfied that it either has the purpose or effect of violating the dignity of the claimant or creating an intimidating, hostile, degrading, humiliating or offensive environment. Case Study 4.4 illustrates this distinction.

---

CASE STUDY 4.4

### HARASSMENT – VIOLATING DIGNITY?

*Morgan v Halls of Gloucester ET*

Morgan, who is black, worked for Halls of Gloucester as a delivery driver. He claimed that he was forced to resign, in part due to suffering serious racial harassment. This had involved being told by another employee to 'stop speaking that jungle talk' and also overhearing a number of instances in which another black employee was referred to in racist terms or racist comments in general. Furthermore, he alleged that the company had done nothing to prevent this behaviour and had failed to discipline one employee, who had expressed extreme racist views despite complaints being made by other staff. The company did have an equal opportunities policy, but it was kept in a cabinet and neither managers nor employees knew of its existence. The tribunal found that even though a number of the comments were not aimed at Morgan, they did violate his dignity and therefore the claim was successful and the company was ordered to pay compensation.

### Heafield v Times Newspaper Ltd EAT/ 1305/12

Heafield was employed as subeditor for the *Times* newspaper and was also a practising Roman Catholic. In 2011, the *Times* was working on a story regarding the alleged involvement of the Pope in a cover-up over the actions of a paedophile priest. As the deadline approached, another employee shouted to other colleagues across the newsroom 'Can anyone tell me what's happening to the fucking Pope?' in an attempt to get some information on the progress of the story.

He then repeated this request. Heafield was offended by this but did not complain at the time and instead raised the issue informally with a manager at a later point. The manager, after getting advice from a colleague, decided to take no further action on the basis that 'these things tended to sort themselves out if left alone'. Heafield brought a claim of discrimination on grounds of his religion or belief, arguing that the repeated comments about the Pope violated his dignity. While the tribunal accepted that the words represented unwanted conduct, they did not agree that the words had the purpose or effect of violating Mr Heafield's dignity. Instead, this was an enquiry about a story and the expletive had been used because of the pressure of the situation. The decision was upheld by the EAT.

Finally, the Equality Act 2010 makes victimisation unlawful. Victimisation occurs when a person is subject to a detriment because they bring proceedings under the Equality Act, give evidence or information in connection with proceedings, or make an allegation that someone has contravened the Equality Act. However, if an employee gives false evidence or information or makes a false allegation (in bad faith), they are not protected.

## 4.6.3 DISABILITY DISCRIMINATION

Slightly different provisions apply to disability discrimination under the Equality Act. Direct and indirect discrimination are both unlawful; however, the Act also places a duty on employers to make reasonable adjustments for staff who may otherwise be placed at a disadvantage because of a disability. This could include adjustments to work equipment, the work premises or shifts and other working arrangements.

In addition, the Equality Act protects people from discrimination arising from their disability. This states that it is discrimination to treat a disabled person unfavourably because of something connected with their disability. Discrimination arising from disability will occur if the following three conditions are met:

● you put an employee at a disadvantage, even if this was not your intention
● this treatment is connected with the employee's disability
● you cannot justify the treatment by showing that it is 'a proportionate means of achieving a legitimate aim'.

### DISCRIMINATION ARISING FROM DISABILITY

*McGraw v London Ambulance Service NHS Trust ET*

McGraw, who worked as a paramedic, was dismissed for gross misconduct for attempting to steal Entonox, an anaesthetic that he had been abusing for a number of years, from his ambulance station. This act was committed while McGraw was absent from work suffering from depression. He was also found to be in breach of the Trust's policy in relation to drug abuse. Among other claims, McGraw argued that in dismissing him the Trust had discriminated against him for a reason arising from a disability. On its part, the Trust argued that it could not tolerate substance abuse and that McGraw could not be relied upon to maintain a proper service to the public. The tribunal could find no link between McGraw's depression and any medication he was taking and the theft of the Entonox, and concluded that the dismissal of McGraw was a proportionate means of achieving a legitimate aim.

However, if, for example, the medication being taken by a worker with a disability resulted in poor performance, it could be unlawful to take disciplinary or other action against them.

### 4.6.4 THE ROLE OF THE EQUALITY AND HUMAN RIGHTS COMMISSION

Employment Relations professionals require a knowledge and understanding of the key legal principles regarding discrimination, the ability to monitor changes and developments in the law, and the will to take on board the practical lessons to be learned from decided cases. A key source of information, guidance and regulatory scrutiny is the Equality and Human Rights Commission (EHRC), which was established in 2007, has a statutory duty to encourage and support the development of a society in which:

- people's ability to achieve their potential is not limited by prejudice or discrimination
- there is respect for and protection of each individual's human rights
- there is respect for the dignity and worth of each individual
- each individual has an equal opportunity to participate in society, and
- there is mutual respect between groups based on understanding and valuing of diversity and on shared respect for equality and human rights.

The EHRC can apply for judicial review of government decisions and intervene in court proceedings. In particular, the EHRC can support claimants in bringing cases under existing equality legislation where it feels that this is a way of meeting its duties outlined above. The EHRC also has powers to assess public authorities' compliance with their positive equality duties under the Equality Act 2010 and can issue 'compliance notices' if it finds a public authority is failing in its duties. The EHRC also has the power to carry out investigations when it has the 'suspicion' of unlawful discrimination taking place. Finally, it provides a 'one-stop shop' for those seeking advice and information on equality issues, legal matters and diversity strategies.

For many managers, discrimination law can be daunting. The cost of dealing with complaints of discrimination and harassment, and resultant tribunal claims, can be high, relative to claims for unfair dismissal. Generally, there is more evidence to be gathered, more witnesses to be heard and, of course, no cap on the possible compensation to be awarded. There are also a number of business risks – firstly, to the organisation's reputation, particularly if the case is covered by the press. Secondly, a discrimination claim is also likely to be personally embarrassing and in all likelihood distressing for those managers named in the claim. If they are found to have discriminated, harassed or bullied, managers are likely to be subject to disciplinary action, may be dismissed and may well find that the claim continues to blight their career. Finally, there is the issue of management time. Frequently, in discrimination claims, an employer will be served with a discrimination questionnaire. The time taken to respond to these questionnaires, together with the time taken to properly prepare for and attend at a tribunal hearing, can be substantial.

By far the best means of minimising the risk of claims is to behave proactively and prevent claims from being brought in the first place. In order to do this, it is essential that employers are sensitive to potential issues of discrimination and harassment within the workplace, and that steps are taken at an early stage when a potential problem arises.

## ?  REFLECTIVE ACTIVITY 4.5

To what extent do you feel that complying with the discrimination legislation, outlined above, is sufficient to achieve equality of treatment and opportunity?

In some cases, if action is taken at an early stage, potential problems can be resolved. For example, mediation can be effective in allowing those subject to discrimination an opportunity to voice their concerns directly to the alleged perpetrator. However, as we note in Chapter 14, there is a danger that using mediation in this context can potentially cover serious mistreatment. More-formal grievance, or specialist dignity at work, procedures can provide individuals with greater protection, but perhaps more importantly, organisations need to have a broad commitment to ensuring equal treatment.

## 4.7 DISMISSAL

Although discrimination law might be one of the most dynamic and complex areas of employment law, the law relating to unfair dismissal and redundancy continues to provide the bulk of the practitioner's workload. In Chapters 11 and 14 we look in much greater detail at the skills that are required to manage these two important issues and the law in this area. Nonetheless, in the context of Kahn-Freund's regulatory function these individual rights are a key area for any employment relations professional.

By virtue of section 94 of the Employment Rights Act (1996), an employee who at the effective date of termination (EDT) of employment has continuous service of two years or more with the employer has a right not to be unfairly dismissed and can make a claim to an employment tribunal. In order to successfully defend an employee's claim for unfair dismissal, an employer must be able to satisfy an employment tribunal of three things:

● that the real or principal reason for the dismissal was one of the potentially fair reasons as set out in section 98(2) of the Employment Rights Act (1996)
● that it was reasonable to dismiss in all the circumstances of the case, and
● that the employer followed a fair procedure.

## 4.7.1 ESTABLISHING THE REASON FOR DISMISSAL

There are a number of reasons for dismissal that are potentially fair:

- Capability problems (including ill-health) or lack of qualifications
- Misconduct
- Redundancy
- Contravention of statute (ie no work permit for the employee), or
- 'Some other substantial reason'

The burden of proof in establishing the reasons for dismissal lies squarely with the employer, although in most cases this burden is not difficult to discharge. However, there are a number of circumstances where an employee's dismissal will be held to be automatically unfair, which include where the employee can show that the real reason for dismissal was related to:

- pregnancy, including all reasons relating to maternity
- parental leave, paternity leave (birth and adoption), adoption leave or time off for dependants
- acting as an employee representative
- acting as a trade union representative
- acting as an occupational pension scheme trustee
- joining or not joining a trade union
- being a part-time or fixed-term employee
- discrimination, including protection against discrimination on the grounds of age, disability, gender reassignment, marriage and civil partnership, pregnancy and maternity, race, religion or belief, sex and sexual orientation (in Northern Ireland, this also includes political beliefs)
- pay and working hours, including the Working Time Regulations, annual leave and the National Minimum Wage
- whistle-blowing.

In such cases, there is no requirement for the employee to have two years' continuous employment. It should also be noted that there is no qualifying period for employees to bring a claim to an employment tribunal that they have been dismissed on grounds of their political affilliation or opinion, although such a dismissal is not automatically unfair.

Establishing the reason for dismissal is normally straightforward – in many cases, there will be agreement between both the claimant and the respondent (the employer) on this issue. There is more likely to be a dispute over the reason for dismissal in misconduct cases – as to whether the misconduct that has been alleged has taken place or not. For example, an employer may allege that an employee is 'guilty' of theft, but this is disputed by the employee.

Here, employment tribunals will be guided by the three-stage test set down in the case of *BHS v Burchell [1978] IRLR 379*. This states that in cases of misconduct, an employer must demonstrate that it has:

- a genuine belief in the claimant's guilt
- reasonable grounds to sustain belief
- conducted a reasonable investigation in the circumstances.

## 4.7.2 FAIR DISMISSAL – THE BAND OF REASONABLE RESPONSES

Having established the reason for dismissal, the tribunal will then go on to look at whether the decision to dismiss is fair or unfair. Section 98(4) of the Employment Rights Act states that this depends on:

'...whether in the circumstances (including the size and administrative resources of the employer's undertaking) the employer acted reasonably or unreasonably in treating it as a sufficient reason for dismissing the employee, and ... shall be determined in accordance with equity and the substantial merits of the case.'

Importantly, the tribunal will ask whether the decision to dismiss falls within the range of responses that would have been made by a reasonable employer. This will require an employer to show that it has considered the seriousness of the offence; mitigating circumstances; the previous record and service of the employee; alternatives to dismissal; and whether warnings have been used appropriately.

This 'band of reasonable responses' test is designed to provide an objective measure of fairness such that the tribunal doesn't attempt to second-guess or put itself 'in the shoes of the employer'. However, some legal commentators have argued that it essentially allows for employers to justify overly harsh decisions and provides a very low 'hurdle' over which employers have to jump (see Collins, 2000).

Finally, in reaching the decision, the tribunal will ask whether the employer has followed a reasonable procedure. Here, the fairness of the procedure as a whole will be considered. The underlying principle is that natural justice is adhered to whereby:

- the employee is made aware of the allegations against them
- they have an opportunity to respond to those allegations, and
- they have a right to appeal against any decision that is made.

As we explain in Chapter 11, this underlines the need to establish 'best practice', which is reflected in the Acas Code of Practice on Discipline and Grievance, and the associated non-statutory guidance.

## 4.8 NATURE AND JURISDICTION OF EMPLOYMENT TRIBUNALS

Individual employees enforce their rights on discrimination, redundancy, unfair dismissal and a range of other matters via employment tribunals. Employment tribunals are independent judicial bodies, 'inferior courts' within the meaning of the Rules of the Supreme Court. What we now know as employment tribunals were first established as industrial tribunals under the Industrial Training Act 1964. Subsequently, under the Redundancy Payments Act 1965, tribunals were given the powers to decide on individual employment disputes. However, the report of the Donovan Commission suggested extending the existing tribunal system into what it termed 'labour tribunals', which were conceived as 'an accessible, speedy, informal and inexpensive' system through which disputes could be resolved.

The traditional composition of the tribunal reflected this approach, comprising three members: an employment judge (a solicitor or barrister of seven years' qualification), an employer representative, and an employee representative (usually a trade union representative). The tribunal, therefore, was seen as representing an 'industrial jury' capable of understanding the reality of the context within which employment disputes originated.

### 4.8.1 TRIBUNAL DEVELOPMENT AND REFORM

Over time, however, it has been argued that the principles outlined in Donovan have been replaced by the growing juridification of a system that has become 'increasingly complex, legalistic and adversarial' (Gibbons, 2007: 21). Tribunals now hear cases from an array of jurisdictions and the development of case law in both domestic and European courts has added a further layer of complexity to many issues and made legal representation increasingly important. In 2014–15, claimants were represented by a lawyer in more than 75% of cases. Furthermore, data from the Survey of Employment Tribunal Applications

(SETA) suggests that respondents are more likely to be legally represented (Peters *et al*, 2010). This not only has implications in terms of cost and time but also shapes outcomes as those parties that are represented (whether claimants or respondents) are more likely to be successful (Buscha *et al*, 2012).

The most vocal critics of the employment tribunal system have been employers, who have argued that the costs system has encouraged speculative claims from former employees. A key principle of the employment tribunal system is that costs are not normally awarded to the successful party. Costs awards (of up to a maximum of £500) were generally limited to cases where an application or actions of a party were 'frivolous' or 'vexatious'. From an employer's perspective, the concern was that this allowed claimants to lodge weak claims in the hope and expectation of settlement. Consequently, in July 2001 the maximum costs award was increased to £10,000 and extended to cases where 'the bringing or conducting of the proceedings by a party has been misconceived'. In short, tribunals now had an explicit power to award costs where cases were without merit. Furthermore, in 2004, the power of a tribunal to strike out a claim was extended to where there was no reasonable prospect of success. However, there is little sign that tribunals have been more willing to use these powers. While there is little data as to the number of weak cases that progress through to a full hearing (which itself is inevitably subjective), there has been little change in the number of cases that fail at the preliminary stages, ranging between 11% and 14% (see Table 4.1).

Table 4.1 Outcomes of unfair dismissal claims, 2009–14

|  | 2009–10 | 2010–11 | 2011–12 | 2012–13 | 2013–14 |
|---|---|---|---|---|---|
|  | % | % | % | % | % |
| Unsuccessful at hearing | 42 | 46 | 43 | 45 | 46 |
| Dismissed at preliminary hearing | 11 | 14 | 12 | 12 | 11 |
| No award made in upheld cases | 20 | 14 | 23 | 21 | 18 |
| Compensation | 27 | 25 | 21 | 21 | 21 |

Source: Ministry of Justice

In response to employer concerns, the Coalition Government has radically reformed the tribunal system. This is discussed and analysed in greater detail in Chapter 10. However, rather than tackle the legal and procedural complexity highlighted previously, it has sought to take measures to enhance conciliation and limit access to the system. Now, before a potential claimant can bring a case to an employment tribunal, they must first notify Acas, who will seek to conciliate. Only if this attempt at early conciliation is unsuccessful will the claim proceed. At that point claimants must pay a fee of up to £250 and an additional fee of up £950 if the claim proceeds to a full hearing (see box for schedule of employment tribunal fees).

**Schedule of Employment Tribunal Fees**

| Type of case | Claim fee | Hearing fee |
|---|---|---|
| Unpaid wages | £160 | £230 |
| Redundancy pay | £160 | £230 |
| Breach of contract | £160 | £230 |
| Unfair dismissal | £250 | £950 |

| Type of case | Claim fee | Hearing fee |
|---|---|---|
| Equal pay | £250 | £950 |
| Discrimination | £250 | £950 |
| Whistle-blowing | £250 | £950 |

In certain cases, claimants will be able to pay for remission for fees. For example, claimants in receipt of any of the following will not have to pay fees:

- Income-based Jobseeker's Allowance
- Income-related Employment and Support Allowance
- Income Support
- Universal Credit with gross annual earnings of less than £6,000
- State Pension Credit – Guarantee Credit
- Scottish Civil Legal Aid.

Claimants can also receive full or part remission of the fee based on their and their partner's gross monthly income.

In addition, the Government has sought to streamline the hearing system itself by providing for employment judges to sit alone on most unfair dismissal cases, thus weakening the notion that the tribunal continues to represent an 'industrial jury'.

## ?   REFLECTIVE ACTIVITY 4.6

Would you manage an issue differently in light of the introduction of employment tribunal fees? If you felt that your own employment rights had been breached, would employment tribunal fees affect your decision as to whether to seek legal redress?

### 4.8.2 THE APPLICATION PROCESS

Before an employment tribunal application can be brought, an individual intending to make a claim must submit an early conciliation notification form to Acas. This asks for details about the individual, their representative, their employer and their dates of employment, but it does not ask for any details of the complaint itself. Acas will then contact the potential claimant and the employer and offer to conciliate.

Normally, claimants have three months in which to bring employment tribunal claims (six months in cases regarding redundancy pay and equal pay); however, this period is suspended while early conciliation takes place. It is important to note that the period of early conciliation starts on the day after the claimant sends Acas their notification form. There is then normally one month in which to conciliate, although this period can be extended by a further 14 days if Acas feels there is a good prospect of the case being settled.

The process is completely voluntary. The role of Acas is to help find a solution that both sides find acceptable instead of going to a tribunal hearing. Acas does not impose solutions but will try to help the parties settle differences on their own terms. If either party does not wish to conciliate or no agreement can be reached, Acas will issue an early conciliation certificate, which indicates the end of early conciliation, and the claimant is then able to make a claim to the employment tribunal. This is done by completing an ET1 application form, which is normally submitted online. Importantly, the ET1 asks claimants to set out the nature of their claim and also the grounds on which it is made.

The ET1 is then sent to the employer (the respondent), who has 28 days in which to respond to the claim. This is done on a specified form, the ET3, on which the respondent is asked whether they wish to defend the claim and to outline their reasons for resisting any application. The completion of the ET3 is extremely important for employers when defending claims, as the arguments made in both the ET1 and ET3 will be presented at any future hearing and will be scrutinised against any additional evidence which is brought. Therefore, it is important that any details in the ET3 are accurate and consistent with the evidence that will be presented at a later stage. This may involve HR practitioners in reinvestigating the case before the ET3 is prepared.

Once the tribunal has received both the ET1 and the ET3, an employment judge will go through a sifting process whereby the tribunal can dismiss a claim or the response made by the employer in full or in part, either because the tribunal has no jurisdiction (for example because the claim is out of time or the claimant does not have the necessary qualifying service) or because they feel that there are no arguable complaints or defences. Before such a decision is confirmed, the parties will have a chance to make written representations. If the claim passes this initial hurdle, an employment judge has powers to manage the proceedings in order to ensure the smooth and efficient running of the case. He or she can issue directions on any matter that he or she thinks is appropriate, either from the parties' application/response or at a preliminary hearing.

Either may make an application – or the tribunal may order – that one or other party must provide further and better particulars of any grounds upon which they rely, or any facts or contentions relevant to their claim. The essence of further particulars is to enable a party to know in advance the nature of the case that they must meet at the hearing. In keeping with the need to provide further and better particulars, a tribunal can order discovery and inspection of documents and set a time and a place for compliance. As with further particulars, 'discovery' is an important step in the process of enabling the parties to know the nature and extent of the case they have to respond to. The rules of procedure allow tribunals the power to strike out applications, or award costs, when a party to the proceedings does not comply with a directions order.

### 4.8.3 THE HEARING AND THE DECISION

In preparing for the hearing, parties will be expected to provide written statements for all the witnesses they intend to call. It is also the responsibility of the parties to ensure that their witnesses are ready and willing to attend at the tribunal and that they, through the process of discovery, have in their possession all necessary and relevant documents. Normally tribunals now direct that the parties prepare an agreed 'bundle' of documents for use during the hearing. This responsibility generally falls to the respondent (employer) because it is considered that they will have the appropriate administrative resources and, in the majority of cases, will have in their possession all, or the majority of, the documents. In most cases bundles will comprise the following:

- ET1, ET3 and any correspondence with the tribunal
- contract of employment of claimant
- relevant policies, procedures and collective agreements
- correspondence (including emails) relating to the case (in chronological order)
- other relevant documents – this could include personnel records, performance appraisal documentation, etc.

It should be noted, however, that in recent years, employment judges have become increasingly critical of the size of 'the bundle' and therefore only those documents that will be directly referred to in evidence should be included.

Individual applicants may appear before a tribunal without representation or may be represented by a lawyer, a trade union official or any other person of their choice. If they are unrepresented, the tribunal does what it can to assist them while ensuring that there is no bias.

Although there is no specific rule that dictates the order in which evidence is given, it usually depends on who has the burden of proof. In unfair dismissal cases where dismissal is admitted, the respondent employer begins. If dismissal is not admitted, or it is incumbent upon the claimant to prove his or her case – for example, in constructive dismissal – the claimant begins. In order to speed up the process of evidence-giving, tribunals' witness statements are generally exchanged prior to the hearing. This helps both parties with their preparation and can avoid lengthy cross-examination.

Witnesses give their evidence under oath, but most witness statements are 'taken as read'. They may then be cross-examined by the other side and may also have to answer questions put to them by the tribunal members. Witnesses may also be re-examined by their own representative if any points need to be clarified. Then, when the parties have called all their witnesses, they are given an opportunity to make their final submissions. Generally, the party who presented their evidence first will have the final word. Finally, the tribunal will withdraw to make its decision. It will usually indicate whether it can announce its decision on the day of the hearing or whether it will be given in writing to the parties afterwards. If the claimant is successful, there will often be a need for the parties to make further submissions in respect of the size of any compensation payment, or the type of relief to be granted.

If the claimant or respondent disagrees with the decision, they can write to the tribunal, within 14 days, to request that it is reconsidered. However, this will only be done if it is 'in the interests of justice', for example where new evidence has come to light. Otherwise decisions of the employment tribunal can be appealed to the Employment Appeal Tribunal. Appeals must be made within 42 days of the date that either the decision or the reasons for the decision were sent to the parties. They cannot simply appeal because you disagree with the decision of the tribunal or because they feel that they made a factual mistake. However, they can appeal if they can show that the tribunal:

- applied the law incorrectly
- failed to follow proper tribunal procedure in a way that affected the final decision
- had no evidence to support its decision
- was unfairly biased towards the other party.

As with employment tribunal claims, parties must pay fees to lodge an appeal (£400) and to bring the appeal to a full hearing (£1,200). However, the EAT can order the other party to pay your fees if you win your appeal and the system of fees remission also applies to EAT actions.

## 4.8.4 AWARDS AND COMPENSATION

A key element of the employment tribunal process is the determination of remedy. Those claiming unfair dismissal may ask for reinstatement, re-engagement or compensation; however, in reality reinstatement and re-engagement are very rarely awarded.

For unfair dismissal compensation, there are two elements: the basic award and the compensatory award. The basic award is calculated in a similar way to statutory redundancy payment. It is made up of:

- 1.5 weeks' pay for each complete year of employment when you were 41 or over
- 1 week's pay for each complete year of employment when you were between the ages of 22 and 40 inclusive
- half a week's pay for each complete year of employment when you were below the age of 22.

The maximum number of years' service one can include is 20 and, as from 6 April 2015, the maximum week's pay was £475. This means that the maximum basic award is £14,250.

The compensatory award is based on actual and future financial loss. Therefore, the tribunal will take into account any earnings between the date of dismissal and the tribunal, and also whether the claimant is in employment at the time of the judgment. At the time of writing, the maximum unfair dismissal award was the lower of a year's salary or £78,335. However, for claims of discrimination on the basis of a 'protected characteristic', there is no limit to compensation and the tribunal can also make an award in relation to 'injury to feelings'.

Awards can be increased by 25% if the employer has not followed the Acas Code of Practice on Discipline and Grievance. However, they can also be reduced by 25% if the employee has not followed the Code, for example, if they have not appealed a decision. In addition, awards can be reduced for three other reasons:

1   If the employee has failed to mitigate their loss. Employees who have been dismissed are expected to look for work following dismissal. If the tribunal finds no or little evidence that they have done so, the compensatory award can be reduced.

2   If the dismissal is due to a procedural flaw – the tribunal can reduce compensation by an amount to reflect the probability that the claimant would have been dismissed if a fair procedure had been used. This reduction can be up to 100%. This is known as the Polkey reduction.

3   The basic award can be reduced if the claimant has: received a statutory redundancy or other *ex gratia* payment; refused re-employment; or contributed to his or her own dismissal.

### 4.8.5 EMPLOYMENT TRIBUNALS – RISK AND REPUTATION

However, it is important to put the risk faced by employers into perspective – only 24% of ET claims reached a hearing in 2013/14 and, of those that did, less than half (42%) were upheld and only one in five resulted in compensation being awarded. Furthermore, while potential compensation is high, the typical successful claim does not lead to substantial awards, as Table 4.2 indicates.

Table 4.2 Employment tribunal compensation, 2014–15

|  | Maximum Award | Median Award | Average Award |
|---|---|---|---|
|  | £ | £ | £ |
| Unfair dismissal | 238,216 | 6,955 | 12,362 |
| Race discrimination | 209,188 | 8,025 | 17,040 |
| Sex discrimination | 557,039 | 13,500 | 23,478 |
| Disability discrimination | 239,913 | 8,646 | 17,319 |
| Religious discrimination | 1,080 | 1,080 | 1,080 |
| Sexual orientation discrimination | 80,783 | 6,000 | 17,515 |
| Age discrimination | 28,428 | 7,500 | 11,211 |

Source: Ministry of Justice

Of course, employment tribunals may have a negative reputational effect and employers may incur significant costs in defending claims. It is important to remember that costs can only be awarded in employment tribunal proceedings where participants act vexatiously, abusively, disruptively, or otherwise unreasonably, or where a case was misconceived or had no reasonable prospects of success. Despite giving tribunals greater discretion to award costs, this occurs in a very small proportion of cases. Moreover, average costs of legal representation are around £7,000–£10,000 per case. As noted above, this leads some employers to argue that it is cheaper to settle cases even where they feel the claim is relatively weak. However, there is no compulsion for employers to be legally represented – and the tribunal system provides for parties to represent themselves. In these circumstances, the tribunal may take a less formal and more inquisitorial approach to proceedings. In our experience, a competent and well-prepared employment relations professional is more than capable of representing their organisation in cases in which the legal issues are relatively straightforward.

## ? REFLECTIVE ACTIVITY 4.7

You are asked by your line manager to explain the procedure used in employment tribunal hearings. What would you tell him or her, and why?

## 4.9 INDIVIDUAL EMPLOYMENT RIGHTS – ENFORCEMENT AND EFFECTIVENESS

Some commentators (see for example Dickens, 2012) argue that the reliance on employment tribunals as the main method of enforcing employment rights is fundamentally flawed and does not provide a framework that promotes good employment relations practice. In particular, Dickens (2012: 206) argues that:

'The approach to enforcement in Britain is flawed in that too much reliance is placed on individuals having to assert and pursue their statutory employment rights, which generally require only passive compliance from employers.'

This is particularly evident in relation to the impact of discrimination law on concrete equality measures such as the gender pay gap. In short, relying on individual complaints does little to address structural and institutional inequalities (Dickens, 2007; Fredman, 2011). There is a clear danger that organisations subject to discrimination claims at the employment tribunal defend such cases in isolation rather than using this as a trigger for reviewing their broader organisational policies and practices. Furthermore, as we discuss later, changes in employment tribunal regulations, and in particular the introduction of employment tribunal fees, have arguably made such enforcement even harder. Certainly, the volume of employment tribunal claims has reduced by more than 80%, but the impact on discrimination claims has been even more acute, with the level of sex discrimination claims less than 10% of its pre-fee levels.

Of course, there are some instances of agency enforcement where the Government takes a more proactive stance. For example, the HMRC has responsibility for taking action to ensure that the National Minimum Wage is observed – enforcement action can be initiated in response to a complaint from an employee or through targeted action in 'high risk' sectors of the economy. In addition, the Equality Act 2010 was particularly significant in that it attempted to shift the responsibility for pursuing equality from the individual to the organisation. The scope of the duty is set out in the following box. However, in addition to the general duty, most public bodies must also set and publish equality objectives at least every four years and publish information to show their compliance with the duty.

---

## THE PUBLIC SECTOR EQUALITY DUTY

The public sector equality duty was contained in the 2010 Equality Act. However, this was based on previous duties in respect of race, gender and disability, which had been established in 2001, 2006 and 2007 respectively. The race equality duty was in response to the Macpherson Report following the murder of Stephen Lawrence. The rationale for this change was to place responsibility from individuals to organisations.

The Equality Act sought to bring these different duties together and extend this to the other protected characteristics within the Act. The duty requires organisations to, in the exercise of their functions, have due regard to the need to:

- eliminate unlawful discrimination, harassment and victimisation and other conduct prohibited by the Act
- advance equality of opportunity between people who share a protected characteristic and those who do not. This in turn is defined as:
  - *removing or minimising disadvantages suffered by people due to their protected characteristics*
  - *taking steps to meet the needs of people from protected groups where these are different from the needs of other people*
  - *encouraging people from protected groups to participate in public life or in other activities where their participation is disproportionately low*
- foster good relations between people who share a protected characteristic and those who do not.

The equality duty covers the nine protected characteristics: age, disability, gender reassignment, pregnancy and maternity, race, religion or belief, sex and sexual orientation. Public authorities also need to have due regard to the need to eliminate unlawful discrimination against someone because of their marriage or civil partnership status.

In essence what this means is that when designing policies and delivering services, public authorities must consider potential impact on equality.

---

However, a review of the equality duty was announced in May 2012 by the Coalition Government as part of its 'Red Tape Challenge', which was introduced *'to give business and the general public the opportunity to challenge the Government to get rid of burdensome regulations, to boost business and economic growth and to save taxpayers money'* (www.redtapechallenge.cabinetoffice.gov.uk/about/). The review, which reported in 2013, concluded that a full evaluation should take place in 2016, but in the meantime made a number of recommendations which were accepted by the Government as a way of what the minister at the time, Maria Miller, referred to as 'gold-plating by the public sector'. This encapsulates a significant tension within the contemporary debate over the legal framework of employment relations in that regulation is not judged in terms of the extent to which it promotes fairness at work but in relation to the potential 'burdens' that are placed on business.

## ? REFLECTIVE ACTIVITY 4.8

Do you think that organisations should have a positive duty to promote equality and fairness? Should the Government try to promote fairness as an end in itself or is fairness only important if it underpins organisational performance and efficiency?

## 4.10 SUMMARY

Over the last three decades there has been a radical change in the legal framework of UK employment relations. We have seen the decline of the auxiliary function of the law, whereby the Government plugged gaps or supplemented existing collective employment relations. The erosion of trade union organisation, arguably helped by legislation restricting union activity and industrial action, has seen increased emphasis placed on individual employment rights. This, in turn, has been accentuated by the influence of European legislation. As a consequence, employment relations practice that once revolved around collective processes of negotiation and accommodation is now dominated by issues of regulatory compliance and the threat of litigation. In some respects, what is seen as 'good practice' is intertwined with what is required to comply with the law.

As Linda Dickens (2012: 212) has argued:

'compliance with many of the employment rights does not require much of employers. The common passive/reactive individualised approach is not only a weak lever for bringing about change ... but in fact may be counterproductive for employers since it means they are only likely to realise ... that they are "not complying" when challenged and facing a potential ET.'

There is, therefore, a danger that employment relations professionals focus solely on what their organisations need to do to achieve minimum levels of compliance. Moreover, the perception that employment rights represent a barrier to greater efficiency and performance has been used to justify changes in which the structure of employment rights in the UK has been weakened and the threat of litigation reduced.

This represents a significant challenge for practitioners. Proactive employment relations strategies that promote equity, organisational justice and trust not only ensure legal compliance but also underpin enhanced engagement and organisational performance. The difficulty is that the current framework is not one that drives employers in this direction. Accordingly, it may be left to employment relations professionals to make both the business and also the moral case for greater fairness at work.

## KEY LEARNING POINTS

- The contract of employment provides the foundation of the employment relationship – in addition to express terms, it also includes implied terms, which include a duty on both employer and employee to maintain 'mutual trust and confidence'.
- Employee status confers important individual employment rights such as the right to claim unfair dismissal. However, this has become more difficult to define because of the increased variety of contractual types.
- The key tests that tribunals use to assess employee status are: control, mutual obligation and whether the other provisions of the contract are consistent with its being a contract of service. Importantly, tribunals will look at the reality of the employment relationship rather than what the written contract states.
- There has been a significant shift from the law playing an auxiliary role to one in which it plays a central role in regulating the employment relationship. Accordingly, the law is a prime concern for employment relations professionals. Furthermore, the policy debate has increasingly revolved around employers' concerns over the extent to which regulation represents a burden on business.
- The prevailing system of individual employment rights in the UK is predominantly passive and reactive. This has produced a focus on legal compliance rather than on practices and approaches that generate high levels of trust and positive employment relations.
- The employment relations professional should not view the law as simply a process of compliance. Good employment relations are achieved by the positive action employers take to win the trust and confidence of their workforce.

## REVIEW QUESTIONS

1   What is the most effective way of ensuring that your own organisation is protected against litigation and adverse employment tribunal decisions?

2   A regional manager has asked to meet you to obtain advice on the status of some workers in her division. Three people have worked on a daily basis as cleaners supplied by an external agency for more than 12 months. The regional manager would like to terminate the cleaning contract. What would be the implications of this?

3   An employee in your organisation belongs to an extreme right-wing political party and he regularly espouses views that other employees find racist and offensive. How would you advise that this situation should be handled?

4   You are asked to draw up a briefing paper for senior managers on the impact of the introduction of employment tribunal fees – what would be the impact on your organisation and how might this shape organisational policies and practices?

5   To what extent does the UK's system of employment regulation encourage organisations to take action to ensure fairness equality at work?

**EXPLORE FURTHER**

DICKENS, L. (ed) (2012). *Making employment rights effective: issues of enforcement and compliance.* Oxford: Hart Publishing.

GIBBONS, M. (2007). *A review of employment dispute resolution in Great Britain.* London: DTI.

LEWIS, D. and SARGEANT, M. (2015) *Essentials of employment law.* 13th ed. London: CIPD.

**Website links**

www.bis.gov.uk is the website of the Department for Business, Innovation and Skills, and will give you access to the main provisions of Acts of Parliament relevant to employment relations.

www.cipd.co.uk provides information about the CIPD Employment Law Service.

www.equalityhumanrights.com is the website of the Equality and Human Rights Commission, created by the merger of the Equal Opportunities Commission, the Commission for Racial Equality and the Disability Rights Commission.

# CHAPTER 5

# The Global Environment

## OVERVIEW

This chapter examines the international context of employment relations. It starts by assessing the development of international and global trade, and particularly the rise of emerging economies and markets. It then goes on to look at the role of multinational corporations and the debate over whether their increased influence and increasing international competition is leading to a convergence of national employment relations systems. The ability of multinational corporations to relocate productive resources and take advantage of low labour costs and permissive regulatory regimes within developing economies is then discussed, and we ask whether this is encouraging 'a race to the bottom' with significant consequences for global inequality. We then turn to attempts to provide social protection through supranational regulation in the form of the European Union (EU) and the International Labour Organization (ILO) and examine key legislation. Finally, we explore the potential of 'soft regulation' in the form of voluntary codes of conduct adopted by multinational corporations in order to regulate labour standards and practices of suppliers in developing economies.

## LEARNING OUTCOMES

When you have completed this chapter, you should be able to:

- identify the implications of globalisation for employment relations
- critically evaluate the role played by multinational corporations and their influence
- understand the influence of the European Union on employee relations management in the UK
- describe the main developments in the social dimension of the European Single Market
- analyse the nature and impact of key EU legislation
- critically evaluate the link between globalisation and concerns over labour standards and the role of the International Labour Organization (ILO)
- critically assess the impact and effectiveness of corporate codes of conduct.

## 5.1 INTRODUCTION

An important feature of contemporary employment relations has been the growing importance and influence of the international context. The greater reach of global markets, the increased mobility of labour and capital, and the extension of European employment regulation, means that anyone working in employment relations needs to have a broader perspective and a clear understanding of how this shapes practices in UK workplaces. Foreign multinational corporations have the potential to influence the conduct of employment relations by exporting particular practices, while the threat of disinvestment can have a fundamental impact on government policy and the balance of workplace bargaining power. In addition, UK governments have sought to attract investment by emphasising the relative lack of regulatory constraints in comparison with competitor countries. For some, this suggests a convergence of national systems of employment relations around a neo-liberal model with an emphasis on deregulation and labour flexibility.

International systems of employment regulation aim to provide some protection against this. In particular, EU legislation plays an important role in defining the framework of employments rights within which employment practitioners in the UK operate. However, here again, there are some signs that the threat of competition from emerging economies is placing pressure on EU countries to dilute their commitment to a social dimension. In this context, international standards, such as those set by the International Labour Organization (ILO), are one way of trying to prevent workers becoming victim to global market forces. More recently, greater emphasis has been placed on the growing role of voluntary labour standards and ethical training initiatives. However, the efficacy and impact of such forms of soft regulation is open to question and a key issue for this chapter.

## 5.2 GLOBALISATION AND INTERNATIONALISATION

Since World War II, there has been a rapid expansion in international trade and economies have become increasingly interdependent. According to a 2009 report prepared for the World Trade Organization (WTO) and International Labour Organization (ILO), global trade comprised more than 60% of world GDP, compared with less than 30% in the mid-1980s (Bacchetta *et al*, 2009). There are a number of reasons for this. First, technical advances in communication, transportation and, most recently, the development of the Internet have increased the mobility of labour and capital. Second, both labour and capital markets have been liberalised with the removal of tariffs and barriers to trade. Third, these developments have, in part, led to rapid growth of economies that were previously underdeveloped. For example, China is currently the leading global economy in terms of purchasing power and second only to the USA in terms of output. In 2015, China, the Philippines, Indonesia, Kenya and India are all forecast to grow by more than 5%, compared with around 3% for the USA and the UK, and less than 2% for the Euro area.

These developments have significant implications for countries such as the UK, as emerging economies provide new markets and are also both a source of, and destination for, new investment. In 2011, the UK was the fourth largest overseas investor ($73 billion) behind only the USA, Japan and Belgium (OECD, 2013). In addition, there has been a significant increase in foreign-owned enterprises investing in the UK. In 1990, the stock of foreign direct investment in the UK was just over $200 billion, but by 2014 it was more than eight times higher at just over $1,600 billion (UKTI, 2014). Furthermore, China invested £11.7 billion in the UK between 2005 and 2013 and is forecast to invest more than £100 billion between 2015 and 2025 (CEBR and Pinsent Masons, 2014). According to Driffield *et al* (2013), foreign-owned enterprises employ 3 million workers in the UK – 13% of the entire workforce. Therefore, their approach to the management of people has the potential to shape the nature and climate of employment relations in the UK.

## 5.3 THE ROLE OF MULTINATIONAL CORPORATIONS (MNCS)

Foreign-owned multinational corporations play an increasingly important role in the UK economy, while UK-owned MNCs have significant influence on economies overseas. MNCs are defined by Mike Leat (2006) as: *'enterprises which in more than one country own or control production or service facilities that add value'*. Investment by MNCs in the UK can be argued to have many positive features: this creates jobs both in the organisations directly but also in the supply chain and adds to local economic development. As noted previously, the UK is one of the main recipients of foreign direct investment, most of which comes from MNCs mainly based in the USA, Europe and the Far East. However, the increased involvement and activity of MNCs is likely to have far-reaching implications for the nature and conduct of UK employment relations. For example, research (Edwards and Walsh, 2009; Marginson and Meardi, 2010) has found that foreign-owned MNCs have a number of distinctive traits. In particular, they are more likely to: look to introduce direct communication and employee involvement strategies; have centralised HR functions; and operate single-union bargaining approaches. However, it is suggested that they argue that, over time, these differences have tended to diminish.

It has long been argued that the growing influence of MNCs will contribute to the convergence of national industrial relations systems as countries develop the kind of rules and institutions necessary to support large-scale industrial development (Kerr *et al*, 1960). As Turner and Windmuller (1998) point out, the 1970s saw some evidence of this; US and European systems coalesced around increased direct intervention in the conduct of employment relations, both in the establishment of individual employment rights, the development of state-sponsored dispute resolution processes and the greater decentralisation and fragmentation of collective bargaining.

More recently, it has been suggested that MNCs facilitate convergence by encouraging different 'regimes' to compete with each other as to who can offer the most conducive environment for profitability (Streeck, 1997). The political pressure on governments to retain employment and attract investment in the context of a global market arguably forces different employment relations systems to move towards a deregulated and neo-liberal model characterised by high levels of flexibility, limited employment protection and weak trade union organisation (see for example Eaton, 2000). For example, successive UK governments have sought to attract investment on the grounds that the UK has a relatively light-touch approach to labour regulation in comparison with other developed economies, particularly those in Europe.

Much of the evidence suggests that despite both the development of EU regulation, broader pressures of global competition and the increased influence of MNCs, there has been relatively little change to national systems of industrial relations within the EU (Marginson and Sisson, 2004). This reflects wider international evidence that different systems are relatively resilient in the face of the pressures of globalisation (Hall and Soskice, 2001). Importantly, the forces of convergence are not necessarily unidirectional and, while increasing international competition and the diffusion of new technology might be expected to lead to pressures towards more deregulated and flexible systems, the emergence of international networks of trade unions and employers and the development of international and regional regulation through bodies such as the EU produce a very different dynamic. One of the key aspects of convergence has been the greater decentralisation of bargaining, which in itself has the seeds for greater diversity as practices develop to fit local conditions. As Turner and Windmuller argue, '*market forces drive convergence in industrial relations, while both a decentralization of bargaining and contrasting national institutions refract change into diverse channels*' (1998: 204).

Nonetheless, there are signs that, in the wake of the global financial crisis of 2008 and ongoing economic problems of the Eurozone, Streeck's prediction (1991) of convergence around a more deregulated neo-liberal political economy may have some substance. As we explore later in this chapter, it could be argued that the EU's commitment to social protection has been progressively diluted as concerns over maintaining employment in the face of competition from less-regulated economies have grown. Furthermore, at the time of writing, the UK is seeking to substantially renegotiate their relationship with the EU in order to, among other things, reduce the impact of EU employment legislation. The outcome of these negotiations may provide a clear indication of the resilience of the EU's social dimension.

There is also little doubt that the increased mobility of capital and productive resources and the consequent threat of multinationals relocating operations to lower-cost economies has reduced the bargaining power of labour. This practice, known as 'whipsawing' (Greer and Hauptmeier, 2015), essentially involves management making coercive comparisons (Muller and Purcell, 1992) between different factories, plants or outlets whereby there is an explicit or implicit threat to move production unless workers (and normally trade unions) make concessions in terms of wages, conditions and/or working practices. Of course, this is nothing new; as Greer and Hauptmeier point out, such tactics were used by large international corporations such as the Ford Motor Company in the 1970s. However, the strength of trade unions and institutions of employment relations in the UK limited the power of such threats. In more recent times, the intensification of global competition, the reduction in union bargaining power and the greater mobility of productive resources have accentuated the threat of disinvestment. The case of GM Vauxhall is an excellent example of this, with trade unions adopting pragmatic approaches and even working in co-operation with politicians with whom they share little in common in order to protect employment. While such agreements may be seen as examples of partnership working, they also reflect in stark terms the relative fragility of union influence in the face of international capital.

---

**CASE STUDY 5.1**

### GM VAUXHALL – LABOUR AGREEMENT SAVES JOBS

In 2012, the Vauxhall car plant at Ellesmere Port was rescued from closure, saving more than 2,000 jobs, when the company announced that the new model of the Vauxhall Astra would be made at the factory. The company had made it clear that the work would go to either Ellesmere Port or its plant at Bochum in Germany. This represented an investment of £125 million.

Securing the future of the plant depended on a new agreement on pay and conditions, which included:

- *a four-year pay deal (including a two-year freeze)*
- *a new shift system to enable 24-hour production*
- *an end to the traditional summer shutdown*
- *a 37-hour week expandable to 40 hours at times of high demand*
- *reform of the pension scheme.*

For Vauxhall, the 'responsible labour agreement' was central to its decision to stay, alongside a commitment from government to support supply chain initiatives and apprenticeships.

---

## 5.4 GLOBALISATION AND DEVELOPING ECONOMIES – A RACE TO THE BOTTOM?

There is significant debate about the impact of globalisation on employment within emerging economies. Foreign direct investment from MNCs has created large numbers of jobs; however, the nature of these jobs and the conditions under which the new global workforce are employed has become a source of increasing concern. An authoritative review of this area, commissioned by the WTO and ILO, summed this up as follows:

'Few would contest that increased trade has contributed to global growth and job creation. However, strong growth in the global economy has not, so far, led to a corresponding improvement in working conditions and living standards for many. Absolute poverty has declined, thanks to the economic dynamism of recent years, the efforts of private companies, migrant workers and their remittances and the international development community. Nevertheless, in many instances, labour market conditions and the quality of employment growth have not improved to the same degree. In many developing economies job creation has mainly taken place in the informal economy, where around 60% of workers find income opportunities. However, the informal economy is characterized by less job security, lower incomes, an absence of access to a range of social benefits and fewer possibilities to participate in formal education and training programmes – in short, the absence of key ingredients of decent work opportunities.' (Bacchetta *et al.*, 2009: 9)

It could be argued that the development of national and supranational systems of employment regulation may lead multinational organisations to move more labour-intensive parts of their operations to relatively low-wage economies. Writing in the early 1980s, Froebel *et al* (1980) argued that there was increasing evidence of a 'New International Division of Labour', whereby manufacturing processes that required relatively low-skilled labour were outsourced to countries in which pay was low, union organisation was weak and in which there was little regulation to protect workers. At the same time, high-value processes such as R&D and those that require high levels of skills and training were retained within developed economies. The case of Dyson outlined in Case Study 5.2 is a classic example of this process, whereby the technically advanced functions of research and design were kept in the UK and production was relocated to Malaysia.

---

**CASE STUDY 5.2**

**DYSON DISINVESTS**

In 2002, Dyson, which makes a range of domestic appliances, attracted considerable publicity with its decision to move production of its vacuum cleaners to Malaysia at the cost of 800 jobs. James Dyson, the owner and founder of the company, claimed that rising labour costs made production unviable. He argued that direct labour costs had doubled in ten years. Production costs in Malaysia were 30% lower, while wages were around one-third of those in the UK.

Dyson told the BBC, 'I don't think I can (see an alternative) ... It's been an agonising decision and very much a change of mind ... Increasingly in the past two to three years our suppliers are Far East based and not over here ... And our markets are there too. We're the best selling vacuum cleaner in Australia and New Zealand, we're doing well in Japan and we're about to enter the US. And we see other Far Eastern countries as big markets as well.'

However, the company's headquarters was kept at Malmesbury in Wiltshire along with its R&D department, employing around 1,300 staff.

Derek Simpson, then General Secretary of the trade union AMICUS (now UNITE), commented: 'This latest export of jobs by Dyson is confirmation that his motive is making even greater profit at the expense of UK manufacturing and his loyal workforce. Dyson is no longer a UK product.'

Speaking two years later to the *Guardian*, Dyson claimed that 'we are a much more flourishing company now because of what we did and it's doubtful if we could have survived in the long term if we had not done so.'

*Sources:* the *Guardian*; the *Daily Telegraph*; BBC

---

However, as the Dyson case suggests, the relocation of production may also be driven by greater proximity to new and growing markets, as well as the pursuit of lower labour costs.

MNCs not only organise their global production chains on the basis of the relative labour costs of developed and less-developed economies, but also encourage competition between less-developed countries over which governments can offer the cheapest labour and the least-regulated labour markets. This so-called 'race to the bottom' is a matter of debate. Some commentators argue that investment from multinationals has a broadly positive impact, not only increasing employment but generally paying wages that are higher than domestically owned businesses. Moreover, as Williams and Adam-Smith (2010) argue, MNC investment can improve equality of opportunity, opening up employment opportunities for women in particular. MNC activity in developing and emerging economies may also speed up the process of industrialisation and improve the transfer of new technology and knowledge.

A 2010 Oxfam report (Oxfam International, 2010) argued that while millions of jobs have been created in the last two decades in developing economies, the precariousness of this work is a major barrier to reducing levels of poverty. The report points to a number of specific problems: first, workers often have no job security and are paid on the basis of piece rates or paid by the day. For example, in the Bangladeshi garment industry, it is claimed that only one-quarter of workers have a written contract. Second, wages are low and often below legal minima. For example, in Moroccan agriculture, less than a third of workers earn the legal minimum wage, which is rarely enforced. Third, working hours are often extreme, with shifts of more than 12 hours a regular occurrence.

## RANA PLAZA – A DISASTER WAITING TO HAPPEN?

The issue of labour standards within suppliers to leading international brands was brought into stark relief on 24 April 2013 when the Rana Plaza, an eight-storey factory, which mainly housed clothing manufacturers, collapsed, killing 1,134 people. The building in the capital of Bangladesh, Dhaka, contained suppliers to a wide range of high-street fashion brands including Benetton, Bonmarché, Monsoon Accessorize, Matalan, Primark and Walmart. Bangladesh is the world's second largest exporter of clothing; however, wages were and are low. In August 2013, the ILO reported that the minimum wage of entry-level garment workers in Bangladesh was just $39 (£25) per month, around half that of India, Vietnam and Cambodia (International Labour Organization, 2013).

A report into the collapse blamed substandard building materials and a disregard for building regulations. In addition, after warning signs led many workers to leave the building on the day of disaster, they were forced back into the building by their employers. In the wake of the disaster, a fund was set up to compensate victims and families. Brands including H&M, Mango, Primark, the Gap and Walmart have contributed $21.5 million to the fund.

According to a report by Amy Westervelt in the *Guardian* on 24 April 2015, there are some signs of change – three-quarters of Bangladeshi garment factories have been through fire and safety inspections, and 35 have been closed for failing to meet the required standards. In addition, the minimum wage was increased by 77% to $68 in November 2013 after strikes and protests by garment workers. Action on workers' rights is less evident – while there has been an increase in the number of unions and union members in the aftermath of Rana Plaza, they still represent just 5% of the workforce overall. At the same time, recommendations to create worker safety committees have been slow to be implemented.

Some brands have taken action, paying for building upgrades and developing stronger guidelines and more effective strategies for improving pay and conditions. However, there are concerns that once the media gaze has been averted from the disaster, the pressure for change will ebb away.

Therefore, it can be argued that without greater regulation and the development of effective trade union organisation, any benefits of the rapid growth in global trade will feed into extreme inequality (Jaumotte and Osorio Buitron, 2015; Oxfam, 2013). Moreover, the prevalence of poor employment conditions has consequences for both employers and their customers. First, growing international concern over labour standards may have an adverse effect on brand reputation, which may hit sales. This may also have a negative impact on the attitudes of staff working in the UK and other developed economies. As we note elsewhere in this book, organisational commitment is a key ingredient of engagement, and pride in the organisation is an important element of this. Secondly, in host countries, continuing employment and income insecurity will make it difficult to sustain and improve productivity, performance and quality. There are already some signs of growing conflict as workers seek to improve pay and conditions. Strikes and protests by Bangladeshi garment workers were responsible, in part, for an increase in the minimum wage paid to entry-level workers. In China there is evidence of greater industrial unrest as labour shortages, increasing bargaining power and growing worker expectations have combined with falling rates of economic growth. While in 2011 there were just 185 strikes or disputes, there were around 1,400 in 2014 and to date more than 1,800 in 2015 (ABC, 2015; China Labour Bulletin, 2015).

Concerns over increasing costs, and particularly quality, have also led to a small but growing trend of what is referred to as 're-shoring' as organisations bring production back to their host countries. In May 2014, mobile phone group EE announced plans to move 250 jobs in customer services from the Philippines back to the UK. According to the chief executive Olaf Swantee, a major reason was that performance in the UK was better than in its overseas contact centres.

A survey conducted by the Engineering Employers' Federation (EEF) in 2014 found that one in six manufacturers had 're-shored' some elements of their operation. Interestingly, the key issues were quality and delivery times, while the main potential problems were tax, availability of skills and energy costs – as opposed to employment relations issues. Only 16% said the erosion of labour cost benefits was a significant factor.

Examples include Symington's, a Leeds foods company, which moved noodle production from Guangzhou back to Yorkshire, and Hornby, the maker of model rail sets, which recently returned the making of aircraft kits from India to East Sussex. UK Trade and Investment, the trade promotion agency, estimated in 2014 that 1,500 jobs had been re-shored since 2011. China was the main area from which companies were re-shoring, followed by Eastern Europe.

## 5.5 REGULATING INTERNATIONAL EMPLOYMENT RELATIONS

The ability of MNCs to work across national boundaries and to relocate all or parts of their operation has led to various attempts at regulation in an attempt to both prevent terms and conditions of employment being used as a source of competition and to ensure certain minimum labour standards. In the next part of the chapter we shall examine three different approaches: first, we will explore the influence of the European Union – this is examined in some detail because of the day-to-day importance of EU legislation for UK-based practitioners. Second, the role of the International Labour Organization is discussed, and finally, we assess the nature and impact of the adoption of voluntary codes of conduct by multinational companies as a means of improving labour standards in emerging economies.

### 5.5.1 THE INFLUENCE OF THE EUROPEAN UNION

In the context of the globalisation of economic activity, the purpose and role of the European Union is particularly important. While the Treaty of Rome, which established the European Economic Community in 1957, provided for the creation of a free-trade area, it also recognised the potential for countries to seek comparative advantage through driving down labour costs. It therefore contained a number of articles that sought to provide some protection against this. For example, article 117 established that there was a need to improve and harmonise working conditions and article 118 called for close co-operation from member states on issues related to labour, employment and health and safety. The treaty also included a clause which established the principle of equal pay for equal work for men and women (Hyman, 2010). In 1989, EU member states, with the exception of the UK Government (led by Margaret Thatcher), accepted the introduction of a 'Charter of Fundamental Social Rights of Workers', known as the Social Charter. While this had limited direct effect, it signalled a commitment to maintaining a social dimension alongside the extension of the single European market. This paved the way for the development of the Social Chapter, which was part of Maastricht Treaty in 1991.

The Social Chapter is designed to ensure that product and service market competition would take place on a 'level playing field' of minimum social and employment conditions in all member states.

---

### THE OBJECTIVES OF THE SOCIAL CHAPTER ARE:

- the promotion of employment
- improved living and working conditions
- proper social protection
- dialogue between management and labour
- the development of human resources with a view to lasting employment
- the combating of social exclusion.

---

It also commits member states, to ensure and maintain the application of the principle that men and women should have equal pay for equal work, or work of equal value. The Social Chapter is not a set of detailed regulations. It is a mechanism that allows the member states to make new rules and legislation at the EU level on a wide range of social and employment issues.

Under the Social Chapter procedures, legislation in any of the following areas can be adopted by qualified majority voting:

- improvements in the working environment to protect workers' health and safety
- working conditions
- information and consultation with workers
- the integration of persons excluded from the labour market
- equality between men and women with regard to labour market opportunities and treatment at work.

The Social Chapter mechanisms can be used to introduce EU-wide legislation on the basis of unanimity amongst member states in the following areas:

- social security and the social protection of workers
- the protection of workers where their employment contract is terminated
- the representation and collective defence of workers' and employers' interests, including co-determination
- conditions of employment for third-country nationals legally resident in the EU.

Critics of the EU nevertheless point out that although some areas are formally subject to unanimity or even excluded altogether, this is by no means a secure safeguard. They argue that EU institutions will seek to apply the broadest possible interpretations in order to maximise the scope for adopting measures by qualified majority voting, despite possible objections from individual member states. From its inception, the Conservative UK Government argued that Social Chapter mechanisms would result in costly, far-reaching and unforeseeable legislation being imposed on the UK, contrary to the deregulated approach to the operation of labour markets that had become dominant since the election of Margaret Thatcher in 1979. As a consequence, the then Prime Minister, John Major, negotiated an opt-out from the Social Policy Protocol of the Maastricht Treaty, which operationalised the Social Chapter. This was important as it meant that the UK Government was not required to transpose EU legislation in this area into UK statute. However, public sector workers, as employees of the Government, were able to seek protection under EU law.

Following the UK general election in 1997, the new Labour Government agreed to opt in to the Social Policy Protocol and the UK again took full part in social policymaking and thus became fully bound by EU employment legislation. Although this undoubtedly led to an extension of the scale and scope of employment protection afforded to employees in the UK, the position adopted by New Labour (as discussed in Chapters 3 and 4) to balance fairness and flexibility saw EU legislation being introduced in a minimalistic fashion, which often placed the responsibility for enforcement on the individual employee (Davies and Freedland, 2007).

### 5.5.2 THE SOCIAL CHAPTER IN PRACTICE

There are four main areas of employment relations management in which EU laws have, and will continue to have, a direct impact on the work of the employment relations professional:

- equal opportunities
- employment protection/working conditions
- employment relations
- health and safety at work.

## EU EMPLOYMENT AND SOCIAL DIRECTIVES THAT IMPACT ON THE WORK OF UK EMPLOYMENT RELATIONS PROFESSIONALS

Equal opportunities

- Equal Pay Directive (1975)
- Equal Treatment Directive (1996)
- Parental Leave Directive (1996)
- Sex Discrimination Directive (1997)
- Part-time Worker Directive (1997)
- Fixed-term Contract Directive (1999)
- Agency Worker Directive (2008)

Employment protection

- Collective Redundancy Directive (1975)
- Transfers of Undertakings Directive (1977)
- Insolvency Directive (1980)
- Proof of an Employment Relationship Directive (1992)
- Posting of Workers Directive (1996)

Employment relations

- European Works Council Directive (1994)
- European Works Council (UK Extension) Directive (1997)
- Information and Consultation Directive (2002)
- European Company Statute (2001)

Health and safety

- Working Time Directive (1993)

In the next section, we examine a number of the key pieces of EU legislation, which have had a significant impact on employment relations in the UK.

## Equal Pay and Equal Treatment

The 1975 Equal Pay Directive sought to strengthen the application of equal pay for men and women, as laid down in the Treaty of Rome, by reducing differences between member states. The Directive essentially set out the principle that men and women should receive equal pay for work of equal value and also that job classification or evaluation schemes should be based on the same criteria for both men and women, and must be drawn up so as to exclude discrimination on grounds of sex. This had a significant impact on equal pay legislation in the UK, which until that point had only guaranteed equal pay for those in like work. This was of little use in countering occupational segregation. In 1983 the Equal Pay (Amendment) Regulations were introduced in the UK to comply with this Directive. These regulations, among other things, introduced provision for 'independent experts' to undertake job evaluation exercises independently of the employer in the case of claims for equal pay based on work of equal value. Although the legislation is time-consuming and cumbersome, this has led to large-scale claims and provided the basis for negotiated settlements for thousands of women, particularly those employed in the public sector (for a detailed review see O'Reilly *et al*, 2015).

The Equal Treatment Directive (1976) was initially designed to give effect to the principle of equal treatment for men and women with regard to access to employment, promotion, vocational training and working conditions, including the conditions governing dismissal. However, subsequent development of the Directive has extended the principles to age, sexual orientation, religion or belief, and disability and has been largely responsible for the protections now consolidated in the 2010 Equality Act (discussed in Chapter 4) and specific measures such as the equalisation of retirement ages for men and women.

## Parental Leave

The Parental Leave Directive (1996) provided an individual right for parents to take up to three months' unpaid leave after the birth or adoption of a child before its eighth birthday. Employees are protected from dismissal for asking for the leave and have the right to return to work on the same conditions as before. The Directive also entitled individuals to a certain number of days off work for urgent family reasons in the case of sickness or accident. The UK Government transposed this Directive into national legislation via the Maternity and Parental Leave Regulations (1999).

In June 2009 the European social partners, including trade unions and employers' representatives, reached an agreement on a number of enhanced provisions, including:

- increasing the length of parental leave from the previous three months to four months
- making part of the leave non-transferable in order to encourage fathers to take advantage of parental leave

- offering a right to request flexible working when returning from parental leave
- calling on member states to establish notice periods that workers should give in exercising the right to parental leave.

This was implemented in 2010 through Council Directive 2010/18/EU and transposed into UK law through the Parental Leave (EU Directive) Regulations 2013. Importantly, the UK Government sought to implement the Directive in a manner that supported *'its wider policy objectives of encouraging shared parenting and maintaining attachment to the labour market whilst minimising burdens to business'* (HM Government, 2012), underlining the unease of many Conservative politicians about the supposed burdens of EU 'red tape' and also the UK's historic approach of enacting EU legislation in a minimalist fashion.

### Agency workers

For governments, employers and trade unions, the status of agency workers has assumed increased importance as their use has grown in recent years. For employers, they provide a degree of important flexibility; however at the same time there were, and are, concerns that the vulnerable position of such workers can be abused. Consequently, the Temporary Agency Work Directive was designed to end the situation in which agency staff can work in a company for a long time but never receive equal treatment with full-time workers. The original draft Directive proposed that agency workers receive the same employment rights to basic pay and other employment conditions as full-time workers once they have spent six weeks in a specific post.

In June 2008, after 6 years and significant opposition from the UK, a revised Directive was agreed which provided that agency workers should receive equal treatment with permanent employees after 12 weeks in a specific job. This therefore means that after the 12-week period, agency workers should have the same pay, holidays and other working conditions, such as overtime and breaks, as directly recruited staff. But sick pay and pensions are excluded. The UK Government gave effect to this Directive via the Agency Worker Regulations (AWR) in October 2011.

### Health, Safety and Working Time

More than 40 Directives have been adopted in this area, making health and safety at work the most regulated area of EU social policy. These Directives have largely been incorporated into UK law via the Control of Substances Hazardous to Health (COSHH) Regulations (2002). However, the majority of these Directives are so-called 'daughter' Directives, aimed at implementing in specific areas the provisions laid down in the 1989 Framework Directive, which itself was intended to 'introduce measures to encourage improvements in the safety and health of workers at work'.

An important EU measure in the health and safety area is the Working Time Directive (1993). At the time of its introduction, the UK Government was the only member state that voted against, complaining that labelling working time as a health and safety issue was a way of bypassing the UK opt-out of social legislation negotiated at Maastricht. This also reflected the general criticism that such measures would be damaging to business. In fact, the Directive allowed for significant flexibility (in part an attempt to meet the concerns of the UK), which included the ability to vary the terms of the Directive through collective agreement and for individual employees to opt out of some of the key elements. The Directive was eventually introduced into UK legislation in 1998 (after the election of the Labour Government) through the Working Time Regulations. However, consistent with the approach of UK governments to EU legislation, the regulations provided for maximum flexibility and the UK was the only member state to provide an unrestricted ability for individual employees to work more than 48 hours by agreement.

Nonetheless, the Working Time Regulations introduced a range of significant new rights and entitlements, such as a minimum of four weeks' paid annual leave (but which can include bank holidays). There is significant scope in the Regulations for employers and employees to enter into collective agreements on how the working time rules will apply in their own particular circumstances. Collective agreements can be made with an independent trade union, while 'workforce agreements' can be made with workers who are not covered by collective bargaining. Certain activities, or sectors of activities, of workers were excluded from the Regulations. These include those whose working time is under their own control – for example, managing executives, family and religious workers, domestic servants and trainee doctors. However, a so-called 'horizontal amending Directive' (HAD) was adopted by the Council of Ministers, extending the Directive on the organisation of working time to the previously excluded sectors and activities (road, rail, air, sea, inland waterways and lake transport, sea fishing, offshore work and junior doctors). These measures were implemented over the period 2003/04.

### KEY RIGHTS PROVIDED BY THE WORKING TIME REGULATIONS

A limit of an average 48 hours a week on the hours a worker can be required to work, though individuals may choose to work longer by 'opting out'. The average is calculated over a 17-week reference period

Paid annual leave of 5.6 weeks a year

Eleven consecutive hours' rest in any 24-hour period

One 20-minute rest break if the working day is longer than six hours

One day off each week

A limit on the normal working hours of night workers to an average eight hours in any 24-hour period, and an entitlement for night workers to receive regular health assessments.

Worker entitlements under the Regulations (eg rest periods and paid annual leave) are enforced by an individual complaint to an employment tribunal. In the case of the mandatory 'limits' on working time (such as the weekly working time and night work limits), employees' rights are enforced by health and safety authorities (the Health and Safety Executive and local authorities). However, workers have protection against detrimental treatment or unfair dismissal for, amongst other things, refusing to work in breach of an acceptable working time limit. Employers are required to keep adequate records, going back two years, to show that the working time limits have been honoured.

The introduction of the regulations appeared to have some impact with the number of UK workers averaging more than 48 hours per week falling from around 3.8 million to around 3 million in 2010. However, according to the TUC, between 2010 and 2014 this increased to 3.4 million, with UK workers averaging 43.6 hours per week compared with 40.3 hours in all EU countries (TUC, 2015). Recent Attempts to reform the Working Time Directive by removing opt-outs in exchange for a maximum 60-hour week, averaged over a 12-month period, have stalled, with discussions still continuing at the time of writing after more than ten years of negotiations. In some respects, these problems epitomise the tension within EU policy between social protection and governments calling for greater flexibility to respond to international competition.

### Redundancy

The Collective Redundancy Directive (1975) introduced the requirement for consultation, in good time, with employee representatives on mass redundancies, with a view to reaching an agreement. The consultations must cover ways and means of avoiding collective redundancies or limiting the number of workers affected, and of mitigating the consequences through help for redeployment or retraining workers made redundant. The employer must provide the workers' representatives with certain information – for example, the reason for the redundancies, the number and types of workers to be made redundant, and the criteria proposed for the selection of workers to be made redundant. This Directive was transposed into UK legislation in the Employment Protection Act (1975). The Directive was amended slightly by a further Directive (1992), which was implemented in the UK in June 1994 in the Trade Union Reform and Employment Rights Act (1993). This ensured that consultation takes place at the workplace affected, even if the redundancy decision has been taken by a controlling body in another country.

### Transfer of Undertakings

The Acquired Rights Directive (1977) sought to protect employees in the event of a change of employer through takeover or merger. It introduced the principle that when a business is sold, employees should transfer to the new owner on the same basic terms and conditions of employment and could not be dismissed for reasons connected with the transfer. In transposing the Directive into UK law (the 1981 Transfer of Undertakings and Protection of Employment Regulations – TUPE), the Government excluded the public sector.

However, in 1992 the European Court of Justice confirmed that the Directive applied to employees in both the private and non-profit sectors. The UK law was therefore amended by the Trade Union Reform and Employment Rights Act (1993) to include public sector employees. In 1998, an amendment to the 1977 Directive was introduced to limit existing law by clarifying that transfer of undertakings legislation applied only when an 'economic activity' that retains its identity is transferred. The UK implemented this amendment in July 2001. The Acquired Rights Directive was consolidated in 2001 and subsequently this was reflected in the revised 2006 TUPE regulations. These were further revised in 2014 by the Collective Redundancies and Transfer of Undertakings (Protection of Employment) (Amendment) Regulations 2014, which involved a number of key changes, including:

- For TUPE to apply to work that is outsourced, the work must be 'fundamentally the same'.
- An employee will be automatically unfairly dismissed if the sole or principal reason for the dismissal is the transfer, but dismissals will not be automatically unfair just because the transfer involves a change in location.
- Terms and conditions agreed through collective bargaining, which transfer, can be renegotiated after one year provided that overall the contract is no less favourable to the employee.

### The European Works Council Directive

This Directive, which was introduced in the UK in 1994 and transposed into UK law in 1998, provides for a Europe-level information and consultation system to be set up in all organisations with more than 1,000 employees in member states and employing more than 150 people in each of two or more of these. A Works Council (or an alternative system) has to be agreed between the central management of the organisation and a special negotiating body (SNB) of employee representatives. If no agreement is reached within three years, a fallback system applies. This requires the establishment of a European Works Council of employee representatives with the right to meet central management at least once a year for information and consultation about the progress and prospects of the company, and to request extra consultation meetings before certain major decisions are taken affecting more than one member state.

## Information and Consultation at National Level

The aim of the Information and Consultation Directive (2002) was to establish a general framework setting out minimum requirements for the informing and consulting of employees in undertakings or establishments within the European Community. Its requirements apply to undertakings employing at least 50 employees in any one member state or establishments employing at least 20 employees. An 'undertaking' is defined as a public or private undertaking carrying out an economic activity, whether or not operating for gain. An 'establishment' means a unit of business in accordance with national law and practice. In short, a multi-site UK company, employing at least 50 individuals across a number of plants in different geographical locations, would be deemed an undertaking. An enterprise could be any of these individual plants, provided that it had a workforce of at least 20 employees.

The right to information and consultation covers information on:

- the recent and probable development of the undertaking's or the establishment's activities and economic situation
- the situation, structure and probable development of employment within the undertaking/establishment
- any anticipatory measures envisaged, in particular where there is a threat to employment
- decisions likely to lead to substantial changes in work organisation or in contractual relations.

This information is to be given at such time, in such fashion and with such content as is appropriate to enable employees' representatives to conduct an adequate study and, where necessary, prepare for consultation.

Under the Directive, consultation should take place at the relevant level of management and employee representation, and in such a way as to enable employees' representatives to meet with the employer and obtain a response, and the reasons for that response, to any opinion they might formulate. In addition, consultation must take place with a view to reaching an agreement on decisions within the scope of the employer's powers likely to lead to substantial changes in work organisation or in contractual relations. In the UK, this Directive was enacted by the Information and Consultation of Employees Regulations (often abbreviated to the ICE Regs), which were introduced on 6 April 2005. However, as we discuss in greater detail in Chapter 10, the experience of the ICE Regulations demonstrate the limitations of EU regulation and the resilience of domestic employment relations regimes. As with much EU legislation, the regulations represent a minimalist interpretation maximising the amount of flexibility that the Directive allowed (Hyman, 2010) and as Hall and, Terry (2004) argue, relying on a 'legislatively-prompted voluntarism' (226) whereby the onus remains on employees to enact any of the procedures laid down in regulations. The wide discretion and flexibility provided to employers has consequently limited the uptake and impact of the regulations (Hall et al, 2011).

CASE STUDY 5.3

## COERCIVE COMPARISONS AND THE EUROPEAN UNION

Planet Corporation employs 4,500 workers who produce a wide range of electronic domestic appliances for the European and North American markets. It is a UK-based multinational company and – apart from the UK, where it employs 1,500 workers – it has establishments in France (1,000 employees), Germany (1,500 employees), Italy (100 employees) and Hungary (400 employees).

The UK workforce feels strongly that their wages are well below what the company can afford. This feeling has grown stronger since the European plants with which they identify most closely (France, Germany and Italy) are part of the euro zone. It is easier now to compare pay and conditions plus living standards with workers in these countries, and it certainly seems to the UK workforce that their colleagues there are getting a much better deal.

The UK trade union that is recognised and is well organised in the plant has asked to meet with the management of Planet Corporation to put forward a claim for an improvement in pay and conditions. This in itself is not unusual because pay and conditions agreements usually last 12 months and the time for a review is approaching in any case. On this occasion there are a number of significant issues which the chief executive officer of the UK operation has highlighted. They are:

1. Planet Corporation's central management has been informed that the European Works Council (EWC) has tabled an item for discussion at the next EWC meeting, which is scheduled to take place in two weeks' time. The item focuses on pay differentials and general rewards and policies throughout the company's European operations.

2. The UK site is more profitable than other sites in Europe.

3. Last year, the organisation invested £3 million in new equipment in the UK plant and as a result attracted new and lucrative business from North America, which could develop into a long-term revenue-generating arrangement. However, delivery dates, quality, maintenance and price are all important considerations. The contract with the North Americans has just been signed.

4. The only other site belonging to Planet Corporation that could technically fulfil the USA requirements is the one in Budapest. Although labour costs are much lower there, its current performance in terms of productivity and delivery reliability are not good.

## ? REFLECTIVE ACTIVITY 5.1

The central management has asked your CEO to attend a strategy meeting to discuss a number of key issues, of which the question of pay and conditions, and employee relations in the UK – along with the North American contract – are the most important. As the HR manager you should use your knowledge and understanding of contemporary research and employee relations policy and practice in other organisations to produce an employment relations strategy, which should include: an analysis of the problem; possible solutions with associated costs and benefits; and justified options/recommendations.

### 5.5.4 GLOBALISATION AND THE EUROPEAN UNION

While EU regulation attempts to create a level playing field between European economies, and between organisations operating within Europe, it cannot be insulated from global competitive pressures. This has led some politicians to argue that EU regulation is a barrier to organisations competing effectively in global markets. In October 2013, the UK Prime Minister, David Cameron, launching a report entitled 'Cut EU red tape: report from the Business Taskforce', said:

> 'It's vital that business can take full advantage of the EU's single market. But all too often EU rules are a handicap for firms, hampering their efforts to succeed in the global race. Business people, particularly owners of small firms, are forced to spend too much time complying with pointless, burdensome and costly regulations and that means less time developing a new product, winning contracts or hiring young recruits. I'm determined to change that and to get the EU working for business, not against it.'

Of course, the view that EU regulation is a burden to business also plays to the domestic political agenda of the UK; nonetheless, it reflects a broader concern among a number of EU member states that the EU's social model could lead to a flow of jobs and investment to less-regulated economies. Andre Sapir, writing in 2006, argued that the understanding of these challenges has shaped EU policy. In fact, some commentators have argued that, over time, the notion of a 'social Europe' has faded and is increasingly being replaced by a neo-liberal emphasis on the supremacy of the free market (Crouch, 2010).

Notably, the Treaty of Amsterdam introduced the promotion of employment as one of the objectives of the European Union. More specifically, Article 2 of the Treaty set the objective of achieving 'a high level of employment' without weakening the competitiveness of the European Union. The Treaty introduced the Employment Chapter, which asserts that:

- employment is a matter of common concern
- the objective of generating high employment is to be taken into consideration when implementing all other common policies
- the achievement of this objective is closely monitored
- the EU considers the employment situation in each member state and in the Union as a whole on an annual basis, and conducts a detailed examination of the steps taken by individual governments to promote employment
- an employment committee promotes co-ordination of national measures and encourages dialogue between employers and employees.

As we write this book in late 2015, the UK Government is attempting to renegotiate its relationship with the EU. A key element of this is to reduce the impact of European social legislation on British business, with some arguing that unless the role of the EU in shaping UK employment legislation (among other things) is significantly reduced, the UK should leave the EU. At the same time, trade union leaders have stated that they will support exit from the EU if the UK Government negotiates away employment protection that they see as vital in protecting their members' interests within a globalised economy. The result of these negotiations and the consequent referendum on EU membership will therefore have a decisive impact on the future of the social dimension of the EU and the way in which this shapes employment relations in the UK.

> **?**     REFLECTIVE ACTIVITY 5.2
>
> Do you think that the UK Government is right that EU legislation places an unnecessary burden on business? What do you think the implications of the UK leaving the EU would be for employment relations?

### 5.5.5 THE ROLE OF THE INTERNATIONAL LABOUR ORGANIZATION (ILO)

Attempts have also been made to improve and harmonise global labour standards through the International Labour Organization (ILO). The ILO is an agency of the United Nations and was set up in 1919 in the wake of World War I; all but eight of the 193 member states of the UN are members of the ILO. It has a tripartite structure with government, employers and workers all represented. Conventions and recommendations are discussed and potentially adopted at the ILO's annual conference at which each member state has four representatives, two from government and one each from employers and workers (normally trade unions).

The main way in which international labour standards are expressed are through conventions. If conventions are ratified by member states, they have a legal obligation to apply their provisions. Recommendations supplement conventions but do not have binding authority. The ILO's Declaration on Fundamental Principles and Rights at Work contains four fundamental policies:

- The right of workers to associate freely and bargain collectively
  - *C87 Freedom of Association and Protection of the Right to Organise Convention, 1948*
  - *C98 Right to Organise and Collective Bargaining Convention, 1949*
- The end of forced and compulsory labour
  - *C29 Forced Labour Convention, 1930*
  - *C105 Abolition of Forced Labour Convention, 1957*
- The end of child labour
  - *C29 Forced Labour Convention, 1930*
  - *C105 Abolition of Forced Labour Convention, 1957*
- The end of unfair discrimination among workers
  - *C29 Forced Labour Convention, 1930*
  - *C105 Abolition of Forced Labour Convention, 1957*

While all member states are obliged to uphold the principles and conventions outlined above, the ILO has very few powers through which this can be enforced and tends instead to rely on working collaboratively with countries to encourage compliance. In addition to ILO standards, another approach has been to include social and labour clauses in multilateral trade agreements, although these have met with little success (Hepple, 2005). There has been more progress in providing for labour standards in bilateral agreements, particularly between developed and emerging economies (Kuruvilla and Verma, 2006).

### 5.5.6 LABOUR STANDARDS AND VOLUNTARY REGULATION

More recently, there has been significant emphasis placed on the development of so-called 'soft regulation' through voluntary codes of practice. According to Ngai (2005: 102), a code is 'a formal statement specifying the ethical standards that a [multinational] company holds and applies to the factories of its suppliers or to its trade partners'. These have become increasingly common as organisations have responded to increasing concern over labour standards. In addition, they have been driven by initiatives and campaigns often involving trade unions and charities. In the USA, the Fair Labor Association was set up in 1999 from a group of universities, companies and civil society organisations. It aims to find sustainable solutions to systemic labour issues by:

- holding affiliated companies accountable for implementing the FLA's Code of Conduct across their supply chains
- conducting external assessments so that consumers can be assured of the integrity of the products they buy
- creating a space for CSOs to engage with companies and other stakeholders to find viable solutions to labour concerns.

Its affiliates include Adidas, Apple and Cornell University.

In the UK, the Ethical Trading Initiative (ETI) describes itself as a grouping of *'companies, trade unions and NGOs that promotes respect for workers' rights around the globe'*. Moreover, it defines its vision as *'a world where all workers are free from exploitation and discrimination, and enjoy conditions of freedom, security and equity'*. Members of the ETI include well-known retailers such as Primark, Marks & Spencer, and Asda alongside the TUC, Fairtrade and charities such as CAFOD. The ETI also has a base code of practice, which has a number of key principles:

- Employment is freely entered into.
- Freedom of association and the right to collective bargaining are respected.
- Working conditions are safe and hygienic.
- Child labour shall not be used.
- Living wages are paid.
- Working hours are not excessive.
- No discrimination is practised.
- Regular employment is provided.
- No harsh or inhumane treatment is allowed.

The code, according to the ETI, helps to 'define best practice', while the ETI also provides training for its members, raises awareness of workers' rights and helps to encourage 'work cultures where workers can confidently negotiate with management about the issues that concern them'. The following box contains an extract from the ETI's Base Code of Conduct, which a number of leading organisations use as a foundation for their own codes for suppliers. It is also worth noting that this draws on existing ILO conventions.

---

## ETI BASE CODE

1 Employment is freely chosen.

*1.1 There is no forced, bonded or involuntary prison labour.*

*1.2 Workers are not required to lodge 'deposits' or their identity papers with their employer and are free to leave their employer after reasonable notice.*

2 Freedom of association and the right to collective bargaining are respected.

*2.1 Workers, without distinction, have the right to join or form trade unions of their own choosing and to bargain collectively.*

*2.2 The employer adopts an open attitude towards the activities of trade unions and their organisational activities.*

*2.3 Workers' representatives are not discriminated against and have access to carry out their representative functions in the workplace.*

*2.4 Where the right to freedom of association and collective bargaining is restricted under law, the employer facilitates, and does not hinder, the development of parallel means for independent and free association and bargaining.*

3 Working conditions are safe and hygienic.

*3.1 A safe and hygienic working environment shall be provided, bearing in mind the prevailing knowledge of the industry and of any specific hazards. Adequate steps shall be taken to prevent accidents and injury to health arising out of, associated with, or occurring in the course of work, by minimising, so far as is reasonably practicable, the causes of hazards inherent in the working environment.*

*3.2 Workers shall receive regular and recorded health and safety training, and such training shall be repeated for new or reassigned workers.*

*3.3 Access to clean toilet facilities and to potable water, and, if appropriate, sanitary facilities for food storage shall be provided.*

*3.4 Accommodation, where provided, shall be clean, safe, and meet the basic needs of the workers.*

*3.5 The company observing the code shall assign responsibility for health and safety to a senior management representative.*

4 Child labour shall not be used.

*4.1 There shall be no new recruitment of child labour.*

*4.2 Companies shall develop or participate in and contribute to policies and programmes that provide for the transition of any child found to be performing child labour to enable her or him to attend and remain in quality education until no longer a child; 'child' and 'child labour' being defined in the appendices.*

*4.3 Children and young persons under 18 shall not be employed at night or in hazardous conditions.*

*4.4 These policies and procedures shall conform to the provisions of the relevant ILO Standards.*

5 Living wages are paid

*5.1 Wages and benefits paid for a standard working week meet, at a minimum, national legal standards or industry benchmark standards, whichever is higher. In any event wages should always be enough to meet basic needs and to provide some discretionary income.*

*5.2 All workers shall be provided with written and understandable information about their employment conditions in respect to wages before they enter employment and about the particulars of their wages for the pay period concerned each time that they are paid.*

*5.3 Deductions from wages as a disciplinary measure shall not be permitted nor shall any deductions from wages not provided for by national law be permitted without the expressed permission of the worker concerned. All disciplinary measures should be recorded.*

Source: Ethical Trade Initiative www.ethicaltrade.org/resources/key-eti-resources/eti-base-code

What evidence is there for the impact of such measures? Some writers, such as Wedderburn (1997), are sceptical about the potential of soft regulation, arguing that workers' rights must be based on enforceable statutory provision, but as Kuruvilla and Verma (2006) point out, one of the main reasons for low labour standards is a lack of will on the part of governments to either enact or enforce 'hard' regulation of this type. In many countries, statutory protections are in place, but they are often ignored.

Barrientos and Smith's (2007) survey of the impact of the ETI among companies in South Africa, Vietnam and India found some positive impacts – particularly where supply chains were more integrated and there was a stronger relationship between customer and supplier. However, suppliers tended to focus on commercial imperatives and in some cases saw the codes as a barrier. Furthermore, suppliers found that it was difficult to comply with codes due to pressures being placed upon them by buyers. This points to a central problem with codes of conduct in that buyers may demand improved labour standards but may expect suppliers to absorb these costs rather than accept any reductions in their margins. Therefore, the purchasing practices of MNC buyers are a critical factor in determining whether codes will have any substantive impact. Importantly, Barrientos and Smith also found that there seemed to be greater impact on visible 'technical' outcomes such as health and safety standards but very little effect on building trade union structures, enhancing workers' rights or combatting discrimination. In part, this reflects the role of auditing as a mechanism of enforcement but also questions whether any improvements in standards can be sustained without the development of independent and robust mechanisms of worker representation.

Yu's (2008) study of the impact of corporate codes on a Reebok footwear supplier in China also suggests that the purchasing practices of the buyer (Reebok) had constrained the supplier's ability to comply. In addition, Reebok was unwilling to reform its purchasing policy or share the cost to improve labour standards. As a result of this, Reebok relied heavily on punishment-oriented techniques in order to force compliance. This potentially means that suppliers displace the costs of compliance on to the workforce. For example, a reduction in working hours can result in greater work intensification.

Therefore, while 'soft regulation' of this type can have benefits, it can be argued that material and sustainable improvements to the terms and conditions of workers are only likely where robust national systems of employment regulation are in place, which underpin strong and independent structures of union representation.

## 5.6 SUMMARY

This chapter has examined the international and global context within which employment relations is conducted both in the UK and overseas. Over the last three decades, this environment has been transformed through the development of the European Union and, perhaps more profoundly, by the emergence of developing economies as both producers and consumers. A key part of this has been the ability of multinational corporations to move or source production across the globe to take advantage of lower labour costs and different regulatory structures or to make 'coercive comparisons' between different European nations, despite EU-wide legislation. Accordingly, successive UK governments have jealously guarded the light-touch approach to employment regulation that they feel attracts inward investment.

The social dimension of the EU was developed in order to remove pay and conditions as a source of competitive advantage; however, as we argue earlier, UK governments have been reluctant to embrace this approach. Even the Labour Government elected in 1997 and which signed the Social Chapter adopted a minimalist approach to the adoption of EU legislation in order to limit the impact on business and so retain what it saw as the UK's competitive advantage in terms of labour flexibility. More recently, there are signs that the instensification of global competition has led to the EU adopting a more market-orientated approach and diluting its commitment to social protection. The outcome of current negotiations between the UK Conservative Government and other EU countries may mark a decisive point in determining the future of a 'social Europe'.

However, it is the extent to which organisations based in Europe have either moved or outsourced production to developing economies where labour costs are significantly lower that is the defining feature of the context of international employment relations. Although some commentators argue that the jobs and investment bring significant benefits to emerging economies, there is also considerable evidence of extreme income inequality and insecurity. This is not only an important moral and ethical issue but also runs counter to many of the arguments made in this book about the centrality of trust and equity to employee engagement and organisational performance. Attempts to improve these conditions through international legislation, such as the conventions of the ILO or through voluntary corporate codes, have made some progress. But, this is essentially limited by the fact that without sustainable structures of representation through which workers can leverage a degree of influence, enforcement is at best problematic.

## KEY LEARNING POINTS

1. Since World War II, there has been a rapid expansion in international trade and economies have become increasingly interdependent. In addition, a key feature of this environment has been the mobility of labour and productive resources.

2. Commentators have argued that globalisation will inevitably lead to the convergence of national employment relations systems. To date, the evidence suggests that national systems have been remarkably resilient, although there are some signs that concerns over employment are pushing developed economies towards more deregulated and flexible approaches to employment regulation.

3. The rapid growth of some emerging economies has created new markets for UK products but has also provided large pools of relatively cheap and unregulated labour.

4. Multinational corporations (MNCs) have increasingly divided their operations, keeping high value-added functions that require high levels of skill in their country of origin while shifting low-cost manufacturing and production into emerging markets in order to reduce costs.

5. The ability to use 'coercive comparisons' can allow MNCs to secure concessions in terms of wages and conditions from employees and trade unions. This also raises the prospect of a 'race to the bottom' as developing countries compete to offer the lowest wages, least regulation and greatest flexibility in return for investment.

6. The social dimension of the European Union has provided a framework of employment regulation that seeks to limit the ability of organisations to use labour conditions as bases for competition. EU Directives in the areas of equal opportunities, employment protection, employment relations and health and safety have had a direct impact on the day-to-day work of the UK HR/ personnel specialist.

7. The International Labour Organization (ILO), an agency of the United Nations, was established in 1919. The ILO has developed a range of conventions in relation to the right of workers to associate freely and bargain collectively; the end of forced and compulsory labour; the end of child labour; and the end of unfair discrimination among workers. However, it lacks any effective powers to enforce these measures.

8. There has been increasing emphasis on the use of voluntary codes of practice as a way of countering exploitation of workers in emerging economies. These are seen as important in countering negative publicity and also creating the conditions for improved productivity and performance. However, the evidence suggests that while there have been modest achievements, particularly in relation to measurable and visible outcomes, they have done little to help develop substantive structures of employee representation.

REVIEW QUESTIONS

**?**

1    You are employed by a communications company which is considering outsourcing all its call centres to the Philippines. What issues does the organisation need to consider before taking this decision?

2    Explain what the term 'race to the bottom' means? Do you think that outsourcing production to emerging economies can be justified from an ethical or a business perspective and, if so, how?

3    Do you feel that European legislation places a burden on your organisation or business? If yes, please explain which measures you feel are problematic.

4    To what extent do you think that the adoption of voluntary codes of conduct are effective in improving labour standards? What do you think are the main barriers to their effective implementation?

EXPLORE FURTHER

ADDISON, J.T. and SIEBERT, W.S. (1991) The social charter of the European community: evolution and controversies. *ILR Review*. Vol 44, No 4. pp597–625.

BARRIENTOS, S. and SMITH, S. (2007) Do workers benefit from ethical trade? Assessing codes of labour practice in global production systems. *Third World Quarterly*. Vol 28, No 4. pp713–729.

EDWARDS, T. and WALSH, J. (2009) Foreign ownership and industrial relations in the UK. In Brown, W., Bryson, A. and Forth, J. (eds). *The evolution of the modern workplace*. Cambridge: CUP.

GENNARD, J. (2009) Is social Europe dead? *Employee Relations*. Vol 30, No 6. pp589–593.

O'REILLY, J., SMITH, M. and DEAKIN, S. (2015) Equal pay as a moving target: international perspectives on forty years of addressing the gender pay gap. *Cambridge Journal of Economics*. Vol 39, No 2. pp299–317.

YU, X. (2008) Impacts of corporate code of conduct on labour standards: a case study of Reebok's athletic footwear supplier factory in China. *Journal of Business Ethics*. Vol 81. pp513–529.

**Website links**

www.ethicaltrade.org/ is the website of the Ethical Trading Initiative.

http://europa.eu/institutions/ is the group website of the EU Commission, the Council of the EU, the European Parliament and the European Court of Justice.

www.eurofound.europa.eu/ is the website of the European Foundation for the Improvement of Living and Working Conditions.

www.labourbehindthelabel.org/ is the website of Labour Behind the Label – a campaigning group that monitors labour standards in the supply chain of leading fashion brands.

# CHAPTER 6

# Employment Relations Strategies, Policies and Change

## OVERVIEW

This chapter is divided into three main parts. The first part deals with the formulation of an organisation's strategy, concentrating on the main elements of business strategy, the levels at which strategic decision-making takes place – the corporate level, the business-unit level, and the levels appropriate to the different functions of the business – and the 'fit' between an organisation's activities and its resources. The second part looks at the associated employment policies necessary to achieve those strategic objectives. The third part of the chapter is concerned with the management of change. This includes why attempts to introduce change often fail and how important it is for management to be able to articulate a clear vision of the objectives of the change programme and to gain the commitment of the workforce. This section also considers the key elements of organisational culture and the role of leadership in effectively managing employment relations strategy.

## LEARNING OUTCOMES

When you have completed this chapter, you should be able to:

- understand what strategy is, and critically evaluate the role that strategy plays overall in defining employment relations strategies and policies
- analyse the ways in which strategic choices are shaped by the values, preferences and power of those who are the principal decision-makers
- explain and evaluate the link between organisational, human resource management (HRM) and employment relations strategies
- identify the key components of each of these elements of strategy
- critically assess the role of leadership and culture in developing employee relations strategy.

## 6.1 INTRODUCTION

In this chapter, we discuss the importance of employment relations strategies, and the type of employment policies that flow from such strategies. However, in many organisations, people management is often still not accorded the same strategic significance as other key business functions, such as financial management or sales and marketing. Although organisations have always had strategies, *only since the 1960s has it been common to explicitly address the question of what their strategy should be* (Kay, 1993: 6). This change in emphasis was one consequence of the fluctuations in economic performance that characterised the decades between the end of World War II and the new millennium. Similarly, the growth in the intensity of competition, at home and abroad, during this period forced organisations to recognise that there is a need for a process of evolution to meet these challenges (see Farnham, 2010). Such evolutionary change has to be managed and requires clear organisational strategies that will then drive functional strategies in respect of human resources generally, and more specifically, the management of employment relations.

## 6.2 PEOPLE MANAGEMENT AND PERFORMANCE

The increased emphasis on HR or people management strategy has grown, in part, from the research and analysis that has claimed a link between HR strategy and organisational performance. For instance, in 2001, Simon Caulkin's review on behalf of the CIPD pointed out that there had been more than 30 studies conducted in the USA and UK since the early 1990s. He argued that there was little doubt that the management and development of people has one of the most powerful effects on overall business performance, including overall profitability. For Caulkin:

'...it would be hard to overestimate the importance of this finding. The empirical results that prove the business case slot the final piece into a new business model that has people squarely at its centre. It completes a historic transition from a mechanistic view of the company to one that sees it as a living system where Tayloristic task management gives way to knowledge management; the latter seeking to be cost-efficient by developing an organisation's people assets, unlike the former which views labour as a cost to be minimised.'

Caulkin further believed that the findings opened up:

'...huge opportunities for competitive improvement through learning, managing and developing people more effectively. The same goes for the UK economy as a whole, where people management has the potential to turbo-charge investment in skills, R&D and new technology, offering a way to jolt the economy out of its low-skills/low-quality equilibrium and claw back the productivity advantage held by its competitors.'

Subsequently, a wide range of studies have similarly suggested a positive relationship between HR practices and performance. For example, Miller (2012) reports on the central role of HR in delivering 'sustainable organisational performance' in SMEs. Balogun *et al* (2014) also conducted an interesting review of the literature on behalf of the CIPD to highlight the key themes, such as managing ambiguity and developing relational leadership skills amongst senior managers, that HR professionals need to focus on when supporting 'transformational change' in their organisations. Loon and Stuart specifically identify the important role that training and development plays, arguing that, increasingly, *'L&D must be more business, organisationally and context savvy as this helps L&D to anticipate and contribute to organisational needs in the future'* (2014: 6).

However, the link between HR strategy and oganisational performance is complex and difficult to define (Marchington and Wilkinson, 2012: 401). As Keith Sisson and John Purcell have pointed out, the 'holy grail' of a definitive causal link has been frustratingly elusive (see also Purcell and Kinnie, 2007). Furthermore, the take-up of more strategic approaches to HRM and employment relations has been relatively slow. The most recent analysis of WERS2011 points to some evidence of a small increase in the extent to which employment relations issues are being included in 'formal strategic plans', but this remains at a relatively low level. Employee development is included in such plans in a majority of workplaces, but only 39% include job satisfaction and just 33% include employee diversity. Furthermore, such a strategic orientation appears to be more common in larger organisations and the public sector (van Wanrooy *et al*, 2013: 54–55).

Therefore, despite the plethora of research into the link between HR and performance, one of the most difficult tasks facing HR professionals is opening the minds of their management colleagues to adopting more strategic approaches to managing people. That is why, in this book, great emphasis is laid on the need to gain commitment from senior management colleagues to employment relations initiatives. This often rests on constructing a convincing 'business case', which relates specific policies and practices to quantifiable outcomes. However, this can be challenging, as shown by the difficulties in demonstrating a clear connection between HR and improved performance. For example, although most practitioners would agree 'good employment relations' underpins high levels of engagement and productivity, this is not easy to evidence.

This task is made even more difficult by the changing context within which employment relations strategies are framed and developed. The erosion of trade union organisation and influence means that employer–union relationships are no longer the prime consideration in many workplaces. This may lead some senior managers to consider that employment relations is no longer important. Therefore, practitioners will need to develop creative, and often patient, approaches to building support for locating employment relations at the heart of organisational strategy. However, as we argued in Chapter 3, unions remain the main source of employee voice in many parts of the economy. Furthermore, high-trust relationships between unions and managers are an important factor in securing employee engagement (Chapter 7) and in minimising the damage that can be caused by workplace conflict (Chapter 11). The emergence of partnership approaches to employment relations in some organisations and industries reflects a change in strategic approach by both unions and employers. In non-unionised settings, developing effective channels of communication and providing employees with greater involvement in decision-making is critical in achieving organisational goals and objectives (Marchington and Wilkinson, 2012).

## ? REFLECTIVE ACTIVITY 6.1

How can employment relations contribute to wider organisational strategies? How would you convince senior managers of the need to locate employment relations at the centre of their strategic priorities?

## 6.3 WHAT IS STRATEGY?

The origin of the concept can be traced back in military history to the Greek word for an army commander, *stratēgos*, and there are many definitions of strategy. In the context of public or private organisations, it reflects the way that senior managers lead the organisation or business in a particular direction (Boxall and Purcell, 2011). Other writers, such as Mintzberg (1987 and 1994) and Ansoff (1991), have sought to define strategy in a way that is relevant to all tiers of management. One of the most comprehensive and detailed texts on strategy is the work by Johnson, Scholes and Whittington (2008), who offer a critical understanding of what corporate strategy is and why strategic decisions are important. They view corporate strategy in two ways – as a matter of economic analysis and planning, and also as a matter of organisational decision-making within a social, political and cultural process. Marchington and Wilkinson (2012: 11–12) term this the 'classical perspective'. Within this context, both sets of writers have identified a number of characteristics that are usually associated with the terms 'strategy' and 'strategic decisions':

- Strategic decisions are likely to be concerned with or affect the long-term direction of an organisation.
- Strategic decisions are about trying to achieve some advantage for the organisation – for example, over the competition.
- Strategic decisions are, therefore, sometimes conceived of as the search for effective positioning to provide such an advantage in a market or in relation to suppliers.
- Strategic decisions are likely to be concerned with the scope of an organisation's activities.
- Strategy can be seen as the matching of the activities of an organisation to the environment in which it operates.
- Strategy can be seen as building on or stretching an organisation's resources and competences to create opportunities or capitalise on them.
- Strategies may require major resource changes for an organisation.
- Strategic decisions are likely to affect operational decisions.
- The strategy of an organisation will be affected not only by environmental forces and resource availability but also by the values and expectations of those who have power in and around the organisation.

Drawing on these key characteristics, we offer the following definition in order to frame the discussion in the context of this chapter:

> Strategy is the direction and scope of an organisation over the long term, which achieves advantage for the organisation through its configuration of resources within a changing environment, to meet the needs of markets and to fulfil stakeholder expectations.

It is clear that strategic development is a complex process. This is particularly true if the organisation operates in a wide geographical area, has a diverse portfolio of products and services, or provides public services in an often uncertain political environment. Throughout the book we argue that employment relations cannot stand alone. It has to be integrated with other management and HR functions. The same is true of strategy, which requires an integrated approach to managing the organisation. Managers must cross functional and operational boundaries in order to engage with strategic problems and reach a consensus with other colleagues who will, inevitably, have different interests and perhaps different priorities.

## 6.4 STRATEGIC FORMULATION

To understand further the nature of strategy it is helpful to consider first the process of strategy formulation. The Aston Centre for Human Resources in 2008 stated that a classic strategic management process consists of a series of steps:

- Establishing a mission statement and key objectives for the organisation
- Analysing the external environment (to identify possible opportunities and threats)
- Conducting an internal organisational analysis (to examine its strengths and weaknesses and the nature of existing management systems, competencies and capabilities)
- Setting specific goals
- Examining possible strategic choices/alternatives to achieve the organisational objectives and goals
- Adoption/implementation of chosen choices
- Regular evaluation of all of the above.

One of the oldest and most influential management viewpoints is to portray strategy as a highly rational and scientific process. This approach is based on one of the characteristics identified above – namely, the importance of the fit between an organisation and its environment. Analyses are made of a firm's environment to assess likely **opportunities** and **threats**, and of its internal resources to identify **strengths** and **weaknesses**. This process is often referred to as a SWOT analysis, and it is argued that through rigorous planning, senior managers can predict and shape the external environment and thus the organisation itself.

Other approaches to strategy formulation argue that the complexity and volatility of the environment may mean that a SWOT analysis is both difficult and inappropriate. This evolutionary approach believes that organisations are at the mercy of the unpredictable and hostile vagaries of the market and the unpredictability of government policy. The environment in which they operate may be changing so frequently that any data they use, either historical or current, may be worthless (see Marchington and Wilkinson, 2012: 14–15).

Some writers, however, argue that it is not possible to apply either a rational or an evolutionary label to the process of strategy formulation. Rather that it is behavioural, and that strategic choice results from the various coalitions that are to be found within organisations. The most dominant of these coalitions will be at senior management level, and it is they who have to 'create a vision of the organisation's future' (Burnes, 1996: 168). Similarly, the extent to which managing people is given a high profile within the organisation will be driven by the values, ideologies and personalities, or culture, of those in positions of power and influence (Hatch, 2012). It is also determined by those individuals who formulate the strategy and the long-term direction of the organisation (Marchington and Wilkinson, 2012: 12).

From this brief summary of strategy and strategy formulation, it is clear that there is no one right way. We have noted that there are a number of approaches that can be adopted by an organisation. Jenkins and Ambrosini (2002) suggest that a useful approach is to consider the different elements of strategy and use these to form an agenda that gives managers a reasonably clear set of concepts. They identify eight primary subjects ('the eight Cs'), which cover the diverse and complicated aspects of strategy that can be considered by an organisation.

---

## THE ESSENTIAL ELEMENTS OF BUSINESS STRATEGY

Context

These issues are concerned with an organisation's external environment: how the external environment is perceived, how it is studied, what the organisation can do to control it and to change it. Context also refers to industry and market structure, and strategic groups.

Competing

These issues are concerned with how organisations gain customers, how they identify their competitors and how they outperform them. This element is also about the competitive strategies organisations can implement to achieve sustainable advantage, and about co-operation and collusion.

Corporate

Corporate strategy typically addresses the multi-business context. So, this heading deals with questions of alliances, diversification, mergers, globalisation, corporate parenting, etc.

Choice

This covers decision-making and the degrees of freedom for an organisation to determine a particular strategy. This aspect deals with questions and issues surrounding the choices made by firms in following a particular trajectory.

Competences

This covers the organisation's resources such as skills, know-how, organisational knowledge, routines, competences and capabilities. This section focuses on the role of a resource in an organisation and in generating competitive advantage. It also deals with issues such as the transferability and the immutability of resources.

Culture

This deals with an organisation's internal environment. It includes the role of organisational culture, its importance and its influence on employees. This heading also covers how culture is created or changed, and how employees perceive organisational culture.

Change

This area covers the types of change an organisation can implement, and how change can take place, or how change is constrained. This section also includes the reasons for change, the change process, and the possible outcomes of change programmes.

Control

This topic deals with organisational structure, power relationships and the way managers control what is happening in their organisation. Control describes the role of managers in the organisation, the extent to which they can 'manage' what is happening inside organisations, and the extent to which they know what is happening around them.

The environment within which any organisation operates will, without doubt, constrain strategic choice. This may be a relatively stable and predictable environment in which planning and predicting the future is not a particularly hazardous exercise. Alternatively, as we witnessed during the recession of 2008 and 2009, an organisation might have to develop strategy in an unpredictable and uncertain environment in which planning is almost impossible. The challenge for senior management is how quickly they can adapt their business model to those changes. While environmental considerations may provide the stimulus for change, there is a clear consensus that the success or otherwise of individual change programmes is governed by the people in each organisation. A useful tool for analysing your organisation's environment is shown in Figure 6.1, which also captures the key elements of the context of employee relations as discussed in Chapter 3.

Figure 6.1 A PESTLE analysis

| POLITICAL | ECONOMIC | SOCIAL |
|---|---|---|
| • Government philosophy<br>• Global forces | • Government economic policy<br>• Inflation<br>• Market trends | • Demographic changes<br>• Social attitudes<br>• Consumer preferences |
| **TECHNOLOGY** | **LAW** | **ENVIRONMENT** |
| • IT innovations<br>• New production processes | • Employment law<br>• Competition regulations | • Energy costs<br>• Government policy on the environment |

---

**?**   REFLECTIVE ACTIVITY 6.2

Use the PESTLE model in Figure 6.1 to consider the environment in which your own organisation has had to operate over the past five years. What changes have had to be made to business plans and strategic objectives and why?

---

## 6.5 LEVELS OF STRATEGY

In Jenkins and Ambrosini's model, the essential elements of strategy ('the eight Cs') can be applied to different levels within the organisation. Therefore, it is important to consider not only the sort of strategic choices that organisations can make but also the levels of strategic decision-making. There are three levels with which we need to concern ourselves (Burnes, 1996) as shown in Figure 6.2.

Figure 6.2 Levels of strategic decision-making

| Corporate | Business unit | Functional |
|---|---|---|
| Determining the overall direction and focus of the organisation | Deciding how to compete in a particular market or provide a specific service | Considering the operation of a specific organisational function such as HR, marketing and finance |

All these levels are interrelated, but equally, each has its own distinctive strategic concerns. It is helpful, therefore, to look at each of them in a little more detail.

### 6.5.1 CORPORATE-LEVEL STRATEGY

Corporate-level strategy concerns itself with a number of questions and is usually formulated at board level. One of these questions will be about the overall mission of the organisation: what is the game plan? How should the business portfolio be managed? Should you make acquisitions or dispose of parts of the business? What priority should be given to each of the individual parts of the business in terms of resource allocation? How is the business to be structured and financed?

Purcell *et al* argue that:

'One of the keys to the HR-performance link is the existence of a "big idea", a clear mission underpinned by values and a culture expressing what the organisation stands for and is trying to achieve.' (2003: ix)

According to Purcell *et al*, organisations with a 'big idea' display five common characteristics: the idea is embedded, connected, enduring, collective, and measured and managed. This means more than just having a formal mission statement, but, in addition, ensuring that the values are spread throughout the organisation so that they are embedded in policies and practices. These values connect the relationships with customers (both internal and external), culture and behaviour, and provide the basis upon which employees should be managed.

However, the mission will fail unless it is capable of being achieved. This means that three things are necessary. First, it must be expressed in language that is understandable to the bulk of employees, which means that attention must be paid to the communication process. Second, it must be attainable and employees should recognise that the organisation has some chance of achieving the objectives it has set itself. Third, the mission must be challenging and needs all of those involved in its achievement to be stretched and for their individual performances to be a condition of the mission's overall success. That is why the current focus on employee engagement – which we examine in more detail in later chapters – is so critical.

> ### ? REFLECTIVE ACTIVITY 6.3
>
> If the organisation in which you work has a declared mission, how does it fit with the criteria we describe? To what extent is the way that employment relations are managed consistent with this mission?

### 6.5.2 BUSINESS-UNIT-LEVEL STRATEGY

Competitive or business-unit-level strategy is concerned with the way a firm or business operates in particular markets: what new opportunities can be identified or created? Which products or services should be developed? In this context, strategy is concerned with gaining an advantage over the competition. Porter (1985) sees this as seeking to obtain a sustainable competitive advantage and answers to a number of key questions: which markets should the organisation attempt to compete in and how does it position itself to achieve its objectives? How does it achieve some form of distinctive capability (Kay, 1993)? What should its product range or mix be? Which customers should it aim for? Decisions about products, markets and customers were central to some of Porter's (1985) theory about strategy. He argued that there are only three basic strategies that dictate the choice to be made. These are set out in Figure 6.3.

Figure 6.3 Porter's three basic business-unit-level strategies

| Cost Leadership | Product Differentiation | Specialisation |
|---|---|---|
| Achieving lower costs than your competitors or comparators without reducing quality | Achieving industry or sector-wide recognition of different and superior products or services compared with those of other suppliers | Developing niche markets or distinctiveness in service provision |

All these considerations have an effect on employment relations as they impact on the way that the organisation structures itself internally and on the way that relationships are managed.

### 6.5.3 FUNCTIONAL-LEVEL STRATEGY

Functional-level strategy is concerned with how the different functions of the business translate corporate- and business-level strategies into operational aims. In HR terms, this means that there has to be a clear alignment between business and HR strategy. In Figure 6.4 we demonstrate how this leads to the formulation of an employment relations strategy.

That is, business strategy drives HRM strategy, which in turn drives employment relations strategy, and from this process are derived the practices and policies that influence the employment relationship. Once you have reached down to this level of functional strategy, it is important that the various functions pay attention to how they organise themselves. This is not only in order to achieve their aims but also to ensure synergy with the rest of the business.

Figure 6.4 Strategic employment relations management: an overview

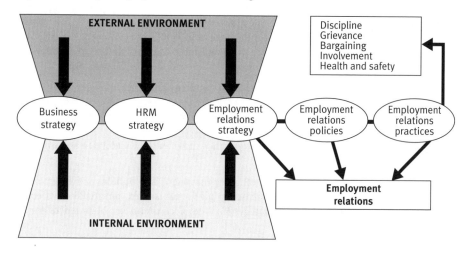

## 6.6 PEOPLE STRATEGY

One aspect of strategy concerns the match between an organisation's activities and its resources. Those resources may be physical, such as buildings or plant, or people. Strategies about people, such as physical resources, require decisions to be made about investment. However, it is a different type of investment decision – not the type that fits easily into the process usually reserved for capital expenditure. A key aim of HRM is to achieve strategic integration within the broader objectives of the organisation. However, difficulties exist in making this happen. Some of the main barriers are:

- the size and complexity of large organisations and the different people management needs of their constituent parts
- the people strategy of most SMEs can and will differ
- the changing nature of business strategy
- the absence of a strictly defined business strategy
- the qualitative nature of HR policies and consequent tensions with the quantifiable objectives of the business
- the incompatibility between the short-term financial goals of many organisations and HR policies

- tensions between 'soft' and 'hard' HRM

Against this backdrop, HRM strategists and writers have sought to capture a model through which HRM can conceptualise and practically address these barriers (Ulrich, 1997; Ulrich and Brockbank, 2005; Boxall and Purcell, 2011; Marchington and Wilkinson, 2012).

### 6.6.1 'BEST FIT' AND 'BEST PRACTICE'

The first two models to consider, best fit and best practice,' while common in many organisations, also differ in their overall approach. Both seek to highlight the central contribution that HR policies can make to business strategy. Best fit, however, is based on a contingent view, that the strategic needs of the business can vary and so an 'it depends' perspective should be adopted by practitioners. To this end, best fit is based on:

- a vertical integration between the organisation's strategy and HRM policies and practices
- the link between business strategy and performance of every individual in the organisation being central to that 'fit'
- the assumption that organisations are more efficient when they achieve fit as compared with when there is no fit.

In contrast, best practice is premised on the view that there is a 'bundle' of HRM policies and practices that, when marshalled together in any organisation, can make an effective contribution to its overall business strategy. It offers a common set of practices for all organisations in terms of:

- selective hiring
- employment security
- self-managed teams or team working
- high pay, contingent on company performance
- extensive training
- reduction of status differences
- sharing information.

The emphasis in best practice is to achieve both vertical and horizontal integration throughout the organisation, through the framework of an 'internally consistent set of HR practices' (Marchington and Wilkinson, 2012).

### 6.6.2 RESOURCE-BASED STRATEGY

While acknowledging the need to integrate HR policy and practice in the formulation of business strategy, a resource-based view focuses more on the specific skills and knowledge of an organisation's workforce, and the added value that 'uniqueness' can have in terms of competitive advantage. For proponents of a resource-based view (RBV) the focus is on internal resources of the organisation, rather than analysing performance in terms of external context. In addition, people are viewed as strategic assets and competitive advantage is gained and sustained through the development of that 'human capital'. Importantly, this is seen as unique – human resources are therefore not only valuable, but they are rare and inimitable. Therefore, the focus is on how organisations can develop strategies which both recognise and make the most of these attributes and build and maintain unique, enviable clusters of human assets (see Boxall and Purcell (2011) Chapters 3 and 4 for an excellent critical in-depth discussion on relative merits and limitations of bestfit, best practice and RBV). In contrast to the resource-based approach, an organisation can choose to adopt a 'hard' HRM approach. Then, rather than focus on the 'inimitability' of your employees, competitive advantage is seen as being better achieved through financial efficiencies; where people are viewed as any other factor of production and as a cost to be minimised wherever possible. Making the business case for a strategy based on a soft HRM approach, when appropriate, remains a key challenge for all practitioners.

> ## ? REFLECTIVE ACTIVITY 6.5
>
> To what degree does your organisation adopt a best-fit, best-practice or resource-based view to people management? Which approach are you more persuaded by and why?

### 6.6.3 ULRICH AND THE RISE OF THE 'BUSINESS PARTNER'

Whichever model is adopted, HR functions within organisations are increasingly expected to demonstrate how they can 'add value to the business'. Our final model, driven by writers such Ulrich (1997) and Ulrich and Brockbank (2005), argues for a greater awareness of the need for clear HR strategies that are aligned to business strategies. Crucially, it calls for HR to transform itself into a more focused **business partner** that can provide line managers with clear advice and information. The main elements of their model are set out in Table 6.1.

Table 6.1 Models of HRM styles

| Mid-1990s | Mid-2000s – present day |
|---|---|
| Admin expert | Functional expert |
| Employee champion | Employee advocate |
| Agent for change | Human capital developer |
| Strategic partner | Leader |

Source: Ulrich (1997) and Ulrich and Brockbank (2005)

It is notable that the model seeks to capture the key roles that HR practitioners can play, both as a strategic partner to senior management and as an operational support to line managers and staff in terms of the practical achievement of that strategy. With respect to employment relations strategy, it is equally of note that Ulrich and Brockbank recognise the key contribution HR practitioners can make in representing the views and interests of employees.

According to the CIPD (2013), the 'business partner' model is the most commonly adopted HR service delivery model. However, this is interpreted in very different ways. In some organisations it may simply be a title conferred on senior HR managers, while in others it reflects a more fundamental shift to a more strategic orientation. Furthermore, the notion of business partners and the Ulrich model itself on which they are based have been increasingly challenged (Stephens, 2015). It could be argued that the development of business partner models has been used in some respects to justify a reduction in HR resource, removing 'on-site' practitioners and creating a more centralised HR function on the basis that this will inculcate a more strategic approach and force operational managers to take responsibility for people management. Recent research into the management of workplace conflict has not only questioned whether HR practitioners see themselves as 'employee advocates' but whether the predominant result of the adoption of business partner models has been to create a more distanced and remote HR function, which is less able to develop and maintain the relationships necessary for more nuanced, creative and informal approaches to conflict resolution (Saundry *et al*, 2016). Interestingly, Ulrich

(2015) himself recently emphasised that 'the new HR operating model' needs to be more about relationships than partners (see also Balogun *et al*, 2014).

Whatever HR management model is in use, there are very few managers that would not subscribe to the view that significant improvement in both productivity and profitability can be achieved if they ensure that people are satisfied with their jobs, rewards, working conditions and career prospects. This then requires the development of a clear and focused strategy for managing people, and one which must have at its heart policies and practices to build trust between employees and their managers. As Boxall and Purcell rightly stress:

> 'The argument is that employees who perceive good organisational support in their employment relationship respond with increased trust in management and greater commitment to the organisation. They are more engaged ... Trust and commitment can be very valuable intangible assets for organisations.' (2011: 224)

## 6.7 CULTURE AND HR STRATEGY

Trust and commitment are significantly informed by employees sharing the values and beliefs of management. Therefore, it is also important in developing strategy to take account of company culture; noting, however, that the degree to which culture can actually be 'managed' is a strongly contested notion among both writers and practitioners (Martin, 2001; Hatch, 2012). Nonetheless, employee attitude surveys conducted by the authors over many years demonstrate that it is important to understand how the organisation is perceived by its various stakeholders. We have found that across a variety of sectors of the economy, a number of key issues were critical in forging a positive culture. Our findings also resonate with Schein's classic three-level model of culture (1985). Furthermore, while we have sympathy with the argument that culture is not easily managed, it can still be a useful tool for identifying organisational issues to be addressed by reformulating employment relations strategy.

At the more superficial level of culture (Schein, 1985: 18–21), the artefacts and symbols of the organisation, such as the layout of the working environment, the technology used, and the use of information, are key clues towards a better understanding of cultural variables. While it is not always apparent, stakeholders, particularly employees, can be strongly influenced towards achieving organisational goals if they believe, for instance, that their working environment is considered to be important by key decision-makers. Similarly, stories and myths are commonly shared in organisations and often reflect the success or failure of strategy and management decisions, and often an inability to communicate and deliver strategy.

At the intermediate level of Schein's model, the rules, systems and procedures of the organisation are said to set the parameters for behaviour and action, ie, that which others have termed the 'espoused values' of the organisation; or those which staff think represent the behaviours they are expected to demonstrate (Brown, 1995: 8–26). For example, if policies, procedures and practices are seen to be time-consuming and overbureaucratic, employees will not only refuse to engage but see this as confirmation of the organisation's lack of appreciation of their interests. Rigid performance review and management systems may simply be seen as a bureaucratic hurdle to overcome, rather than as an opportunity to voice important issues and develop staff potential. Furthermore, where policies and practices are not consistent with the overall strategic objectives of the organisation, they are likely to have a negative impact on people's willingness to 'go the extra mile'. In contrast, where operational managers communicate with their staff, offer opportunities for employees to shape decisions and handle difficult issues in a fair and transparent manner, a positive and open 'culture' can be created, which builds trust and underpins engagement. Therefore, the beliefs, values and attitudes that are expressed and displayed in everyday activity are fundamental in establishing and maintaining an effective people management strategy.

Finally, at the deepest level of the culture, the basic assumptions (Schein, 1985) that are made about human behaviour, human nature, relationships, reality and truth can inform the overall behaviour of organisational members. These, it is argued, are the values that really inform the behaviour of employees. They can be hard to change but are too often easy to overlook by management.

## 6.8 STRATEGY IN PRACTICE

Everything we have outlined is important in formulating strategy, but nothing must be viewed in isolation – as the example from a private sector organisation following the last recession demonstrates. It has not been possible to publish the document in full. Nevertheless, the extract demonstrates the ways in which organisations can attempt to ensure that the whole range of people management activities – recruitment and selection, reward and recognition, training and development, and employment relations – are integrated into the strategic planning process.

---

### FIVE-YEAR HUMAN RESOURCE PLAN

Executive summary

The environment in which all our companies have to operate has, because of the recession, changed beyond recognition. In recent months we have had to go through the painful process of reducing our headcount, while at the same time continuing to be very competitive in our various marketplaces. Our staff are, with good reason, feeling insecure and nervous about the future and, in this context, it is important to recognise the importance of the 'people contribution'.

People's contribution is influenced by the way that they are managed and whether they perceive that they are valued for their individual contributions. To this extent it is vitally important that managers, at all levels, acquire and develop expertise and knowledge in management skills. To achieve these aims means that we must:

- take a strategic view of managing people
- involve people in the business
- continue to invest in communication
- manage people's performance effectively
- focus on employees as individuals.

If we do these things, we are much more likely to develop enhanced employee commitment. In turn, this will mean that individuals are encouraged to move beyond their basic contractual commitment and develop a strong sense of loyalty to the organisation. Creating the climate where people are prepared to give more by 'going the extra mile' will ensure that their contribution to the business is maximised. But by itself this is not enough. We need to concentrate on certain key factors, which can be summarised as follows:

*Employee reward systems*

Our basic reward system is currently a combination of basic pay, performance- or profit-related bonus (for some individuals) and an optional pension benefit. If we want to motivate individuals to deliver our declared business strategies, we have to develop our current reward system so that it is capable of meeting individual employee aspirations. To achieve this, we need to ensure that we have a reward system that is both flexible and fair and that is perceived as such by employees. Although our ownership structure does not allow for any 'equity share' arrangements, we need to expand on the successful Long-term Incentive Plan (LTIP) that has been in place in one subsidiary for the past five years. Part of the HR remit over the lifetime of this plan is to ensure that 'reward' is related to real growth in our businesses and not simply to the short-term attainment of artificial budgetary targets.

*Recruitment and selection*

There are two major issues that we need to be concerned with. One is to ensure that the level of labour turnover in each part of the business is properly managed and kept within acceptable norms. The second is the need to attract sufficient numbers of high-calibre candidates for declared vacancies. Because of the changing nature of the labour market we must consider what changes we need to make in our employment practices if we are to meet this objective.

*Performance management*

The recent difficulties in trading across the whole group have highlighted the need to constantly improve levels of individual performance. This can only be achieved if we seek ways to 'engage' staff so that they feel valued. Without developing strategies for the effective engagement of people, we will not improve organisational performance generally. Staff engagement, therefore, has to be a key priority. This is a complex process with no easy solutions, and there are a number of steps that can be taken to enhance both individual and collective performance.

*Career development*

If we are to retain competent employees within our workforce, we need to develop the process of career planning. While this will not be appropriate for everyone, it will be an important factor for some in deciding whether to remain in our employment. Added to this will be a continuing requirement to develop the skills of all our employees. Every group business should have a development plan and provide appropriate budgets for this purpose, which should be driven by the appraisal process. Beyond this, there is also a need to develop those individuals who might have the capability of taking on senior management roles in the future. Our annual succession planning exercise is crucial to meeting this objective, but we also need to provide a senior management development programme.

*Employment relations*

It is clear that developments in employment law will not slow down and that during the lifetime of this plan further changes will take place, either because of government intervention (new statutes) or through the development of case law. Cases relating to holiday pay, sickness and retirement ages might require us to amend policies and practices. While relationships with our principal trade unions remain relatively benign, we cannot take these relationships for granted. Union representatives must be part of the communication process.

Overall, our human resource activities over the lifetime of this plan have to meet the following objectives:

- to generate commitment of all employees to the success of the organisation
- to enable the business to better meet the needs of its customers and adapt to changing market requirements
- to help the business to improve performance and productivity, thus generating appropriate levels of growth
- to improve the satisfaction that employees get from their work
- to provide all employees with the opportunity to influence and be involved in decisions which are likely to affect their interests.

The importance of adopting an integrated approach, as demonstrated above, is supported by the research carried out for the CIPD and others. This confirms that companies achieving the best results in productivity, profitability and growth have people management strategies that make a real difference. The conclusions of Purcell *et al* (2003), for instance, are compelling. They state that the most successful organisations were those that could sustain their performance over the long term by demonstrating a clear relationship between people management and performance. However, the challenges facing employment relations are significant; it is notable that in the case above, employment relations is not only a minor part of the overall strategy but is limited to transactional issues with a particular emphasis on legal compliance. In addition, the role of trade unions is relegated to communication. As we argue in Chapter 11, placing employment relations issues – such as representation and voice, and effective conflict management – at the centre of HR strategy is critical in achieving increased commitment and consequent improvements in organisational productivity and performance.

## ? REFLECTIVE ACTIVITY 6.6

How does the strategy outlined above fit with key elements of strategic design outlined earlier in the chapter? Is there anything that you would either add, amend or remove from this strategy if you were applying it to your own organisation?

## 6.9 EMPLOYMENT RELATIONS STRATEGY

Having examined the process of strategy formulation, we now turn to look at how this links into employment relations in particular. Whatever means organisations choose for formulating their strategy, either at corporate or business level, the design and management of employment policies and processes, it can be argued, will figure prominently in delivering and sustaining business improvement. Furthermore, a critical analysis of any of the key HR strategic models we considered earlier suggests also the centrality of employment relations as part of that strategy. For instance, Ulrich (1997) and Ulrich and Brockbank (2005) highlight the importance of employee voice, while the general role of effective communication is a recurring theme.

In addition, the process of change, and its impact on the development of strategy, also presents many challenges for the employment relations professional. As we discuss later in Chapter 9, there is the issue of trade unions and the provisions for recognition. Where trade unions already exist and are recognised within an organisation, the trends towards individualism, as opposed to collectivism, means that strategic choices will inevitably be made. For instance, what should be the stance of the organisation in relation to unions and do alternative or complementary voice mechanisms need to be developed? Where trade unions are not recognised, the organisation may need to consider how it responds to any requests for recognition (Boxall and Purcell, 2011: 173–178; Williams, 2014: 146–153). Of course, context is critical in deciding the strategic response to these issues. However, as we discuss in Chapter 7 and also in Chapter 10, effective structures of representation and high-trust relationships with trade unions can be beneficial both in terms of developing employee engagement and facilitating effective responses to workplace conflict.

The key is to develop an employment relations strategy that is responsive to the needs of the organisation. It must provide an overall sense of purpose to the employment relations professional and assist employees to understand where they are going, how they are going to get there, why certain things are happening, and most importantly, the contribution they are expected to make towards achieving the organisational goals (Marchington and Wilkinson, 2012; Boxall and Purcell, 2011). An interesting example can be found in the experiences of Transport for London (Jeffery, 2015).

CASE STUDY 6.1

TRANSPORT FOR LONDON

As HR director of Transport for London (TfL) – the public authority that manages transport across the capital – Tricia Riley must balance the needs of more than 27,000 employees in diversified roles, around 30 million passenger journeys each day, and multiple trade unions whose complex history with transport chiefs has in the past led to strikes. And all of it in the glare of the city's media, which delights in detailing the organisation's perceived failings.

Since she took over the role in 2011, after a lengthy period of flux in TfL's HR department, Riley has focused on ensuring the structure, at least, isn't overly complex. There is now one HR function reporting to TfL's commissioner through a single HR director, organised into four key areas to underpin the people strategy. 'We have strategic people priorities rather than an HR strategy because the people strategy is owned by the senior leadership team, not by HR,' she says. 'We help pull it together, facilitate it and make sure it's aligned to the business strategy, but it is very much a people strategy for the business.'

As part of that, she adds: 'We've come to realise you don't need the leading-edge HR practice in the world because that may not be appropriate. We're in the public eye all the time and what we do has to be right for the business. That means the Mini Cooper version may sometimes be more suitable than the Rolls-Royce version.'

Change, it's fair to say, has become a constant at TfL, which is why the delivery, support and change function includes a flexible pool of HR professionals – primarily OD and delivery experts – who are assigned to areas of the business going through transitions. As well as offering a dedicated resource ('it helps us specifically support change rather than adding it on top of business as usual,

which just doesn't work'), this ensures best practice principles of change management become embedded.

'People think change means redundancy, and that's not always the case,' says Riley. 'We have been working on reaching out to people going through change, learning from our past mistakes and bringing people with us, and this is ongoing. We are supporting the delivery teams who are out there day in, day out.' That brings benefits for HR professionals too. She adds that undertaking a project role in the change team offers a change of pace and the chance to develop new skills.

Even so, it doesn't make the industrial relations backdrop any easier. The introduction of pay for performance for staff in support roles in 2014 led to a strike being called; and plans later this year for five tube lines to operate around the clock will bring changes in working patterns. Most notably, the Fit for the Future London Underground modernisation programme – which will see better stations and service but closures of manned ticket offices, replaced by roving staff armed with tablets, and more machines – has been a point of contention.

'We deal with multiple trade unions and it's fair to say we are working towards a professional, honest and transparent relationship,' says Riley. 'We're not always going to agree – we acknowledge that and so do they – but it's about how you work through the issues.'

'There's a much greater understanding of the current changes. There will still be people who don't like them because they are used to the ticket offices, and this is a big change. And not everybody is comfortable on an iPad or iPhone; but we are trying to put everything in place so when we implement it, it is embedded properly. With some companies, projects are about getting to the implementation date and that's it. Our phased approach ensures all staff receive all the training and help they need.'

A 'simple, pragmatic and honest' internal communications strategy helps ensure key messages get across, adds Riley, and marks a break with the 'formal and matter-of-fact' style of the past. And it's backed by a raft of progressive initiatives: a leadership development programme that is being cascaded to senior managers; clear 'role families' to show how careers can progress 'and dispel the myth that going up the career ladder is the only option'; and a focus on customer service under the 'every journey matters' banner.

Source: JEFFERY, R. (2015) Transport for London: you don't always have to be the best. *People management*. April. pp18–20.

As the Transport for London example demonstrates, the overall philosophy of an organisation will be supported by its HR strategy, which will reflect the importance placed on employment relations. Furthermore, this will be operationalised through specific policies and practices. This will also be shaped by the political, economic, societal, technological and legal context. For example, within a highly unionised environment, such as Transport for London, improving performance and achieving a greater focus on customer service cannot be divorced from developing positive relationships with trade unions. Therefore, the way in which policies and practices are developed and implemented, in relation to staff involvement, performance management and discipline and grievance, will need to take this into account.

## ? REFLECTIVE ACTIVITY 6.7

What challenges will your organisation face over the next five years and how will these impact on employment relations strategy? How might you pre-empt and, therefore, offer solutions to resolve the 'unforeseen' consequences of these challenges?

## 6.10 MANAGING CHANGE AND EMPLOYMENT RELATIONS

The development of HR and employment relations strategy is inextricably linked with change. The effective management of change may need to be supported by new strategies, while the implementation of such strategies often has a significant impact on the working lives of those employees involved. However, change is frequently difficult to implement successfully, despite most organisations embarking on a change programme with honourable motives. They want to make life better, both for the organisation and for the people who work in it. Although it is always dangerous to generalise, the reasons for failure may include:

- misunderstanding what change is
- lack of planning and preparation
- no clear vision
- looking for quick fixes
- poor communication
- a legacy of previous change programmes.

Given the importance of people to the change process, it is essential that management is able to articulate a clear vision of the objectives of the change programme in order to gain the support of the workforce. Crucially, managers need to persuade the employees of the rationale for change. We accept that a consensus cannot always be achieved when change becomes necessary, but it is a basic principle of good employment relations that consent, however grudgingly given, is better than control. In this context, managers might have to accept that change will sometimes have to be negotiated, with or without trade unions. Even without negotiation, allowing employees to participate in the decision-making process through proper consultation is much more likely to lead to effective implementation.

A further factor to be taken into account is that, during the change process, responsibilities might have to be altered and the boundaries of jobs clarified. This may mean examining organisational structure because some change programmes will challenge traditional hierarchies – a change that can give rise to considerable resentment and individual resistance. It is also important to ensure that other policies that might be required to underpin change are themselves in place – for example, equal opportunities or single-status workforce. Furthermore, it cannot be assumed that the process is complete just because an initiative has been evaluated and then properly communicated to all employees.

Organisations of all sizes are embroiled in change, and increasingly that includes changing, to the degree to which this is possible, the established culture (Martin, 2001; Hatch, 2012). This means asking questions such as, 'How can we get our people to be more innovative, more focused, more assertive, more in line with our values?' In some cases, a fundamental shift in culture is needed in order to fit a new set of values to meet the organisation's intentions. Our second case study offers some valuable learning points with respect to this process.

---

**CASE STUDY 6.2**

### INTRODUCING A CULTURE OF LEARNING AND DEVELOPMENT AT JAGUAR LAND ROVER

Kirsty Scott is head of talent and development at Jaguar LR. Her job is to make sure that all 30,000 employees worldwide are on their own journey, she says, to become everything they can under its tutelage.

'That every employee has potential to develop – whether in their current role, in an adjacent role or in a more senior role – is one of our fundamental principles,' says Scott, who took up her current post in April 2012 after four years in HR roles across the business. 'An important part of that is understanding the individual's ambitions and where they want to go at work. Some organisations, ourselves included, can be quick to overlook that.'

Potential development, she insists, is distinct from performance management. 'Performance is a historic record of what

you've done in your current job,' says Scott. 'This is about your potential to contribute in the future. We're embedding that as a fundamental belief, which underpins how we do business, and how we treat our people.'

Scott's aim is to create tailored development plans for every employee globally, but she acknowledges this is a 'five-year plan, not something that can happen in the next six months.' High-potential senior managers are being targeted first, with a two-year intensive development programme designed to fit with their ambitions and areas of strength. This is rooted in what Scott calls 'breakthrough development plans'.

'Employees are really conscious of the intended outcomes of their plans, whether that's to be better in their current jobs tomorrow, to take on a different role in a different function, or if they want to progress through the ranks of seniority,' she says.

Managing talent development on such a scale means HR needs to upskill line managers, especially those whose expertise lies in technical rather than people skills. 'We're offering them more training that helps integrate coaching into their normal role as a manager, because when a senior manager has a great experience, they'll be more compelled to give their team a great experience as well.'

Development strategies can't just be tailored for the British workforce: they have to make sense for staff in JLR's sales organisations across the world. 'We were very UK-centric before becoming part of [Indian conglomerate] Tata in 2008,' says Scott. 'Now, everything we do has to have a global focus. That old mindset isn't going to develop future business leaders in a global environment. Scott is also adamant that schools and universities need to play a bigger role in developing the right sort of talent needed for the future.

JLR offers A-level leavers a six-year higher apprenticeship delivered in partnership with nearby Warwick University, meaning 'students get great experiential learning, a salary and a Russell Group degree,' says Scott. Although the scheme has only been in place for three years, it's already proving extremely popular, with numbers set to rise from the initial intake of 50 per year. 'It's definitely gaining momentum, and I think we'll be taking on more and more students.'

It's just one of the ways Scott's team is responding to business challenges. 'People here really do see the value of HR,' she says. 'We're fortunate that the HR director sits on the board, and the board members are fully engaged with our development strategy.' Achieving this level of respect, says Scott, is down to the team's 'focus on pragmatic solutions and business outcomes. Because we speak their commercial language, rather than preaching from the HR textbook, we have become a fundamental part of a cross-functional leadership team.'

Partnering with the wider business to deliver results is a philosophy mirrored in JLR's approach to learning suppliers: Scott has overseen a rationalisation of the company's agencies from more than 50 to a select few genuine partners.

Staff from across the business now actively approach Scott's team when thinking about their L&D requirements. 'We've built that reputation by working with the functions to create pragmatic solutions and improve the quality of training. It all comes back to visibility and support. We don't sit in our offices: we're out on the shop floor where people need us.'

Source: NEWBERY, C. (2015) Jaguar Land Rover: talent development isn't a process – it's a philosophy. *People Management*. March. pp18–20.

**?    REFLECTIVE ACTIVITY 6.8**

Reflecting on Case Study 6.2 and our discussion so far, what for you are the key cultural elements of an organisation that can impact on strategic choices over employee relations? Justify your reasoning.

The experience at JLR suggests that through the strategic guidance of their head of talent and development, it is possible over the longer term to develop a culture that reflects more the HR needs of a global workforce. Furthermore, this first requires managers at all levels of the organisation to develop the skills and attitude to deliver this change.

## 6.11 THE ROLE OF LEADERSHIP IN EMPLOYMENT RELATIONS POLICY AND PRACTICE

The study of leadership is a complex and extensively researched element of management theory and practice. Our discussion here must be brief. However, for a more detailed understanding, we would direct you in particular to the valuable conceptual contributions of Grint (2005) and Rickards and Clark (2006). From a more practical perspective, Zheltoukhova's (2014) recent report for the CIPD gives real insight into the contemporary people management challenges facing most leaders in organisations. The research is based on more than 120 interviews and focus groups with managers, employees and HR practitioners in seven large organisations. The main challenges identified include:

- addressing the hierarchical and bureaucratic culture still prevalent in many of our organisations
- how excessive individualism can hinder collaborative work among the workforce
- the ongoing problem of short-termism in terms of organisational strategy
- a 'them and us' mentality.

We would argue that these challenges can all affect the effective management of employment relations. However, the cultural challenge for organisational leaders to change attitudes from confrontation and mistrust, to partnership, is fundamental, and is a central theme of both section 2 and 3 of the book.

For instance, the importance of understanding the impact of different forms of management styles, particularly of line managers, on the employment relationship, is key for HR practitioners tasked with breaking down the 'them and us' perception of that relationship. We address this particular area indepth in Chapter 8.

Short-termism, we would argue, remains the malaise of British business. It is a strategy, as we will discuss in section 3 of the book, that can, and does, lead to workplace conflict. For example, short-term strategies to reduce headcount through redundancy need to always be measured against the long-term logic of retaining the skills and loyalty of staff affected through redeployment and retraining. Furthermore, leaders with strategic responsibility for developing employment relations policy and practice need to fully understand the context of organisational structure. The barrier of bureaucracy and hierarchy, as we discussed in Chapter 2, can perpetuate a power imbalance between management and workers. We would argue that only conceptual tools from employment relations, such as the unitary, pluralist and radical perspectives, can assist the practitioners in better understanding and addressing, where possible, the effects of such imbalances of power. The discussion in Chapter 9 focuses on how greater employee voice through channels such as employee representation could, to some degree, help address the 'dead weight' of bureaucracy. It is also of note that Zheltoukhova's focus on excessive individualism highlights the potential to address such tendencies in the workplace and is considered in Chapter 10, where we critically analyse the value of greater employee involvement and participation, both individually and collectively, to the organisation and its workforce. Effective line management and, therefore, good practice in all elements of leadership, are central to that endeavour. In closing, we set out in the following box what in our experiences, as both writers and practitioners, remain the most practical leadership techniques that all managers must develop. The significance of these skills and approaches are discussed in more depth in the remaining chapters of the book.

KEY TECHNIQUES IN EFFECTIVE EMPLOYMENT RELATIONS LEADERSHIP

*Give consistent and regular feedback on performance*

Motivate staff by acknowledging good work through positive feedback. Conversely, do not leave issues of concern to build up, which can often result in the type of disputes we discuss in section 3 of the book, or until the next formal appraisal, when in contrast swift action can often address those issues.

*Make relationships human as well as professional*

The insightful leader is one who recognises the core management skills of empathy, seeing an issue through the eyes of your employee, and good listening. As discussed in section 3, in a dispute situation, for instance, really ensure that you gather all the facts and different opinions; do not make assumptions and be prepared to question and change your own set views if necessary.

*Be tolerant and know the strengths and weaknesses of each member of your team*

Set reasonable and achievable objectives, and give team members the support and development to successfully and consistently reach those goals. As we discuss in Chapter 10, ideally, let staff have a real input into setting those objectives.

*Management of the employment relationship is contingent on many issues*

As we consider in Chapter 8, managers typically can adopt a range of styles, both effective and less so. In addition to deciding which style or approach may be appropriate for a given situation, the astute leader also recognises that any situation is dependent on many factors. Therefore, good practice is to fully analyse the data relating to the issue in question, and then to systematically consider all the possible options available before deciding on what, for you, is the best solution.

## 6.12 SUMMARY

In recent years, there has been much discussion on the need for HR practitioners to align their role with wider business strategy. The increased prominence of business partner models has been a defining feature of the contemporary HR function. This is seen by some as a way of HR taking on a more strategic role and moving away from transactional activities. However, as we note above, evidence suggests that the business partner concept is interpreted and implemented in many different ways. Nonetheless, if employment relations is to significantly shape both business performance and the working lives and experiences of employees, it must engage with broader organisational concerns and objectives. Furthermore, if employment relations is to retain and build influence among senior managers, it must be seen to be relevant to the needs of the business.

The discussion above, however, has shown that this is no easy task for the HR or employment relations practitioner. Often, short-term operational considerations crowd out the need to consider the role that effective people management can play. Therefore, it is up to practitioners to develop and demonstrate the relationship between good employee relations and fundamental organisational outcomes. In so doing, employment relations cannot operate in a vacuum but must be integrated not only with others aspects of HRM, such as employee development, reward and resourcing, but also attempts to improve employee engagement, productivity and performance.

1 Strategy is about the way that senior management lead their organisation or business in a particular direction. The development of strategic objectives enables leaders to influence and direct an organisation as it conducts its activities.

2 Whatever method of strategy formulation is adopted, it is important to be aware that it will be constrained by societal, environmental, industry-specific and organisational factors, many of which will conflict with each other.

3 The key is to develop an employment relations strategy that is responsive to the needs of the organisation. It can provide an employment relations professional with an overall sense of purpose and that will assist employees to understand where they are going, how they are going to get there, why certain things do not happen, and most importantly, the contribution they are expected to make towards achieving the organisational goals.

4 In recognising the centrality of people in successfully managing change, it is essential that management is able to articulate a clear vision of the objectives of the change programme. To gain commitment to change, that vision has to be expressed clearly and unambiguously. Commitment will thus be obtained if management takes the right steps in managing the process. In this respect, leadership is crucial.

1 Describe the strategic planning process. Why is it important for the employment relations professional to be aware of this?

2 What is your understanding of the different models of HRM strategy? Which one do you think is most suited to your organisation and why?

3 To what extent does the existence of HR business partners imply a strategic approach to the management of people? How can HR business partners ensure that they contribute to maximising organisational performance?

4 How can employment relations policies and practices be designed so that they contribute to the strategic objectives of the organisation?

5 Your line manager tells you that the organisation is likely to be planning major changes in the coming months. She tells you that she wants you to be a member of the change team. In this regard she would like you to produce a proposal outlining how the commitment of the employees to this organisational change might be obtained. In relation to HRM and employment relations strategy, what will you say in your paper, and why?

BALOGUN, J., HOPE HAILEY, V. and STUART, R. (2014) *Landing transformational change*. London: CIPD.

BOXALL, P. and PURCELL, J. (2011) *Strategy and human resource management*. 3rd ed. Basingstoke: Palgrave Macmillan.

CIPD (2013) *Organising HR for partnering success*. London: CIPD.

ULRICH, D. (2015) The new HR operating model is all about relationships, not partners. *People Management*. April, 2015.

ZHELTOUKHOVA, K. (2014) *Leadership: easier said than done*. London: CIPD.

**EXPLORE FURTHER**

# CHAPTER 7

# Employee Engagement

## OVERVIEW

This chapter begins by explaining the nature of employee engagement and in particular by asking with whom, and in what, employees are engaged. Evidence in relation to the extent of employee engagement is then assessed. A crucial aspect of this chapter is to identify the conditions under which engagement can be developed. In particular, Macleod and Clarke's influential 'enablers of engagement' model is examined. The factors that they argue underpin employee engagement – leadership, engaging managers, employee voice and organisational integrity – are discussed. Next, it considers the barriers to engagement with a particular focus on the critical role played by managerial attitudes and behaviours. The chapter then outlines and examines three case studies of effective employee engagement before closing by reflecting on the ten key steps in conducting an effective employee engagement survey.

## LEARNING OUTCOMES

When you have completed this chapter, you should be able to:

- understand and explain the nature and extent of employee engagement
- critically evaluate the case for organisations engaging with their employees
- identify the necessary conditions to make employee engagement a success
- examine and critically analyse the link between employee engagement and organisational performance
- describe the main barriers to securing employee engagement
- critically assess the techniques and processes designed to secure employee engagement.

## 7.1 INTRODUCTION

The management of the employment relationship is central to good human resource management practice. Furthermore, many professional practitioners believe that employment relations now needs to focus on gaining and retaining employee commitment, particularly in terms of giving employees greater input into the decision-making process. Nevertheless, engaging employees' hearts and minds can be a major challenge for many organisations, where the mix of human resources and other factors of production are vital to sustained business performance. Greater employee engagement for many is seen as the solution, gained through 'high commitment' work practices such as teamworking, functional flexibility, employee involvement and reward packages (Williams, 2014: 161).

Rayton *et al* (2012: ii) not only argue that there is a clear link between employee engagement and productivity and performance, but that *'if the UK is to move its engagement levels to the middle of the top quartile, such as that for the Netherlands, this would be associated with a £25.8b increase in GDP.'* They go on to claim that their analysis of a large number of case studies drawn from across industry supports:

> the existence of a strong longitudinal synergistic connection between employee engagement and performance. Engaged employees perform better: perhaps by working harder, longer and/or smarter. Engaged employees have been shown to work more vigorously, offer innovative suggestions, and to pursue their work objectives in the face of even quite substantial obstacles. The value of these behaviours undoubtedly varies across contexts, but every organization has employees whose engagement makes a meaningful difference to organizational success, and understanding how to manage engagement is therefore a crucial business issue. (2012: 24)

There is clearly a significant role for human resource management professionals in most workplaces to drive the engagement agenda at senior and line management level and translate it into everyday reality. However, the causal relationship between HR practices and improved business performance is not clear. For example, Truss *et al* (2013) warn against attributing improved performance solely to engagement initiatives while ignoring the contribution of 'work intensification' and 'worker compliance'.

Furthermore, although clear and consistent leadership is a crucial factor, employee engagement cannot simply be 'imposed' through top–down mechanisms. Instead, as we shall argue, it is dependent on engaging employees through creating an environment characterised by high levels of support, security and trust. This in turn requires the development of front-line managers who have the skills to communicate with and motivate their staff, and also on effective structures of direct and indirect employee voice.

## ? REFLECTIVE ACTIVITY 7.1

What does the term employee engagement mean to you in the context of your organisation? What do you think are the key factors that maximise your own engagement with your organisation and with your job?

## 7.2 DEFINING EMPLOYEE ENGAGEMENT – ENGAGED WITH WHOM OR WHAT?

Defining employee engagement is not straightforward. MacLeod and Clarke, in their influential 2009 review 'Engaging for success: enhancing performance through employee engagement', identified fifty different definitions. They argued that employee engagement encompasses:

- unlocking people's potential at work and the measurable benefits of doing so for the individual employee, the organisation and the UK economy
- retaining and building on the commitment, energy and desire to do a good job to maximise individual and organisational performance
- making the employees' commitment, potential creativity and capability central to the operation of the organisation – it is how people behave at work that can make the crucial difference between business success or failure
- enabling people to be the best they can at work, recognising that this can only happen if they feel respected, involved, heard, well-led and valued by those they work for and with
- employees' having a sense of personal attachment to their work and organisation – they are motivated and able to give their best to help it succeed, and from this will flow a series of positive benefits for the organisation and the individual

- ensuring that employees are committed to their organisation's goals and values, are motivated to contribute to organisational success and are able at the same time to enhance their own sense of well-being
- providing clear evidence of trust and fairness based on mutual respect through which two-way promises and commitments between employees and management are understood and fulfilled.

Some commentators see employee engagement as a set of approaches or strategies designed to elicit organisational commitment. However, for others, employee engagement is an outcome of managerial actions and activity (see for example Purcell, 2012). Acas (2014) suggest that employee engagement describes the positive attitude or behaviour of someone at work. However, to whom, or with what, are employees engaged? Purcell (2010) draws attention to the importance of this, since the policy implications vary according to the nature and direction of engagement. Management consultants who undertake employee engagement surveys give the impression that engagement is mainly or wholly to do with engagement *with the employer and the organisation* for which people work (Dromey, 2014). It is normally measured as the extent to which employees wish to stay with their employer, are proud to work for the firm, and are prepared to exert extra effort on behalf of the organisation. This can sometimes be brought together as an 'engagement index' (see also CIPD, 2014). However, it could be argued that commitment to the job, the team or a particular individual may have a more powerful influence on performance than commitment to the organisation. In reality, employees have multiple loyalties. In some circumstances, employees – such as a nurse or a teacher – may be indifferent towards an employer but be passionate about their job, patients, pupils or colleagues.

This multifaceted nature of employee engagement has also been noted by Alfes *et al* (2010) in a report commissioned by the CIPD, their findings suggested that engaged employees perform better than others, take less sick leave and are less likely to leave their employer. They point out that central to the concept of employee engagement is the idea that all employees can make a contribution to the successful functioning and continuous improvement of organisational processes. Therefore, employment is about creating opportunities for employees to connect with their colleagues, managers and the wider organisation. Importantly, Alfes *et al* argue that engagement is not homogenous and distinguish between three types (or dimensions) of employee engagement: intellectual engagement; affective engagement; and social engagement.

Figure 7.1 Dimensions of employee engagement

| Intellectual engagement | Affective engagement | Social engagement |
|---|---|---|
| The extent to which individuals are absorbed in their work and think about ways in which performance can be improved | The extent to which people feel positive emotional connections to their work experience and thus with the company | The extent to which employees talk to colleagues about work-related improvements and change |

Similarly, Gourlay *et al* (2012) identify two types of engagement: emotional and transactional. They argue that employees may seem engaged on a behavioural level, but what motivates that behaviour is different. Accordingly, when individuals are intrinsically motivated by the love of their job, their relationships with colleagues or the values of the organisation, they are likely to encourage emotional engagement. In contrast, transactional engagement occurs when an employee is driven to achieve more extrinsic rewards by a fear that if they do not perform they may lose their job or be unable to afford a certain standard of living. In this case, motivation is dependent on organisational expectations and the external context. Therefore, this research suggests that employee engagement has a number of dimensions and that which secures the engagement of one group of employees is likely to differ from another. As Kinnie *et al* (2005) have stressed, one size does not fit all. This means that employers have to understand the different motivators of engagement in different parts of their organisation and their workforce.

The Acas policy discussion paper authored by John Purcell on *Building Employee Engagement* (2010) puts forward two reasons for suggesting that a focus on employee engagement is crucial. First, it has been accepted for many years that employees who are committed to their work and to their employer have a higher probability of behaving in positive, co-operative ways, to the benefit of the firm and of themselves. They are also less likely to take sickness absence or quit. Second, the concept of engagement stems from a recognition that work in the modern enterprise is more complex and changes more frequently than was earlier the case. This makes the task of management more challenging. Command-and-control management styles in most companies are now much less effective since employees tend to know the intricacies of the job better than their managers. Increasingly, what makes a competitive difference is not technology but the way in which employees choose to undertake their job in terms of how co-operative, how innovative, how caring and how responsive to customers they are. Putting employees at the centre of the policy and practice debate means that greater focus is placed on the management behaviour required to build engagement rather than on rules and regulations.

## 7.3 THE EXTENT OF EMPLOYEE ENGAGEMENT

MacLeod and Clarke (2009) found a wide variation in engagement levels in the UK within and between organisations and companies. John Purcell (2012), in reviewing a range of studies, also concluded that around a third of employees are not engaged, or disengaged, with the remainder showing some attributes of engagement. Alfes *et al* (2010) found in their study that 8% were strongly engaged and a further 70% 'moderately' or 'somewhat' engaged. More recently, with reference to Table 7.1, the latest analysis of WERS data shows an increase across all sectors in terms of employee commitment since the last survey. This is significant in that commitment has also been seen to have a clear link to levels of engagement (MacLeod and Clarke, 2009; Dromey, 2014; Williams, 2014).

Table 7.1 Changing nature of organisational commitment

|  | Public Sector | Manufacturing | Services | All |
|---|---|---|---|---|
|  | % | % | % | % |
| **Agree: 'I feel loyal to my organisation'** | | | | |
| *WERS2004* | 70 | 76 | 72 | 71 |
| *WERS2011* | 72 | 72 | 77 | 75 |
| **Agree: 'I share many of the values of my organisation'** | | | | |
| *WERS2004* | 60 | 44 | 57 | 55 |
| *WERS2011* | 65 | 56 | 67 | 65 |
| **Agree: 'I am proud to tell people who I work for'** | | | | |
| *WERS2004* | 59 | 53 | 63 | 61 |
| *WERS2011* | 65 | 63 | 70 | 68 |

Source: Workplace Employment Relations Survey 2004 and 2011

Dromey's (2014) analysis of WERS2011 also found that, between 2004 and 2011, there had been a 'significant improvement' in positive indicators of increased engagement: organisational commitment; discretionary effort; and a sense of achievement by staff. However, if one digs deeper beneath these headline statistics, a more nuanced picture begins to develop. As Robinson and Hayday's (2009) survey on behalf of the Institute of Employment Studies found, engagement in organisations varied between age groups, between the type of organisation, and between different job roles. Dromey (2014) also found higher levels of engagement among women and younger people, while disabled workers were far less engaged. It is, therefore, perhaps surprising that issues of equality and diversity have received little consideration in the engagement literature (Truss *et al*, 2013).

In contrast, engagement also varies with job type and seniority. Managers and professionals exhibit higher levels of engagement arguably due to the fact that they enjoy greater discretion and autonomy (Boxall and Purcell, 2011). This was also supported by WERS2011, which found that 84% of managers and professionals agreed that they used their initiative to carry out tasks that are not required of their job; whilst only 57% of process, plant and machine operatives did so (van Wanrooy *et al*, 2013). In addition, organisational commitment was higher among employees in smaller workplaces, which could relate to the personal nature of the employment relationship in small firms.

---

**?   REFLECTIVE ACTIVITY 7.2**

Critically assess the extent of employee engagement at your workplace. What are the main factors that explain this and what could your employer do to secure higher levels of engagement?

---

## 7.4 ENABLERS OF ENGAGEMENT

MacLeod and Clarke, in their influential review of the evidence in relation to employee engagement, concluded that there were four main factors which were critical to securing high levels of employee engagement: leadership, engaging managers, employee voice, and integrity. Dromey's (2014) analysis of WERS2011 data found support for the influence of these four enablers (2014: 37).

---

### MACLEOD AND CLARKE'S ENABLERS OF ENGAGEMENT:

Leadership that ensures a strong, transparent and explicit organisational culture, which gives employees a line of sight between their job and the vision and aims of the organisation

Engaging managers who offer clarity, appreciation of employees' effort and contribution, who treat their people as individuals and who ensure that work is organised efficiently and effectively so that employees feel they are valued, and equipped and supported to do their job

Employees feeling they are able to voice their ideas and be listened to, both about how they do their job and in decision-making in their own department, with joint sharing of problems and challenges, and a commitment to arrive at joint solutions

A belief among employees that the organisation lives its values and that espoused behavioural norms are adhered to, resulting in trust and a sense of integrity

MacLeod, D. and Clarke, N. (2009) *Engaging for success: enhancing performance through employee engagement: a report to government.* London: Department for Business, Innovation and Skills.

## 7.4.1 LEADERSHIP

MacLeod and Clarke argued that effective leadership ideally defines a clear mission, which has widespread ownership and commitment from managers and employees at all levels. A strong narrative provides a shared vision for the organisation at the heart of which lies employee engagement. It is a story that explains the purpose of an organisation, the breadth of its vision, and sets out the contributions that individuals can make. Employees must understand not only the goals of the organisation for which they work but also how they can make a contribution (see also Acas, 2014).

CASE STUDY 7.1

A TRADITIONAL LOAN BUSINESS PREPARES ITSELF FOR A NEW WAY OF WORKING

When Sarah Dickins joined Provident in 2012 as the new people director, she found an organisation ready for an 'aggressive' turnaround programme to meet the changing needs of 2.5 million customers, and grow into new markets. With more than 8,000 agents – and 11,000 employees in total – Provident's staff pound the streets visiting borrowers in their homes to discuss their needs, deliver cash loans to their door and collect repayments, which puts people at the heart of the business. But Dickins says staff were still reliant on paper-based records for customer accounts and there was a higher-than-ideal turnover of sales and collection agents. It was time to modernise and change the culture.

'We were struggling to attract agents, find them and keep them in that first year. So we put in place structured recruitment processes and an induction, which we called "Best Welcome".'

This involved reviewing whether Provident was finding the right people for the roles, and whether these recruits understood what the job would entail. Under 'Best Welcome', new recruits go out with an accredited agent to witness the job first-hand before they start with the firm. The lender also introduced a standard induction for agents and field leaders. Twelve academy branches have

now been launched to deliver training. In the first year after the changes were introduced, the results were dramatic, with a 25% improvement in agent turnover.

Ensuring workforce engagement throughout the process has been crucial, she adds, with leadership training playing its part: 'I put a good case forward about investing in people and investing in leadership. . . we knew we were not going to embed the change effectively without equipping our people to take their people with them.'

The people department brought in practical leadership training around leading people and teams through change, with actors and role-play sessions. Board members went through the training personally to ensure they understood it. As the training is rolled out, a board member opens and closes each session with managers and function heads, to demonstrate their commitment to development and get employee feedback.

Dickins says the training has helped 'blend together' existing, experienced staff with those who have just joined the business. This had the added benefit of improving relationships across departments, which aided the move to a matrix organisation, combining functional and divisional structures to bring together employees and managers to accomplish a common goal. New communication methods have helped further engage staff in the change. They include a regular radio chat show with the managing director and other senior leaders answering staff questions, and weekly in-office 'huddles' to keep staff up to date on how the business is doing and what their immediate goals should be to keep the turnaround on track.

'Our leaders really got the simple people strategy because it gave them a different perspective on why we're here as a people team. It gave our team a unique opportunity to be able to say "What's our strategy? What are we trying to do?" By keeping things simple we've been able to achieve a lot by connecting what we want to do with the operational agenda.'

Source: CHURCHARD, C. (2015) Provident Financial: we couldn't change without helping our people change too. *People Management*. February. pp18–19.

---

**?**  REFLECTIVE ACTIVITY 7.3

---

What does the experience of Provident tell us about the role of senior management in establishing an effective engagement strategy? What lesson could you learn for your own organisation?

## Engaging Managers

Front-line managers also play a critical role in giving local context to that vision and employees' place within it. For MacLeod and Clarke, 'engaging managers' are at the heart of organisational culture. They facilitate and empower rather than control or restrict staff. They treat their staff with appreciation and respect and show commitment to developing, increasing and rewarding the capabilities of those they manage. Engaging managers offer clarity for what is expected from individual members of staff. They treat their people as individuals with fairness and respect and with a concern for the employee's well-being, and have a very important role in ensuring that work is designed efficiently and effectively. However, the extent to which 'engaging managers' are a feature of British workplaces is debatable and an issue that we discuss in greater detail later in this chapter.

## Employee Voice

In an organisation that affords effective and empowered employee voice, the views of employees are sought out. According to many surveys, feeling listened to is the most important factor in determining how much employees value their organisation. Being heard reinforces a sense of belonging within an organisation and a belief that one's actions can have an impact. 'Engaging managers' will therefore be able to open up clear and accessible channels of 'direct voice' whereby employees will feel safe and confident to raise issues of concern. A key driver of engagement, according to MacLeod and Clarke (2009), is the ability for employees to feed their views upwards. In this sense, also feeling well-informed about what is happening in the organisation and thinking that one's manager is committed to the organisation. Management's action on feedback is critical. There are also synergies between engagement approaches and partnership agreements working between unions and employers where trust, co-operation and information-sharing are key.

Dromey's (2014) analysis of WERS2011 concluded that successful engagement is premised on giving genuine voice to employees in terms of influencing overall decision-making in the organisation. The analysis by Van Wanrooy *et al* (2013) of the same data found that 91% of those employees who were satisfied with their influence over decisions also agreed that they were loyal to their organisations. However, among those who were not satisfied with their influence over decisions, less than half said they were loyal. This also reflects the findings of Kular *et al* (2008), whose critical review of the literature at that time identified employee involvement as a key prerequisite for effective engagement.

'Voice' can be enabled directly through one's line manager, for instance by way of team meetings or one-to-ones. A key element of this direct aspect of employee voice is that individuals also have a greater say over the design and carrying out of their own work tasks. Alternatively, indirect channels, such as employee forums, can help to involve workers in the decision-making process, as Case Study 7.2 demonstrates.

---

**CASE STUDY 7.2**

👁 THE INNOVATIVE WORKPLACE: EMPLOYEE ENGAGEMENT PROJECT

The Health Store is a co-operative warehouse and distribution centre for health foods. It employs over 100 people and is based in Nottingham. What was the problem?

Many of the communication problems experienced by the company seemed to go back to their change of premises. On the surface, moving from cramped and dingy conditions to a spacious, purpose-built warehouse facility could only be beneficial. But the change had an unintended consequence, as 'the new environment became sterile and people didn't feel as involved as they were.' (Operations Director)

The company realised that, to respond to market pressures and continue to increase sales, it had to involve managers and staff, and improve levels of engagement.

What did they do?

The Health Store worked with Acas in a project aimed at 'giving the company back its personality' by establishing more two-way (face-to-face) communications. Employee representatives were elected and training was provided by Acas to give

them a clear idea of their roles and responsibilities. The communication and consultation forums have enabled everyone to get back to talking and listening to each other more, and improvements have been made in work processes and health and safety procedures.

Twelve months down the line, absenteeism has been reduced, staff morale improved and there has been a marked reduction of instances of formal disciplinary action.

'By engaging with our staff we are able to steal a march on our competitors. We are a co-operative, not just with our customers but also with our staff.' (Operations Director)

Source: Acas (2014) *The people factor – engage your employees for business success*. Available at: www.acas.org.uk/media/pdf/0/0/Advisory-booklet-The-People-Factor.pdf [Accessed 16 November 2015].

Contains public sector information licensed under the Open Government Licence v3.0

---

**?  REFLECTIVE ACTIVITY 7.4**

Reflecting on Case Study 7.2, what made the use of an employee forum particularly effective? What difficulties might organisations encounter in trying to use such bodies as part of an engagement strategy?

In Chapter 9, we identify the potential weaknesses of non-union employee forums. It is argued that they are commonly under-resourced and representatives often lack training. Crucially, if employers are not committed to developing them as a genuine source of employee voice, they may find it hard to gain the legitimacy they need to play an active role in securing engagement. Trade unions have traditionally been sceptical about engagement strategies, seeing them as a way to intensify work and bypass traditional forms of representation. However, as Purcell states (2014), the potential for collective union voice to promote elements of organisational justice and therefore underpin employee engagement is often overlooked in the literature. Case Study 7.3 provides an example of where partnership working in an NHS trust between employers and unions overcame initial suspicion over a wide-ranging engagement initiative. The active involvement of the unions was critical in proving to staff that this was not simply a 'tick-box exercise'.

## CASE STUDY 7.3

### AN NHS TRUST BECOMES AN AWARD-WINNER BY GETTING TO GRIPS WITH EMPLOYEES' CONCERNS

When Nicole Ferguson joined Wrightington, Wigan and Leigh (WWL) NHS Foundation Trust as staff engagement lead, she could have been forgiven for thinking her job would be straightforward. The organisation was known for having an open relationship with its unions and was one of ten pioneering trusts leading the NHS Listening into Action programme. With chief executive Andrew Foster – former HR director at the Department of Health – championing the process at board level, it seemed safe to assume everything was rosy.

But the NHS national staff survey in 2011 brought some dispiriting news: 55.3% of employee engagement measures were under par, and just 21% were above average. In response to this 'wake-up call', the HR team needed to deliver 'a kick up the backside' to the relationship between the trust and its 4,500 staff.

The answer was to delve more deeply into the engagement scores and to understand where problems had arisen at a local level. The process began with a new Staff Engagement Pathway model: every quarter, employees answer questions about working relationships, recognition, resources, perceived fairness and personal development, with each team using their individual scores to identify specific needs and development tools.

'I wanted to establish a measurable framework of engagement, something that we could track and then act on,' Ferguson says. 'The trust was very keen to establish its own brand of staff engagement – the "WWL way" – and had a number of initiatives working on an organisational and team level. My role was to pull everything together and make sure the staff had access to an extensive toolkit of engagement methods.'

But understanding where improvements could be made is pointless if nothing changes – and it's implementation that has seen the plaudits rolling in for WWL. The trust has created a 26-week 'Pioneer' training and support programme for teams to design and introduce new measures. The results can be seen on every ward in the form of display boards, which help teams measure their daily activities.

'Every day, staff get together to talk about the immediate issues of the day: how they are doing, what's gone well and wrong the previous day, and what they need to do to address the issues,' says Jon Lenney, director of HR and organisational development. 'If you walk through our x-ray department or any of the theatres, you'll see the boards, in open view of patients, staff and visitors.'

An initiative designed by 'Staff Side' union reps – called Staff Involvement Delivers (SID) – sees Foster and other directors hold Q&A events with employees. 'Walkabout' sessions put senior staff back on the front line. It all adds up to a complete culture shift. Above-average scores reached 59% in the 2012 national staff survey, and 69% in 2013. Sickness absence fell from 4.62% to 4.17% in 2013 and the trust saved around £3 million on temporary staffing. The team's efforts were recognised with the overall prize at the 2014 Healthcare People Management Association Excellence in HRM awards. And other local trusts are benefiting from the WWL toolkit.

More importantly, Ferguson and Lenney have been able to quantify what they always knew – that better staff engagement correlates to optimal organisational performance, which in turn drives better outcomes for patients. The challenge has been to communicate that to trust employees.

'It's the NHS; people are challenged for time, they face constant pressures, and their priority is always patient care, so the challenge for them is to invest time and effort into this "selfish" notion of staff engagement,' says Ferguson. The team created an animated video to explain why engagement benefits patients, and developed an accredited leadership training programme for those managers to whom 'openness and engagement don't necessarily come naturally,' Lenney says.

Getting unions on board has also been crucial. 'Our original staff engagement model was something we developed in partnership with our unions and they were a real key partner in this. In a way, the organisation had left it to them to make staff engagement activities work, and we weren't putting enough thought and imagination into it from a management perspective,' says Lenney.

'When we decided to take more of a role in 2011, I think Staff Side were a bit suspicious about our intentions. They thought we were trying to undermine their position in relation to the staff.'

Ferguson agrees: 'The things we try and do to engage staff are much more authentic when they have that endorsement from Staff Side. It doesn't appear to employees that this is just a tick-box exercise – they can see that their reps are buying into it and can see the value.'

It seems the remaining danger for WWL may be for teams to be almost too engaged. 'I really am starting to see a highly engaged workforce but as the pressure mounts, and employees are giving everything to their role, I think the risk of burnout is ever more present,' says Ferguson. 'We've got to be really careful that we are equipping staff to deal with both internal and external pressures, and going forward we'll look at employees' well-being and how we can manage and support that alongside the engagement initiatives.'

Source: LEWIS, G. (2014) Our staff engagement needed a kick up the backside: [Wigan and Leigh NHS Foundation Trust]. *People Management*. September. pp20–21.

## REFLECTIVE ACTIVITY 7.5

Analyse Case Study 7.3 and list three key arguments for having the unions 'on board' as part of an employee engagement strategy.

While this is a positive example of the role played by collective employee voice, the erosion of representational structures in British workplaces raises worrying questions as to the consequent implications for sustaining employee engagement.

## Integrity

Behaviour throughout the organisation should be consistent with its stated values, leading to trust and a sense of integrity. Most organisations have stated values and accepted behavioural norms. Where there is a gap between the two, the size of the gap is reflected in the degree of mistrust within the organisation. If this gap is closed, high levels of trust usually result. If an employee sees the stated values of the organisation embodied in the leadership and by colleagues, a sense of trust in the organisation is more likely to be developed, thereby constituting a powerful enabler of engagement. Sanders (2012: 2) also identifies the importance of increasing employee trust in underpinning successful engagement; however, as she further notes, trust is a complex notion:

> 'Trust resides within relationships and it comes from seeing and experiencing behaviours which enable us to trust the other party. In organisations, these relationships are often complex. For example, evidence shows that a relationship built on trust between the line manager and an employee is crucial to positive employee engagement... As an employee [therefore], you also need to feel trusted by your manager and your colleagues.'

Purcell (2012) recognises this complexity but questions the extent to which employee engagement can simply be generated through engagement mechanisms. Crucially, he argues that this is dependent on the extent to which process, practices and strategies are seen to provide and reinforce organisational justice, both 'procedural' and 'informational'. Procedural justice is seen as a measure of the 'fairness' of the management procedures exercised in coming to decisions within the organisation, and the level of consultation of employees that involves. Informational is the justification by management of the actual procedures they chose to that end and the outcomes of those choices for their workforce.

## 7.5 ENGAGEMENT AND THE ROLE OF MANAGERS

Given the crucial role of the line-management relationship in developing employee engagement, Robinson and Hayday (2009), working for the Institute of Employment Studies (IES), embarked on a research project entitled 'The Engaging Manager', to better understand how managers inspire and engage their teams to perform and behave well in their dealings with people. The project involved seven organisations: the Association of Chartered Accountants, Centrica, Corus, HM Revenue and Customs, the London Borough of Merton, Rolls-Royce and Sainsbury's. Researchers identified 25 'engaging managers', and the IES interviewed them, their own managers and their teams. The interviews centred on engaging behaviour rather than on personality. The 25 managers had little in common except their ability to engage their teams via very similar behaviours. Their jobs and roles varied, their span of control ranged from four people to over 5,000, and they were very different in terms of personality, background and training.

All the managers interviewed said that an important way to learn about management was to observe others. One remarked:

> I think my style is more looking at managers I worked with before, and stealing the bits that work for me and losing the bits that don't.

A very strong theme was the belief that they should be clear about goals and expectations, as summed up by the comment:

> I try to encourage people to think of the wider objectives and how they fit in . . .

The managers in the IES research had been selected by their organisations because their teams had high engagement scores. It was noticeable that these managers were good at the difficult matters – tackling poor performance quickly and effectively and breaking bad news. The consensus was that honesty and openness were essential, along with empathy and demonstrating that the manager had an understanding of the possible impact on staff. However, this had not always been the case; managers had acquired new behaviours and developed their skills, becoming more self-aware of the impact of their own actions.

Figure 7.2 Behaviours of engaging and disengaging managers

| Engaging managers | Disengaging managers |
|---|---|
| Communicates, makes clear what is expected | Self-centred – lacks empathy and interest in people |
| Listens, values and involves team | Fails to listen and communicate |
| Supportive and backs up team members | Doesn't motivate or inspire |
| Target-focused with clear strategic vision | Doesn't deliver – blames others, doesn't take responsibility |
| Shows active interest in others | Is aggressive |
| Displays good leadership skills and commands respect | Lacks awareness |

Source: *People Management*, 5 November 2009

There was a feeling amongst engaged teams that they were happy and enjoyed their work, and that there was a good atmosphere, compared with other teams. An important feature was teams' openness and ability to discuss a wide range of topics.

As well as describing engaging behaviours, respondents were asked to describe disengaging managerial behaviour (see Figure 7.2). The factors associated with disengagement or low levels of engagement can expose basic failings in employment policy and practices. It is accepted, for example, that where people work in jobs with very short task cycle times, perhaps a minute or less (as found in some telephone contact centres and some manufacturing assembly work), where there is high stress related to little autonomy and inflexibility, and where there is a feeling of job insecurity, employees will also tend to have lower engagement levels. Lower levels of engagement are also more likely to be found where there is perceived unfairness in rewards, where there is bullying and harassment, and where people believe they are stuck in their jobs and feel cut off from open communications. Furthermore, this is likely to be exacerbated by the external context. For example, van Wanrooy *et al* (2013) found, in their analysis of WERS2011, a clear link between lower levels of engagement and the extent to which workplaces had been affected by recessionary pressures. They argue that there is a clear relationship between employee engagement and workplace conflict, with less effective employee engagement in workplaces where either industrial action had taken place in the previous 12 months, or where respondents felt that there was a poor overall climate of employment relations within their organisation.

Purcell's (2010) analysis of WERS2004 data underlined the importance of the role played by front-line managers. Having trust in their manager was a significant predictor of higher levels of employees' organisational commitment for all occupations, closely followed by job satisfaction (doing the work itself) and involvement in decision-making, sometimes referred to as 'employee voice'. Interestingly and also worryingly, analysis from

WERS2011 found that only 57% of employees agreed that their managers were 'sincere in understanding their views' and this fell to as low as 38% among low and middle earners (van Wanrooy *et al*, 2013).

### 7.5.1 ENGAGEMENT, EQUALITY AND DIVERSITY

The discussion on engagement in the previous section highlighted a number of issues, none the least the key role of 'engaging managers'. However, the fact that the gender, for instance, of those managers was not seen as a factor in the research suggests that we often fail to consider the implications of equality and diversity for engagement. Challenging this omission, a number of contemporary writers have been critical of the lack of action by employers in addressing issues of inequality in the workplace, particularly in relation to 'soft' HRM approaches such as employee engagement (Kirton and Greene, 2005; Cassell, 2013).

It would appear that issues of equality and diversity affect engagement levels. A recent study conducted by Yarlagadda *et al* (2015) found that engagement varied depending on gender, age and disability. Women tended to be more engaged than their male colleagues, while engagement appeared to decrease with age. Furthermore, disabled workers were significantly less engaged than those without a disability. The authors argue that there are strong links between policies and practices aimed at increasing diversity and employee engagement, through, for example, the provision of flexible working. In addition, they claim that discrimination can undermine and erode engagement, and accordingly adopting clear approaches to challenging discriminatory behaviours and actively promoting the benefits of workforce diversity will have a positive impact on engagement levels.

This again could point to the importance of organisational justice providing a foundation for trust and therefore engagement. If workers feel that they can depend on their managers to support them if they encounter discrimination, their commitment to the organisation may be deepened. However, there is less evidence that the links between diversity and engagement are appreciated by employing organisations, as Yarlagadda *et al* found that only around one-third of organisations connected strategies in these areas.

The research conducted by Yarlagadda *et al* highlighted the case of Northern Gas Networks' innovative approach to employee engagement through equality and diversity. This was based on employees being encouraged to develop and put into place their own solutions to problems facing the company. This process was furthermore facilitated by regular forums where employees came together to discuss these issues. Crucially, a central premise of the initiative is that effective problem-solving is a key business benefit of employing a diverse and inclusive workforce. Their case study is reproduced in full in Case Study 7.4.

---

CASE STUDY 7.4

### NORTHERN GAS NETWORKS' APPROACH TO EMPLOYEE ENGAGEMENT

Northern Gas Networks (NGN) is one of the main gas distribution companies in the UK, and is responsible for distributing gas to 2.6 million customers across Yorkshire, the North East and Northern England. NGN's 2,000-strong workforce (a mix of direct employed and contract resources) – from emergency engineers who are on the street seven days a week, 365 days a year – to their customer care officers who work closely with their customers and stakeholders, all play a crucial role in delivering excellent customer care. NGN has been recognised at various forums for its work on employee engagement. It was a winner at the 2014 UK Employee Experience Awards and at the 2014 UK Customer Experience Awards.

NGN's innovative approach to employee engagement gives its employees the freedom to develop and implement their own solutions to problems faced within the business, as well as creating opportunities to discuss their ideas. As Susan Wareham, HR Director at NGN, described: 'We try to do things far more informally and organically. We don't dictate from the top and we are pleased to let our people take the lead.' Susan believes that a diverse workforce is very important to the success of the organisation, but that it is crucial for Northern Gas to have a holistic approach to engagement and treat all colleagues with respect and dignity.

A Young Persons' Network exists for the under-35s to network and create their own development and learning opportunities. This, together with the embryonic development of a Women's Network, provides discreet opportunities for two diverse groups within the business. Following a recent women's event, it was reported that women feel that they are treated in exactly the same manner as their male colleagues and that opportunities were available equally for all.

The company believes in having a direct approach to engaging with their diverse workforce. As Susan Wareham explained: 'We are not keen on undertaking big surveys, we find that they are accurate at one point in time. We prefer to work with smaller groups where we can engage and involve colleagues on localised issues that are important to them. We engage with our colleagues in a range of different ways and are always seeking feedback.' The company encourages informal discussions between its colleagues and the leadership teams. The senior leadership team operates an open-door policy and welcomes everyone who wants to discuss any issues. This has created an environment where colleagues feel empowered to make a difference.

NGN also has various forums in place to encourage dialogue between the management team and its colleagues. For example, the Colleague Involvement Group (CIG) was established a few months ago to provide a voice for people-related issues on the things that matter to the colleagues of NGN. As Susan Wareham explained: 'We have an existing forum in place with trade union representatives, and the CIG is in addition to that. We had a lot of colleagues who weren't represented by a structured forum. Now, through the CIG, they have a voice.' Danny Godward, who is the CIG representative for Bradford and Pennines, believes that the forum has played a crucial role in enhancing employee engagement and improving work–life balance for members. As Danny explained: 'A lot of our members were upset about their working patterns. They were too onerous. We brought the issue into the CIG and talked to our leadership team. We understood the company's point of view, and the senior management understood the colleagues' point of view. We managed to land on a balance of what's acceptable for both of us, which was a very positive outcome.'

NGN supports its employees in gaining important skills to help them grow within the organisation. It invests £2.4 million each year for the growth, development and career aspirations of its employees. NGN's Inspire Academy takes a leading role in training and developing its employees. Through the academy and the 'inspire approach', they offer employees a structured way to make their thoughts, feelings and observations about the business known. As Susan Wareham explained: 'We would like to see ourselves as a coaching and mentoring organisation. We want to give our people the opportunity to grow within the company.' As Paul Sadler, Customer Operations Area Manager said: 'There have never been as many opportunities as there are now at NGN for people who want it.' (IPA, 2015)

However, there are dangers associated with promoting a business case for equality and diversity on the basis that it contributes to engagement. Linda Dickens (1994, 1999) has argued the growing prominence given to the business case in the equality and diversity discourse means that equality initiatives are dependent on perceived business gains and more likely to be short term and contingent in nature. Therefore, by relying on an argument that equality and diversity is 'good for engagement', the longer-term social and moral arguments for fairer pay and job opportunities may be neglected.

## ?    REFLECTIVE ACTIVITY 7.6

From an equality and diversity perspective, how persuaded are you by the idea of establishing a young person's and a women's network in an organisation? Would it work in your organisation and, if so, what could be the business benefits? Which other minority groups might also benefit from such networks and why?

## 7.6 BARRIERS TO ENGAGEMENT

MacLeod and Clarke (2009) identified four broad barriers to effective management by an organisation's leaders, which occurred across both the private and public sectors. They argued that some leaders were not aware of employee engagement while others do not believe that it is worth considering or do not fully understand the concept and the benefits it could have for their organisation. Often, the potential of engagement is underestimated. Respondents to the MacLeod and Clarke survey (2009) expressed concern that some senior managers regarded employee engagement as another job on the to-do list that could be ticked off once an annual staff survey had been carried out, and the results perhaps delegated to HR and line managers to fix.

They also found leaders who were interested in employee engagement but did not know how to address the issue within their organisation. This lack of certainty about how, and where, to start was compounded by the feeling that employee engagement was something that was 'out there' – a product one buys, often at great expense. There was also concern about the scale of the challenge. The impression can be given that building employee engagement means that action is needed on every aspect of people management. This may include designing better jobs; building more effective employee voice systems; adopting a radical change in the manner in which line managers are selected, rewarded and trained; or transforming top management vision, values and leadership. Making improvements in all these areas is a daunting challenge and the return on investment of time, effort and resources may not be realised in the short term.

Even when leaders placed great emphasis on the idea of employee engagement, managers may not share that belief, or may be ill-equipped to implement engagement strategies. As a result, the organisation is unable to secure employee engagement. Alfes *et al* (2010) identified these deficiencies as:

- reactive decision-making that fails to address the problem in time
- inconsistent management style based on the attitude of individual managers, which leads to perceptions of unfairness
- lack of fluidity in communications and knowledge-sharing due to a rigidity in communication channels or in cultural norms
- low perceptions of senior management visibility and the quality of downward communication
- poor work–life balance due to a long-hours culture.

Many respondents told MacLeod and Clarke of the need for better training for managers in so-called soft or people skills. A large proportion of them felt that current skills training concentrated too heavily on qualifications and too little on how people skills were implemented within the workforce. In addition, managers were often promoted on the basis of their technical competence rather than their ability to manage people and develop high-trust relationships among their team. These problems, which are a recurring theme of this book, are particularly important given the devolution of HR management to the front line, which accentuates the critical role played by line managers in engaging their staff.

More broadly, Purcell (2010) warns that employee engagement will be a short-lived fad if it is used by employers to get their employees merely to work harder. Exception has been taken, for example, by some trade unions to the engagement agenda because its emphasis on discretionary behaviour can be seen as no more than inveigling people simply to do more, to make more of an effort – for example, in unpaid overtime. It is also the case that in the implementation of high-performance working, there have been incidences of increased stress and intensification of work. There is also evidence that some managers think that engagement is just about listening to their employees via an engagement attitude survey as a form of two-way communication (Lewis *et al*, 2012). Employee engagement, its supporters contend, is about much more than this. It is about building trust, involvement, a sense of purpose and identity in respect of which the employees' contribution to organisational success is regarded as essential. Critically, HR and employment relations practitioners have a major role to play in convincing boards of directors and senior managers of the need to focus more on their employees and customers, and not just on their shareholders.

---

### ?    REFLECTIVE ACTIVITY 7.7

Reflecting on your own organisation, how do you think these barriers to engagement outlined above can be overcome?

---

### 7.7 THE EMPLOYEE ENGAGEMENT SURVEY

So far we have considered both the strategic and theoretical aspects of engagement. In this final section, we focus on a key practical element: how do we actually measure the degree to which our staff are engaged? Van Wanrooy *et al* (2013) report in their analysis of WERS data that workplace surveys took place in 38% of workplaces in 2011, 3% up on 2004, in the two years prior to WERS. Surveys were more likely in the public sector (75%) than the private sector (33%) and were more frequently found in large workplaces. It is difficult to assess in any useful way the level of employee engagement without systematically consulting the employees themselves. The upside of surveys is that they not only provide data which gives evidence on levels of employee engagement and variations between parts of the organisation, but they can also highlight the factors that contribute to engagement, supported by statistical evidence. Survey results can, when used constructively alongside other data – for example, absence and labour turnover, customer satisfaction, quality measures – help to explain differences in the data.

To be effective, the engagement survey has to be well designed and have the confidence of the employees as well as the senior managers. Purcell (2010) sets out ten key steps in running an effective and authoritative employee engagement survey.

Ten steps to running an effective employee engagement survey:

1 Obtain active support from top management.

There must be strong support from top management for conducting the survey, publishing the results and taking action in the light of the issues identified. Top management must also be committed to repeating the survey at regular intervals. The survey's aims and design, and the actions to be taken following the results, should be on the agenda of the executive board and/or the board of directors.

2 Ensure alignment with the business strategy.

The survey must be closely aligned with the business strategy so that key areas of importance to the business can be identified. This could be innovation, leadership, quality, absence, or whatever. To do this will involve discussions with appropriate senior managers.

3 Involve employees in the design.

Equally, the survey needs the support of the employees and should cover items of importance from their perspective. This means discussing the survey with the recognised trade union or employee representatives. Focus groups with employees can help identify key issues that should be covered in the questionnaire.

4 Decide on the arrangements for the survey.

The decision must be taken whether to survey all employees or to rely on a sample. In very large organisations sampling is possible although the authenticity of the survey then tends to suffer in the eyes of the employees, since people may say, 'Well, they didn't ask me.' Will the survey be filled in by hand on hard copy or be completed online? Employees may be given a choice over which method suits them best. It is useful for around two weeks to be afforded to complete the survey (see Anderson, 2013).

5 Encourage everyone to take part.

Deliberate and considered action must be taken before and during the survey to publicise it and encourage everyone to take part. Most surveys can achieve a response rate of around 60% to 70% if there has been a concerted effort via all communication media to 'sell' the survey.

6 Ensure confidentiality.

Confidentiality is essential. Staff must be confident that their answers cannot be traced back to them, and that they are able to say what they really think and feel. Using an external agency to conduct the survey helps protect confidentiality. If the survey is online and an agency is not being used, a remote external server is essential. Confidentiality is also achieved by following the rule that data is never broken into groups of fewer than ten people. Although it may be important to collect some demographic data such as ethnicity, age, gender and disabilities, it is vital to ensure that this does not inadvertently identify someone from a minority group.

7 Take care in selecting the questions to ask.

The range of questions should include measures of engagement and those key parts of people management and employment relations which theory and practice suggest are likely to be causal factors. These are likely to include:

- attitudes towards the nature of the work (autonomy, discretion, responsibility, control)
- attitudes towards the nature of the job (workload, pace, monitoring, skills)
- attitudes towards management and unions (communication, involvement, representation)

- attitudes towards management (trust and the climate of employee relations)
- attitudes towards the company (advocacy, pride, loyalty).

Examples of the type of questions you can put in an engagement survey are shown in Table 7.2 and are drawn from the bi-yearly CIPD Outlook Survey.

Table 7.2 Engagement measures and survey questions

| Going the extra mile | I will often take on more work to help relieve my colleagues' workloads. I will often work for more hours than those I am paid or contracted to do. |
|---|---|
| Alignment to organisation purpose | I know very clearly what the core purpose of my organisation is. I am highly motivated by my organisation's core purpose. |
| Work–life balance | I achieve the right balance between my home and work lives. I feel under excessive pressure in my job. |
| Relationships with colleagues | I have positive relationships with my colleagues. |
| Satisfaction with role | My job is as challenging as I would like it to be. My organisation gives me the opportunities to learn and grow. |
| Attitude to senior managers | Senior managers have a clear vision of where the organisation is going. Senior managers consult employees about important decisions. |
| Attitude to line manager | My manager treats me fairly. My manager makes me feel my work counts. |

8 Benchmark the questions to compare results.

The design of the survey should not be seen as a one-off event but as part of a continuous effort to monitor and build employee engagement. It is important to be able to benchmark the results over time to plot changes in levels of engagement and compare the results with those in the same sector and the economy as a whole. External survey agencies can provide this service and ensure that the questions replicate those asked elsewhere. An important additional reason for using standard questions is that they are likely to have been tried and tested. This suggests that a core number of questions will be used in every survey. It is possible to add additional questions to cover areas of particular concern or interest. The only caveat is that the questionnaire should not take more than 15 minutes overall to complete, or response rates will fall. Most surveys use a five-point scale, giving the respondents a choice of how satisfied or dissatisfied they are, plus a neutral position.

9 Analyse the results.

Simple descriptive analysis of the results provides a basis for understanding the overall picture of employee engagement. More sophisticated statistical analysis will allow questions to be grouped together to explore patterns of behaviour and attitudes, what factors contribute to engagement, and how these differ – for instance, between types of employee, department or locations.

10  Report back and take action.
    It is good practice to report the results of the engagement survey within two months of
    the closing date. Full results must be reported to senior management and in some
    instances to union or employee consultative committees.

There must be discussion of areas in which action should be taken to help build levels of
engagement or deal with weaknesses identified through the survey results. It is common
practice – and a good one – for the results to be relayed to employees using various forms
of company media but especially via team meetings or briefings at which there can be a
discussion of the measuring of the results and reports on planned actions. Some
employers make the engagement results one of the key performance indicators for line
managers.

## 7.8 SUMMARY

Up to and since the influential MacLeod and Clarke report (2009), it is of significant note
that a large number of studies from academics, consultancies and organisations have
looked at the impact of high levels of engagement on outcomes for the business or
organisation. Covering a wide range of industries, it suggests that there is a strong story to
be told about the link between employee engagement and positive outcomes. In particular,
there are a number of studies that demonstrate that private sector organisations with
higher levels of employee engagement enjoy better financial performance, and that high
levels of engagement are also associated with better outcomes in the public sector
(Rrayton *et al*, 2012; Dromey, 2014).

However, caution is necessary in the assessment and interpretation of 'evidence' about
the processes and benefits of engagement. Many studies of the subject lack empirical detail
and devote excessive attention to the views of those who have a vested interest in
reporting progress and success. We must guard against any tendency towards overblown
rhetoric. Nonetheless, we would argue that employee engagement, if properly understood,
carefully implemented and objectively measured, is potentially a powerful tool for
delivering positive reputational and 'bottom-line' outcomes. In addition, the evidence of
the impact of successful employee engagement in practice is that the relationship between
engagement, well-being and performance is too strong and is repeated too often for it to
be a coincidence.

Nonetheless, employee engagement is difficult to pin down, with MacLeod and, Clarke
(2009) identifying 50 different definitions. While some commentators see engagement as a
set of processes and strategies, it is perhaps more useful to see engagement as an outcome
of managerial behaviors. However engagement is defined, it is clear that it has a number
of dimensions and that what motivates one group of employees may differ from what
motivates another. One size does not fit all. Managers have to understand the motivators
of engagement in the different parts of the business.

MacLeod and Clarke (2009) have suggested that engagement is underpinned by four
key enablers: organisational integrity, leadership, engaging managers and employee voice.
Subsequent recent research has underlined the importance of these factors (Dromey,
2014). There is a strong story to be told about the link between employee engagement and
positive outcomes – better financial performance, lower absence and sickness rates and
higher productivity. The research shows that in unlocking discretionary effort from staff,
respected leadership and a strong sense of organisational identity are important. But while
senior leaders within an organisation can set the context for high levels of employee
engagement, this will ultimately depend on the experiences of employees on the front line.

Disengaged employees tend to feel insecure; have little autonomy in doing their work;
feel they are treated unfairly, especially in rewards; may be subject to bullying and
harassment; and are not listened to or respected. Given the increased role for managing
people assigned to line managers, whether they communicate with and support their staff,

create a sense of fairness and equity and crucially involve staff in decision-making would seem to be critical in influencing the degree of engagement.

## KEY LEARNING POINTS

1 Employee engagement is difficult to define; however, it is most accurately seen as an outcome of managerial actions and activity. While it can be secured by specific 'engagement strategies', it is also underpinned by the way in which organisational processes and activities are designed and enacted.

2 MacLeod and Clarke (2009) identify four broad enablers/drivers which are critical to successfully building employee engagement. These are leadership, engaging managers, employee voice and integrity.

3 John Purcell has argued that organisational justice is a basic antecedent of employee engagement. Where workers feel that they are treated fairly and have an opportunity to make their views heard, they are more likely to trust their employer, and this in turn provides a foundation for high levels of engagement.

4 In reality, employees have multiple loyalties – to their job, team leaders, customers, employer. They may be passionate about some of these but indifferent to others. Consequently, equating employee engagement with organisational commitment is too simplistic.

5 Leaders play a key role in enhancing engagement by providing a strong narrative about the values and vision of the organisation. However, it is vital that this is reflected in the way that employees are treated and managed 'on the shop floor'.

6 Employee voice, and particularly having an influence on decision-making, is a key element of any successful engagement strategy. While having an open culture (ie open and transparent communication between line managers and their staff) is important, robust structures of representation are vital in ensuring that workers can shape their working lives.

7 In many respects, front-line managers play the most critical role in determining levels of employee engagement. 'Engaging managers' have good communication skills and listen to the views of their staff. They provide support and back the judgement of team members where appropriate. They empower rather than control or restrict staff, and give them a real say in decision-making.

8 Given the importance of employee voice and effective line management, the growing representation gap and lack of skills and confidence of many operational managers in managing people threatens to limit and erode employment engagement in British workplaces.

REVIEW QUESTIONS

?

1   Using arguments that draw on appropriate evidence, explain how you would persuade your organisation that investment in improving employee engagement would be beneficial.

2   You have been asked by your line manager to carry out an employee engagement survey. What would you include in this survey? Justify your answer.

3   Outline the main barriers to effective management by an organisation's leaders and explain what action you might be able to take to overcome these barriers.

4   Explain why leadership and employee voice are critical 'enablers' to gaining employee engagement.

5   Why are many front-line managers deeply sceptical about employee engagement strategies? As an employment relations practitioner, what arguments could you use to overcome these attitudes?

6   To what extent is employee engagement a way of managers reasserting control over the labour process and intensifying work?

EXPLORE FURTHER

ACAS (2014) *The people factor – engage your employees for business success.* London: Acas.

DROMEY, J. (2014) *MacLeod and Clarke's concept of employee engagement: an analysis based on the workplace employment relations study.* London: Acas.

MACLEOD, D. and CLARKE, N. (2009) *Engaging for success: enhancing performance through employee engagement: a report to government.* London: Department for Business, Innovation and Skills.

PURCELL, J. (2012) The limits and possibilities of employee engagement, *Warwick papers in industrial relations.* No 96, April 2012. Industrial Relations Research Unit, University of Warwick.

RAYTON, B., DODGE, T. and D'ANALEZE, G. (2012) *The evidence: employee engagement task force 'nailing the evidence' work group.* Available at: www.engageforsuccess.org/ideas-tools/employee-engagementthe-evidence/ [Accessed 7 October 2015].

ROBINSON, D. and HAYDAY, S. (2009) *Engaging managers.* London: Institute of Employment Studies.

TRUSS, C., SHANTZ, A. and SOANE, E. (2013) Employee engagement, organisational performance and individual well-being: exploring the evidence, developing the theory. *International Journal of Human Resource Management.* Vol 24, No 14. pp2657–2669.

**Website links**

www.acas.org.uk/engagement covers Acas web pages on employee engagement.

www.engageforsuccess.org is the website of Engage for Success, a 'movement' set up in the wake of the MacLeod and Clarke review of employee engagement.

www.ipa-involve.com/ is the website of the Involvement and Participation Association.

# CHAPTER 8

# Managing Employment Relations

## OVERVIEW

This chapter examines the way in which employment relations are managed. We start by exploring the changing context within which managers operate and the shift from environments that are predominantly regulated through collective institutions to those where direct relationships with individual employees are the norm. We therefore look at the different issues associated with managing with, and without, trade unions. The changing landscape of employment relations has also reshaped the role of employers' associations and the next section of the chapter briefly explores the way in which they support their members. The analysis then turns to the way in which different managerial approaches to employment relations can be conceptualised in terms of management styles (authoritarian, paternalistic, consultative, constitutionalist and/or opportunist), which in turn define the roles played by individual managers. The last part of the chapter examines the implications of the rise of HRM for the management of employment relations and the fundamental shift of responsibility for people management from the HR function to the line.

## LEARNING OUTCOMES

When you have completed this chapter, you should be able to:

- understand and describe the main roles undertaken by line managers in the context of employment relations
- critically assess recent developments in the management of employment relations
- understand how employers' organisations support managers in their day-to-day work
- identify different management styles and use these to critically evaluate organisational approaches to the management of employment relations
- critically analyse the implications for employment relations of the greater devolution of HR duties to front-line managers.

## 8.1 INTRODUCTION

When examining the role of managers in employment relations, it is tempting to see management as a homogenous entity, with no distinction made between the employer, senior managers, supervisors and practitioners responsible for managing human resources. In some organisations, this is the case; around four out of five workers are employed by SMEs in which the owner or director of the business is also often the line manager. However, as organisations grow in size, there is a need for additional managerial layers and the introduction of functional specialisms such as HR. Ultimately, in very large private corporations there is a separation between ownership and management as the business is often owned by shareholders, with professional managers employed to run the business.

Accordingly, the values and attitudes of managers at different levels, and in different parts, of the organisation may vary. For example, it might be expected that directors of a company will have values that closely reflect objectives of major shareholders. This is also likely to be cemented by the fact that it is common for senior managers to have relatively large shareholdings as part of their remuneration package. However, as one moves down the managerial hierarchy, managers may identify more closely with their 'team'. In fact, the evidence tends to suggest that managers' values (and therefore their attitudes) tend to align with those of the organisation more generally. Furthermore, while the traditional view of the 'personnel' manager may have been as a neutral referee between employees and employer, HR practitioners increasingly see their role as supporting managerial and organisational strategy.

Consequently, it is possible to discern identifiable organisational approaches to the management of employment relations, whether in relation to trade unions, employee involvement and participation or the determination of pay and conditions. We examine these management 'styles' later. Perhaps, more importantly, as Marchington and Wilkinson rightly note, HRM responsibilities do not 'reside solely or even primarily' with specialist HRM staff but rather with the line manager (2012: 165). In this context, this chapter considers the theoretical and practical implications of the increasing trend to devolve HR duties, and therefore responsibility for the management of the employment relationship, to line managers. Seen thus, the choice of management style they adopt is crucial, and for many organisations, this will require a fundamental reappraisal of the key knowledge, skills and attitude their managers will need.

## 8.2 WHO MANAGES EMPLOYMENT RELATIONS?

Findings from WERS2011 (van Wanrooy et al, 2013) allow us to paint quite a detailed picture as to who manages employment relations. As we noted above, most organisations are small and do not have specialist managers with responsibility for either HR or employment relations. In fact, van Wanrooy et al found that 86% of the individuals that had responsibility for dealing with employment relations issues were employed in a more general role and had nothing in their job title relating to HR or employment relations. In almost eight out of ten workplaces, issues such as discipline and grievance, health and safety, and pay were handled by a general manager or owner. Therefore, most managers who deal with employment relations do so as part of a wider role within the organisation.

WERS2004 had suggested that there was in increase in the use of staff with specialist HR knowledge or who spent a large proportion of their time on such issues (Kersley et al, 2006), perhaps in response to the growing demands of employment legislation in the late 1990s. However, WERS2011 found no evidence of this continuing. Not surprisingly, as Figure 8.1 clearly shows, the presence of employment relations specialists was much greater in larger workplaces; they were found in almost three-quarters of workplaces with 100 employees or more but just 15% of those with between five and 19 employees.

Given that managers with specialist knowledge are much more likely to be found in larger workplaces, more than half of all employees work somewhere that has an employment relations manager with a relevant formal qualification. It should also be noted that van Wanrooy et al's analysis confirmed a longer-term trend of an increasing proportion of women HR and employment relations managers. Women make up almost half of employment relations managers and this reflects faster progression for women within HR than other managerial disciplines. This is interesting in two respects: it is arguably an illustration of occupational segregation in that HR is often (inaccurately) stereotyped as the 'caring' side of management; also, regression analysis of WERS2011 conducted by van Wanrooy *et al* (2013) found that women managers were more likely to adopt a consultative approach to decision-making than their male counterparts.

Figure 8.1 Presence of employee relations specialist

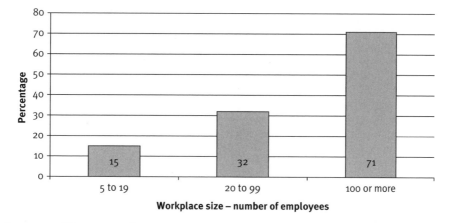

**Workplace size – number of employees**

Source: van Wanrooy *et al*, 2013

WERS2011 data also shed light on the amount of discretion given to managers in terms of employment relations, whether from HR or from more senior managers in the organisation. The main terms and conditions of employment tend to be set centrally at a relatively high level in the organisation, but line managers tend to have much more control over the day-to-day handling of issues such as performance and recruitment. Furthermore, this degree of freedom has increased since the previous survey in 2004 in respect of appraisals, grievances and equal opportunities, reflecting the devolution of responsibility for certain HR and employment relations issues.

Over half of British workplaces in the private sector (56%) had an individual on the board of directors of their company who had responsibility for employment relations and there was a notable increase in the likelihood of board representation among medium-sized enterprises between 2004 (39%) and 2011 (60%). However, we need to treat such statistics with some caution; the representation of HR in the boardroom does not necessarily reflect the relative importance of employment relations within the organisation. In most cases, board representation will be through HR directors, and recent research conducted by one of this book's authors suggested that within HR teams, employment relations are rarely the responsibility of the most senior practitioners (Saundry *et al*, 2016).

## 8.3 WHAT DO MANAGERS DO?

This debate can be traced back to Fayol's (1990) classic and highly technical model of the general principle of management, with its emphasis on the notion of chains of command within a hierarchy. This is in contrast to Mintzberg's (1990) later and more revealing exposition of the 'folklore' of the manager's job, and the reality of its contingent and episodic nature. For many years, writers have focused on the degree to which management has moved from being a traditional bureaucratic function whereby employees are managed through tightly defined rules and regulations, to playing a more facilitative role, providing employees with more autonomy to carry out their work. However, as critics have argued, this shift can mask the way in which de-layered structures have the potential to subtly reassert control over the labour process and intensify work (see Thompson and McHugh (2009) for a critical discussion).

In more practical terms, writers such as Mullins (2010: 434) suggest that the key functions of the line manager are: clarifying the objectives of their team; planning work; organising activities; directing and guiding; and controlling performance.

Figure 8.2 Key functions of a line manager

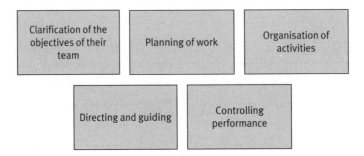

Similarly, Acas (2014), in their guide for line managers, suggest that the key aspects of the role include:

- managing people
- managing budgets
- organising work rotas
- monitoring quality
- managing performance
- ensuring customer care.

Watson (2006: 167) offers a broader perspective of the role of management and argues that management can be understood as three distinct categories:

- management as the function of shaping relationships, and understanding the processes needed to bring about tasks to achieve the overall objectives of the organisation
- managerial work as the activity of bringing about that shaping
- managers as the people who have the responsibility to ensure that the tasks are carried out successfully.

Watson implicitly criticises the whole notion of managing 'human resources'. Instead, the role of the manager is to manage relationships in order to ensure the achievement of particular tasks of value to the organisation through the facilitation of her or his team's efforts and other material resources. As Dundon and Rollinson point out, this is in stark contrast to the dominant notion of 'managerial prerogative', which in turn is based on a 'property rights' argument of the manager as owner with the necessary competence to decide on issues as a 'professional manager' (2011: 109). Indeed, the employment contract is founded, in part, on the notion of 'obedience' and reflected in organisational rules, the management of performance and, ultimately, the application of discipline, through which managers seek to enforce a degree of control and compliance.

However, as we discussed at some length in Chapter 2, in most organisations, this is insufficient to achieve necessary levels of performance, efficiency and quality. Therefore, managers must also try to secure the commitment and co-operation of their team. They can attempt to do this by adjusting reward and remuneration or by ensuring that they communicate and consult over important decisions. This is not straightforward, particularly as managers often have limited influence on either broader organisational strategy or the changing competitive conditions in which they work. Consequently, attempts to secure the consent of their staff will be compromised by pressures to reduce costs and increase efficiency. It is this basic contradiction at the heart of the capitalist employment relationship (Hyman, 1987) with which managers have to contend.

## 8.4 WORKING WITH, AND WITHOUT, UNIONS

The contradiction between control and consent that characterises the management of employment relations is clearly reflected in the historical relationship between managers and trade unions, and the scale and scope of collective bargaining.

### 8.4.1 THE EROSION OF COLLECTIVE BARGAINING

As we outlined in Chapter 2, the reach of collective bargaining expanded rapidly in the post-war period so that by 1980, almost two-thirds of British workplaces (with 25 or more employees) and half of those in the private sector negotiated pay and conditions with trade unions (Brown *et al*, 2008). This was partly due to the fact that collective bargaining offered significant advantages for management in terms of reducing the transaction costs of determining wages and conditions. However, it was also driven by a desire to maintain managerial prerogative in the face of collective action and organisation by workers. By creating processes and procedures through which pay and other terms could be negotiated, the eventual outcomes had greater legitimacy.

Relationships with trade unions also enabled managers to manage and resolve individual issues more easily. Trade unions played a self-disciplinary role in many workplaces, ensuring that their members adhered to rules in relation to absence and other matters (Edwards, 1994). If disciplinary disputes and employee grievances escalated, managers could work with trade unions to work towards informal resolutions.

**Figure 8.3 Percentage of workplaces with 25 or more employees recognising unions, 1980–2004**

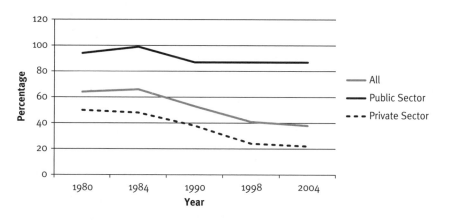

Source: Brown *et al* (2008)

However, as can be seen from Figure 8.3, the extent of union recognition fell rapidly between 1984 and 1998 and then at a slower rate to 2004. By this time, just 38% of workplaces employing 25 or more employees recognised unions, and only 22% in the private sector. In some respects, this mirrors the decline in union density and organisation during this period, which we discuss in greater detail in the next chapter. But, Brown *et al* (2008) have argued that the decline in union recognition and collective bargaining was rooted in decisions made by managers in newly established workplaces not to recognise unions between 1950 and 1960, and again between 1970 and 1980. Of course, after the election of the Thatcher Government in 1979, the disappearance of workplaces in highly unionised industries in manufacturing exacerbated this, but 'the demise of collective bargaining was already well-advanced' (Brown *et al*, 2008: 8). Of perhaps greater importance was the programme of privatisation and wider intensification of competition, which created conditions wherein managers, faced with the option of working with or without unions, generally chose to do the latter.

### 8.4.2 MANAGERIAL ATTITUDES TO COLLECTIVE EMPLOYMENT RELATIONS

This is possibly rooted in the ambivalent attitude that British managers have always had to the collective regulation of labour in general, and trade unions specifically. Clegg's seminal text on the systems of industrial relations in the UK in the 1970s, for instance, identified the 'philosophical' nature of management as being broadly unitarist (1976: 188–189). There is some support for this in recent data from WERS2011, with four out of five managers preferring to consult directly with staff rather than through employee representatives (van Wanrooy *et al*, 2013). In addition, only 23% of managers either actively encouraged or were in favour of union membership, 17% were against and 60% were neutral. However, managerial attitudes towards trade unions also vary in relation to sector and size of workplace. In workplaces with 500 or more employees, 48% had positive attitudes to union membership, which increased to 73% in all public sector workplaces. In the private sector, just 12% were in favour while 20% held negative views about union membership. Therefore, the attitudes of managers would appear, to some extent, to reflect the organisations in which they work.

---

### ?    REFLECTIVE ACTIVITY 8.1

What are the attitudes of managers to unions where you work? If your managers could choose to work with or without unions, what do you think they would do and why?

---

### 8.4.3 RECOGNITION, RESISTANCE AND CONTINUING INDIVIDUALISATION OF EMPLOYMENT RELATIONS

In general, despite some of the potential benefits of working with unions, British managers have generally only done so when placed under some pressure to do so, either by government policy or, perhaps more importantly, by trade unions themselves. The most recent attempt to promote collective bargaining through state policy was the introduction of a statutory procedure for union recognition as part of the Employment Relations Act 1999. However, even this was introduced rather reluctantly by a new Labour Government, keeping a pre-election pledge to the trade union movement. As Williams and Adam-Smith (2010) point out, its terms were extremely limited. It did not apply to small workplaces (fewer than 21 employees) where union recognition was traditionally extremely low. In addition, the procedure required trade unions to reach a threshold of support of 40% of the entire 'bargaining unit' before union recognition would be granted, as seen in Figure 8.4.

Figure 8.4 Statutory union recognition procedure

- Union request recognition in respect of a group of at least 21 workers
- Central Arbitration Committee (CAC) determines whether there is sufficient support
- If more than 50% of the group are union members, CAC can order recognition
    - *If not, at least 10% of the group must already be union members*
    - *There must be a likelihood that a majority of the group would be in favour of recognition*
- CAC can then order a ballot of the relevant group

    - *To win recognition, the union must get a majority of those voting and be supported by 40% of the total constituency*

Worked examples

USDAW applies for union recognition at Foodmart PLC. Out of a total of 10,000 employees, 990 are union members. The claim fails as less than 10% are members of the relevant union.

UNITE applies for union recognition at ABC Haulage. Out of a total of 100 employees, 52 are UNITE members. The claim succeeds (without a ballot) as a majority (52%) are members of the relevant union.

UNISON apply for union recognition at Dobbins Retirement Care Ltd. Out of a total of 100 staff in the bargaining unit, 20 (20%) are already members of UNISON. A ballot is held of all 100 staff. The turnout (total vote) is 60 (60%) staff. Of these, 39 vote for union recognition. The claim fails – although a majority of those voting have voted in favour, less than 40% of the total electorate (39 out of 100) have voted in favour.

There is some evidence that new union recognition agreements increased both prior to, and after, the introduction of the procedure. In 2001, there were 685 new deals; however, the number of new agreements fell significantly after this high point, as unions were forced to move into areas of industry that were more difficult to organise, and as Gregor Gall (2007) has pointed out, employers have become more active in resisting unionisation. Figure 8.5 shows the number of new applications received by the CAC between 2001 and 2015; while there is some variation, the general trend is clearly downwards.

Overall, the number of new agreements triggered by the Statutory Recognition Procedure has not been sufficient to prevent the continuing erosion of collective bargaining, as newly established workplaces chose not to work with unions and, within unionised workplaces, the scope of bargaining continued to shrink. There are perhaps four dimensions through which the trend to work without unions can be seen.

First, small workplaces are highly resistant to union organisation. Kersley *et al*'s analysis of WERS2004, which covered the period over the introduction of statutory recognition, found that the greatest fall in the incidence of collective bargaining occurred among workplaces with between 10 and 24 employees. In 1998, 28% of these workplaces had recognised unions, but by 2004, this was just 18%. It has long been acknowledged that owners of small and medium-sized enterprises are generally hostile to union membership and involvement (Rainnie, 1989). Trade unions are perceived to be antithetical to the notion of paternalistic and informal employment relations, based on close personal ties between employer and employee, which characterise smaller workplaces and organisations (Ram *et al*, 2001). This does not mean that employment relations are necessarily harmonious. Wood *et al*'s (2014) analysis of WERS2011 found that very small organisations (five to nine employees) had the highest rates of disciplinary sanctions and employment tribunal applications. Furthermore, conflict is also more likely to be suppressed in small firm environments in which employees are less likely to have the protection of formal procedure.

Figure 8.5 New applications to the CAC for statutory union recognition, 2001–15

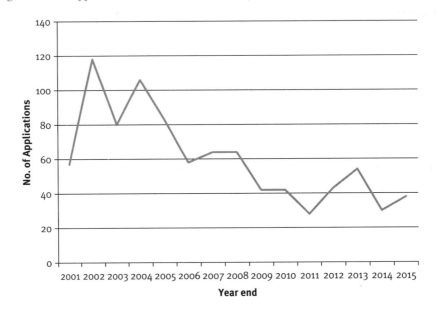

Second, large non-union businesses adopt a policy of union substitution by offering relatively generous terms and conditions and developing channels of direct employee voice. We provide the example in Chapter 9 of Marks & Spencer, whose BIG representatives are, unlike most non-union representatives, trained to accompany colleagues into disciplinary and grievance hearings. Although non-union representatives have failed to come even close to filling the gap left by trade union decline, there are some signs of growth (albeit from a very small base) in large private sector workplaces; from 6% in 2004 to 13% in 2011 (van Wanrooy *et al*, 2013). In addition, van Wanrooy *et al* (2013) found that levels of mutual trust between non-union representatives and managers was higher than between managers and union representatives. Of course, this may reflect the fact that non-union representatives are less likely to challenge managerial prerogative, but could also be explained by a preference among managers for non-union forms of voice.

Third, some organisations are actively hostile and aggressive towards trade unions, using threats and intimidation in an attempt to resist attempts to organise. For example, Williams and Adam-Smith (2010) give the example of BSkyB, which suggested to workers at one of its call centres that a vote in favour of recognition would make it more likely that their work would be 'offshored'.

Finally, even within those workplaces that recognise trade unions, there would appear to be a clear trend towards more individualised approaches to employment relations. Brown *et al* (2008) noted in their analysis of the WERS series of surveys (up to 2004) that 'there has been a fundamental shift in attitudes, towards individualism and away from collectivism' (354). This would appear to be continuing. For example, there was a small but significant reduction in the proportion of employees who felt that their managers were in favour of union membership between 2004 and 2011. Notably, some of the biggest sectoral reductions were in the public sector in areas such as public administration, health and education (van Wanrooy *et al*, 2013).

While this does not appear to have been reflected in any reduction in the scope of the issues that managers negotiate with trade unions, the picture is very different in the private sector. Van Wanrooy *et al* (2013) report that in private sector workplaces in which trade unions are recognised, the scope of issues that are subject to bargaining has narrowed substantially, with the mean number of items over which they negotiated falling from 1.6 to 1.1. They argue that:

'these findings on the scope of collective bargaining in the private sector are reminiscent of those in earlier WERS studies (for example, Millward *et al*, 2000) in suggesting that formal recognition of unions for pay bargaining may often resemble a "hollow shell" in which unions and their members have little influence over the setting of terms and conditions.' (van Wanrooy *et al*, 2013: 82)

## 8.5 THE CHANGING ROLE OF EMPLOYERS' ASSOCIATIONS

The individualisation of the management of employment relations has also been reflected in the changing role of employers' associations. Employers' associations are voluntary, private bodies, which exist to provide information and co-ordination in areas of common interest. However, they traditionally played a key role in industry-wide collective bargaining. Employers' associations developed in the late nineteenth and early twentieth century to respond to the increasing power and influence of newly formed and fast-growing trade unions. By negotiating industry-level agreements, employers' associations removed bargaining from the workplace and prevented trade unions from isolating particular employers. However, multi-employer bargaining declined as large organisations demanded the ability to negotiate terms and conditions that reflected their needs and circumstances. This also mirrored declining union power, which enabled employers to break away from national agreements. The consequent decentralisation of bargaining further undermined the ability of trade unions to mobilise large-scale solidaristic action.

Employers' associations, like unions, have seen their influence fade in recent years. In 1983, there were 375 employers' associations, but by 2014, this had shrunk to just 56. This is largely a result of mergers but also reflects the contraction of industry-wide, multi-employer bargaining (Dundon and Rollinson, 2011). According to WERS2011, just 7% of all British workplaces, and only 2% of private sector workplaces, were covered by multi-employer collective bargaining. Industry-wide agreements remain more common in the public sector, for example in higher education and local government, and overall 43% of public sector workplaces have some element of multi-employer collective bargaining. However, this proportion has fallen sharply due to the extension pay of review bodies in the NHS, and primary and secondary education. Between 2004 and 2011, the proportion of workplaces covered by multi-employer bargaining fell by more than one-quarter to 43%, while by 2011 pay review bodies determined pay in over one-third of public sector workplaces (35%), compared with 28% in 2004. These changes were reflected in substantial reduction in the proportion of public sector employees who were covered by collective bargaining, from 69% in 2004 to 44% in 2011 (van Wanrooy *et al*, 2013). While this may not reflect derecognition, it does constitute a rapid and radical shift away from the joint determination of pay and conditions.

For employers' associations like the Local Government Association (LGA), which has traditionally negotiated pay at national level in respect of local authority workers, it also represents a major change. The LGA acts as the voice of the local government sector and as an authoritative and effective advocate on its behalf, covering 414 local authorities across England and Wales. Like all employers' associations, a major function of the LGA is to lobby national government over issues relevant to its members. In regard to employment relations, although collective bargaining on behalf of their members is still part of their remit, they now play a much wider 'consultancy' role. The LGA website states that:

'We provide advice and guidance on workforce issues and employment law, and help councils develop a framework for their roles and responsibilities as employers. And from strategy through to action and evaluation, our consultancy service delivers advice and support to help local authorities solve their HR problems.'

Increasingly, employers' associations, rather than bargaining collectively, provide their members with the support and information to bargain individually. Many of them therefore provide a commercial employment relations service that offers members advice and support on wage rates and conditions of employment, disciplinary procedures, redundancy procedures and even representation at employment tribunals. Most employers' organisations also provide employee relations information services. Prominently featured in such information are pay and benefits data based on regularly conducted surveys, which are useful for salary and pay comparisons and local negotiations.

---

## THE ENGINEERING EMPLOYERS' FEDERATION

The EEF provides a wide range of business support services – a small part of this is set out below. The EEF can help negotiate with unions, respond to recognition demands or mediate in the event of a dispute:

We provide a comprehensive range of consultancy services to help you manage arrangements with trade unions.

*Employee relations audit* – we offer employee relations audit services to help you develop an employee relations strategy.

*Mediation and dispute resolution* – we can help you mediate and resolve disputes quickly, preventing employment tribunal costs.

*On-site employee and industrial relations support* – we provide interim employee relations services on-site or help you manage one-off projects.

*Pay negotiations* – we can help you manage pay negotiations with your trade unions.

*Trade union recognition* – we offer consultancy services to help you deal with the challenges of unions seeking recognition agreements.

*Working successfully with trade unions* – we provide trade union support services to ensure you're confident and successful in your negotiations with trade unions.

*www.eef.org.uk/business-support/our-services/hr-and-employment-law/employee-relations-and-trade-unions*

---

In some ways, the growing business consultancy role of employers' associations could be argued to represent a marketisation of the HR function with the public sector. It is also another potent indication of the erosion of institutional employment relations and its replacement with a fragmented and individualised system dominated by concerns over legal compliance.

## ? REFLECTIVE ACTIVITY 8.2

In what ways has the role of employers' associations, like the EEF, changed over the past 20–30 years? What does this teach us about the changing nature of employment relations?

Employers' bodies, whether in the public or private sector, organise themselves in different ways. The priority each gives to employment relations, as opposed to trade matters, differs according to tradition, the nature of the industry it represents and the degree of unionisation in its particular sector. Perhaps the best-known UK-wide employers' organisation in the UK is the CBI. It sees its overall task as the promotion of policies for a more efficient mixed economy. Currently, the confederation represents over 140 trade associations made up of 190,000 members drawn from across all industries and organisations of all sizes. They estimate that this equates to around 7 million employees, including a third of all private sector employees. An important political lobbying organisation, the CBI's major function is to provide for British industry the means of formulating, making known and influencing general policy in regard to industrial, economic, fiscal, commercial, labour, social, legal and technical questions.

Although it does not specifically engage in employment relations activities, the CBI's lobbying activities can (and do) have an impact on issues that affect workplace employment relations. In recent years, the CBI has lobbied successfully on behalf of employers on issues such as the National Minimum Wage, statutory trade union recognition procedures, the reform of the employment tribunal system and the implementation, in the UK, of EU directives. As an organisation, the CBI does not engage in negotiations with employee representatives, but it does maintain a direct working relationship with the Trades Union Congress (TUC) as well as an indirect one via joint membership of bodies such as Acas and the Health and Safety Executive.

---

**CASE STUDY 8.1**

### EMPLOYERS' ASSOCIATION VIEWS ON PROPOSALS FOR NEW TRADE UNION LEGISLATION

**CBI**

The CBI welcomed the introduction of the Trade Union Bill and supported the idea of thresholds for industrial action ballots. Katja Hall, CBI Deputy Director, said that:

'We're glad the Government has brought forward this Bill, as the CBI has long called for modernisation of our outdated industrial relations laws to better reflect today's workforce and current workplace practices. The introduction of thresholds is an important, but fair, step to ensure that strikes have the clear support of the workforce. Placing time limits on ballot mandates is an important measure to ensure industrial action is limited to the original dispute and not extended to other matters. We welcome the

consultation on modernising picketing rules. Intimidation or harassment of individuals is never acceptable – and we want to see the current Code of Practice put on a statutory footing and penalties increased to drive out bad behaviour.'

Source: http://news.cbi.org.uk/news/cbi-response-to-strike-law-reforms/ [Accessed 17 November 2015]

**EEF**

The EEF were more cautious. Discussing the inclusion of the reforms in the Queen's Speech in 2015, Tim Thomas, Head of Employment Policy, argued for 'a measured legislative approach'. This needs to balance the objectives of ensuring that ballots properly reflect the views of all trade union members, and provide a mandate for timely, specific industrial action, with the unintended potential to undermine the constructive relations that currently exist between trade unions and many employers in the private sector.

Source: www.eef.org.uk/about-eef/ media-news-and-insights/media-releases/2015/may/eef-comments-on-todays-queens-speech [Accessed 17 November 2015]

**Welsh Local Government Association**

The Welsh Local Government Association, which represents local authority employers in Wales, was highly critical of the trade union reforms, arguing that 'the Government's proposals were aimed at tackling problems that do not reflect the reality of modern industrial relations in Wales. The number of days lost to strike action has dropped by over 90% in the last twenty years and industrial action today increasingly takes the form of protest action rather than all-out strikes, which makes the legislation even less warranted. As employers, we have disagreements and disputes with the trade unions, but we seek to work with them in a mature and responsible manner. The purpose of this Bill, however, seems to harken back to an outdated "I'm all right Jack" caricature of the way business is conducted, with a set of proposals on strike laws that are probably unworkable and which represent a deeply unfair curtailing of trade union rights. As such, the WLGA is firmly opposed to the introduction of the Trade Union Bill as it is currently drafted.'

Source: www.wlga.gov.uk/media-centre-l-wlga-e-bulletins/councils-voice-opposition-to-draft-trade-union-bill [Accessed 17 November 2015]

## REFLECTIVE ACTIVITY 8.3

Case Study 8.1 provides the views of three employers' associations on proposals, now contained in the Trade Union Bill, to, among other things, introduce a threshold for strike ballots (see Chapter 4). In what way are these views different, and what does this suggest about the membership of the three associations and their outlook on employment relations?

## 8.6 MANAGEMENT STYLES

We have already noted in Chapter 6 the impact that the values and preferences of organisations' dominant management decision-makers have on strategy formulation. These values and perceptions will in part be determined by whether the organisation adopts a unitary or pluralist approach to its employment relations. Recalling the discussion in Chapter 2, the unitary approach portrays organisations as harmonious and integrated, all employees sharing the organisational goals and working as members of one team. The pluralist approach, in contrast, recognises that different groups exist within an organisation and that conflict can, and does, exist between employer and employees (Fox, 1985).

These are broad definitions, and it must be noted that simply because an organisation is described as unitarist does not mean that management and employees share the same agenda. Organisations with a unitarist philosophy can be either authoritarian or paternalistic in their attitudes, and this can have a major impact on management style. Alternatively, organisations that adopt a pluralist approach will tend to embrace collective relationships and, while accepting that conflict will inevitably occur, will emphasise the need to develop co-operative and constructive relations between interest groups. It is this distinction in approach to the management of people that leads to variations in employment relations policies, ranging, for instance, from the paternalistic non-union approach of Marks & Spencer through to the single-union no-strike philosophy of Japanese firms such as Nissan, or the multi-union sites of companies such as Ford (see Salamon, 2001).

Although external constraints on employment relations policy formulation are an important element, the internal constraints are probably of greater significance. Factors that often determine management style are organisational size, ownership and location. Style can be an important determinant in defining employment relations policy and practice, and is as much influenced by organisations' leaders as it is by business strategy. Since Fox (1985) first developed the frames of reference approach for conceptualising employment relations, others have sought to define the topic in greater detail. However, it is important to consider Bacon's warning that 'there are no simple methods to assess whether managers hold one frame of reference or another – individual managers may have a complex range of views' (2013: 244).

Dundon and Rollinson usefully define management style, in contrast to the notion of the leadership traits we considered in Chapter 6, as 'a manager's preferred approach to handling employment relations, which reflects the way that he or she exercises authority over subordinates' (2011: 114). From this broad definition, we can (following Purcell and Sisson, 1983) identify a number of types of styles.

Figure 8.6 Management styles

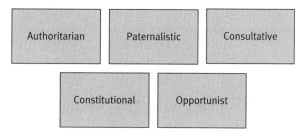

The authoritarian approach sees employment relations as relatively unimportant. Although policies and procedures may exist, they are often there because of some legislative necessity (eg grievance, discipline), and as a consequence people issues are not given any priority until something goes wrong. Typically, firms with an authoritarian approach can be small owner-managed businesses, and it is not unusual to find that the things that go wrong revolve around disciplinary issues. In many of the small firms that we have contact with, complaints against them of unfair dismissal have been a common problem. For example, an employer who has paid little attention to setting standards of performance dismisses an employee who makes a mistake, and then finds that the dismissed employee wins a tribunal claim for compensation. This is usually because no previous warnings were issued and no disciplinary procedure is followed.

Paternalistic organisations may share some of the size and ownership characteristics of the authoritarian type, but they tend to have a much more positive attitude towards their employees (as noted previously with respect to Marks & Spencer). Employee consultation is a high priority, irrespective of whether unions are present in the workplace, and staff retention and reward are seen as key issues (the John Lewis Partnership is a good example of an organisation whose constitution includes this type of staff involvement).

The type of 'constitutional' organisation described by Purcell and Sissons assumes a trade union presence. Here, although sharing some of the characteristics of the previous types of organisation, management style in employment relations is often more adversarial than consultative. In the opportunist organisation, management style is determined by local circumstances. These would determine, for example, whether it was appropriate to recognise trade unions or not, or the extent to which employee involvement was encouraged. Purcell (1987: 535) later moved the analysis of management style forward and redefined it as:

> 'the existence of a distinctive set of guiding principles, written or otherwise, which set parameters to and signposts for management action in the way employees are treated and particular events handled.'

## 8.7 INDIVIDUAL AND COLLECTIVE DIMENSIONS OF MANAGEMENT STYLE

Writing at the time, Poole, like Purcell, also notes the clear distinctions in the styles adopted by many managers. For him, the unitarist dimensions of style were simply 'directive' under authoritarian approaches or 'directive but welfare-oriented' when the style was more paternalistic. Towards the more pluralistic end of the spectrum, Poole defined the constitutional style as 'negotiational and based on reaching agreements with organized labour', with participative going beyond this to the 'involvement of employees in decisions' (Poole, 1986: 42–44).

Purcell (1987) agreed, suggesting that management style has two dimensions – individualism and collectivism – each dimension having three stages. Individualism is concerned with how much policies are directed at individual workers and whether the organisation takes into account the feelings of all its employees and 'seeks to develop and encourage each employee's capacity and role at work'. The three stages in the individual dimension are: commodity status, paternalism and resource status (see Figure 8.7).

Figure 8.7 Managing the individual

In the first, the employee is not well regarded and has low job security; in the second, the employer accepts some responsibility for the employee; in the third, the employee is regarded as a valuable resource. The collectivist dimension is, in a sense, self-explanatory. It is about whether or not management policy encourages or discourages employees to have a collective voice and collective representation. The three stages in this dimension are: unitary, adversarial and co-operative (see Figure 8.8).

Figure 8.8 Managing the collective

At the unitary stage, management opposes collective relationships either openly or by covert means. The adversarial stage represents a management focus that is on a stable workplace, where conflict is institutionalised and collective relationships limited. The final – co-operative – stage has its focus on constructive relationships and greater openness in the decision-making process.

As Dundon and Rollison rightly stress, Purcell addresses the limitation of Fox's model in that whilst Fox better explains 'the attitudes and values of individual managers ... style is a more useful tool to describe [the different types of management styles used in] an overall approach to employment relations' (2011: 115), and thus captures the 'different shades of both unitarism and pluralism within any organisation' (ibid.). Fundamentally, it also highlights that managers can and do adopt different styles depending on the context, the employment relations issues and the balance of power that exists in the organisation. Specifically, in terms of a key employment relations concept and practice, these variations in approach by management can and do have a major impact on the level and extent of employee voice. This core element of giving degrees of access to employees to decision-making in the organisation is investigated in depth in Chapter 10, where we look at employee involvement and participation.

Identifying a particular management style is not simply a question of labelling an organisation 'individualist' or 'collectivist'. Purcell (1987) points out that the interrelationship between the two is complex; for instance, simply because an organisation is seen to encourage the rights and capabilities of individuals does not necessarily mean that it is seeking to marginalise any representative group.

## ? REFLECTIVE ACTIVITY 8.4

Can you identify the management style that operates within your organisation? Do you think that it changes to meet different needs, or is it static?

## 8.8 THE GROWING INFLUENCE OF HRM

In recent years, the approach of many organisations to the management of employment relations has been shaped by the growing influence of human resource management (HRM). It is difficult to see whether the growth of HRM has contributed to a shift away from more pluralistic management styles or whether it is a reflection of the decline of collective employment relations. Either way, there is little doubt that it represents a profound change in the way that organisations consider the management of employment. As we noted in Chapter 6, HRM contends that people management is central to the strategy of the business and consequently implies a reorientation of practitioners away from a concern with the negotiation and accommodation of collective relationships and towards a closer identification with 'business' objectives and the individual worker or work group.

In this way, people management (and by extension employment relations) is seen as supporting 'bottom-line' objectives by delivering high levels of organisational commitment (so-called 'soft' HRM) and cost efficiency through increased work flexibility ('hard' HRM). Interestingly, this reflects the contradictory nature of employment relations, but the overarching philosophy underpinning this is essentially a unitarist one; collective relationships and institutions are subordinated to the primacy of promoting the identification of individual and work group with the organisation. Therefore, for the contemporary, employment relations professional, the onus is on strategies to secure employee engagement rather than to regulate and manage conflict through collective bargaining and consultation.

Of course, within unionised workplaces, HR practitioners and employment relations professionals play a key role in maintaining and developing relationships with union representatives, but as we implied earlier in this chapter, this is often out of necessity rather than choice. At the same time, there is an emphasis on developing direct communication and involvement. The growing peripheralisation of structures of collective bargaining and consultation, which has been charted through the WERS series (Brown *et al*, 2008), and discussed before, needs to be seen in this light.

Overall, Williams (2014: 154–155) argues that the predominant model of 'sophisticated HRM and the management of employment relations' is a strategy that seeks to:

- develop a climate where employees feel valued and thus work more effectively
- put more of a 'fit' between employment policies and the overall business objectives
- manage employees to enable them to better contribute to overall business goals
- increase worker commitment through strategies of employee engagement.

It is important to note that this approach is based on a preference for none or weak unions and is, therefore, again highly unitarist in nature. If, as it is increasingly argued, more 'people management' tasks are falling within the remit of the line, what then are the implications for effectively managing employment relations in the workplace?

## 8.9 DEVOLVING THE MANAGEMENT OF EMPLOYMENT RELATIONS

It has been recognised for many years by both employment relations writers and practitioners that a key effect of the rise of HRM has been a transfer of HR duties and responsibilities to the line. As we noted in Chapter 6, it is argued that this is a logical outcome of HR practitioners taking on a more strategic role within the organisation. Consequently, the day-to-day managing of operational employment relations issues has been seen as more appropriate to the line manager (Ulrich, 1997). Interestingly, others would argue that managing people has always been a central part of the remit of the line manager (see for example Legge, 2005).

Renwick also argued that the role 'seems such a common occurrence in work organisations today that it might be seen as an essential aspect of a HRM-approach to employment relationships' (2013: 264). The degree to which front-line managers themselves have embraced or rather contested this 'new' role, however, is a key element of our discussion (Whittaker and Marchington, 2003; Renwick, 2003, 2013). Significantly, as Boxall and Purcell argue, the line manager plays an important role in that *'the HR practices that employees perceive and experience will be heavily influenced by the quality of their relationship with their direct manager'* (2011: 248).

---

### MANAGERIAL CONFIDENCE – KEY FINDINGS FROM ACAS RESEARCH PROGRAMME

Since 2010, Acas have funded a range of projects examining the management of workplace conflict (see Saundry and Wibberley, 2014). These have highlighted a lack of managerial confidence and competence in managing people. Findings include:

- *Managers who tend to be reactive in their approach are promoted purely for their technical skills and success and not their people management skills – this relates to those that Marchington and Wilkinson term 'reluctant managers' (2012: 171).*
- *Managers receive inadequate training and development to manage people.*
- *Lack of confidence, or a propensity linked to their chosen management style, drives many managers to formalise the dispute early rather than to address the issues at an early stage.*
- *A surface-level informality and collegiality often hides a more autocratic, target-driven and non-empathetic style adopted by the manager.*
- *The management style or strategy of senior managers can have a major influence on the extent to which managers can take time to explore more creative resolutions to problems. Senior management often prioritise short-term targets and objectives at the expense of less tangible goals of good employment relations and effective conflict management.*

Purcell and Hutchinson's (2007) research results build on this, identifying the key link between employee commitment to their organisation, and the quality and consistency of HR policy as delivered by the line managers. This raises the question of whether all line managers have the time and/or inclination to consistently and effectively implement HR policy across the organisation. Alternatively, is it the reality that perceived operational imperatives, or even 'management style', impacts negatively on managerial practice? Consistency of HRM policy and practice is one of a number of key issues for Boxall and Purcell, and highlights for them the crucial role that the line manager also plays in delivering HRM. As they argue:

'Line managers are not ciphers or simple conduits. Line manager action or inaction is often responsible for the difference between espoused HR policies and their enactment. Many HR policies can only be converted to practice by line managers.' (2011: 247)

As students and practitioners of employment relations, the implications of these typical assertions in the 'devolution debate' are significant for us. For instance, what duties should be devolved? Equally crucial, what support does the line then need to effectively perform those duties? From a developmental perspective, can we assume that all managers have the knowledge, skills and attitude to carry out those duties (Marchington and Wilkinson, 2012; Teague and Roche, 2012)? If not, how does the organisation address this deficit of capability?

Reflecting back on their research in the 1970s, Marsh and Gillies conclude that:

'It is generally agreed that the day-to-day conduct of industrial relations must inevitably lie with line and staff managers and subordinate supervisors.' (1983: 27)

This recognises the long-standing role of line managers in managing employment relations. This is important because it suggests that the key change is not the centrality of the role played by line managers but the extent to which they undertake these duties in isolation from the support of HR and employment relations specialists and also institutions of employment relations. We noted at the start of the chapter that line managers have growing autonomy to make decisions over a range of issues without reference to more senior colleagues or HR. As Table 8.1 shows, there have been increases across a wide range of duties from 2004 to 2011, but particularly in terms of appraisal, equality issues, grievance, discipline and health and safety.

Table 8.1 HR issues where decisions can be made at branch sites without consulting managers elsewhere in the organisation

|  | 2004 | 2011 |
|---|---|---|
|  | % | % |
| Training of employees | 72 | 78 |
| Performance appraisals | 60 | 74 |
| Staffing plans | 66 | 72 |
| Recruitment and selection | 63 | 68 |
| Health and safety | 42 | 63 |
| Grievances | 44 | 55 |
| Working hours | 53 | 54 |
| Discipline | 46 | 52 |
| Equality and diversity | 34 | 43 |
| Holiday entitlements | 25 | 27 |
| Rates of pay | 30 | 23 |
| Union recognition | 17 | 18 |
| Pensions | 12 | 7 |
| None of these | 11 | 9 |

Source: van Wanrooy et al, 2013

## 8.10 BARRIERS TO DEVOLUTION – HR AND 'THE LINE'

Reporting over 30 years ago on his research on line managers and employment relations, Smith (1983: 43) argued that managers then, as now, fought to protect their 'right to manage'. He concluded at the time that managers felt that specialist (HR/personnel) colleagues could often wrongly give concessions – certainly to the trade unions – that undermined their authority. This illustrates a tension between the approach and the concerns of HR practitioners and operational managers, which remains evident and represents a substantial barrier to the effective devolution of people management responsibilities.

More recently, Marchington and Wilkinson (2012) have identified the key criticism made by many managers of their HR colleagues. It is important here to stress that the HR practitioners face the difficult task of reconciling some of the criticisms listed, rightly or wrongly in the following section, whilst also satisfying the demand for their services still expected by those same managers.

---

MANAGERIAL PERCEPTIONS OF HR

- HR is out of touch with commercial realities.
- HR constrains the autonomy of line managers to make decisions.
- HR is 'slow to act' and always wanting to check options.
- HR produces procedures that appear sound in theory but are hard to apply in practice.

Source: Marchington and Wilkinson (2012: 166)

---

Whittaker and Marchington's (2003) study both compounds and, in part, contradicts these criticisms, offering evidence that many line managers actually found it difficult to find sufficient time to carry out HR duties when focusing primarily on more immediate business goals. Watson *et al* also discovered in their study of the hospitality sector that 'the two main barriers to supporting line managers with their HR role are heavy workloads and short-term job pressures' (2006: 43).

Addressing these criticisms are of course paramount for the HR specialist in terms of evidencing their contribution to the business and legitimising their advice and guidance to the line. In defence of HR policy, line managers often do not fully appreciate that employment rights need to be upheld, particularly when they appear to be in conflict with business goals. Moreover, they may not see the importance of recognising the representative rights of trade unions or of acting consistently across the organisation as a whole. Furthermore, the concerns of line managers contain a fundamental paradox; they want to have greater autonomy and flexibility, but at the same time they want clearer and detailed guidance from HR practitioners. This highlights the difficult balance that HR practitioners have to achieve between respecting the independence and authority of line managers to take action while ensuring that damaging precedents are not set with respect to employment relations practice.

Whitttaker and Marchington (2003) conclude that a partnership approach between the line and HR is key to addressing many of these barriers. While the managers in their study were agreeable to take on HR tasks, they still valued being able to contact HR for advice and support in deciding their actions. Interestingly, in this study the line managers reported that HR was becoming more remote. Given the continuously changing nature of the demands made on all line managers, might we concur with the view of the Chair of Acas, Sir Brendan Barber (2014), that in the context of the increasing overcentralisation of HR and the consequent distancing of support from the line, that we are '[simply] expecting too much of our managers?'

Renwick (2013) notes the importance of assessing and developing the HR and employment relations skills of line managers, and the importance of linking this to their career development and progression. In terms of employment relations, Saundry and Wibberley's (2014) research identifies a clear skills deficit in respect of conflict management and also a lack of support from senior management (see the box on Marchington and Wilkinson's 'Managerial perceptions of HR'), the lack of key skills amongst line managers, and also the lack of suitable support. Saundry et al's (2014) critical review of the existing studies in this area concludes that many line managers face the concurrent barriers of:

- not having the confidence and competence to deal with difficult people issues
- this lack of skills and 'emotional' insight leading to a tendency to prefer more formal HR mechanisms rather than trying to first 'nip issues in the bud'
- crucial lack of support from senior management who do not see conflict management as a key business issue
- increasing isolation as HR devolves day-to-day tasks of its role to the line.

The role played by the line manager in addressing workplace conflict is covered in greater depth in section 3 of the book. However, there is some evidence that organisations are beginning to realise the need to give managers on the front line the skills to deal with the new tasks they are expected to take on. One organisation that has recognised the key role of training and development in equipping their managers with the skills and knowledge to effectively manage the employment relationship, as autonomous operational managers, is Countrywide Estate Agents, part of Countrywide Plc. Its branch manager's training programme is outlined in Case Study 8.2.

---

**CASE STUDY 8.2**

### COUNTRYWIDE ESTATE AGENTS

As the largest estate agency in the UK, Countrywide Estate Agents recognised the key role of the branch in delivering the strategic objectives of the organisation, crucially through the provision of a quality service to its customers. In-house research identified the central role of the branch manager in facilitating consistently excellent service via the branch team. To this end, the company's training and development team developed a bespoke programme for current and potential branch managers focusing in particular on:

Management training programme

1   *Style*

2   *Organisation*

3   *People management*

Professional estate agent qualifications

The programme is split into different modules depending on where the

manager is in their development. Before becoming a branch manager, individuals undertake a management development programme. This consists of four modules that cover what they should do when they take over a branch with respect to customer service, sales meeting and sales management, SWOT analysis and observing staff or 'walking the job'.

When they are promoted, they move on to the second stage of their development, which consists of a further five modules. These modules in particular equip the manager in terms of people management skills and knowledge in the areas of:

1   Management style and leadership

2   Time management

3   Managing one-to-ones

4   Observation and feedback skills

5   Coaching skills.

They also run development modules (often referred to as 'refreshers'), which are run depending on the need of the business; they are for managers who have completed the management development programme.

In addition, and reflecting their position as innovative leaders in the area of learning and development for the sector, Countrywide Estate Agents have also developed specific NVQ level 2 and 3 qualifications for the industry. Furthermore, acknowledging the concomitant professional development of their staff, completion of the qualification, together with relevant work experience, leads to membership of the professional body for the sector – the National Association of Estate Agents (NAEA).

## ? REFLECTIVE ACTIVITY 8.5

Reflecting on your own experiences, identify the key knowledge, skills and attitude needed for line managers to effectively manage employment relations in your organisation. Justify your choices. To what extent are 'soft' skills – such as emotional intelligence, empathy and listening skills – appropriate for effective line management?

## 8.11 SUMMARY

The management of people cannot be seen as a neutral activity. The management style or styles adopted by the line manager is crucial. It is influenced by many factors, including the nature of the organisation and the sector it is in, the culture of employment relations that have evolved within the organisation and the preferences, to a degree, of individual managers.

Managers in the UK have, at best, had an ambivalent attitude towards trade unions and collective regulation of labour. While they have traditionally operated within a system of employment relations informed by a pluralist perspective, their own outlook tends to be unitaristic. In recent years, the contextual changes outlined in the first part of this book have provided conditions in which managers have increasingly been able to dictate the terms on which employment relations are conducted. This has seen the progressive erosion of collective bargaining and the joint regulation of pay and conditions, and the promotion of direct strategies of communication and involvement. Weak attempts by government to provide a statutory underpinning for union recognition have had limited success and failed to arrest the charge towards more individualised employment relations.

In this context, the importance of the role played by line managers is brought into stark focus and has been accentuated by attempts to devolve greater responsibility for the management of employment relations. This presents HR practitioners with both conceptual and practical challenges. They have to respect the autonomy of the line manager at the same time as trying to ensure equity and consistency of outcomes across the organisation. Linked to this is the clear need to ensure that all managers have the appropriate knowledge, skills and attitude to effectively manage all aspects of the employment relationship. The evidence suggests that this is not the case, but there are tentative signs that organisations are realising the importance of the acquisition and utilisation of 'soft' skills such as facilitated management, emotional intelligence, listening, mediation of conflict and empathy. However, as we go on to explore in the following chapters, developing the employment relations competencies of line managers will have little impact unless broader organisational approaches provide a consistent context in which these new-found skills can be utilised.

KEY LEARNING POINTS

1   The management of employment relations has been transformed in the last 30 years. We have seen the rapid and progressive erosion of collective bargaining and joint regulation, and the growth of individualised approaches and practices designed to secure employee commitment and engagement.

2   Attempts by government to provide statutory support for union recognition have been half-hearted and have had limited impact.

3   Management style is not only shaped by the individual preferences of managers but by the context of the organisation, its culture, and the balance of workplace power. Recent years have seen a clear shift from collective to individual styles.

4   Responsibility for the management of employment relations has been increasingly devolved to line managers. There are clear tensions between the desire of line managers for flexibility and autonomy, and the obligations of HR practitioners to promote consistency and organisational integrity.

5   There are significant doubts as to whether line managers have the necessary skills to manage employment relations effectively. In addition, they operate in a context in which operational imperatives crowd out less tangible, but nonetheless important, objectives of fairness, equity and trust.

REVIEW QUESTIONS

1   Critically explain the concept of management style in the context of employment relations.

2   What have been the main changes to scale and scope of collective bargaining in the UK? What does this suggest about the way in which management styles have changed, and are changing, in the UK?

3   Your organisation is a small to medium-sized firm and has recently been invited to join a well-known and respected employers' association for the industry. The owner is sceptical of what value the association could add to the organisation. Explain to him or her the main functions of employers' associations and, using evidence, show the possible value to employment relations.

4   You have been invited to give a talk at a one-day workshop organised by the local branch of the Chartered Institute of Personnel and Development on the skills and knowledge front-line managers need to effectively manage employment relations in the workplace. Outline, with appropriate evidence, what you would include in your talk.

5   What are the main tensions in the relationship between HR practitioners and line managers? What can HR practitioners do to resolve these issues?

EXPLORE FURTHER

ACAS (2014) *Front-line managers' booklet*. London: Acas.

BACON, N. (2013) Industrial relations. In WILKINSON, A. and REDMAN, T. (eds). *Contemporary human resource management: text and cases*. 4th ed. Harlow: Pearson.

BARBER, B. (2014) Do organisations expect too much of line managers? *Personnel Today*. 3 June.

CBI (2015) *What do we do?* News.cbi.org.uk/about/ [Accessed 25 June 2015].

LEGGE, K. (2005) *Human resource management: rhetorics and realities*. London: Palgrave.

PURCELL, J. (1987) Mapping management styles in employee relations. *Journal of Management Studies*. Vol 24, No 5. pp533–548.

PURCELL, J. and HUTCHINSON, S. (2007) Front-line managers as agents in the HRM-performance causal chain: theory, analysis and evidence. *Human Resource Management Journal*. Vol 17, No 1. pp3–20.

RENWICK, D. (2013) Line managers and HRM. In WILKINSON, A. and REDMAN, T. (eds). *Contemporary human resource management: text and cases*. 4th ed. Harlow: Pearson.

WHITTAKER, S. and MARCHINGTON, M. (2003) Devolving HR responsibility to the line: threat, opportunity or partnership. *Employee Relations*. Vol 23, No 3. pp245–261.

**Website links**

www.cbi.org.uk is the official website of the Confederation of British Industry.

www.eef.org.uk is the website of the Engineering Employers' Federation.

www.lga.gov.uk is the website of the Local Government Association.

# CHAPTER 9

# Employee Representation

## OVERVIEW

This chapter examines the way in which employees' and workers' interests are represented in employment relations and in particular focuses on the changing role of trade unions, which, despite their declining influence, still provide the main source of representation in UK workplaces. The chapter begins by outlining the historical development of trade unions and traces their growing power up to the election of the Conservative Government under Margaret Thatcher in 1979. It then explores, in some detail, the main explanations for the decline in union membership and organisation since that time, and also the responses of trade unions to this challenge. This decline has created a representation gap (Towers, 1997) and the next part of the chapter examines the extent to which this has been filled by alternative non-union mechanisms. Finally, in summarising, the chapter discusses the future of trade unions and the implications of this for the management of employment relations.

### LEARNING OUTCOMES

When you have completed this chapter, you should be able to:

● understand and explain the main purposes, functions and development of trade unions
● critically assess the key explanations for the decline in trade union density from 1979
● describe and critically evaluate the strategies adopted by trade unions to renew and revitalise union organisation
● discuss the nature and extent of non-union forms of employee representation and critically assess their effectiveness
● debate the implications of the changing nature of employee representation.

## 9.1 INTRODUCTION

According to section 1 of the Trade Unions and Labour Relations (Consolidation) Act 1992, trade unions are:

> 'organised groups of employees who: consist wholly or mainly of workers of one or more description and whose principal purposes include the regulation of relations between workers and employers.'

Until relatively recently, the management of employment relations was largely conducted between employers and trade unions. In 1979, around seven out of every ten workers were dependent on unions to represent their interests in bargaining over pay and conditions, and over half the workforce were union members. Therefore, in both the public and private sectors, trade unions were not only the primary source of employee representation and voice but played a major role in shaping the life of the nation. However, following the election of the Conservative Government in 1979, there was a sharp and profound decline in union membership and also the scale and scope of collective bargaining. Today, around one-quarter of all workers in the UK are union members and even fewer are covered by collective bargaining.

Although it is easy to link trade union decline to the policies of the Thatcher Government and subsequent Conservative administrations, a number of factors combined to create an increasingly hostile environment for organised labour, including deindustrialisation and the increased globalisation of economic activity. In the UK, while this decline slowed significantly in the late 1990s, there has been little sign of trade unions, outside of the public sector, regaining any significant measure of power and influence. That is not to say that trade unions have not responded to the challenges they have faced; they have sought to reshape their approach to employment relations through pursuing workplace partnership and promoting the business case for trade unions. At the same time, recent efforts have focused on rebuilding capacity and influence through grass-roots organisation. However, it would seem that, at best, these strategies have enabled unions to consolidate rather than make any substantial gains. Crucially, there is also little evidence that non-union forms of representation have emerged to fill the 'representation gap' that has opened as a result of union decline. While non-union representation is more common, it is limited to a relatively small minority of workplaces and research has suggested that it generally fails to provide a strong voice for employees. This chapter looks at these developments in detail and in doing so assesses the future for employee representation in the UK.

## 9.2 ORIGINS AND DEVELOPMENT OF TRADE UNIONS

The roots of modern trade unions in the UK can be found in the industrial revolution of the late eighteenth century and the dramatic migration of workers from the land and from cottage industries into urban centres to work in factories, mills, ironworks and mines. This resulted in the creation of large urban workforces of men, women and children often working for low wages in extremely poor conditions. It should be remembered that there was no health and safety legislation until the Factory Act of 1833, and no organised system of state welfare support until the introduction of the National Insurance Act of 1911. The power imbalance of employment relationships was stark and, for employees, work was a necessary condition for survival. Employers, on the other hand, could draw their labour from a rapidly growing population. In this context, workers joined together in an attempt to improve conditions; however, such actions were made unlawful by the Combination Acts of 1799 and 1800.

Although this legislation was repealed in 1824, it was not until the 1871 Trade Union Act that unions were recognised under the law. By this time, there were around 1 million trade union members and a number of larger national trade unions had been formed, such as the Amalgamated Society of Engineers (ASE). In addition, the Trades Union Congress (TUC), the representative body of trade unions, was established in 1868. The subsequent years up to the end of World War II saw a rapid growth in union membership, which coincided with rising industrial militancy and political activism, particularly in the pre-war years. By 1920, there were over 8 million trade union members (see Figure 9.1). Furthermore, this period saw the emergence of growth of general or so-called new unions that extended union membership into semi-skilled and unskilled work. For example, the Gas Workers and General Union (which went on to become what is today the GMB) was formed in 1889, while the Transport and General Workers Union (part of what is today UNITE) was formed in 1922.

Economic decline and the 'great depression' between 1929 and 1933 saw high levels of unemployment and declining union membership. However, from the mid-1930s union membership grew, almost unabated, for more than 40 years to a peak of over 13,000 in 1979, which represented around 55% of the labour force. The reasons for this growth are complex; however, four key factors can be identified. First, increased industrialisation and high levels of economic growth prior to World War II, and full employment in the post-war years, created high levels of demand for labour, and therefore, conditions for unions to grow.

Figure 9.1 Trade union membership, 1892–2013

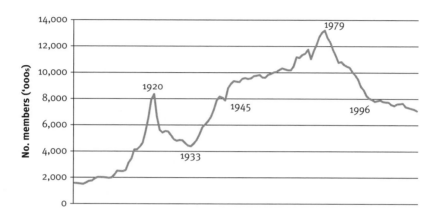

Source: Office for National Statistics

Second, unions themselves became more organised, professional and effective, using their bargaining power in certain industries to make union membership effectively compulsory through what were known as 'closed shops'. Third, post-war governments of different political colours adopted a pluralist approach to employment relations in which trade unions were seen as playing an important role in establishing stable employment relations. Finally, increasingly well-organised unions were able to win improved terms and conditions for members – this union 'premium' was attractive to workers who had hitherto been unlikely to join. In particular, in the late 1960s and 1970s, in the face of rising inflation and growing economic concerns, membership grew particularly rapidly as workers turned to trade unions to negotiate pay rises that would maintain or increase living standards.

This last point reflects an important contradiction, which, as we shall see later in this chapter, is still very relevant to the contemporary challenges facing trade unions. As we discussed in Chapters 3 and 4, industrial militancy was unpopular with many people in the UK and was one reason why Margaret Thatcher's Conservative Government was elected in 1979. However, at the same time, the effectiveness of unions in using industrial sanctions (or the threat of them) to win improved pay and conditions was crucial in demonstrating the value of union membership.

## ? REFLECTIVE ACTIVITY 9.1

Do you think that the reasons for the development and growth of trade unions still apply today? To what extent are unions relevant to the issues facing workers today?

## 9.3 WHAT DO UNIONS DO?

This question was asked by US academics Richard Freeman and James Medoff in their classic book of the same name in 1984. Their answer was that unions are: 'beneficial to organised workers, almost always; beneficial to the economy, in many ways; but harmful to the bottom line of company balance sheets' (1984: 190). In essence, they argued that unions are a vital source of collective voice, which in turn reduces labour turnover, encourages investment in capital and skills, and improves managerial decision-making. At the same time, unions are good for members as they are able to negotiate higher wages than would have been paid in their absence (wage premium). However, while unions may reduce inequality, they may also have a negative impact on profitability.

Although Freeman and Medoff's work, and in particular, the productivity effects of trade unions, has been a subject of significant debate (see for example Hirsch, 2004), it reflects the fact that the primary purpose of trade unions is to protect and to enhance the living standards of their members. In doing this, they inevitably represent a challenge to managerial prerogative and a source of increased labour costs. It is notable that van Wanrooy *et al* (2013) in the their detailed analysis of WERS2011 found that unionised workplaces were less likely to be adversely affected by the recession than non-unionised sites. While this may reflect the growing competitiveness of unionised organisations, it may also demonstrate the ability of unions to protect the interests of their members by constraining employers from taking hasty action over such issues as redundancy.

The British academic Alan Flanders, in 1970, argued that union behaviour was characterised by:

- 'sword of justice' objectives
- the advancement of job interests and not class interests
- according the highest priority to delivering their objectives by industrial methods rather than political methods
- pragmatism – dealing with matters in a sensible, flexible and realistic manner rather than being influenced by fixed theories or ideology.

Flanders argued that throughout their history trade unions have sought for their members not only more income, more leisure time and more security but also an enhancement of their status by establishing employment rights for them – for example, the right to a certain wage, the right not to have to work longer than so many hours, the right not to be subject to arbitrary dismissal. For this reason, Flanders contended that trade unions can be viewed as a 'sword of justice' seeking fairness of treatment for their members from employers and from the state.

This 'sword of justice' behaviour is seen in the impact of trade union behaviour, for example, on pay distribution. The Office for National Statistics reported in 2014 that the union wage premium was 19.8% for public sector workers and 7% for those in the private sector. Moreover, the activities of trade unions in negotiating higher wages have a disproportionate effect on groups at the lower end of the pay spectrum. Therefore, this tends to reduce pay inequality as Freedom and Medoff argued. For example, Metcalf (2005) has estimated that if there were no trade unions market, the wage differential between male and female employees would be 2.6% higher than its present level. The corresponding figures he presents for non-manual/manual worker differentials and between white and black workers are +3.0% and +1.4% respectively.

However, according to WERS2011, only 23% of employees are covered by collective bargaining, while only just over a quarter of unionised workplaces have an on-site representative. The dramatic contraction of collective bargaining since 1979 has seen trade unions revert to strategies based around individual representation and the enforcement of individual rights (Dickens and Hall, 2010). In fact, most shop stewards and workplace representatives devote the majority of their time providing advice to individual members over specific problems at work or providing representation in absence meetings, disciplinary and grievance hearings, and redundancy consultations. More than three-quarters of union representatives spend their time representing members on disciplinary and grievance issues, whereas just 61% spend time on rates of pay (van Wanrooy *et al*, 2013). This shift from an emphasis on collective bargaining to the provision of individual services also creates challenges for trade unions, with some commentators arguing that this has generated a passive and consumer-based relationship between members and their union, which is ultimately unsustainable (see Saundry and McKeown, 2014; Jarley, 2005).

Trade unions also attempt to defend and further the interests of their members through political methods, including 'pressure group' activities in relation to the UK Government and the EU decision-making bodies, whether they are conducted by campaigns, delegations, lobbying or sitting on governmental and EU advisory committees. At a national level, this role is played by pressurising the UK Government to pass legislation favourable to trade unions, which is often done through the Trades Union Congress (TUC). The TUC has 53 affiliate unions with a total membership of 6.8 million. It performs two broad roles. Its main function is to act as the collective voice of the UK trade union movement to governments, intergovernmental bodies and international trade union bodies. The supreme authority in the TUC is its Annual Congress, which is held in September, and to which affiliated organisations send delegates on the basis of one for every 5,000 members or part thereof. Congress policy is decided on the basis of motions, submitted by affiliated unions, being accepted by a majority vote of delegates. The implementation of policy decided at Congress is the responsibility of the General Council, which is serviced by the General Secretary.

Individual trade unions are also able to exert an influence over UK policy through their relationship with the Labour Party. Although the links between Labour and the unions have been weakened in recent years, fees from affiliated unions currently make up over one-quarter of Labour Party funding and, in 2014, a further £11 million was donated by trade unions, In addition, many Labour MPs have a trade union background and are union members. However, while the ties between unions and the Labour Party remain close, trade unions have often expressed disappointment that Labour governments have not provided greater support to their campaigns over issues such as employment legislation.

## ?  REFLECTIVE ACTIVITY 9.2

What do you think the main priorities of trade unions should be? To what extent do trade unions play a positive role in ensuring effective organisations?

## 9.4 TRADE UNIONS – A DECLINING FORCE?

The defining feature of employment relations over the last four decades has been the decline in trade union membership and density. Total union membership in the UK peaked at an all-time high of 13.2 million members in 1979, but by 2014 this had more than halved to just 6.4 million – around one-quarter of the UK workforce. While the rate of decline slowed markedly with the election of the Labour Government in 1997 and the subsequent sustained period of economic growth, the broad trend remains downward.

Figure 9.2 provides a breakdown of union density by sector, which clearly shows the concentration of union membership in public services such as health, education and public administration. Trade union density is much larger in the public sector (54%) than the private sector (14%). Density is particularly low in the private service sector, in industries such as food and accommodation, but even in manufacturing, once a stronghold of union organisation, fewer than one in every five workers is a union member.

The decline in density has been particularly steep among men, and women are now more likely to be union members. In addition, there is evidence that unions are failing to recruit workers entering the labour market in sufficient numbers – among 16 to 24-year-olds, less than 9% are union members and only 19% of workers between the ages of 25 and 34 have joined a trade union.

Figure 9.2 Union density by industrial sector

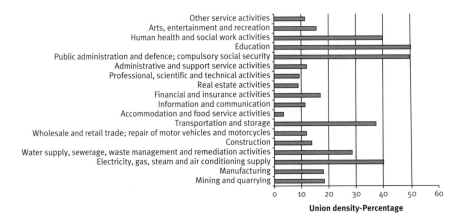

Source: Office for National Statistics, Labour Force Survey

However, falling membership and density is only one aspect of trade union decline. Just as important is the erosion of union organisation and representative capacity. Between 1984 and 2004, the estimated number of trade union representatives decreased from 335,000 to 128,000 (Charlwood and Forth, 2009). While more than half of workplaces with 25 employees or more had an on-site representative of a recognised trade union, this had fallen to less than a quarter by 2004 (Terry, 2010). Although WERS2011 seems to show that this decline has been halted, if one takes all workplaces, just 7% have an on-site union representative (van Wanrooy et al, 2013).

## 9.5 EXPLAINING TRADE UNION DECLINE

There are a number of explanations for the progressive decline in trade union membership and density.

### 9.5.1 BUSINESS CYCLE

Some commentators have argued that trade union decline can be matched to the business cycle, with periods of economic growth being associated with increasing union density as workers feel confident but also need pay to keep pace with rising prices. However, in times of recession and rising unemployment, unions will lose members who are made redundant, while those in work may also see union membership as both a risk and a cost, particularly if inflation is relatively low. Certainly, Figure 9.1 shows that the two major reductions in union membership coincided with sustained periods of high unemployment between in the 1920s and early 1930s, and again in the 1980s. However, union membership and density did not recover in the late 1990s despite sustained economic growth and the election of a Labour Government.

## 9.5.2 ROLE OF THE STATE

Many people, particularly those in the Labour movement, have blamed hostile government policy for reduced membership and influence. The fact that the decline in union membership coincided with the election of a Conservative Government, which enacted a programme of legislation designed to restrict union activity, has given some superficial credence to such beliefs. The state can influence membership directly through laws on recognition and the closed shop, and indirectly by creating the environment in which employee–management relations are conducted. In this way, the state can undermine or promote collectivism. Freeman and Pelletier (1990) calculated a 'legislation index' according to how favourable or unfavourable various strands of labour laws were to unions in each year. The changes in the law in the 1980s were held to be 'responsible for the entire decline' in union membership during this period. However, this theory fails to explain why there have also been substantial declines in union membership in countries such as the Republic of Ireland in which such 'anti-union' legislation has not been introduced.

Nonetheless, it is likely that the approach of successive governments to industrial action and the marginalisation of trade unions within policy development has sent a clear signal to employers in the private sector – that they have complete discretion over how they choose to manage employment relations. This in turn has shifted the balance of power against trade unions, thus reducing their effectiveness in the eyes of potential members.

## 9.5.3 BENEFITS OF UNION MEMBERSHIP

Fernie (2005) has argued that a key contributing factor is that for many workers the benefits of trade unions are now less clear than they once were. As we pointed out previously, an important advantage to the individual who joins a trade union is the wage premium compared with an equivalent non-member. However, since 1995, the premium has fallen by 10.5% and 8.3% for public and private sector workers respectively, as union influence and bargaining power has been curbed. Therefore, even where unions are recognised, there is less incentive for workers to join (Metcalf, 2005). In addition, it is also argued that the extension of employment rights (outlined in Chapter 4) has undermined the rationale for unions. At the same time, there has been an expansion of alternative sources of advice, whereby employees with problems at work can ring the Acas helpline, visit the Citizens Advice Bureau or consult an employment lawyer (usually for no initial charge).

## 9.5.4 CHANGING ATTITUDES

Millward et al (2000) argue that workers have lost their taste for belonging to a union, but the data we examined from the British Social Attitudes survey in Chapter 2 suggests that this is not necessarily the case. Generally, workers are not negative to the idea of trade unions and what they represent. As Towers (1997) has argued, this represents a 'frustrated demand', but nonetheless trade unions find it increasingly difficult to recruit new members to replace those leaving employment. WERS data showed that between 1983 and 2004, there was a large rise in the proportion of the workforce that had never been a union member – up from 28% in 1983 to 60% in 2004 – suggesting that unions are experiencing difficulties in getting individuals to take out membership in the first place. Research also suggests that younger employees are much less likely to belong to a union than older workers, and that this gap in membership rates by age has grown sharply in recent years.

In 2003, Bryson and Gomez (2003) and Blanden and Machin (2003) reported that young workers were much less likely to be in a trade union than at any time since 1945. Their 'age of employee' effect corresponds to the 'age of workplace' factor discussed previously. In 1975, 55% of employees aged 18–64 were union members, but by 2001 this figure had fallen by 29%. Membership rates were lower in both years for employees aged below 30. In 1975, union membership density was only 11 percentage points lower for younger people (48% compared with 59%), but by 2001 the gap had risen to 19 points (15% compared with 34%). Union density among young men has fallen by 39 points over the last quarter of a century, and for young women by 23 points. Metcalf (2005) argues that young workers probably are the main factor in explaining falling union density in workplaces where unions are recognised. Between 1983 and 1998, he points out, in workplaces where unions are recognised, the density of those aged 30 remained virtually unchanged at 70%, but the density of those aged 18–25 almost halved from 67% in 1983 to 41% in 1998.

One reason for the increasing gap between membership rates between younger and older workers is said to be the transmission of membership across generations. Blanden and Machin (2003) have shown that there is a 30% higher probability of being a union member if your father is also a union member. Fewer parents are union members today than was previously the case so – given the cross-generation correlation in trends of taking up union membership – fewer younger people are likely now, and in the future, to join trade unions.

### 9.5.5 EMPLOYER ATTITUDE AND ACTION

It is also argued that employers have become more hostile to unions. To examine this view, one could look at plant closures, derecognition activity and the new recognition of trade unions. There is no research evidence to support the hypothesis that union activity has resulted in a higher rate of plant closures amongst unionised workplaces relative to their non-union counterparts, nor that management have embarked on the wholesale derecognition of trade unions. Research by Machin (2000) and Blanden and Machin (2003), however, suggests that union decline is linked to the inability of unions to achieve recognition in newer workplaces. It shows that union recognition in workplaces with 25 or more employees fell from 64% in 1980 to 42% in 1998. In 1980, establishments less than ten years old had a recognition rate of 0.59 – almost as large as the fraction of workplaces aged ten or more years, which recognised unions. However, over the next 20 years, unions found it increasingly difficult to organise new workplaces. By 1998, just over a quarter of workplaces under ten years of age recognised a trade union – only half the corresponding figure of older workplaces. This inability of unions to make an impact on new workplaces is not, as often thought, restricted to the private services sector. Only 14% of manufacturing workplaces opened after 1980 recognised a trade union, compared with 50% of those establishments in 1980 or before.

Blanden and Machin's (2003) research demonstrates clearly that workplace age is a central factor in explaining the decline in union membership over the past 30 years. It also indicates that lower recognition rates in newer workplaces is not the end of the story, since even where union recognition was achieved, union density was some 11 percentage points lower than it was in older workplaces. It could be argued that this is related to changed managerial attitudes to trade unions. According to WERS2011, four out of five managers said that 'they would rather consult directly with employees than with unions', a slight increase from 2004. This arguably reflects the spread of unitaristic perspectives among British managers, intensified and underpinned by the growth of HRM in which a focus on communication and engagement has replaced more traditional approaches to collective employment relations. In short, managers would rather not deal with trade unions and, therefore, in new workplaces and enterprises, managers are likely to avoid union recognition where possible.

## 9.5.6 HOSTILE TERRAIN?

A fundamental challenge confronting trade unions has been the changing composition of industry and the labour market. What Blyton and Turnbull (2004) refer to as the 'Mountain Gorilla hypothesis' argues that, like the mountain gorilla, the natural terrain that supports trade unions has progressively disappeared. The industries from which trade unionism grew – textiles, coal mining, ironworks and steelworks, port transport, shipbuilding and car manufacturing – have been decimated through deindustrialisation, globalisation and, arguably, a lack of government support. These dangerous and physically demanding jobs, often in state-owned industries, in which trade union membership was extremely high, have been replaced by low-paid, unskilled service sector jobs with little tradition of trade union organisation and membership. At the same time, the growth of non-standard employment contracts has also hampered the ability of trade unions to recruit. Booth (1989) attributes over two-fifths of the decline in union membership in the 1980s to such compositional factors.

## 9.5.7 THE CHALLENGE FOR TRADE UNIONS – A LETHAL COCKTAIL?

While it is difficult to attribute the rapid decline in trade union membership and density to a single explanation, together, the factors discussed provide a potentially lethal cocktail for organised labour. The terrain in which they operate has been transformed, and the environments in which union organisation thrived have all but disappeared. At the same time, the enterprises that have replaced them and their managers have embraced a unitarist perspective, which reflects a preference for engaging directly with their employees. Therefore, in the absence of a regulatory framework that supports the role of trade unions in providing a source of collective voice, organisations choose to work without unions rather than with them. Where trade unions are not recognised, it is more difficult to demonstrate their potential effectiveness, and their lack of workplace presence means that potential members have little contact with, and are therefore less likely to join, trade unions. More broadly, trade unions are caught in a catch-22, in which falling density and presence reduces union bargaining power and, therefore, effectiveness, which in turn undermines the rationale for union membership.

### ?  REFLECTIVE ACTIVITY 9.3

Has trade union density and presence increased or reduced in your organisation? Why do you think this is?

### 9.6 THE UNION RESPONSE – STRATEGIES FOR SURVIVAL, RENEWAL AND REVITALISATION

Given the scale of the challenge outlined in the previous section, developing strategies to survive in an increasingly hostile terrain and to renew and revitalise workplace organisation has become a central issue for British trade unions. Some measures, such as mergers with other unions, have been, in part, forced by economic and practical necessity.

However, the debate over the provision of services, workplace partnership and grass-roots organising highlights questions over the fundamental purposes of unions.

### 9.6.1 UNION MERGERS – EFFICIENCY AND IDENTITY

As union membership declined, so did the revenue from subscriptions used to support organisational infrastructure. As with any other organisation, one response was to seek efficiencies by merging trade unions and so making significant savings on operational costs. In fact, mergers have been a constant part of trade union history, but over the last 35 years, as a result of trade union mergers, the number of unions affiliated to the TUC has fallen from 112 in 1979 to 52 in 2014.

Furthermore, the trend in union mergers has been towards the formation of 'mega-unions' aspiring to represent whole sectors of the economy. This trend was confirmed by the merger in 2007 of Amicus (which itself was a result of a previous merger between Manufacturing Science and Finance, the AEEU (Amalgamated Engineering and Electrical Union) and two smaller unions, UNIFI and the GPMU) and the Transport and General Workers Union to form UNITE, which now represents approximately 1.4 million members employed across the private and public sectors. The second largest union in the UK, with approximately 1.3 million members, is UNISON, which was formed from NALGO (which traditionally represented local government officers), NUPE (which represented low-paid workers in the public services), and COHSE, which organised health service workers. A further aspiration underpinning mergers was to provide increased influence at both a national and international level, both with employers and government.

However, mergers have not been straightforward. Roger Undy's (2008) empirical study of union mergers found that potential transformative gains were difficult to achieve in practice, and that there was little impact in terms of union renewal. A key problem has been the resilience of very different cultures and even structures of constituent trade unions post-merger. Furthermore, it could be argued that the development of large super-unions not only created increased distance between members and the union but have eroded the professional and occupational identities on which trade unions were built. Some potential members may see large unions as being too diffuse to represent their specific concerns.

### 9.6.2 WORKPLACE PARTNERSHIP – INCREASED INFLUENCE OR COLLUSION?

One of the main responses of trade unions to their declining fortunes was the development of workplace partnerships with employers. In some respects this was underpinned by the importance placed on partnership by the New Labour Government elected in 1997. The Fairness at Work White Paper published in 1998 set out the new administration's philosophy. In relation to trade unions it argued that:

> 'Trade unions can make the task of forging effective partnerships easier for employers and employees. In recent years they have changed to reflect change in business. Many trade unions now focus much more strongly on working with management to develop a flexible, skilled and motivated workforce. Trade unions can be a force for fair treatment, and a means of driving towards innovation and partnerships.'

In order to facilitate the expansion of workplace partnership, the Government established a Partnership Fund. By 2003, the DTI had provided support to 160 projects, totalling £5 million in funding. Case Study 9.1 was produced by the DTI, which focuses on a joint project undertaken by Gate Gourmet, which supplied airline meals, and the TGWU.

## PARTNERSHIP

The following is an extract from a case study published on the Department of Trade and Industry website featuring projects funded by the Partnership at Work Fund:

Anyone who has flown from Heathrow has probably eaten a meal prepared by Gate Gourmet's staff at one of three locations on the Heathrow site. It is a fast-moving business with around 2,500 mainly Asian staff catering for some prestigious airlines such as British Airways and Virgin Atlantic, and providing some 75,000 meals a day. But the outsourcing of BA's catering service to Gate Gourmet in late 1997, plus the merger of Gate Gourmet and Dobbs International two years later, led to unprecedented levels of staff turnover and organisational change.

Major restructuring and cost cutting took place involving swingeing cuts in overtime, training and the abolition of some grades. The result was plummeting staff morale, poor staff/management and management/trade union relationships, unacceptably high levels of grievances, disputes and extremely high turnover. At one point in the late 1990s, turnover reached 50% per year. As Director of HR, Lisa Clilverd, said, 'The case for tackling these problems through a partnership approach was compelling.'

Lisa explained that, unusually for the company, this project was genuinely a joint undertaking with the trade unions. Alan Green, Regional Industrial Organiser for the TGWU, has worked jointly with Lisa to set up and then drive through the programme. Not only did the union sit on the Project Steering Committee, but they took part in a joint review of basic HR procedures (discipline, grievance, appeal, disputes etc). They were also invited to attend a series of off-site joint workshops with management, enabling both sides to speak in an unconstrained way about issues of mutual concern and sometimes frustration. As Lisa said, 'These were sometimes "blood on the wall" sessions,

but they have produced action plans and have really made a difference to the degree of trust between the two sides. This was particularly important with so many new managers and new union representatives in place.'

Other initiatives launched under the auspices of the project were improved training for TU representatives (previously this was rather ad hoc), and the development of a new behavioural standard called 'Dignity at Work', which is being integrated into training courses for both managers and operators.

Although the project only started in earnest in August 2001, Lisa says that already it is bearing fruit. 'One test was the extent to which this partnership approach would survive the staffing cuts imposed on the company following September 11. It was gratifying that neither side wanted to put the new approach aside. As a result, I think we achieved a far higher proportion of voluntary rather than compulsory redundancies, and in a much better atmosphere than we might previously have expected.'

'The test will come when we compare statistics on turnover, disputes and so on, and when we look at the results of a new staff survey. But I think we are already seeing less industrial action by staff, a greater willingness to talk first. Early results from one unit show some promising signs – turnover levels amongst staff have dropped to a much healthier level of 13.5%. The number of formal grievances has reduced by 18% and dismissals for gross misconduct have reduced by 43%.'

Source: Department of Trade and Industry – http://webarchive. nationalarchives.gov.uk/ 20041129050451/http://dti.gov.uk/ partnershipfund/gate.htm

Contains public sector information licensed under the Open Government Licence v3.0

**?    REFLECTIVE ACTIVITY 9.4**

What are the main characteristics of the approach outlined in the Gate Gourmet case study that suggest a move towards a partnership approach? What do you think the union's motivations were in entering into this, and what might have been the potential pitfalls?

Partnership was also enthusiastically embraced by the TUC, which believed that more confrontational approaches to employment relations had failed to deliver benefits for unions or members. Perhaps more importantly, trade unions no longer had the industrial bargaining power to 'take on' employers; therefore, if unions were to rebuild, they had to do this by regaining their influence through constructive engagement.

The message that underpinned this approach was that trade unions were 'good for business'. In 2002, the TUC published a report entitled 'Partnership Works' (TUC, 2002), which argued that effective partnership working led to increased productivity and profitability at the same time as making work more rewarding and fulfilling. The report highlighted the work of the TUC's Partnership Institute in facilitating the development of partnerships across public and private sectors. The research detailed in the report claimed that 'partnership workplaces' were one-third more likely to have financial performance that was a lot better than average; and were a quarter more likely to have labour productivity that was a lot better than average.

The report also set out six key principles that make up a meaningful partnership agreement:

- A joint commitment to success of the enterprise
- Unions and employers recognising each other's legitimate interests and resolving difference in an atmosphere of trust
- A commitment to employment security
- A focus on the quality of working life
- Transparency and sharing information
- Mutual gains for unions and employers, delivering concrete improvements to business performance, terms and conditions, and employee involvement.

There is little doubt that partnership enabled trade unions to retain a foothold in organisations and its supporters would argue that, as a consequence, unions were able to shape organisational decision-making (Tailby and Winchester, 2000). This in turn could demonstrate to members and potential members that unions could have a demonstrable effect on their working lives.

However, most unions did not enter partnership from a position of strength; but from one that reflected the weakness of union organisation. Therefore, it is not surprising that partnership tended to reflect managerial rather than union aspirations and was, arguably, a way of controlling potential union opposition to restructuring and change. Consequently, partnerships could be fragile. Gate Gourmet was a case in point; just three years after the case study was written by the Department of Trade and Industry, industrial relations at the company deteriorated, culminating in a bitter industrial dispute following the dismissal of 670 workers who had previously protested about restructuring at the company and the hiring of temporary seasonal workers. British Airways staff also took unofficial industrial action in support of the Gate Gourmet workers, grounding flights for two days at an estimated cost of £40 million.

Furthermore, it has been suggested that while partnership was seen as a necessity by senior full-time officials keen to retain a place at the negotiating table, it could also create a gulf between the unions' rank and file, and their leadership (Wills, 2004). In this context, workers might find it difficult to see tangible evidence that partnership has any demonstrable impact on increasing their job security or involvement with decision-making. Thus, while partnership strategies may consolidate union influence within a particular organisational setting, its impact on union renewal and revitalisation may be more questionable (Kelly, 2004; Stuart and Martinez Lucio, 2005).

Despite these reservations, partnership remains a central aspect of employment relations and, a number of commentators argue that, given an increasingly hostile environment for organising, it still provides an opportunity for trade unions to develop specific areas of influence and shape important issues that affect their members. One particular example of this has been the development of partnership to identify and address the learning needs of their workforce, through the Union Learning initiative. This has been embraced by trade unions, who have developed networks of union learning representatives (ULRs) and drawn on government support through the Union Learning Fund to provide learning opportunities for their members. This not only provides benefits for workers but can also strengthen union organisation by establishing a connection between union membership and employability, and strengthening relationships between the unions and their members (Rainbird and Stuart, 2011).

Research by Bennett into learning partnerships in the north-west of England revealed that the collaborative work of managers and ULRs not only increased the skills, knowledge and, therefore, effectiveness of the workforce, it also reduced individual and collective conflict within those organisations, which had signed up to learning partnerships. Table 9.1 summarises the key findings.

Table 9.1 The effectiveness of learning partnerships: a summary of the findings

| Impact of learning on workplace conflict | Key findings |
| --- | --- |
| Context for the conflict | Ongoing government support for union learning projects<br>Pressure to deliver learning outcomes<br>Pressure of current economic climate and in particular job losses |
| Facilitative nature of the learning partnership | Based on a learning agreement<br>Agreed funding arrangements<br>Time off for lead ULR<br>Support for learners<br>Clear joint objectives identified<br>On-site learning centre<br>Ongoing project worker support<br>Inter-union collaboration<br>Role of 'key players' in organisation |
| Managing individual conflict | Encourages members to share workplace problems with their ULR<br>Pre-empts performance issues through early intervention in training<br>Addresses disadvantage<br>Engenders employee commitment<br>Promotes well-being<br>Supports career development |
| Managing collective conflict | Facilitates systematic deployment of ULRs to manage redundancy and redeployment<br>Promotes better trust between partners<br>Develops inter-union co-operation<br>Enhances branch organisation |

Source: Bennett, 2014

### 9.6.3 THE SERVICING AGENDA

The role and significance of servicing has become a central theme within the debate over the effectiveness of unions' renewal strategies. However, it is important to stress that providing 'services' to individual members in terms of advice and representational support over discipline, grievance and redundancy is not a new phenomenon and has always been an important element of union activity, and particularly the work of local shop stewards and representatives.

Nonetheless, the erosion of collective bargaining and reduction of union influence over collective issues has meant that greater emphasis has been placed on individual representation. As we noted in Chapters 3 and 4, in the 1960s and 1970s, disputes relating to individual workers and employees were often resolved through collective channels and the threat of industrial action. As we point out in Chapter 11, disciplinary and grievance issues were a major source of days lost through industrial stoppages. However, as the threat of industrial action became less acute and the scope of individual employment legislation expanded following the election of a Labour Government in 1997, trade unions redirected efforts to enforcing these rights and the threat of employment tribunal litigation replaced that of industrial action (Dickens and Hall, 2010).

This has had important consequences for the role played by local representatives and the relationships between unions and their members. For many representatives, individual 'casework' takes up the bulk of their time, arguably crowding out other activities, in particular recruitment and organising. Given the shrinking number of representatives (as noted previously), this places particular stress on the representative capacity of trade unions. Furthermore, it has been argued that this creates a passive relationship between (Saundry and McKeown, 2014) the member and union, in which the former does not necessarily see the union as a living and breathing entity of which they are a part, but as a provider of services. Given the limited resources of trade unions, some would argue that this is unsustainable.

In addition to the traditional services provided to union members, one response to declining membership was the development of a range of discounted benefits. While trade union members had long been able to access legal advice on work-related matters, they were now able to get discounted advice over other personal matters, cheap car and home insurance, and retail discounts. The following box shows the benefits that UNITE members can currently access.

**Member Benefits Offered By UNITE**

| | |
|---|---|
| Unite credit union service | Mortgage advice |
| Unite pre-paid Mastercard | Discounted domestic appliances |
| Free financial advice | Union energy |
| Discounted home insurance | Unite travel insurance |
| Tax refund service | Reduced cost airport parking |
| Unite debt helpline | Free foreign currency card |
| Discounted life insurance | Shopping discounts |
| Unite funeral care | Unite assist breakdown cover |

It is this aspect of servicing that critics often point to in arguing that it cannot provide a substantive basis for union renewal. In particular, research is cited which clearly shows that such benefits are not among the main reasons why members join trade unions. The most compelling evidence to support this contention is the seminal research conducted by Jeremy Waddington and Colin Whitson (1997), who surveyed over 11,000 new union members in 12 unions between 1991 and 1993. The key results of this survey (see Figure 9.3) show that the main reason for joining was 'support if I had a problem at work', cited by almost three-quarters of respondents, followed by 'improved pay and conditions' (36.4%).

Figure 9.3 Reason for joining trade unions

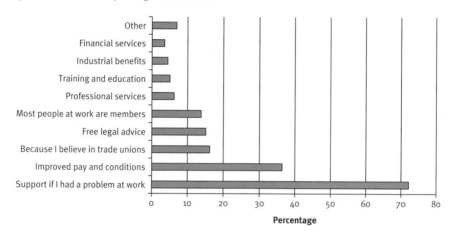

Source: Waddington and Whitson (1997)

Therefore, Waddington and Whitson argued that their findings confirmed *'the centrality of collective reasons for joining, and support among new members for traditional trade union activities'* (1997: 520). Furthermore, the fact that individual benefits rank very low has been seen as evidence that trade unions should focus on traditional bargaining activities as opposed to narrow servicing strategies. However, 'support' for problems at work does not necessarily infer collective activity and is consistent with individual representation in regard to disciplinary, grievance, absence and redundancy issues. Indeed, if unions were not able to provide effective representation over individual issues, both recruiting and retaining members would prove particularly challenging.

### 9.6.4 UNION ORGANISING – A NEW APPROACH

There is little doubt that the provision of individual representational services has become central to union strategies to recruit and retain members. Moreover, while few union organisers would claim that member benefits, such as those listed previously, are primary reasons for joining trade unions, they may be important as added incentives to 'seal the deal' with new recruits. However, a reliance on individual services is unsustainable and counterproductive in the longer run. These services have to be provided by an increasingly small group of (often older) union activists (see Charlwood and Terry, 2007; Charlwood and Angrave, 2014). Therefore, unions will find it difficult to meet the growing demands of their members. This in turn could lead to dissatisfaction and consequently problems in retaining both new and existing members if the union is unable to provide them with the support that they require. Perhaps, more fundamentally, it has been argued that this servicing agenda has hollowed out union organisation, severing bonds between union officials and members (Jarley, 2005).

In response, an alternative approach seeks to focus on 'union organising'. While this covers a wide range of strategies and practices (Simms and Holgate, 2010), the essential components are to:

- identify, recruit and develop new workplace union leaders and by doing this rebuild the representative capacity of local branches
- mobilise workers and develop collective consciousness around local concerns and issues
- encourage a culture of self-organisation through which members become more empowered and take responsibility for addressing and resolving issues
- increase membership density, strengthen bargaining power and consequently secure demonstrable improvements in terms and conditions.

Most organising strategies contain these elements, however, different unions place an emphasis on certain aspects. For example, Simms and Holgate distinguish between approaches that are based on the 'political imperative of worker self-organisation' (2010: 164), pursued in the UK by unions such as the GMB and UNITE, compared with unions such as USDAW, who focus on increasing membership density and strengthening existing representative structures.

Evidence of the impact of organising from the UK is mixed – unions have been successful in some instances in securing recognition and it could be argued that the slowing of the rate of decline of union density and membership, even during the recession following the financial collapse in 2008, is due, in some part, to more effective organising efforts (van Wanrooy *et al*, 2013). However, long-term increases in union density have been elusive (Gall, 2007), and the most authoritative review of union organising in the UK, conducted by Mel Simms, Jane Holgate and Ed Heery, concluded 'that thirteen years of organising activity has made comparatively little impact on formal aggregate measures of union power' (2013: 163).

Debates over the effectiveness of union organising have tended to focus on the different approaches that unions have taken and the relationship between organising and the use of other servicing and partnership approaches (Heery, 2002). It can be argued that as organising is based on developing grass-roots campaigns around collective grievances with the employer, this is incompatible with workplace partnership. Therefore, the impact of organising is restricted by concerns that union officials have over maintaining relationships with the employer. It is certainly the case that most trade unions use partnership and organising strategies concurrently, even if they may adopt different approaches for different settings. Saundry and Wibberley's (2014) study of a major organising campaign in the public sector in the UK found that outcomes were improved where there were positive employer–union relationships, which provided access to workers and workplaces. However, the research found two main obstacles to successful organising. First, there is a tension between short-term pressures on unions to curb declining membership and the longer-term sustainable returns that an organising-led approach aims to achieve. Therefore, there is a danger that engagement, empowerment and the development of grass-roots leadership are sacrificed at the *'altar of quantitative recruitment goals'* (Hurd, 2004).

Second, there is friction between the competing visions of the servicing and organising approaches. While engaging and empowering rank and file members is undoubtedly a positive aspiration, the reality (at least in the shortterm) for many local representatives is that they face a demand for representational services. Moreover, retaining members recruited through an organising campaign depends largely on whether the local union can respond effectively to members' requests for support. Unless they are seen to be able to defend their members effectively, there is little prospect of building a sense of engagement, which is arguably a prerequisite for the development of self-organisation.

It could be suggested that the balance, within union organising strategies, between the recruitment of new members and more relational approaches to stimulating grass-roots activism, reflects the challenges posed by different organisational contexts. But within both approaches, the union must have the commitment and the resources to support the mentoring, development and training of new representatives and to provide a context in which strong, trusting relationships between members and the union, and crucially between union activists and officers, can be built.

A further criticism of union organising has come from US academic Paul Jarley, who argues that union organising is essentially insular and does not extend outside the workplace to the hard-to-reach groups with which unions must engage. Therefore, he argues that union renewal strategies need to *recreate community in the workplace'* by focusing on people rather than issues and building *'personal relationships among all members of the work group in ways that create an emotional bond among the workers and between the workers and the union leadership'* (Jarley, 2005: 12–13).

More recently in the UK, there has been a greater focus on 'community organising' whereby trade unions have attempted to develop strategic alliances with community groups (McBride and Greenwood, 2009; Wills and Simms, 2004). By forming networks in this way, it is hoped that unions can achieve key goals – for example, increasing wages for the lowest paid – but also engage with groups of workers who otherwise are resistant to, or have little inclination towards, joining trade unions. Perhaps the best-known recent example is the successful campaign conducted by London Citizens to persuade employers in the capital to pay the Living Wage – here, trade unions such as UNISON joined a coalition of church and other groups to lobby major corporations to pay their lowest-paid workers in London a wage significantly above the National Minimum Wage. Importantly, many of the workers involved were migrants to the UK, often employed on a part-time or temporary basis, and therefore typical of the groups that trade unions need to attract but often struggle to reach. Jane Holgate's (2014) international study of community organising found that there were opportunities for trade unions to extend organisation through building broader community alliances and, importantly, to find out the real needs, views and aspirations of their members and potential members. However, in the UK, there was a tendency for unions to adopt an instrumental attitude, looking for short-term organising gains, which hampered their ability to develop long-term and mutually beneficial relationships with community groups.

## 9.7 THE NON-UNION ALTERNATIVE?

The decline of trade unions in the UK has created what Towers (1997) called the 'representation gap', with no union members in more than three-quarters of workplaces and no on-site union representatives in more than nine out of ten workplaces. However, a key question is, have alternative, non-union forms of representation expanded to fill this gap? The short answer to this is no. Although there has been some growth in the incidence of non-union representatives in large private sector organisations, from 6% in 2004 to 11% in 2011, non-union representatives can be found in just 7% of British workplaces (van Wanrooy *et al*, 2013). These were more likely to be found in larger workplaces and, unlike union representatives, there was little difference in coverage between the public and private sectors, in which 13% and 18% of employees respectively had access to a non-union representative.

Interestingly, the roles played by union and non-union representatives appear to be very different. WERS2011 found that the three most common issues that union representatives spent time on were discipline and grievance (78%), health and safety (69%) and pay (61%). In contrast, 44%, 52% and 50% (respectively) of non-union representatives spent time on these matters.

## NON-UNION REPRESENTATIVES IN MARKS & SPENCER PLC

One of the foremost examples of non-union representation is operated by Marks & Spencer PLC. Marks & Spencer do not recognise trade unions and have actively resisted attempts by USDAW, UNITE and the GMB to organise their employees. The company has a network of elected employee representatives, who form their Business Involvement Group (BIG).

According to Marks & Spencer, 'through the BIG network, the Company informs, involves and consults with its people on the matters that affect them. The Company's commitment to BIG means that colleagues have the chance to voice their opinions and ideas, get answers and have their views represented when the business considers changes that affect them. This means everyone has an opportunity to positively influence the business we work in.'

BIG representatives are elected at business unit, regional and national level every five years. Formal consultative mechanisms at business unit, regional and national level are supplemented by regular informal meetings between employee representatives and managers. However, BIG representatives do not negotiate as such.

Importantly, unlike most non-union representatives, BIG representatives are trained by the company and have a relatively wide role, which includes accompanying employees at disciplinary or grievance hearings; representing employees' views either by raising issues on behalf of other staff, or by asking for colleagues' feedback as requested by management; and acting as a channel for communicating changes to employees. In addition, staff are encouraged to discuss their concerns with a representative before raising a grievance or appeal, and if they are facing disciplinary action.

At a CIPD event on 'the future of collective voice' held in 2007, Malcolm Heaven, then Chair of the Marks & Spencer National Business Involvement Group, outlined the details of a consultation exercise over significant changes to staff pensions. This involved a two-day workshop attended by the Chief Executive, HR Director and 850 employee representatives and the consideration of proposals and counter-proposals were considered over a 60–day period. He argued that this was an illustration of 'true consultation on a grand scale'. However, trade unions such as USDAW have argued that the BIG has done little to protect the terms and conditions of staff at Marks & Spencer.

The research to date also casts doubt on the effectiveness of non-union representation. One of the main difficulties facing non-union representatives is that, unlike their union counterparts, their rights to paid time off and protection against detriment or dismissal are limited to specific situations and contexts:

- Acting as a health and safety representative
- Representative duties in relation to health and safety
- Acting as a representative under the Information and Consultation of Employees (ICE) regulations
- Membership of a European Works Council
- Representative duties in relation to pensions.

Therefore, non-union representatives have no rights to time off in regards to the core representative roles in discipline and grievance, and also no rights in relation to day-to-day organisational consultative structures. Furthermore, if an employer was to take disciplinary action against or dismiss a non-union representative for activity that fell outside those contexts outlined previously, they would not be protected.

This has three effects: first, it may deter employees from taking on a representative role; second, it means that non-union representatives are dependent on the support and patronage of the employer; and third, it will inevitably restrict the representative in their activities. The independence of non-union representatives is also questionable given the fact that fewer than 40% are elected, with the majority either taking on the role unopposed or selected by the employer (Moore *et al*, 2008). In addition, while trade union representatives have potential sanctions, such as strike action or litigation, at their disposal to lever concessions from management, this is not the case for non-union representatives. If a non-union representative encouraged fellow employees to withdraw their labour, they would not have the immunity given to industrial action officially sanctioned by trade unions. In addition, they are in no position to support employees in taking legal action against their employer.

There is clear evidence from the WERS series of data that non-union representatives generally have more positive views about the state of employment relations in their organisations compared with their unionised counterparts. Furthermore, WERS2011 found that non-union representatives were more likely to trust managers to act with honesty and integrity (93%) than their union counterparts (66%), and mutual trust between managers and non-union representatives was much higher than between union representatives and managers (van Wanrooy *et al*, 2013). This could simply be because relationships are more positive in non-unionised workplaces or reflect the fact that trade unions are more likely to be organised in workplaces in which there are employment relations challenges. However, it could also reflect a greater acquiescence on the part of non-union representatives. Certainly Charlwood and Forth (2009) found that non-union representatives appeared not to be valued and appreciated by the employees they covered.

There is evidence that the non-unionised channels of representation tend to be more effective when there is a threat of greater union presence (Gollan, 2006). For example, it could be argued that Marks & Spencer has made a serious commitment to its BIG representatives, because of the consistent attempts by unions, such as USDAW, to organise its staff and so force recognition. In addition, research conducted by Charlwood and Angrave (2014) for Acas suggests that although there has not been a substantial growth in non-union representation:

'following the introduction of the ICE regulations, there were noticeable signs of a more extensive and formal role for non-union representatives following their introduction; more regular meetings between management and representatives, representatives spending more time on representative activities and being provided with more facilities by management to undertake their representative role.' (7)

## 9.8 SUMMARY

This chapter has focused in some detail on the challenges facing trade unions in the UK. This may seem questionable given the fact that they represent only one in four workers; however, they remain the main source of employee representation in British workplaces and retain significant influence in many larger organisations. Although there has been some increase in the prevalence of non-union forms of representation, these have not filled the gap left by union decline, and there are significant questions over their ability to provide effective and independent support for employees. The key problem is that non-union employee 'voice' is currently almost totally dependent on the patronage of the employer, and representatives lack credibility and the power to threaten and enforce any realistic sanctions.

In the absence of the development of any alternative, the role of trade unions in providing effective representation remains a core issue in employment relations. As we argue throughout this book, representation does not just provide support to employees but can facilitate the management and resolution of conflict and underpin notions of justice and fairness, which form the basis of employee engagement. The future of trade unions and employee representation is therefore an important question for both employees and employers. However, unions face significant challenges: the nature of work in the UK has changed rapidly in recent years, moving away from the full-time, male, skilled manual workers who formed the bedrock of union organisation. The 'tradition' of trade union membership is also fading as future generations enter workplaces with no visible signs of unionisation, and who have little familial link with the labour movement. Interestingly, evidence suggests that young workers are not necessarily anti-union and often exhibit a collective identity around shared problems (Tailby and Pollert, 2011). The problem for unions is that young workers often neither understand nor identify with trade unions. At the same time, unions are often seen as ineffective or irrelevant, but there is little public appetite for measures to give unions greater influence.

Unions have placed significant faith in renewing organisation by rebuilding grass-roots organisation. However, while there are some examples where this has generated positive results, organising has tended to consolidate union density and influence where it was already relatively strong. Therefore, if unions are to have a future and if structures of employee representation are to survive, it could be argued that unions need to rebuild a sense of 'community in the workplace' and reach out to 'communities of workers' in wider society by both developing campaigns over a broad range of issues and becoming more strategic and flexible in the way they seek to connect with potential members.

## KEY LEARNING POINTS

1  Trade unions developed in response to the rapid industrialisation of Britain in the nineteenth century. They subsequently grew to represent the majority of workers in British workplaces by the end of the 1970s.

2  The main functions of trade unions are to negotiate on behalf of their members in order to defend and improve their terms and conditions of work. They also provide support and representation to individual members who may have a problem at work. This latter role has come to dominate the work done by unions as the scale and scope of collective bargaining has been curtailed.

3  The membership of trade unions and their influence in employment relations has been rapidly eroded in the last four decades. This is due to a combination of factors: deindustrialisation; more ambivalent (or even hostile) attitudes to trade unions on the part of government and employers; globalisation; and reduced power and effectiveness.

4  Trade unions have adopted a variety of approaches in an attempt to manage, arrest and reverse this decline. This includes: union mergers to reduce costs and increase political influence; the provision of a wide range of member benefits and incentives; the development of workplace partnerships with employers; investment in grass-roots organising in an attempt to build capacity and union activity. The evidence suggests that while a greater focus on organising may have slowed the rate of decline, it has not, as yet, significantly strengthened union power and influence.

5  Non-union forms of representation have not filled the gap left by trade unions. Furthermore, research suggests that they often lack credibility with employees. This is in part due to the fact that they have relatively few statutory protections and lack independence from the employer. They also tend to be less well-trained than their trade union counterparts.

6  Perhaps the most significant developments in the representation of employee interests has come through broad community alliances such as London Citizens, who waged a successful campaign for the Living Wage in the capital. Trade unions are now placing greater emphasis on building coalitions with such groups, and this may be one way that they can begin to rebuild some of the influence that they have lost.

REVIEW QUESTIONS

**?**

1   What were the main reasons for the development of trade unions? To what extent does the rationale for trade unions still exist today?

2   Do you think that effective representation has benefits to the employer? From the perspective of an employer, what are the main advantages and disadvantages of recognising, and managing with, trade unions?

3   What are the main reasons for trade union decline? Why do you think that employees in your workplace are not trade union members?

4   If you were employed as a marketing specialist by a trade union to enhance their image and boost their appeal to younger workers, what would be the main elements of your campaign?

5   Do you have non-union representatives in your workplace? If yes, how effective are they and why do you think this is?

6   Do you think that non-union representatives can fill the place left by trade unions?

7   What are the main barriers to trade unions successfully revitalising their workplace capacity and organisation? To what extent do you think that alliances with broader community groups offer a way forward for trade unions?

**EXPLORE FURTHER**

BAILEY, J., PRICE, R. and ESDERS, L. (2010) Daggy shirts, daggy slogans? Marketing unions to young people. *Journal of Industrial Relations.* Vol 52, No 1. pp43–60.

CHARLWOOD, A. and TERRY, M. (2007) Twenty-first century models of employee representation: structure, processes and outcomes. *Industrial Relations Journal.* Vol 38, No 4. pp320–337.

FERNIE, S. (2005) The future of British unions: introduction and conclusions. In FERNIE, S. and METCALF, D. (eds). *Trade unions: resurgence or demise?* London: Routledge. pp1–18.

FREEMAN, R. and MEDOFF, J. (1984) *What do unions do?* New York: Basic Books.

GOLLAN, P. (2006) Representation at Suncorp – what do the employees want? *Human Resource Management Journal.* Vol 16, No 3. pp268–286.

HOLGATE, J. (2014) An international study of trade union involvement in community organising: same model, different outcomes. *British Journal of Industrial Relations.* Vol 53, No 3. pp460–483.

JARLEY, P. (2005) Unions as social capital: renewal through a return to the logic of mutual aid? *Labor Studies Journal.* Vol 29, No 4. pp1–26.

SAUNDRY, R. and MCKEOWN, M. (2014) Relational organising in a healthcare setting: a qualitative study. *Industrial Relations Journal.* Vol 44, No 5–6. pp533–547.

SAUNDRY, R. and WIBBERLEY, G. (2014) Contemporary union organising in the UK – back to the future. *Labor Studies Journal.* Vol 38, No 4. pp281–299.

SIMMS, M., HOLGATE, J. and HEERY, E. (2013) *Union voices – tactics and tensions in UK organising.* Ithaca, NY: ILR Press.

TAILBY, S. and POLLERT, A. (2011) Non-unionised young workers and organising the unorganised. *Economic and Industrial Democracy.* Vol 32, No 3. pp499–522.

**Website links**

www.citizensuk.org/ is the website for Citizens UK, which contains details in relation to community organising and campaigning activity.

www.livingwage.org.uk/what-living-wage is the website for the Living Wage Foundation in which information regarding the campaign for the living wage can be found.

www.tuc.org.uk/ is the website for the Trades Union Congress, which contains a wealth of information and useful research relating to trade unions in the UK and their role in contemporary workplaces.

www.tuc.org.uk/union-issues/organising-academy is the website for the TUC Organising Academy. This provides details of the work of the TUC in training and developing new union activists.

# CHAPTER 10

# Employee Involvement and Participation

## OVERVIEW

In recent years, employers have looked to find new ways of improving performance by developing mechanisms to encourage the involvement and participation of employees in the life of the organisation. In the context of union decline, methods of employee involvement and participation (EIP) have taken on an added significance and provide the employer an opportunity to engage directly with their employees. This has been driven by clear business imperatives, and in the first part of this chapter we explore and analyse the business case for EIP. This includes: improved economic performance, improved quality of product/service, increased productivity, and a more informed workforce that is more likely to accept the legitimacy of management action. We then explore the breadth and depth of EIP before going on to consider the attributes of specific processes and practices such as team briefing, profit-sharing and joint consultation. In particular, we focus on the example of the introduction of the Information and Consultation of Employees (ICE) Regulations. Finally, we examine the evidence in relation to the impact of EIP before concluding by offering a model that incorporates EIP within the broader conceptual framework of employment relations and offers a bridge to the next part of the book.

## LEARNING OUTCOMES

When you have completed this chapter, you should be able to:

- understand and critically evaluate the business case for EIP
- identify and explain specific employee involvement and participation practices, and critically assess their importance and impact
- develop an informed view as to the appropriate employee involvement and participation practices for different organisational contexts
- explain the legal framework surrounding the provision of information and consultation arrangements
- understand the role of EIP within the overarching concept of employee voice.

## 10.1 INTRODUCTION

The term 'employee involvement and participation' (EIP) captures a range of techniques ranging from direct communication with employees to indirect or representative participation through workplace committees or working with trade unions. These types of EIP vary according to the level of influence they give to employees, the scope of the subject matter for discussion and the level in the organisation at which the mechanisms operate. The amount of influence employees have in decision-making, in particular, is regarded as important because it is likely to shape broader organisational outcomes (Marchington *et al*, 1992).

Employee involvement is generally seen as directed at individual employees. By introducing employee involvement mechanisms, management seeks to gain the consent of the employees to their proposed actions on the basis of shared objectives rather than purely control (Walton, 1985; Hyman and Mason, 1995). These mechanisms are aimed at enabling individual employees to inform management decision-making processes. Typically, they are based on management sharing information directly with individuals or groups of employees in return for their views. Alternatively, employee involvement (EI) can also involve 'task-based' control of decision-making for employees at the individual job level of the organisation. This encompasses the notions of 'job enlargement' and 'job enrichment' (Dundon and Wilkinson, 2013: 492). Although critics might rightly suggest that these types of EI initiatives remain largely unitarist in design, it can also be argued that they increase job satisfaction by reducing the routinisation of work and allowing greater autonomy. However, employee involvement is not about employees sharing power (jointly regulating the employment relationship) with management; the decision whether to accept, or reject, the views of the employees rests with management alone.

In contrast, employee participation concerns the extent to which employees play an active role within the decision-making machinery of the organisation. This is generally achieved through indirect collective representation in the form of joint consultation, collective bargaining and board-level worker representation. These systems focus on collectively representative structures (Hyman and Mason, 1995). This approach is often termed 'power-based' control as employees 'have a real say' in the decision-making process across all levels of the organisation. It is also underpinned by legal rights and the bargaining power of labour (Dundon and Wilkinson, 2013: 488–490). Crucially, the context of employment relations and the balance of workplace relations will determine the extent to which EI and EP exist in an organisation. In general, employers are unlikely to invest in EIP practices unless there is a clear business case. Otherwise, powerful trade unions may demand robust structures of employment participation. At the same time, employers may seek to challenge the influence of unions by developing direct channels of employment involvement (Ramsay, 1977, 1980; Marchington, 2005).

## ? REFLECTIVE ACTIVITY 10.1

Explain the difference in meaning between the terms 'employee involvement' and 'employee participation'.

## 10.2 WHY INVOLVE EMPLOYEES?

In contrast to the traditional bureaucratic control of employees underpinned by a largely 'Taylorist' approach to employment relations, it is argued that increasing international competition and technological change means employees need to have higher skill levels and must be able to work more flexibly. According to Walton (1985), in this environment, employers need to maximise employee commitment by: broadening the scope of jobs (job enlargement) to combine planning and implementation; giving employees new skills so that they can work across different functions; and allowing teams to control how they deliver their objectives, making them accountable for employee performance.

Under an employee commitment strategy, according to Walton, performance expectations are high and serve not to establish minimum standards but to emphasise continuous improvement and reflect the requirements of the marketplace. As a result, pay and reward strategies focus less on the principles of job evaluation and more on the importance of group achievement and concerns for gain-sharing and profit-sharing. Equally important, argues Walton, is the challenge of giving employees some assurance of security by offering them priority in training and retraining, as old jobs are destroyed and new ones created. This also involves providing them with the means to be heard on such issues as production methods, problem-solving and HR practices.

This rests on a management philosophy that accepts the multiplicity of interests within an organisational community – owners, employees, customers and the public. At the heart of this approach is an acceptance that growing employee commitment will lead to improved performance. Furthermore, there is clear evidence that employees want to be part of a successful organisation which provides a good income and an opportunity for development and secure employment (Bennett, 2014a; IPA, 2003, 2004, 2015).

There are a number of reasons why greater employee involvement should deliver efficiency gains. First, employees generally are better informed about their work tasks and processes than their managers, and are therefore better placed to achieve enhanced performance. Second, advocates of employee involvement hypothesise that its associated practices provide employees with greater intrinsic rewards from work than from other forms of workplace management. It is said that these rewards will increase job satisfaction and in turn enhance employee motivation to achieve new goals. It is also argued that by granting workers greater access to management information, mutual trust and commitment will be increased, thereby reducing labour turnover. In addition, empowering workers reduces the need for complex systems of control and hence leads to improved efficiency.

Similarly, financial forms of employee involvement are said to improve productivity and performance for a number of reasons. First, it is argued that employees will work more effectively because they can all gain by co-operating with each other rather than competing amongst themselves. Second, some argue that performance-related pay schemes indirectly enhance employee effort and commitment by improving communication about company performance and by educating employees about the significance/importance of profitability. There are also those who suggest that such payment schemes increase employees' identification with the organisation (Gilman, 2013: 189–190).

The potential organisational benefits are summarised by Ramsay (1996) along a number of different dimensions: attitudes; business awareness; incentives and motivation; employee influence and ownership; and trade unions. Therefore, employee involvement can improve attitudes through higher morals and greater loyalty. Better information about the rationale for decisions can help employees to understand decisions and reduce resistance to change. The impact on employee incentives and motivation is varied and can simply result in passive acceptance of managerial authority and change, or more active engagement whereby employees will increase productivity and performance. Effective involvement can also have personal effects by making work more interesting and satisfying. It can also be argued that involvement can provide employees with greater 'ownership' of their role, giving them greater control and tying their interests to those of the company.

Table 10.1 Management objectives in introducing employee involvement practices

| Attitudes | Improved morale<br>Increased loyalty and commitment<br>Enhanced sense of involvement<br>Increased support for management |
|---|---|
| Business awareness | Better, more accurately informed<br>Greater interest<br>Better understanding of reason for management action<br>Support for/reduced resistance to management action |
| Incentive and motivation | *Passive*<br>Accept changes in working practices<br>Accept mobility across jobs<br>Accept new technology<br>Accept management authority<br><br>*Active*<br>Improve quality/reliability<br>Increase productivity/effort<br>Reduce costs<br>Enhance co-operation and team spirit<br><br>*Personal*<br>Greater job interest<br>Greater job satisfaction<br>Employee development |
| Employee influence and ownership | Increase job control<br>Employee suggestions<br>Increase employee ownership in the company<br>Increase employees' ties to the company performance and profitability |
| Trade unions | *Anti-union*<br>Keep unions out<br>Representative needs outside union channels<br>Win hearts and minds of employees<br><br>*With union*<br>Gain union co-operation<br>Draw on union advice<br>Restrain union demands |

Source: Ramsay (1996)

However, as we can see in relation to trade unions, employee involvement can have complex and contrasting objectives. It can be used to try to develop co-operative partnership with unions, but at the same time can be seen to bypass traditional representative channels and win the 'hearts and minds' of employees.

**?    REFLECTIVE ACTIVITY 10.2**

Outline the business case for introducing employee involvement practices in an organisation.

## 10.3 CONCEPTS AND PRACTICES OF EMPLOYEE VOICE

A term increasingly used by practitioners and writers to capture the type of theory and practice associated with EI and EP is employee voice. Figure 10.1 shows Marchington and Wilkinson's (2012: 348) conceptualisation of the four key aspects of involvement and participation in the context of employee voice. This suggests that the ability of employees to influence decision-making is a function of: the scope and subject matter of EIP; the level in the organisation at which involvement and participation takes place, and also the specific form of EIP.

Figure 10.1 The key elements of EIP

| The degree of involvement indicates the extent to which workers or their representatives are able to influence management decisions | | |
|---|---|---|
| The scope of decisions open to influence by workers relates to the type of subject matter dealt with in the participation arena, ranging from the trivial to the strategic. | The level in the organisation at which workers (or their representatives) are involved in management decisions. | The different forms – for instance, from face-to-face meetings to collective bargaining. |

To this we can usefully add the concept of 'breadth' of participation (Cox *et al*, 2006) with respect to how many schemes are running at the same time, or as 'multi-complimentary practices' (Cox *et al*, 2007: 18). Marchington *et al* (2007) have subsequently identified the breadth or form of these EIP practices to include:

- Direct downward communication from managers to employees
  - *newsletters*
  - *email*
  - *intranet*
  - *noticeboards*
- Direct two-way communication between management and employees
  - *team briefings*
  - *workplace meetings*
  - *staff newsletters*
  - *cascading of information via the management team*
- Direct upward feedback from employees
  - *problem-solving groups*
  - *suggestion schemes*
  - *employee/staff attitude surveys*

- Direct financial participation
  - *profit-related bonus schemes*
  - *deferred profit-sharing schemes*
  - *employee share ownership schemes*
- Indirect participation
  - *employee representative structures, eg Works Councils*
  - *joint consultative committees.*

We can further include the 'depth' of EIP as measured by their regularity, the power actually given to employees (Cox *et al*, 2006) or how 'embedded' the aspect of voice is in the workplace (Cox *et al*, 2007: 18). As Dundon and Wilkinson note, depth is a crucial concept in analysing the extent to which employees, 'either directly or indirectly, can influence those decisions normally reserved for management' (2013: 489).

---

### INDICATORS OF DEPTH OF EIP (EMPLOYEE INVOLVEMENT AND PARTICIPATION)

*Proportion of employees participating in problem-solving groups.* This reflects management's commitment to involving as many people as possible in EIP, and employee interest in participating.

*Amount of time allocated to employee questions during team briefings.* This reflects management's willingness to give employees the opportunity to clarify their understanding of information received and to hear employee views. It can also indicate the degree of employee willingness to voice their opinions and their level of trust in management.

*Frequency of team briefings.* Greater frequency may indicate greater importance of the group. Less frequency may indicate waning interest in them or the onset of using them only for considering less urgent priorities.

*Permanence of problem-solving groups.* This indicates commitment to sustaining EIP over time and perceived utility to management.

*Free and open method of selecting employee representatives for joint consultative committees* (JCCs). This demonstrates management's willingness to let employees choose their own representative and is indicative of commitment to fairness and efforts to build trust.

*Frequency of JCC meetings.* Greater frequency may indicate greater importance of the JCC. Less frequency may indicate less interest in it or the onset of using JCCs only for considering less urgent priorities.

Marchington *et al* (1992)

---

These levels of distinction are extremely helpful from both a theoretical and practical basis in analysing more completely the type, impact and 'concurrence' of employee voice initiatives (Bennett, 2010). Using these conceptualisations, we can see more clearly the distinction between EI, or direct approaches, to facilitating employee voice and EP, or indirect strategies.

More recently, Marchington's (2015) transnational study of 25 organisations, and the extent to which EIP was embedded within them, offers further insight into the differences in channels used for employee voice. In particular, his analysis suggests that the 'breadth'

## DIRECT AND INDIRECT ELEMENTS OF EMPLOYEE VOICE IN THE PUBLIC SECTOR

**Bennett's (2010) research on EIP, based on a survey of over 140 organisations in the public sector, revealed a mix of 'concurrent' direct and indirect initiatives. The results indicated a healthy 'breadth' of complementary direct voice mechanisms in the 141 organisations surveyed:**

- 'Downward communication' techniques such as newsletters were present in 72% of workplaces surveyed, while 75% used the company intranet.
- 'Upward problem-solving' – 44% of organisations had suggestion schemes, 72% utilised email for employee voice purposes and 69% conducted employee surveys.
- Face-to-face meetings with a supervisor or line manager occurred at 78% of sites, and team briefings at 81% of the organisations surveyed.

**There was also evidence in respect of 'depth' of EIP:**

- 53% of the study's respondents reported monthly team briefings and 32% weekly meetings.
- Over 59% of the organisations surveyed offered employees their input for at least 25% of the meeting.
- The 'scope' or typical content of meetings is discussed later in the section on team briefings.

**Finally, there was also widespread use of indirect voice through trade unions:**

- 91% reported that terms and conditions were covered by negotiation and 72% by consultation.
- Health and safety was negotiated on at 90% of the organisations and was a topic for consultation at 86%.
- Equal opportunities issues figured in 73% of negotiations and 77% of consultations.
- Training and development was a subject of negotiation at 66% of the organisations and 75% on the consultation agenda.
- The organisation of work figured in negotiations in 61% of organisations and at 77% for the purpose of consultation.
- Financial plans were the subject of negotiation at just 36% of organisations researched and consulted on at 44% of those organisations.

Overall, the figures suggest the presence of a substantial negotiation and consultation agenda and are evidence that the unions in the public sector continue to play a valuable role in providing a route for employee voice.

Source: Bennett (2010: 451–452)

and 'depth' of EIP is shaped in part by the existence of high-trust relations between management and unions. Where management was willing to work with unions, employee voice had greater breadth and depth, particularly in terms of representative EIP. In contrast, devolution of HRM to line managers was 'associated with greater breadth and depth of direct and informal EIP, especially if "engagement" was a criterion for performance management of line managers' (2015: 15). This confirms the growing importance of line managers in maintaining channels of direct voice, as discussed in Chapters 7 and 8.

?    REFLECTIVE ACTIVITY 10.3

What employee involvement and participation practices operate in your organisation (or one with which you are familiar)? How, and why, have the various practices been introduced? Has the distribution of the employee involvement practices changed over time?

## 10.4 EIP IN PRACTICE

The next section takes a more detailed look at how EIP processes work in practice. Ramsay (1996) usefully divides employee involvement and participation initiatives into four broad types:

- Communications and briefing systems – which include downward and upward communications systems
- Task and work group involvement – which includes teamworking, quality circles and total quality management programmes
- Financial participation – which embraces profit-sharing, profit-related pay and share ownership schemes
- Representative [involvement and] participation.

### 10.4.1 COMMUNICATION AND BRIEFING SYSTEMS

Employee communications involves the provision and exchange of information and instructions, which enable an organisation to function effectively and its employees to be properly informed about developments. It covers the information to be provided, the channels along which it passes, and the way it is relayed. Communication is concerned with the interchange of information and ideas within an organisation. This can take the form of 'one way' communication from management to their workforce, or 'two way', which while also a form of direct voice, is based on an element of information exchange between the two parties (Dundon and Rollinson, 2011: 284).

With the trend towards flatter management structures and the devolution of responsibilities to individuals, it is increasingly important that individual employees also have the opportunity to influence what happens to them at work (Acas, 2014).

## ADVANTAGES OF GOOD EMPLOYEE COMMUNICATIONS

**Improved organisational performance** – time spent communicating at the outset of a new project or development can minimise subsequent rumours and misunderstanding.

**Improved management performance and decision-making** – allowing employees to express their views can help managers arrive at sound decisions that are more likely to be accepted by the employees as a whole.

**Improved employee performance and commitment** – employees will perform better if they are given regular, accurate information about their jobs such as updated technical instructions, targets, deadlines and feedback. Their commitment is also likely to be enhanced if they know what the organisation is trying to achieve and how they as individuals can influence decisions.

**Greater trust** – discussing issues of common interest and allowing employees an opportunity of expressing their views can engender improved management– employee relations.

**Increased job satisfaction** – employees are more likely to be motivated if they have a good understanding of their job and how it fits into the organisation as a whole, and are actively encouraged to express their views and ideas.

Acas (2014)

The mix of methods selected to form a communication strategy will be determined by the size and structure of the organisation, its employment relations perspective and, to a degree, where the relative balance of power lies within that company. Two main methods of communication can be distinguished. First, there are face-to-face methods, which are both direct and swift and enable discussion, questioning and feedback to take place. The main formal face-to-face methods of communications are:

- *group meetings* – meetings between managers and the employees for whom they are responsible
- *cascade networks* – a well-defined procedure for passing information quickly, used mainly in large or disparately widespread organisations
- *large-scale meetings* – meetings that involve all employees in an organisation or at an establishment, with presentations by a director or senior managers; these are a good channel for presenting the organisation's performance or long-term objectives
- *interdepartmental briefings* – meetings between managers in different departments that encourage a unified approach and reduce the scope for inconsistent decision-making, particularly in larger organisations.

Second, there are written methods. These are most effective where the need for the information is important or permanent, the topic requires detailed explanation, the audience is widespread or large, and there is a need for a permanent record of it. The chief methods of written communications include company handbooks, employee information notes, house journals and newsletters, departmental bulletins, notices and individual letters to employees. Electronic mail is useful for communicating with employees in scattered or isolated locations, and audio-visual aids are particularly useful for explaining technical developments or financial performance.

Crucially, communications strategies, policies and techniques need senior management support and they require discipline to follow them through. We have noted elsewhere the potential for social media to be utilised in HRM practice. It is also being advocated specifically with respect to communication strategy. Silverman *et al*'s (2013) recent report for the CIPD, for instance, sets out a strong case for making surveys more interesting and user friendly, particularly if conducted online. They also identify the potential of 'blogs' and 'discussion forums' to facilitate online communities, through which employees can share their views collectively on issues of interest to them and the organisation. Significantly, the trend to also use more conventional online methods of communication is supported by WERS findings. They show that the use of emails to staff in all workplaces is up 14% from 2004 to 49% in 2011 (van Wanrooy *et al*, 2013: 65).

### ? REFLECTIVE ACTIVITY 10.4

What sort of communications strategy has your organisation adopted? Critically assess its effectiveness. How do you think social media could be used in your organisation to enhance EIP?

## 10.4.2 TEAM BRIEFINGS

Of all the communication methods in use, team briefing is perhaps the most systematic in the provision of top–down information. The latest findings from the WERS series show that they remain popular. In fact, briefings that set aside 25% or more time for questions from team members showed an increase across all workplaces from 37% in 2004 to 40% in 2011 (van Wanrooy *et al*, 2013: 65). Briefings work by information cascading down through various management tiers, being conveyed by each immediate supervisor or team leader to a small group of employees, the optimum number being between four and 20. In this way, employee queries are answered. This takes place throughout all levels in the organisation, the information eventually being conveyed by supervisors and/or team leaders to shop-floor employees.

On each occasion, the information received is supplemented by 'local' news of more immediate relevance to those being briefed. Meetings tend to be short but designed to help develop the 'togetherness' of a work group, especially where different grades of employees are involved in the team. Each manager is a member of a briefing group and is also responsible for briefing a team. The system is designed to ensure that all employees from the managing director to the shop floor are fully informed of matters affecting their work. Leaders of each briefing session prepare their own brief, consisting of information that is relevant and task-related to the employees in the group. The brief is then supplemented with information passed down from higher levels of management. Any employee questions raised that cannot be answered at once are answered in written form within a few days. Although team briefing is not a consultative process, question-and-answer sessions can clarify understanding and give employees the feeling of a measure of input. In terms of the range of topics covered in team briefings, Bennett's research findings on employee voice in the public sector are typical in the experiences of the authors. They included 'top down' issues, such as company strategy and performance, future plans, organisational finance and new initiatives. There was also discussion on 'day-to-day' issues, such as reaching KPIs, team plans and workloads, and customer and technical issues (2010: 451–452).

There are, however, practical problems to be borne in mind in introducing team briefing. First, if the organisation operates on a continuous shift-working basis, is it technically feasible for team briefings to take place, since the employees are working all the time except for their rest breaks? Second, management has to be confident that it can sustain a flow of relevant and detailed information, and also, managers need the skills and support to deliver information in a coherent and clear manner. Third, if the organisation recognises unions, the management cannot act in such a manner that a union believes management is attempting to undermine its influence. Team briefings are highly unlikely to succeed if the relations between management and the representatives of its employees are distrustful.

## 10.4.3 EMPLOYEE ATTITUDE SURVEYS

As we have already noted in our discussion on employee engagement in Chapter 7, surveys are an important upward channel of communication from the employees to management. Like team briefings, they continue to be a popular method of facilitating direct employee voice in the UK. The latest WERS data indicates that across all workplaces, a survey had taken place in the last two years at 38% of workplaces. This was up 3% from 2004. Interestingly, and supporting the findings of Bennett's (2010) researched discussed earlier, in the public sector the proportion of workplaces using surveys was up to 75% in 2011 from 61% in 2004.

Management normally uses an employee attitude survey to obtain specific data on employee perceptions of fairness, pay systems, training opportunities and employee awareness of an organisation's business strategy and long-term goals. Employee attitude surveys can:

- gather staff's views on management proposals for organisational change; ideally to identify and thus pre-empt any unwanted consequences that may lead to major employment relations difficulties
- help managers make internal comparisons of employee morale and behaviour across a number of departments and sites
- provide employee views on specific HRM policies such as the operation of the disciplinary and grievance procedures
- provide data that can be used in problem-solving, planning and decision-making.

However, as Silverman *et al* note in their report on the use of social media in communications strategy, the traditional employee survey can be tedious to complete, too 'tick box' and not able to capture real qualitative feedback. In addition, their findings may seem less relevant to employees if, as often is perceived to be the case, the results are delayed in their publication (2013: 11). However, fundamentally, we must remember that it is not the results alone that are the aim of the process; feedback must be acted upon by senior management if the process is to retain its legitimacy.

### 10.4.4 TASK AND WORK GROUP INVOLVEMENT

The objective of task and work-group involvement practices is to tap into employees' knowledge of their jobs, either at the individual level or through the mechanism of small groups. These practices are designed to increase the stock of ideas within the organisation, to encourage co-operative relations at work and to justify change. Task-based involvement encourages employees to extend the range and type of tasks they undertake at work. It involves practices such as job redesign, job enrichment, teamworking and job enlargement. Job enrichment involves the introduction of more elements of responsibility into the work tasks. Job enlargement centres on increasing the number and diversity of tasks carried out by an individual employee, thereby increasing his or her work experience and skill.

Teamworking is seen by its advocates as a vehicle for greater task flexibility and co-operation, as well as for extending the desire for quality improvement. However, Geary (1994) noted that, in reality, at one level it merely involves the rotation of members of a team between tasks with no real upskilling or greater independence on offer. In contrast, in its advanced form it offered the opportunity for a team of workers to work with a real measure of autonomy in terms of planning and design of the work process. Teamworking provides management with the opportunity to remove and/or amend the role of the supervisor and to appoint team leaders. However, research by Gapper (1990) has indicated that management time saved in traditional supervision and control may be more than offset by the need to give support to individuals and groups.

### ? REFLECTIVE ACTIVITY 10.5

What is the extent of teamworking in your organisation? Critically reflect on its utilisation.

### 10.4.5 TOTAL QUALITY MANAGEMENT (TQM) AND QUALITY CIRCLES (QCS)

Total quality management programmes derive from a belief that competitive advantage comes from high and reliable quality, achieved through the associated welding of more stable and mutual relationships between suppliers and customers. Largely unitarist in design, albeit utilised in both union and non-union workplaces, the total quality ethic is a philosophy of business management, the aim of which is to ensure complete customer satisfaction at every stage of production or service provision. Although TQM was initially driven by the demands of external customers, the concept was evolved into a more wide-ranging principle to encompass internal operations. TQM programmes are designed to ensure that each level and aspect of the organisation is involved in continuously improving the effectiveness and quality of the work to meet the requirements of both internal and external customers. A key element of TQM is the problem-solving function of employee quality circles.

QCs provide an element of 'upward problem-solving' that goes beyond the more limited communications techniques considered above, by allowing employees to discuss, identify and put forward as a group their ideas to management for improving working practices (Dundon and Wilkinson, 2013: 291). Typically, employees meet in small groups led by their supervisor on a regular basis for an hour or so to suggest ways of improving productivity and quality and reducing costs. The group meet 'offline' away from their immediate workplace (Marchington and Wilkinson, 2012: 352) in order to select the issues or problem they wish to address, collect the necessary information, and make suggestions to management on ways of overcoming the problem.

In some cases, the group is itself given authority to put its proposed solutions into effect, but more often it presents formal recommendations for action, which management then consider whether or not to implement. Quality circles encourage employees to identify not only with the quality of their own work but also with the management objectives of better quality and increased efficiency throughout the organisation. Members of a quality circle are not usually employee representatives but are members of the circle by virtue of their knowledge of the tasks involved in their jobs. Although prevalent to a degree in UK workplaces, their use has declined in recent years. The latest WERS survey indicated that this type of 'face-to-face' meeting fell from 18% of all workplaces in 2004 to 14% by 2011 (van Wanrooy et al, 2013: 64–65). Taken together with the increased use of direct communication processes, this tentatively suggests a worrying trend away from EIP processes which allow employees to actively shape their working experiences.

### 10.4.6 FINANCIAL PARTICIPATION

Offering employees a direct stake in the ownership and prosperity of the business for which they work is one of the most direct and tangible forms of employee involvement and participation. It is argued by its proponents that employees can acquire and develop a greater sense of identity with the business and an appreciation of the business needs. Employers also benefit. It is suggested that a financial stake gives employees increased enthusiasm for the success of the organisation and often for a voice in its operation. In its most developed form, employee share ownership means that employees become significant shareholders in the business, or even their own employer. Financial employee involvement and participation schemes link specific elements of pay and reward to the performance of the unit or the enterprise as a whole. They provide an opportunity for employees to share in the financial success of their employing organisation.

Profit-sharing schemes aim to increase employee motivation and commitment by giving employees an interest in the overall performance of the enterprise, by demonstrating that rewards accrue from co-operative effort even more than from individual effort. However, there are practical problems that must be addressed if profit-sharing schemes are to have the desired effect. A scheme has to contain clearly identifiable links between effort and reward. Individuals must not feel that no matter how hard they work in any year, that effort is not reflected in their share of the company's profits. Due account also has to be taken of cross-employee performance, or there is a risk of intergroup dissatisfaction in that some employees might believe other groups have received the same profit-share payment but have made less effort.

Profit-related pay is a mechanism through which employers can reward employees for their contribution to the business. It works by linking a proportion of employees' pay to the profits of the business for which they work. According to WERS2011, around one-third of workplaces had some form of profit-related pay. While the use of such schemes in the private sector looks to be fairly steady, their take-up in the public sector increased to 5% in 2011 compared with just 1% in 2004 (van Wanrooy et al, 2013). Employers may also seek to go a step further by giving employees a stake in the ownership of the enterprise. It grants them shareholder rights to participate in decisions confined to shareholders who vote at the Annual General Meeting. Employee share ownership schemes seek to give individual employees a long-term commitment to the organisation and not just to a short-term financial gain from a sharing of profit. However, employees may view the shares as simply a source of income and so lose the thread of the 'shared ownership' concept. There has been a significant reduction of the use of share ownership schemes, with the proportion of workplaces using such approaches falling from 16% in 2004 to just 9% in 2011 (van Wanrooy et al, 2013).

> **?    REFLECTIVE ACTIVITY 10.6**
>
> Do you have any financial participation schemes in your organisation? If you do, why were those particular schemes chosen? To what extent and why are they effective? If your organisation does not have any financial participation schemes, why doesn't it?

## 10.4.7 EMPLOYEE PARTICIPATION

Setting aside the key role played by trade unions in employee voice discussed in the previous chapter, the next main form of representative participation, we would argue, is joint consultation. Consultation is a process by which management and employees or their representatives jointly examine and discuss issues of mutual concern. It involves seeking acceptable solutions to problems through a genuine exchange of views and information. Unlike negotiation, consultation does challenge managerial prerogative – management must still make the final decision – but it does impose an obligation that the views of employees will be sought and considered before that final decision is taken. It affects the process through which decisions are made in so far as it commits management first to the disclosure of information at an early stage in the decision-making process, and second to take into account the collective views of the employees.

Consultation does not mean that employees' views always have to be acted upon – there may be good practical or financial reasons for not doing so. However, whenever employees' views are rejected, the reasons for rejection should be explained carefully. Equally, where the views and ideas of employees help to improve a decision, due credit and recognition should be given. Consultation requires a free exchange of ideas and views affecting the interests of employees. Almost any subject is therefore appropriate for discussion. However, both management and employees may wish to place some limits on the range of subjects open to consultation – because of trade confidences, perhaps, or because they are considered more appropriate for a negotiation forum – but whatever issues are agreed upon as being appropriate for discussion, it is important that they are relevant to the group of employees discussing them.

Although the subject matters of consultation are a matter for agreement between employer and employees, there are a number of laws and regulations that specifically require an employer to consult with recognised trade unions and other employee representatives. These include: health and safety matters, collective redundancies, transfers of undertaking and certain issues relating to occupational pension schemes. In addition, all organisations with more than 1,000 employees in European Union states and employing more than 150 people in each of two or more of these must establish a European Works Council with which the employer must consult at least once a year.

### 10.4.8 JOINT CONSULTATIVE COMMITTEES

As we note in Chapter 2, joint consultative committees (JCCs) have long been used as a means of employee consultation. They are composed of managers and employee representatives who come together on a regular basis to discuss issues of mutual concern. They may also be referred to as 'Works Councils', 'Employee Forums' and a range of other titles. They usually have a formal constitution that governs their operations. The number of members on a JCC depends on the size of the organisation. Management in organisations that operate over a number of different establishments sometimes prefer to consult with employees on a multisite basis rather than have a consultative committee for each establishment. These are referred to as 'higher-level committees'. The latest WERS results show that 46% of branch sites 'reported that a consultative committee operated at a higher level in their organisation' (van Wanrooy et al, 2013). This is down from 58% in 2004 but suggests that the JCC still remains a significant mechanism for consultation.

In their analysis of the latest WERS2011 data, Adam et al (2014) also highlight that JCCs tend to be more prevalent in: larger workplaces, workplaces that are part of a wider organisation and public sector workplaces (despite a marked decline since 2004 in the case of the latter).

From a practical perspective, the JCC should have as its focus a well-prepared agenda and all members should be given an opportunity of contributing to that agenda before it is circulated. The agenda is normally sent out in advance of the meeting so that representatives have a chance of consulting with their constituents prior to the committee meeting. Well-run JCCs are chaired effectively. It is important that employee representatives know exactly how much time they will be allowed away from their normal work to undertake their duties as a committee member and the facilities to which they are entitled. Employee representatives should not lose pay as a result of attending committee meetings. If joint consultation is to be effective, the deliberations of the committee must be reported back to employees as soon as possible. This can be done via briefing groups, news sheets, noticeboards and the circulation of committee minutes.

---

**?   REFLECTIVE ACTIVITY 10.7**

Do JCCs exist in your organisation? If so, what forms do they take, and are they successful? How could they be improved? If there are no JCCs, what mechanisms are in place to consult with the workforce?

---

## 10.5 THE INFORMATION AND CONSULTATION OF EMPLOYEES (ICE) REGULATIONS

In addition to the legal obligations to consult set out previously, the Information and Consultation of Employees (ICE) Regulations provide an obligation on all employers with more than 50 employees to establish consultation mechanisms where requested to do so by employees. Over a decade ago, the ICE Regulations introduced an added legal imperative for promoting greater employee involvement in the UK, which presented employers with new and specific obligations with respect to managing employment relations. These Regulations gave effect to the EU Directive establishing a general framework for informing and consulting employees in the European Union. They came into force on a sliding scale, depending on the number of employees in the organisation. Only undertakings employing fewer than 50 employees are exempt from the Regulations. An 'undertaking' means a legal entity, such as an individually incorporated company, whereas an 'establishment' is a physical entity such as a factory, plant, office or retail outlet.

### 10.5.1 REQUESTS FOR INFORMATION AND CONSULTATION ARRANGEMENTS

The Regulations require that where employees request the establishment of information and consultation arrangements in their undertakings, the request must be made in writing by 10% of the employees in the undertaking, subject to a minimum of 15 and a maximum of 2,500 employees (see Figure 10.2). In addition, if the employees making the request wish to remain anonymous, they may submit the request via the Central Arbitration Committee or a qualified independent person. An employer has one month in which to challenge the validity of this request. If there are any disputes about the validity of the employees' request, the final decision rests with the CAC.

### 10.5.2 REQUESTS IN THE CASE OF EXISTING AGREEMENTS

In a case where a valid request has been made by less than 40% of the workforce but an agreement providing for information and consultation already exists, the employer may, if he or she wishes, hold a ballot of the workforce to determine whether or not the workforce endorses the request. The ballot should be held as early as practicable but no earlier than 21 days after the request was made. If 40% of the employees endorse the employee request in the ballot, the employer is obliged to negotiate a new agreement on information and consultation. If fewer than 40% of employees endorse the request, the employer is under no obligation to negotiate a new agreement. Complaints may be brought to the CAC concerning the fact that there is no valid pre-existing agreement in place or that the ballot requirements have not been met. The Regulations also permit the employer to take the initiative to enter into negotiations for an information and consultation agreement without waiting for a request from employees. The negotiation process must start within one month of the employer's notifying the workforce of the intention to negotiate an agreement.

### 10.5.3 THE THREE-YEAR MORATORIUM

There are a number of circumstances in which an employee request (or an employer notification of an intention to negotiate an agreement) is not valid. These include where there has already been a request that has resulted in a negotiated agreement, or where, in the case of existing agreements, a request was not endorsed by a workforce ballot. Here, subsequent requests would not be allowed for a period of three years, unless there are material changes to the organisation or to the structure of the undertaking. This moratorium is intended to avoid repeated requests being made by employees and to prevent the employers from unilaterally overturning agreed agreements.

Figure 10.2 Procedures for establishing information and consultation agreements

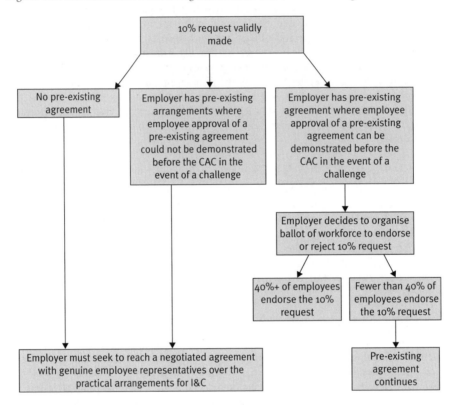

## 10.5.4 NEGOTIATIONS

Where a valid request has been made or an employer has notified the workforce that it intends to start negotiations, the employer must take the necessary steps to trigger the process. This includes making arrangements for employees to appoint or elect negotiating representatives. All employees must be entitled to participate in appointing or electing representatives, and must be represented by one of those appointed or elected. Negotiations are required to start within one month of the request/notification and may last for up to six months. This period can be extended without limit by agreement between the negotiating parties. Acas and other organisations can help the parties in reaching agreements.

The Regulations also set out a number of requirements that negotiated agreements must meet. These are that they must:

- be in writing and dated
- cover all the employees of the undertaking
- set out the circumstances in which employees will be informed and consulted – this may be either directly or via information and consultation representatives
- be signed by or on behalf of the employer
- be signed either by all or by a majority of the negotiating representatives and approved in writing by at least 50% of the employees or by 50% of employees who vote in a ballot.

Where the parties do not reach an agreement within the six-month time limit, or any extended period agreed by the parties, standard information and consultation provisions become applicable. The default requirements make it necessary for the employer to inform/consult elected employee representatives on business developments, employment trends and changes in work organisation or contractual regulations, including redundancies and business transfers. They also require the employer to arrange for a secret ballot to elect one information and consultation representative for every 50 employees or part thereof up to a maximum of 25.

## 10.5.5 ENFORCEMENT

Enforcement of agreements reached under these statutory procedures, or of the standard information and consultation provisions where they apply, is via complaints to the CAC and the Employment Appeals Tribunal. The maximum penalty that can be awarded against employers for non-compliance is £75,000. Employee representatives must not disclose information or documents designated by the employer as confidential. Employers may withhold information or documents if their disclosure could seriously harm or prejudice the undertaking.

## 10.5.6 VOLUNTARY AGREEMENTS

The Regulations accept that there is no single static model for information and consultation – no 'one size fits all'. The underlying principle of the Regulations is that UK experience in the area of information and consultation is built up through a wide variety of existing practices, all of which should be accommodated. Essentially, individual organisations are encouraged to develop their own arrangements as tailored to their particular circumstances, by means of voluntary agreements. Accordingly, the general thrust of the Regulations is on voluntarily negotiated agreements. However, in the final analysis, if such negotiations fail, employers come under an obligation to inform and consult in accordance with a set of fallback (default) provisions.

---

**?    REFLECTIVE ACTIVITY 10.8**

To what degree are you aware of the ICE Regulations? Has your organisation implemented consultation arrangements, or might it be based on the Regulations? Critically reflect on the advantages and disadvantages of adopting such arrangements.

---

## 10.5.7 IMPACT OF THE ICE REGULATIONS

After strong lobbying by UK employers and the Government to block the introduction of the EU Directive on national information and consultation (I&C), its implementation in the form of the Information and Consultation of Employees Regulations (2004) grabbed few contemporary headlines. Bennett's (2010) research in the public sector, for instance, highlighted a lack of knowledge amongst HR practitioners, but particularly union representatives with respect to the Regulations. Nevertheless, other early research on the initial effects of the legislation by Hall *et al* (2007), looking at a cross-section of 13 private sector companies with 150 or more employees where change was taking place, revealed some interesting findings. The researchers found that the key driver for the introduction or overhaul of information and consultation arrangements was an interest in effectively managing a crisis or major change, and that the companies studied had histories of commitment to employee involvement. For them, the Regulations provided both a stimulus to overhaul and extend information and consultation arrangements, and an indication of the direction and nature of the reform.

Management, in particular HR management, drove the detailed change, with little or no influence exerted by employees or unions. Voluntary arrangements (pre-existing agreements), often drawn up by management with little employee input, were the preferred route. The new structures, providing representation on a new or changed forum for all employees, reflected strong, managed acceptance of the link between effective employee participation and corporate performance through building trust and improving two-way communications. Employer commitment was reflected in the participation of top management.

Other factors shaped management behaviour, most particularly the presence of trade unions. Where unions were well established and accepted, little changed. Hall *et al* (2007), however, found cases where management hoped to use the new arrangements to move beyond trade-union-based 'bureaucratic' relationships into a wider and more flexible set of arrangements. However, this tended to meet with resistance from trade unions. They also found other cases where the new arrangements were used to repel attempts at union organising by providing employees with a non-union alternative form of representation.

The interaction between the new information and consultation arrangements, and the views found, gave rise to several interesting developments. Generally, where unions were recognised, companies agreed – not always readily – that existing union-based structures for negotiation should be protected and operate alongside the new, universal systems: a novel sort of 'dual channel'. A further conclusion was that information and consultation bodies established as part of union-exclusion strategies were engaging in extensive discussion of pay-related issues as part of a demonstration that they constituted viable alternatives to union-based arrangements. Most companies with a universal type system, with union representation sitting alongside others representing non-union employees. Hall *et al*'s (2007) research concluded that despite some initial misgivings, the union and non-union representatives appeared to work well together, sharing information and experience. The researchers pose the question whether such developments represent a 'toe in the door' for unions to extend their influence, as some employers fear, or whether they constitute a demonstration that unions are redundant since an equivalent representative function can be performed without them, as some unions fear.

Nonetheless, the information and consultation systems appeared to be appreciated by most managers and representatives, union and non-union, who had taken part. Employee representatives felt better informed. The new forums presented, in some cases for the first time, an opportunity to raise and resolve employees' concerns – for example, mobile telephone allowances, car-parking arrangements – for which there had previously been no obvious place to air them. Quick agreement on such matters raised the standing of the new arrangements in the eyes of affected employers. On the other hand, a number of employee representatives complained that on larger issues they were not being consulted and merely informed of decisions already taken. Some managers complained that after an initial flurry of interest, employee representatives were no longer raising agenda items and the system was increasingly employer-driven – again posing a risk to its long-term viability.

The same writers' subsequent and final report for the new Department of Business, Innovation and Skills, based on a longitudinal study of 25 organisations from across sectors in the UK, updated the initial analysis with some significant findings. Crucially, Hall *et al* concluded that:

'The statutory framework emerged as a factor of only limited significance in the case study organisations. Employees did not utilise their rights to "trigger" the Regulations and management, in most cases, did not regard their decision to introduce I&C arrangements as compliance driven.' (2010: 5)

In short, in most cases, new consultation arrangements would have been developed irrespective of the Regulations. This finding concurs with more recent evidence from WERS2011, which suggests that 'the ICE Regulations appear to have had no real effect on the spread of formal consultation arrangements' (van Wanrooy *et al*, 2013: 192; see also Adam *et al*, 2014). As van Wanrooy *et al* further argue, this could be explained by the way in which the regulations were drafted – providing employers with maximum flexibility and placing the onus on employees to initiate a request for the consultation arrangements. As we saw in Chapter 5, this is symptomatic of the way that UK governments of all parties have tried to limit the impact of EU legislation.

More recently, Dundon *et al*'s (2014) analysis of employers and trade unions in Ireland found that, aside from union ambivalence over the ICEs, the balance of power held by employers at all three levels of a transnational company allowed them to draw up a 'hegemonic' agenda for consultation with employees. This was underpinned by a neo-free market philosophy reflected in an emphasis on direct communication with staff and limited union involvement in decision-making. Burke's review of the efficacy of the ICEs, as a senior trade union officer, concludes by also stressing that 'setting up an ICE structure within a company can be extremely onerous with workers having to establish a 10% interest of the workforce by a petition and they almost certainly face a negative response from their employer' (2015: 1). Unsurprisingly, but legitimately for many, he calls for formal rules for requests to be negotiated between a recognised union and the employer.

Hall *et al* (2010: 3) also highlight this perceived 'advantage' to the employer, who remains the dominant partner in consultation. Nonetheless, they argue that the ICE Regulations do not threaten union organisation and instead offer an opportunity to extend their influence.

'It is arguably time for trade unions to reappraise their ambivalent approach to ICE. Fears of loss of recognition for collective bargaining and declining membership have not been borne out in the research. The operation of "hybrid" I&C bodies has generally been effective, subject to management willingness to consult, and has provided unions with access to senior management.' (2010: 7)

## 10.6 THE IMPACT OF EIP MECHANISMS

What is the evidence that EIP outcomes achieve the positive results claimed at the beginning of this chapter? The research of Marchington *et al* (2001) demonstrated that employers in the 18 organisations they studied valued the voice of the employee in contributing to management decision-making because they believed it contributed to business performance. Employee voice (by communication systems, project team membership and joint consultation) was perceived to lead to better employee contributions, improved management systems and productivity gains. This was seen to be the result of the number of ideas that emerged through employee feedback and joint problem-solving teams. Marchington *et al*'s (2007) more recent quantitative analysis using WERS2004 data found a strong positive link between the 'breadth' and 'depth' of some information and consultation practices and employee commitment. Employee ratings of the helpfulness of some consultation and communication methods were positively linked to job satisfaction and commitment. Employee ratings of managers' effectiveness in consulting employees and employees' satisfaction with their involvement in decision-making were also positively linked with job satisfaction and commitment, suggesting that the way in which information and consultation are implemented is just as important as the type of practice used.

A good deal of research has been done to investigate the links between the use of information and consultation methods, and organisational performance. Much less is known about the links between them and broader employee outcomes such as organisational commitment and job satisfaction. These may be important as part of the links in a chain by which information and consultation methods can ultimately influence organisational performance. Marchington *et al* (2007) found that there were no links between any single information and consultation method and employee commitment and job satisfaction in workplaces with 25 or more employees in 2007. However, significant and positive links were found between the 'breadth' of information and consultation (the number of different practices used together in a workplace) and the 'depth' of direct communication methods and employee commitment. Using a range of complementary EIP practices may be important because a single EIP practice is likely to have less impact on its own than a number of practices operating together. An individual EIP practice can be more easily dismissed as 'bolted on' or out of line with other HR practices and not be taken seriously by workers. In contrast, a multiplicity of EIP mechanisms may complement each other and provide opportunities for employees to be involved at work in different ways. For example, information received by employees from a team briefing may be useful when they are working in problem-solving groups.

No links were found between the breadth of information and consultation methods and the depth of direct communication methods and job satisfaction. A negative association was found between the depth of indirect communication methods and job satisfaction. Employee perceptions of the helpfulness of most methods of keeping them informed about the workplace were positively linked to employee job satisfaction and commitment in workplaces with 25 or more employees. For workplaces with 10 to 24 employees, positive significant links were found between employee perceptions of the helpfulness of noticeboards and meetings and organisational commitment and job satisfaction. Very strong positive links were found between employee perceptions of managers' effectiveness in consulting employees, employees' satisfaction with their involvement in decision-making and job satisfaction and organisational commitment in both small and larger workplaces.

The results of the research of Marchington *et al* (2007) suggest that the way in which information and consultation methods are implemented is just as important as the type of practice used. There are two reasons why management style and approach matter. There is a continuing trend in increasing workplace coverage of direct EIP. This means that individual managers are being given increasing responsibility for the implementation of EIP practices. Second, the links between management effectiveness in consultation through either formal or informal EIP and employee outcomes are particularly noticeable. The cross-sectoral nature of Marchington's data means that a direct causation in the relationship cannot be proved – that is, whether or not effective management implementation of EIP leads to improved organisational commitment and job satisfaction or vice versa.

Purcell and Hall argue that for EIP to be effective, in this case in the context of indirect representation, employers must genuinely share information on major changes and listen to employees; wider-ranging and more significant issues must be discussed; senior managers need to attend; representatives need the support to carry out their role effectively; the link between direct and indirect EIP needs to be clear to all; all EIP needs to be supported by a culture of 'mutual cooperation and trust' (2012: 10–11). Purcell and Hall's conclusions reflect the fact that EIPs are increasingly implemented in non-union settings. For instance, their point on supporting representatives, say through time off and training, is particularly pertinent in a non-union setting where facility time is not a notion normally under consideration. They also note that representatives in such settings find it difficult to be seen to represent the 'collective voice' of their colleagues.

## 10.7 A CONCEPTUAL MODEL FOR ANALYSING THE FACILITATION OF EMPLOYEE VOICE THROUGH EIP

This final part of the chapter builds on Marchington and Wilkinson's (2005) model of an 'escalator of participation' in terms of EIP to develop an overall framework for the analysis of EIP, which draws on a number of the central concepts introduced in Chapter 2 and serves as a bridge to the final section of this book. The five stages: information, communication, consultation, co-determination and control are all reflected in our earlier discussion. For instance, information examples include newsletters and noticeboards, 'direct' team briefings is a communication example, and consultation, as we have seen, is epitomised by the workings of the joint consultation committee. The 'indirect' representation of workers by their union falls within the co-determination step and, finally, worker ownership – such as co-operatives – captures the practice of control.

However, as Dundon and Wilkinson rightly state:

'This framework [Marchington and Wilkinson's] allows for a more accurate description not only of the type of involvement or participation [or voice] schemes in use, but the extent to which they may or may not empower employees...[It] is more than a straightforward continuum from no involvement (information) to extensive worker participation (control). It illustrates the point that schemes can overlap and coexist. For example, the use of collective bargaining and joint consultation does not mean that management abandons communication techniques.' (2013: 490)

Therefore, in Figure 10.3, we have built on this insight, and added the two elements discussed at length in this chapter, EI and EP, to reflect their influence across the spectrum in facilitating employee voice. Furthermore, a third concept of industrial democracy (ID) is located at the control end of the model. Fox's (1974, 1985) frames of reference have proved a valuable analytical tool in our discussions throughout the book. We have introduced those to the model to demonstrate how those perspectives can and do influence the choice and co-existence of EIP initiatives in the workplace. So, for instance, in an organisation with a unitaristic perspective of employment relations, it is likely that employee voice initiatives are often limited to the first two or three stages of the spectrum. In contrast, organisations with a more pluralist perspective are more likely to use voice initiatives across the spectrum concurrently. Finally, in Chapter 3, we considered the concept and impact of the relative balance of bargaining power. Adding this to the revised model, it is clear that if the balance of power errs towards the employer, for instance if the government of the day takes action that restricts trade union activity, then it will be more likely that EIP mechanisms will be towards the lower end of the 'escalator' (Figure 10.3).

Figure 10.3 Conceptual framework of EI/EP

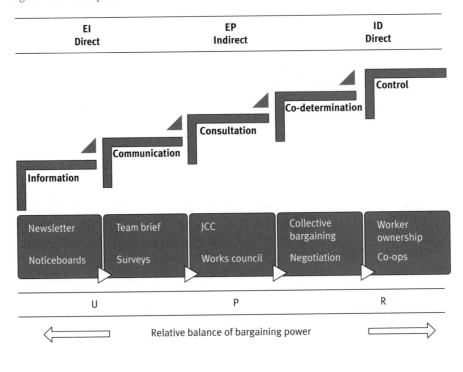

## 10.8 SUMMARY

Through the introduction of employee involvement initiatives, management seek to gain consent from their employees for their proposed actions on the basis of commitment rather than control. To this end, employee involvement and participation cover a wide range of practices designed to increase employee information about the organisation, and thereby to produce a committed workforce. Employee involvement mechanisms tend to involve employers engaging directly with the workforce through communication mechanisms and task-centred initiatives such as teamworking. In contrast, employee participation is indirect, typically through either union or non-union representatives. These are processes by which management and their representatives jointly discuss issues of mutual concern through consultation or negotiation with respect to decision-making at higher levels of the organisation.

The key distinction between involvement and participation is the extent to which employees have a real say in, and control over, the managerial decisions that affect their working lives. This in turn would appear to shape the impact of employee involvement and participation. For such mechanisms to underpin increased commitment to the organisation and consequent improvements in performance, employers need to do more than simply inform their staff – they need to provide them with a meaningful and genuine voice in the decision-making process. It is therefore worrying that the use of more 'participative' mechanisms seems to be declining while channels of upward and downward communication are becoming more widely used in British workplaces.

In this context, statutory underpinning for consultation becomes increasingly important, particularly where the bargaining power of employees is limited. The evidence in relation to the introduction of the Information and Consultation of Employees (ICE) Regulations, discussed at some length in this chapter, suggests that they tended to be adopted by those employers who already recognised the benefits of consultation. Moreover, where structures were established, these were beneficial for all parties. The problem, however, is that the existing regulations, by placing the onus on employees, are unlikely to trigger consultation in those workplaces where there are currently no channels of indirect voice.

## KEY LEARNING POINTS

1   Employee involvement concentrates on individual employees and is designed to produce a committed workforce more likely to contribute to the efficient operation of an organisation. Employee participation is concerned with the extent to which employees are involved with management in the decision-making machinery of the organisation. Crucially, employee involvement is focused on giving direct employee voice with respect to workplace-based 'task' issues. Participation, in contrast, typically through indirect representation by trade unions, presents a 'power related' voice on issues decided at the higher levels of the organisation.

2   The main objective of EIP mechanisms is to tap into employees' knowledge of their job, either at the individual level or through the mechanism of small groups. These practices are designed to increase the stock of ideas within the organisation, to encourage co-operative relations at work and to justify change.

3   Better information about the rationale for decisions can help employees to understand decisions and reduce resistance to change. Effective involvement can also have personal effects by making work more interesting and satisfying. It can also be argued that involvement can provide employees with greater 'ownership' of their role, giving them greater control and tying their interests to those of the company.

4   In implementing employee involvement and participation practices, the employment relations business-oriented thinking performer has to bear in mind a number of basic principles. These include: ensuring that arrangements and procedures are appropriate to the needs of the organisation; providing education and training to enable those who participate in the arrangements to perform effectively; selecting the appropriate EIP mechanisms; and obtaining adequate resources and commitment from top management.

5   Significant and positive links have been found between the breadth of information and consultation (the number of different practices used together in the workplace) and the depth of direct communication methods and employee commitment.

6   Evidence suggests that the adoption of practices and structures that provide employees with meaningful input into management decision-making is less widespread, while organisations are increasing their use of direct communication and other employee involvement strategies. In this context, statutory support – such as that provided by the ICE Regulations – is increasingly important.

### EXPLORE FURTHER

ACAS (2014) *Employee communications and consultation*. London: Acas.

ADAM, D., PURCELL, J. and HALL, M. (2014) *Joint consultative committees under the Information and Consultation of Employees Regulations: A WERS analysis*. Acas research paper, No 04/14. London: Acas.

DUNDON, T., WILKINSON, A. and MARCHINGTON, M. (2004) The meanings and purpose of employee voice. *International Journal of HRM*. Vol 15, No 6. pp1149–70.

DUNDON, T., DOBBINS, T. and CULLINANCE, N. (2014) Employer occupation of regulatory space of the Employee Information and Consultation (I&C) Directive in liberal market economies. *Work, Employment and Society*. Vol 28, No 1. pp21–39.

HALL, M., HUTCHINSON, S. and PARKER, J. (2010) Information and consultation under the ICE Regulations: evidence from longitudinal case studies. *Employment Relations Research Series*. No 117. September. London: Department for Business, Innovation and Skills.

MARCHINGTON, M. (2005) Employee involvement patterns and explanations. In HARLEY, B., HYMAN, J. and THOMPSON, P. (eds). *Participation and democracy at work – essays in honour of Harvie Ramsay*. Basingstoke: Palgrave.

MARCHINGTON, M. (2015) Analysing the forces shaping employee involvement and participation (EIP) at organisation level in liberal market economies (LMEs). *Human Resource Management Journal*. Vol 25, No 1. pp1–18.

MARCHINGTON, M.P., COX, A. and SUTER, J. (2007) *Embedding the provision of information and consultation in the workplace*. London: Department for Trade and Industry.

MARCHINGTON, M., WILKINSON, A. and ACKERS, P. (1993) Waving or drowning in participation? *Personnel Management*. March. pp46–50.

PURCELL, J. and HALL, M. (2012) *Voice and participation in the modern workplace: challenges and prospects*. London: Acas.

RAMSAY, H. (1977) Cycles of control: worker participation on sociological and historical perspectives. *Sociology*. Vol 11, No 3. pp481–586.

SILVERMAN, M., BAKHSHALIAN, E. and HILLMAN, L. (2013) *Social media and employee voice: the current landscape*. London: CIPD.

**Website links**

www.acas.org.uk is the Advisory, Conciliation and Arbitration Service website and gives access to Acas publications on employee involvement and participation, including its *Employee communications and consultation* advisory booklet and its *Teamwork: success through people* booklet, plus its *Getting it right* (communications with your employees) factsheet.

www.etuc.org/european-works-councils is the website for the European Trades Union Council. Its website provides valuable information on employment legislation and issues affecting employees on a trans-EU basis.

www.ipa-involve.com is the official website of the Involvement and Participation Association, which specialises in assisting both unionised and non-unionised organisations to develop effective information and consultation processes and workplace partnership.

# CHAPTER 11

# Managing Workplace Conflict

## OVERVIEW

This chapter examines the management of workplace conflict and in doing so provides a foundation for the next section of the book, which goes on to examine some of the practical challenges faced by employment relations professionals in responding to disciplinary issues, employee grievances and redundancy situations. The chapter initially defines conflict and sets out a basic conceptual framework, which we then use for exploring the nature and pattern of workplace disputes. This includes tracing the incidence of collective industrial action and employment tribunal applications, and exploring the factors that shape individual conflict in the workplace. The changing legal context of conflict management is then discussed, with a particular focus on the ways in which governments have sought to reduce the risks of litigation faced by employers. Finally, the chapter looks at the way in which conflict is managed in the workplace and the way in which changes to the nature of the HR function and employee voice have exposed the critical and often problematic role of front-line management.

### LEARNING OUTCOMES

When you have completed this chapter, you should be able to:

- understand and explain the definition of workplace conflict
- identify and critically assess the key factors that shape the nature and pattern of workplace conflict and employment disputes
- explain and critically evaluate the development of the legal framework underpinning employment dispute resolution
- critically analyse the changing role of HR practitioners, line managers and employee representatives in the management of conflict
- describe the key elements of integrated conflict management systems.

## 11.1 INTRODUCTION

A key feature of contemporary employment relations in the UK has been the sustained reduction in the scale and scope of collective industrial action and the increased emphasis on individual employment disputes and litigation through the employment tribunal system. Consequently, the resolution of individual workplace conflict has become a main focus of employment policy and practice, primarily driven by concerns over the cost of litigation and the perceived burden that this places on employers.

However, the preoccupation with the employment tribunal system is perhaps misplaced. In reality, the source of the 'problem' of individual workplace conflict arguably lies in broader changes to the nature of workplace relations. The gradual shift away from a voluntaristic approach to employment regulation that we identified in Chapter 4 triggered the rapid spread of written procedures for dealing with disciplinary and grievance issues. At the same time, the erosion of union organisation and bargaining power made industrial action less likely but also led trade unions to focus their attention on individual representation (Dickens and Hall, 2010). Furthermore, changes in the nature of the HR function and, in particular, the devolution of responsibility for the management of conflict and the growing representation gap have narrowed the informal pathways through which conflict was traditionally resolved in the workplace.

## 11.2 DEFINING AND CONCEPTUALISING WORKPLACE CONFLICT

Before considering how conflict is managed we need to briefly examine how it is understood. Often, in both policy and practice, 'conflict' and 'disputes' are used interchangeably, while within academic literature the 'links between wider processes of conflict and overt disputes are rarely discussed' (Edwards, 1995: 434). Furthermore, there is often little distinction between different types of disputes.

Dix *et al* (2009) define conflict as 'discontent arising from a perceived clash of interests'. The root cause of this 'clash of interests' depends on your perspective of the employment relationship. In Chapter 2 we discussed the unitarist, pluralist and radical frames of reference. These produce very different views as to the basic cause of conflict and its potential resolution. From a unitarist perspective, the interests of employer and employee are identical. Therefore, conflict is a function of either miscommunication by management or due to agitation by individuals deliberately 'making trouble'. A radical perspective sees that the interests of capital and labour are irreconcilable within a capitalist system – not only is conflict between employers and employees inevitable, but any settlement or resolution is only a 'sticking plaster'. A pluralist frame of reference also sees conflict as an inherent part of the employment relationship but emphasises that different interests can be accommodated and resolutions reached through negotiation and consultation.

Irrespective of the underlying causes, conflict can be triggered by a wide range of different factors, as shown in the following box, but as the definition suggests, this 'discontent' is not always visible and can be expressed in informal and often covert ways. For example, individuals or groups of workers may choose not to voice concerns and/or may indirectly articulate them through absence, quitting or lower levels of performance. Furthermore, these consequences can also be seen through petty theft (pilfering), mischief or misbehaviour – where rules are deliberately breached – and even through industrial sabotage.

---

### TRIGGERS FOR WORKPLACE CONFLICT

Issues that can lead to workplace conflict include:

- poor management
- changes to terms and conditions
- low levels of pay
- unfair treatment
- lack of clarity of job role
- lack of communication or miscommunication
- poor working conditions
- inequality in treatment and opportunity
- bullying and harassment
- work intensification

CASE STUDY 11.1

**BANG GO THE COMPUTERS! A CASE OF SABOTAGE**

One explanation of the derivation of the term sabotage is that it comes from the practice of Belgian workers throwing their 'sabots' or wooden clogs into machinery to stop or slow down production. However, the modern workplace is dependent on information technology, and systems are particularly vulnerable to the actions of employees who have a particular grievance – while some may simply resign or go through company grievance procedures, others take more direct action. In 2013, the *Daily Telegraph* reported on the case of Edward Sobolewski, who was given an eight-year prison sentence for spraying Cillit Bang (a cleaning fluid) into company computers over a three-year period. This not only caused system failures but £32,000 worth of damage. Sobolewski claimed to have taken the action in response to being denied a series of pay rises.

Conflict may also be expressed through more formal channels. Dix *et al* draw a crucial distinction between conflict and disputes, which are 'manifest expressions' of that discontent. At an individual level, these normally take one of two forms: a grievance brought by the employee, or disciplinary action taken by the organisation against an employee, and as we see in Chapters 12 and 13 they are likely to have a 'different character' (Lucy and Broughton, 2011: 24). Discontent can also develop into collective disputes in the form of industrial action. This can take a wide variety of forms, such as strike action, where a group of workers remove their labour by stopping work for a limited or an indefinite period. Other forms include refusal to work overtime or working 'to rule', whereby workers refuse to work beyond the terms of their contract. Workers may also choose to cease a particular part of their contractual duties.

Whether conflict escalates into individual employment disputes, collective industrial action, or is expressed through more informal action, it is likely to depend on a number of critical factors, which are summarised below and represented in Figure 11.1:

Figure 11.1 The dynamics of individual employment disputes

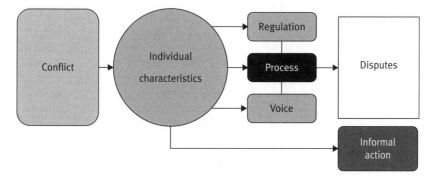

1    Political and legal context – if the regulatory framework underpins employment rights and provides a clear route through which rights can be enforced, discontent is likely to be converted into disputes. Whether this is in the form of individual grievances and litigation will depend on the extent to which collective action is supported or constrained by legislation.

2   Organisational processes – if there are accessible processes through which employees can raise concerns and managers can deal with issues of conduct and capability, discontent is likely to be expressed through formal grievances and disciplinary action. Where such processes are not present, conflict is more likely to be expressed through informal and indirect channels, such as quitting, absence and poor performance.

3   Employee voice – while formal processes may act as channels for employee voice, access to representation may be critical in mobilising discontent and articulating this as an individual or collective grievance.

4   Personal characteristics and emotional contexts – emotional contexts can influence conflict escalation. Issues outside the workplace, often shaped by economic circumstance, may affect how individuals respond to conflict. Both manager and managed will rely on 'attributions' to make sense of the situation they find themselves in.

## ?   REFLECTIVE ACTIVITY 11.1

What are the main sources of conflict in your workplace? How is this conflict expressed?

## 11.3 THE PATTERN OF WORKPLACE DISPUTES IN THE UK

The conceptual framework outlined above provides us with a way of understanding the changing pattern of workplace disputes in the UK. The most distinctive feature of this has been the significant reduction in the incidence and scale of collective industrial action and the increase in the prominence of employment tribunal applications. While this has been seen as reflecting the individualisation of workplace conflict, the evidence suggests a more complex picture revolving around changes in the nature of employee voice mechanisms and the regulatory framework of dispute resolution.

### 11.3.1 STRIKE ACTION IN THE UK

As outlined above, collective grievances can be expressed in a number of ways – groups of workers can take strike action where they withdraw their labour completely for a limited or an indefinite period. In addition, they can take industrial action, short of strike action, by refusing to work overtime, declining to complete certain parts of their normal duties or by strictly limiting their work to the terms of their employment contracts – sometimes known as 'working to rule'.

The Office for National Statistics (ONS) publishes three measures – number of strikes, workers involved in strike action, and also the number of workdays lost. These statistics reveal a clear pattern of change. Firstly, there has been a sharp fall in the incidence of stoppages. Between 1965 and 1979 there were, on average, well over 2,000 strikes every year. However, from the high point between 1970 and 1974 there has been a broadly continuous decline, and between 2010 and 2014, the average had fallen to just 129.

Table 11.1 Strike action in the UK, 1965–2014

| Year | No. of strikes | Workers involved (000) | Days lost (000) |
|---|---|---|---|
| 1965–69 (avg) | 2,397 | 1,215 | 3,929 |
| 1970–74 (avg) | 2,917 | 1,573 | 14,077 |

| Year | No. of strikes | Workers involved (000) | Days lost (000) |
|---|---|---|---|
| 1975–79 (avg) | 2,345 | 1,658 | 11,663 |
| 1980–84 (avg) | 1,363 | 1,298 | 10,486 |
| 1985–89 (avg) | 895 | 783 | 3,939 |
| 1990–94 (avg) | 337 | 223 | 824 |
| 1995–99 (avg) | 213 | 180 | 495 |
| 2000–04 (avg) | 163 | 350 | 750 |
| 2005–09 (avg) | 132 | 454 | 633 |
| 2010–14 (avg) | 129 | 606 | 647 |

Source: Office for National Statistics

The scale of strike action also contracted sharply through the 1980s and 1990s. However, there has been an increase in the number of workers involved in and the number of days lost due to strike action over the last 15 years. This can partly be explained by the changing shape of strike action. Although strikes may be less common, when they do occur they are more likely to take place in the public sector and involve relatively large groups of workers.

CASE STUDY 11.2

## PUBLIC SECTOR WORKERS ON THE MARCH?

On 30 November 2011, up to 2 million public sector workers took part in a one-day strike to protest proposed changes to pension entitlements.

This was in response to government plans to reform pensions in the public sector so that the amounts workers would have to pay into occupational pensions would increase and the age at which workers could retire and claim a full pension would rise.

However, the biggest change was that pensions would be calculated on the basis of a worker's average salary throughout their career rather than their final salary – meaning a substantial reduction in pensions for many. The pension changes were part of the Coalition Government's wider attempts to reduce public sector spending, which also included restrictions on pay and widespread job reductions.

The Government also argued that the cost of funding public sector pensions was 'unsustainable' as people are living longer, while unions claimed that the proposals would leave their members paying more into their pensions but receiving less on retirement.

While the dispute involved all the main public sector unions such as Unite, Unison, the NUT, and the PCS, a key feature of the dispute was the wide range of workers involved. For example, this included the National Association of Head Teachers (NAHT), which had not been on strike for 114 years, and dispatchers and paramedics employed by the London Ambulance Service, who had not been on strike since the 1970s.

Table 11.2 provides a breakdown of strike data in the public and private sectors. Since 2005, although there is a balance between the number of strikes in the public and private sectors, the public sector was responsible for the vast majority of working days lost. The contrast is even more apparent when one examines the 'strike rate' – the number of working days lost per 1,000 employees – which accounts for differences in levels of employment in the two sectors.

Table 11.2 Strike activity in the public and private sector, 2005–14

| | Number of strikes | | Working days lost (000s) | | Strike rate (working days lost per 1,000 employees) | |
|---|---|---|---|---|---|---|
| | Total | Percentage in public sector | Total | Percentage in public sector | Private | Public |
| 2005 | 116 | 52 | 157 | 63 | 3 | 16 |
| 2006 | 158 | 55 | 755 | 87 | 4 | 108 |
| 2007 | 142 | 63 | 1041 | 96 | 2 | 166 |
| 2008 | 144 | 52 | 759 | 94 | 2 | 117 |
| 2009 | 98 | 50 | 455 | 81 | 4 | 58 |
| 2010 | 92 | 51 | 365 | 86 | 3 | 50 |
| 2011 | 149 | 60 | 1390 | 92 | 5 | 210 |
| 2012 | 131 | 48 | 249 | 80 | 2 | 34 |
| 2013 | 114 | 44 | 444 | 82 | 3 | 64 |
| 2014 | 155 | 44 | 788 | 91 | 3 | 133 |

Source: Office for National Statistics

The factors that have triggered changes in the shape of strike activity have been widely discussed. It may be suggested that reduced strike activity reflects a broader reduction in discontent and improving employment relations as organisations have focused on high-involvement work practices and employee engagement. However, this is not supported by the evidence, which shows that the sharp decline in levels of strike action during the late 1980s and early 1990s actually coincided with a general deterioration in perceptions of employee relations and attitudes to work (Dix et al 2009). Therefore, it could be suggested that while discontent was higher, for some reason this wasn't being translated into industrial disputes.

Following the model above, a key factor may be the nature of the regulatory framework. Certainly, it could be argued that the introduction of a range of far-reaching measures restricting the ability of trade unions to win support for and prosecute industrial action suppressed strike activity during this period (see Chapter 4 for a detailed discussion). Although these measures undoubtedly made it more difficult for trade unions to organise and enforce industrial action, strike activity fell in other countries, where similar legislation was not introduced. Therefore, it is unlikely that the changing legislative framework was the main, or even a major, factor in triggering the rapid decline in the incidence of industrial action.

Even if individuals and groups of workers are unhappy about their pay and conditions, whether they are prepared to withdraw their labour and go on strike will be affected by the their own personal circumstances in the context of the broader economic climate. For example, during periods of high unemployment and low inflation, such as the UK economy experienced in the 1980s and 1990s, the incentive for those in work to go on strike may be reduced. Workers may be more concerned about keeping their jobs and prepared to put up with a squeeze on their pay or changes to their working conditions. Therefore, the threat of unemployment may also deter workers from taking industrial action. This may well have been the case in the 1980s and in subsequent periods of recession. But, if this was the main factor, one might have expected to see greater militancy during periods of falling unemployment between 1997 and 2007. However, this did not happen. There are three related factors that could explain this. First, this period also saw very rapid industrial restructuring and the increased globalisation of production. This contributed to the decline of industries that had traditionally experienced relatively high levels of strikes and other industrial action (including coal mining, shipbuilding, and motor manufacturing). Second, the increased mobility of capital meant that the threat of organisations relocating production, sometimes referred to as 'coercive comparisons', made workers and trade unions less likely to take industrial action. Third, these forces combined to create a more hostile environment for trade union organisation, as trade union density and collective bargaining structures were progressively eroded (Charlwood and Terry, 2007).

Overall, in terms of the model above, it could be argued that fundamental changes to the structure of employee voice mechanisms within British workplaces meant that it was much less likely that discontent could be mobilised into collective action (Kelly, 1998). This can also be seen in the changing pattern of strike activity in that the relative resilience of trade union organisation in the public sector is a major reason why there have been higher levels of strike activity in that sector than in the private sector. Furthermore, public sector workers have arguably borne the brunt of attempts by central and local government to drive through organisational change, reduce costs and increase efficiency.

---

### ? REFLECTIVE ACTIVITY 11.2

Industrial action is now overwhelmingly concentrated in the public sector – what do you think are the main reasons for this?

---

## 11.3.2 THE INDIVIDUALISATION OF WORKPLACE CONFLICT

A critical feature of contemporary employment relations has been the increased emphasis on individual expressions of conflict and particularly on employment litigation. Indeed, the rapid decline in strike action in the UK was mirrored by a growth in the number of employment tribunal applications. The number of registered employment tribunal applications grew rapidly during the 1990s and 2000s from 34,697 in 1989/90 to a high point of 236,100 two decades later (Dix *et al*, 2009; Ministry of Justice, 2011).

Figure 11.2 Employment tribunal applications, 1978–2015

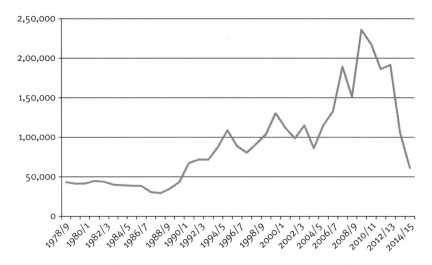

Source: 1978–1979: Employment Gazette (1984); 1980–1998: Hawes (2000); 1998–2010: Employment Tribunal Service Annual Reports; 2011–2015 Ministry of Justice[1]

Understanding the growth in employment tribunal volumes is important as it became the focus of government employment relations policy and a key justification for radical reform of the employment tribunal system and the structure of employment rights in the UK. The evidence suggests that the increase in litigation is related to changes to workplace structures of industrial relations and, once again, the erosion of trade union voice. For example, Burgess *et al* (2000) found that increasing employment tribunal volumes were positively related to falling union density. This suggests that as union influence and presence were reduced, workers were less able to resolve conflict through collective channels. In addition, it could be argued that this also had a negative effect on informal processes of resolution through which management and union representatives negotiated settlements on individual issues. The decline of collective bargaining meant that trade unions were forced to rely on the legal enforcement of individual rights to represent their members' interests. Furthermore, employees who were not union members had little alternative but to turn to the law.

Therefore, in terms of the conceptual framework set out at the start of this chapter, the pattern of employment disputes has been shaped by fundamental changes to the structure of employee voice. It could also be argued that regulatory change between 1997 and 2010 created an environment in which litigation was more likely. Under the New Labour Government, the scope of employment protection was widened. This was partly due to domestic measures, such as the reduction in qualifying periods for claiming unfair dismissal from two years to one year. However, much more influential was the signing of the Social Chapter and the consequent increased influence of European law. By 2012, employment tribunals had the authority to make decisions on more than 60 different types of claim or jurisdiction. Critically, between 2013 and 2015, there was a dramatic fall in the number of employment tribunal applications from 191,541 to just 61,308 in the wake of a range of measures introduced by the Government to reduce the risk of employment litigation. This is discussed in detail later in the chapter.

---

[1] This series is an update from that quoted in Dix *et al* (2009), which provides a detailed discussion of this area.

While high employment tribunal volumes were consistently cited as evidence that individual employment disputes represented a substantial and increasing challenge for both business and government, it could be argued that the scale of this 'problem' has been somewhat inflated. The peaks in employment tribunal applications in recent years were closely linked to waves of co-ordinated claims brought by large numbers of employees relating to issues such as equal pay, redundancy, and working time. For example, in 2009/10, more than 130,000 claims (56% of the total) were made in respect of breaches of the Working Time Regulations and equal pay legislation. In fact, the number of claims for unfair dismissal has remained relatively stable in recent years, while the number of single claims has been falling across the last decade. In addition, there has been a growth in individuals bringing claims under more than one jurisdiction – for example, claiming unfair dismissal, sex discrimination and unfair deduction of wages. This would be registered as three claims although they would relate to a single claimant and normally a single set of circumstances. This also suggests that many employment tribunal claims are actually triggered by collective issues. Therefore, it could be argued that it is not conflict that has become more individualised – after all, the issues are fundamentally the same – but the collective channels through which that conflict can be expressed, managed and resolved have been progressively blocked (Saundry and Dix, 2014).

This picture is also reflected in other measures of workplace conflict. For example, there is relatively little evidence that individual disputes in the workplace are becoming more prevalent. According to the 2011 Workplace Employment Relations Study (WERS) (van Wanrooy et al, 2013), the proportion of workplaces that reported any formal employee grievances in the previous 12 months fell from 38% in 2004 to 30% in 2011. There was also a small reduction in the incidence of disciplinary action – 17% of managers dismissed at least one employee in 2011, compared with 19% in 2004, and 39% of managers used sanctions other than dismissal in 2011, compared with 43% in 2004.

This does not necessarily mean that there has been any reduction in conflict – discontent could simply be expressed in other ways, such as higher turnover or increased absence. In fact, this might be more likely if workers are unable to turn to trade union or other employee representatives. However, these measures show no signs of having worsened. Between 2004 and 2011, the average proportion of staff leaving their employment voluntarily fell from 14% to 9%. At the same time, there was little change in the rate of absence – 3.4% in 2004 compared with 3.7% in 2011 (van Wanrooy et al, 2013).

So, how can we explain this? It might simply reflect that despite the recession and work intensification, workers are more contented. Survey evidence would seem to point in this direction – Dix et al's (2009) evaluation of evidence from the British Social Attitudes Survey, British Household Panel Survey and the WERS series suggests that although perceptions of employee relations and job satisfaction fell during the early to mid-1990s, they have steadily improved in the intervening period. Interestingly, according to WERS 2011, this trend appears to have been sustained. In fact, nearly two-thirds of employees rated relations between workers and managers as either good or very good – a slight increase on 2004. While the figures were slightly lower in public sector and unionised workplaces, there was no evidence of any deterioration (van Wanrooy et al, 2013). Furthermore, WERS2011 found an increase in the proportion of employees reporting organisational commitment across three measures – loyalty, pride and shared values. For example, the proportion of employees who agreed that they shared the values of their organisation increased from 55% in 2004 to 65% in 2011.

In contrast, the Skills and Employment Survey (SES) 2012 (Gallie et al, 2013) found that fear of dismissal, discrimination and victimisation had increased since 2000, with a rise in anxiety levels among public sector workers in particular. At the same time, a CIPD survey of its members, conducted in 2011, found that workplace conflict had increased during the recession. Almost half of those responding reported an increase in the use of disciplinary action and employee grievance procedures since 2009 (2011: 2). In addition,

WERS2011 pointed to a sharp rise in the proportion of workplaces imposing disciplinary sanctions for poor performance (van Wanrooy *et al*, 2013).

This contradictory picture suggests the need for a more nuanced analysis of the incidence of workplace conflict. First, the relationship between organisational commitment and conflict may not be straightforward. Workers may share the values of their organisation and may also have great pride in the work of that organisation but may still be discontented with their pay and conditions or the attitude of their managers. For example, members of the Royal College of Midwives (RCM) took industrial action in October 2014 for the first time in the history of their trade union. This was in protest at the refusal of the Government to apply a 1% pay increase that had been recommended by the NHS Pay Review Body. However, there was no question that this reflected in any way on their commitment to their profession or the NHS.

Second, conflict may be suppressed because of employee concerns over recriminations or job security, particularly at times of recession or high unemployment. Workers may be unwilling to challenge the behaviour of others or to protest at managerial actions if they feel that this might harm their long-term interests. Moreover, employees may have limited options – WERS2011 found that that there were lower rates of staff turnover in organisations adversely affected by recessionary conditions (van Wanrooy *et al*, 2013). In addition, as we highlight in Chapter 12, the 2014 CIPD Absence Management Survey suggested that staff are increasingly likely to attend work even when ill because of fears over job security.

Third, aggregate measures may mask developments within particular sectors. For example, WERS2011 found that disciplinary sanctions were higher in organisations affected by the recession – which possibly points to employers adopting more robust approaches to managing conflict in response to competitive and cost pressure (van Wanrooy *et al*, 2013).

---

### ?   REFLECTIVE ACTIVITY 11.3

How would you explain the reduction in the incidence of disciplinary action and employee grievances in British workplaces? Does this reflect the situation in your workplace?

---

### 11.3.3 THE CONTOURS OF INDIVIDUAL EMPLOYMENT DISPUTES

While the precise levels of workplace conflict may be difficult to establish, interpret and explain, we do know a little more about the key factors that shape the incidence of individual employment disputes (Knight and Latreille, 2000; Antcliff and Saundry, 2009). For example, grievances and disciplinary action are both more likely to occur in workplaces with larger numbers of employees. This could reflect the more impersonal nature of employment relations in larger organisations. It could be further argued that in smaller workplaces and organisations conflict is more likely to be resolved informally, and there is good evidence that in smaller and medium-sized organisations managers are more likely to use disciplinary warnings than dismissals (Forth *et al*, 2006). Similarly, we know that employees in smaller workplaces have more positive perceptions of employment relations (van Wanrooy *et al*, 2013). Nonetheless, the relative absence of disputes in smaller organisations may reflect the fact that conflict is more likely to be suppressed because of the highly personal nature of employment relations in such environments.

The link between personal characteristics and the incidence of employee grievances has not been explored in great detail. Lucy and Broughton (2011), reporting on the Civil and Social Justice Survey 2007 and Fair Treatment at Work Survey 2008, argue that certain types of employee are 'more likely to report experiencing problems in the workplace' (15). This included workers who are: younger; female; have a disability or long-term illness; are lesbian, gay or bisexual; are black; are parents, especially single parents; work in routine and manual occupations; have short tenure; and earn less than £25,000 per annum.

However, there is much more extensive evidence of the relationship between workforce characteristics and rates of disciplinary sanctions and dismissals. For example, the employment of women, older workers and those in more skilled occupational groups is associated with a lower incidence of disciplinary disputes. This could in part be explained by conformity to organisational norms and rules (Ward and Beck, 1990). One could suggest that the same could be true of older workers and those in more senior positions, who may have more to lose by breaching organisational norms. A further reason may reflect the ability and willingness of workers to challenge managerial authority. Those in professional occupations and management grades have a relatively high awareness of legislation in relation to discipline and grievance (Casebourne *et al*, 2006) and hence may be able to contest decisions more effectively. Highly skilled professionals and managers may also feel that they have greater bargaining power and so may be more confident in standing their ground.

Ethnicity also appears to be an important factor – more specifically, workplaces with higher proportions of 'non-white' employees have been found to have higher rates of disciplinary sanctions and dismissals (Knight and Latreille, 2000; Saundry and Antcliff, 2006). This is perhaps a function of discriminatory behaviour from fellow workers and employers but could also be linked to the relatively low level of knowledge of employment rights among employees from minority ethnic groups (Casebourne *et al*, 2006).

Employment relations within an organisation will also shape the nature and extent of workplace conflict. More specifically, the approach taken by management to issues such as conduct and performance will be important, as conflict will inevitably form around managerial attempts to both control the labour process and secure the consent of workers and employees (Hyman, 1987). Furthermore, the way in which organisational actors seek to manage conflict will, in part, determine the incidence of individual employment disputes. For example, managers who adopt a 'problem-solving' approach are more likely to resolve conflicts. Strong trade union organisation is also associated with lower rates of disciplinary sanctions and dismissals, as a result of unions either restraining managerial prerogative or facilitating informal paths of resolution (Edwards, 2000; Saundry *et al*, 2011). At the same time, employee grievances are more likely within unionised workplaces (Kersley *et al*, 2006), in which employees may well receive support in making formal complaints. Certainly, there is evidence to suggest that unrepresented workers are less likely to use formal grievance procedures (Pollert and Charlwood, 2009). Given the role played by union representation, it could be argued that adversarial employment relations could increase discontent within an organisation. Conversely, positive employment relations can help to resolve issues that might otherwise result in formal grievances. For example, high-trust relations within unionised environments can facilitate informal processes that help to resolve issues that threaten to escalate into formal disputes (Oxenbridge and Brown, 2004; Saundry and Wibberley, 2014).

Overall, it would appear that key variables impact upon employee grievances and disciplinary disputes in very different ways. Indeed, those industries with low levels of individual employee grievances tend to be characterised by higher rates of disciplinary action. The extent to which conflict becomes transmitted as disciplinary action is a function of the degree to which worker behaviour contravenes rules and norms, and the consequent managerial response. Moreover, whereas a grievance is initiated by an employee, disciplinary action is fundamentally subject to managerial prerogative. This distinction is not simply theoretical but is crucial in understanding the way in which different types of disputes are resolved and therefore the efficacy of policy instruments designed to facilitate or encourage resolution.

## REFLECTIVE ACTIVITY 11.4

Thinking about a conflict you have witnessed or been involved in – what were the key factors that led to its escalation and resolution?

## 11.4 THE LEGAL CONTEXT OF CONFLICT MANAGEMENT

Of all the different aspects of employment relations, workplace conflict has arguably attracted the most attention from government. Concerns over its impact on efficiency, employment and economic growth have led successive administrations to attempt to develop regulatory frameworks which minimise and/or help to resolve workplace conflict. In this way, the UK has generally moved from a 'voluntaristic' approach, which essentially placed the responsibility for the resolution of conflict in the hands of employers and trade unions, to one which imposes regulatory constraints on trade unions in respect of collective disputes and on employers in terms of individual employment rights. While a settled political consensus has developed over legislative restrictions on collective industrial action, the thrust of recent policy towards the resolution of individual conflict has seen a return to what might be described as a neo-voluntaristic agenda, which provides employers with greater freedom to manage but in a context in which trade union organisation and structures of free collective bargaining are absent from most workplaces.

### 11.4.1 REGULATING INDUSTRIAL ACTION

From the end of World War II until the 1980s, conflict was essentially managed through structures of collective bargaining. This took place within a legal framework, which was based on a system of immunities protecting unions from employer claims under common law if they called on their members to take industrial action. As we noted previously (and in Chapter 4), the election of the Conservative Government under the leadership of Margaret Thatcher in 1979 heralded a programme of intervention to restrict the ability of trade unions to organise and implement industrial action. While this undoubtedly represented a radical break from the past and drew criticism that the UK had breached minimum international standards (Ewing, 1989), a political consensus developed with the Labour Government elected in 1997, leaving the key legislation regulating industrial action intact. Subsequently, the relative decline in the incidence of industrial action and the rapid contraction in the scale and scope of collective bargaining saw the legal regulation of collective industrial conflict fall down the public policy agenda until the election of the Conservative Government in 2015 and the introduction of the Trade Union Bill, which seeks to further regulate and restrict union action and activity (see Chapter 4 for a detailed discussion).

### 11.4.2 INDIVIDUAL DISPUTES – FORMALITY, FLEXIBILITY AND FAIRNESS

As collective industrial action has waned, public policy attention has focused on individual employment disputes and particularly the growth of employment litigation discussed in the preceding section. In this context, a significant source of concern has been the growing formality of dispute resolution in the UK and increased influence of the law and the tribunal system.

In fact, these developments have their roots in the report of the Donovan Commission, published in 1968, and the subsequent introduction of the right to claim unfair dismissal. In 1977 the Acas Code of Practice on 'Disciplinary Practice and Procedures' was introduced to provide guidance for employers and employees. This code, while not legally binding, defined good practice. Perhaps more importantly, it was used by industrial tribunals as a guide as to what could be expected of a reasonable employer. Paragraph 11 summed up the essence of procedural fairness as follows:

> 'Before a decision is made or imposed the individual should be interviewed and given the opportunity to state his or her case and should be advised of any rights under the procedure, including the right to be accompanied.'

Therefore, although there was no legal compulsion to implement disciplinary and grievance procedures, the code of practice became a key benchmark of what organisations needed to do in order to avoid claims for unfair dismissal. As a result, procedures spread rapidly. Prior to 1971, as few as 8% of establishments used formal procedures for dealing with discipline and dismissals. By 1990, they were present in approximately 90% of workplaces employing 25 employees or more (Millward *et al*, 1992), but growth was much slower in smaller non-unionised organisations, perhaps reflecting a general hostility towards regulation. By 2004, written disciplinary procedures could be found in 80% of organisations with fewer than 100 employees (Kersley *et al*, 2006).

The importance of written procedures for dealing with disciplinary and grievance issues was also increased by the decline in union presence. Consequently, informal relationships between trade union representatives and managers, which could help in managing individual conflict, were less likely to be found. Instead, decisions over workplace discipline and on employee grievances were increasingly made unilaterally by management. Crucially, disciplinary and grievance procedures were and are subject to negotiation with trade unions in a minority of unionised workplaces (Kersley *et al*, 2006; van Wanrooy *et al*, 2013).

It is slightly ironic that the formalisation of workplace dispute resolution took place during a period when successive Conservative administrations were promoting a more deregulated approach to employment policy. For example, the Thatcher Government increased the qualifying period for claiming unfair dismissal from one to two years, providing employers with greater freedom to dismiss employees and contributing to a small fall in employment tribunal applications between 1980 and 1988 (Dix *et al*, 2009).

This measure was reversed by the incoming Labour Government elected in 1997. Furthermore, continued standardisation of dispute resolution procedures was seen as an important way of combating rising employment tribunal applications. In particular, the Government felt that a major problem was the lack of basic employment practices in smaller workplaces and organisations. Findings from WERS2004 (which overlapped with the introduction of the regulations) confirmed that while formal procedures were widespread in larger workplaces, in small workplaces a significant minority still had no formal grievance (37%) or disciplinary procedure (31%) (Forth *et al*, 2006).

In an attempt to fill this gap, the Employment Act 2002 introduced minimum compulsory procedures for dealing with dismissals and employee grievances. These regulations stipulated that employers (and employees) should follow three key steps when dealing with a dismissal or employee grievance. First, the issue should be set out in writing; second, there should be a hearing or meeting to discuss and decide on the issue; and third, the employee should have the right to an appeal. If an employer dismissed an employee without following the necessary three steps, the dismissal was deemed to be automatically unfair. In addition, if either the employer or employee failed to follow the minimum procedure, compensation in the event of a finding of unfair dismissal could be increased or reduced by between 10% and 50%. The Government argued that these measures were designed to ensure basic procedural standards and that parties in dispute exhausted all possibilities of resolution before litigation. However, some commentators (that is, Hepple and Morris, 2002) pointed out that the majority of workplaces operated procedures that were more extensive and offered employees greater protection. Therefore, there was a danger that there would be a levelling down of overall standards. Either way, the main driver behind these measures was the desire to reduce employment tribunal volumes.

**? REFLECTIVE ACTIVITY 11.5**

Why do you think that disciplinary and grievance procedures are necessary? Do you think they are designed to protect the interests of employees or employers? Do you believe that they help to resolve conflict and disputes?

### 11.4.3 THE GIBBONS REVIEW – FROM LITIGATION TO EARLY RESOLUTION

In fact, there was little evidence that the introduction of statutory procedures had the desired effect of reducing the volume of employment tribunal applications. In particular, they were unpopular with employers, who complained that the regulations increased the associated administrative burden and made it more likely that conflict would escalate into formal disputes. In response to these criticisms, the Government commissioned a review chaired by Sir Anthony Gibbons to 'identify options for simplifying and improving all aspects of employment dispute resolution' (Gibbons, 2007: 7). Gibbons argued that the three-step procedures encouraged employers to adopt defensive positions in disputes and to turn to formal processes at an early point to avert the threat of legal action. Having to put issues in writing was counter to the personal nature of employment relations in small workplaces and so helped to escalate rather than diffuse disputes.

There were two main aspects to the recommendations of the Gibbons Review. The first was to urge the Government, employers and trade unions to promote the greater use of mediation to resolve workplace disputes (mediation is examined in greater depth in Chapter 14). Second, it called for the repeal of the statutory dispute resolution procedures and the development of 'clear, simple, non-prescriptive guidelines' for employers and employees in relation to grievances, discipline and dismissal. The Government accepted the need for a greater focus on the early resolution of disputes and repealed the statutory dispute resolution procedures as part of the Employment Act 2008. At the same time, a revised Acas Code of Practice on Discipline and Grievance was introduced in 2009. This was much shorter than the previous version and provided employers, in particular, with a greater degree of flexibility and discretion in handling individual employment disputes backed by more detailed non-statutory guidance. Importantly, the Government increased the influence of the Code by allowing tribunals to adjust tribunal awards by up to 25% if either party acted unreasonably in not complying with its provisions.

### 11.4.4 NEO-VOLUNTARISM AND DEREGULATION?

The Gibbons Review and the repeal of the Dispute Resolution Regulations arguably marked a return to a more voluntaristic approach to the management and resolution of individual conflict. From the perspective of employers, this was needed, given what they saw as the burdensome nature of the existing system of dispute resolution. This inevitably revolved around the issue of employment litigation.

Employers' organisations argued that the existing employment tribunal system encouraged weak and speculative claims from employees. The fact that legal costs were rarely awarded to the successful party in employment litigation meant that employees without strong cases could pursue claims in the hope that employers would agree to a financial settlement rather than incur the legal costs associated with defending a claim through the tribunal system. Moreover, it was argued that the fear of facing a possible employment tribunal application discouraged employers from taking on new employees and also from dealing with conflict in informal ways. It is clear that this perception was widely held by employers. BCC's 2011 survey of small business found that 61% believed that employment tribunals were weighted unfairly against the employer (British Chambers of Commerce, 2011).

There is general consensus that employment tribunals, which were originally conceived as industrial juries, providing an accessible and relatively informal source of workplace justice, have become 'increasingly complex, legalistic and adversarial' (Gibbons, 2007: 21). However, the argument that the system was unfairly weighted in favour of claimants is questionable. Although tribunals rarely awarded costs to the successful party, their powers to do so had been significantly expanded in that respect. Prior to 2001, costs awards (of up to a maximum of £500) were generally limited to cases where an application or actions of a party were 'frivolous' or 'vexatious'. But in 2001, the maximum costs award was increased to £10,000 and extended to cases where 'the bringing or conducting of the proceedings by a party has been misconceived'. This meant that tribunals now had an explicit power to award costs where cases were without merit. However, there has been little sign of a substantial and sustained increase in the use of these powers. Ewing and Hendy (2012) argue that the system is in fact weighted against the employee. They point out that only a very small proportion of cases are successful and, even then, levels of compensation are generally low. In 2014/15 just over 14% of all unfair dismissal cases disposed of were upheld, while the median compensation in these cases was around £7,000.

Nonetheless, in October 2013, employment tribunal fees were introduced to 'prevent poorly conceived claims from progressing through the system, wasting time and cost for all' (BIS, 2011: 28). While these changes (which are discussed in detail in Chapter 4) have generally been welcomed by employers' organisations, trade unions have warned that they would reduce access to justice. Certainly, their introduction has triggered a significant fall in tribunal volumes, as noted above. Unfortunately, we currently have little definitive evidence as to whether this reflects weak claims being squeezed out of the system or those with strong cases being dissuaded by the costs involved.

At the same time, the Government introduced settlement agreements, which represented a streamlining and codification of the previous system of compromise agreements. In effect, these are designed to allow employers and employees to safely negotiate the terms of terminating employment without the risk of litigation. Typically, employees will agree not to bring a claim for unfair dismissal in return for financial compensation and/or agreement to provide a reference.

This package of measures, together with an increase in the qualifying period required to claim unfair dismissal, substantially reduces the risks of litigation faced by employers. This would also seem to provide employers with greater freedom and flexibility in respect of conflict management. However, whether this will translate to earlier and more active intervention on workplace conflict by employers is open to question. A study commissioned by the Government into the impact of employment regulation suggested that 'anxiety' over regulation rather than its direct effect tended to shape responses (Jordan et al, 2013: 44). In short, many employers tended to exaggerate the extent to which they were constrained by legislation – therefore the fear of litigation tended to drive employers to adopt more formal and risk-averse approaches to workplace conflict. Critically, small and medium-sized enterprises, which are more likely to find themselves subject to litigation (Saridakis et al, 2008), are also less likely to be aware of the detail of employment law. Consequently, it could be argued that the impact of legislation will be dependent on changing perceptions of the law and increasing awareness of its detail. However, there is also a danger that reducing the risks associated with dismissal will narrow the incentives for employers to take steps to resolve disputes when the least costly option may simply be to terminate the employment relationship.

---

### ?    REFLECTIVE ACTIVITY 11.6

What do you think the impact of employment tribunal fees will be on the way that organisations respond to problems in the workplace? Are they a barrier to justice or a necessary way of 'weeding out' speculative claims?

---

Interestingly, while the 'problem' identified by policymakers has been the growing complexity of the regulatory system and the threat of appearances before the employment tribunals, there has been little detailed consideration of radical reform to the nature of adjudication over employment cases. While the Acas Arbitration Scheme (launched in 2001 and still in operation) was not intended to replace the employment tribunal system, it offers an alternative means of deciding claims of unfair dismissal and those relating to requests to work more flexibly. To date, the voluntary nature of the Scheme, its jurisdictional reach and a lack of incentives for potential users (among other factors) has limited its use and significance (see Dickens, 2012). Nonetheless, it potentially provides a model for a less adversarial and more accessible means by which workplace disputes can be decided.

### 11.4.5 MEDIATION AND CONCILIATION

In addition to the reform of employment tribunals, the other area of policy attention in recent years has been the promotion of mediation and conciliation as a way of resolving workplace conflict. The Gibbons Review recommended the promotion of workplace mediation, which we examine in much greater detail in Chapter 15. While the Government has stopped short of concrete measures to increase its use, it has supported workplace mediation and, there is evidence that it is becoming an increasingly important part of the management of employment relations.

There has been greater policy emphasis on the use of pre-claim and early conciliation conducted by Acas. In fact, Acas already had an existing statutory duty to conciliate between employment tribunal claimants and respondents in order to promote settlement. In most cases, once a claim had been registered with the employment tribunal, Acas would be provided with details and a conciliator would contact both parties to explore the possibility of settlement. This approach was remarkably effective, with around four out of every ten cases being settled and only around 20% of cases referred to Acas proceeding to a full hearing (Peters *et al*, 2010).

The relative success of Acas in encouraging settlements in such cases prompted the development of pre-claim conciliation (PCC) in disputes that were 'likely' to result in a tribunal claim. The key difference between this and standard conciliation was that it represented an earlier intervention, before litigation had commenced and therefore offered the hope of repairing employment relationships. Crucially, the process was voluntary, confidential and (unlike mediation) free of charge. The scheme was successful – and in addition, often helped organisations to improve their practices and procedures (Acas and Infogroup/ORC International, 2010). Importantly, organisations that used the service tended to be smaller, non-unionised and with little access to HR expertise – in short, the type of organisation that tended to be more vulnerable to legal challenge.

Around half of the cases referred to PCC were resolved and fewer than 30% of cases subsequently progressed to litigation. However, the hopes that PCC would improve the chances of preserving or restoring the employment relationship were misplaced. Only a small minority of workers taking part in PCC subsequently stayed in employment. Thus, PCC provided an effective way of avoiding costly and time-consuming litigation, but did not necessarily offer an alternative approach to the management of conflict in the workplace.

More recently, in April 2014, in a further attempt to reduce tribunal volumes, the structure of individual conciliation was revised to provide 'early conciliation' in respect of all tribunal applications. The new process is outlined in Chapter 4. In most respects, the role of the conciliator, and the methods used, are unchanged. The key difference is the timing of the intervention – instead of referring cases to Acas after claims have been lodged, all tribunal applications are first sent to Acas, who attempt to facilitate a settlement before the claim is officially lodged with the employment tribunal. In the first eight months of the scheme, 22% of cases progressed to the tribunal, 15% reached a written, legally enforceable agreement, while a further 63% of cases did not progress to the tribunal – this could mean that employer and employee reached an unwritten settlement or, alternatively, that the employee simply decided not to pursue their claim.

---

### ? REFLECTIVE ACTIVITY 11.7

Is mediation used in your workplace? If so, how effective has it been? To what extent does early conciliation represent a significant change in the way that potential employment tribunal claims are resolved?

---

## 11.5 THE MANAGEMENT OF CONFLICT IN UK WORKPLACES

Interestingly, the policy debate over conflict and dispute resolution in the UK has almost entirely focused on the potential of reform of the regulatory framework. Much less attention has been given to the way in which conflict is managed within the workplace. While the Government has acknowledged that a lack of capability and competence among line managers is a barrier to early and effective interventions to address and manage workplace conflict, there has been little detailed consideration of this issue and the way in which managers interact with HR practitioners and employee representatives.

### 11.5.1 HR PRACTITIONERS AND THEIR ROLE IN CONFLICT MANAGEMENT

The traditional role played by personnel managers within the management of conflict was interventionist. In short, personnel, or later HR, were generally called on to resolve or handle disputes. Therefore, workplace conflict was seen as an issue for HR or personnel, who were generally expected to provide solutions to problems that had often arisen between workers and operational managers.

This tended to be seen as reactive and stereotyped as 'firefighting'. Furthermore, conflict-handling came to be seen as a largely administrative and low-status function, while there was a perception that personnel managers lacked the training and expertise necessary to fulfil this role effectively. Whatever the truth of this, there is less doubt that as the role of personnel managers in collective issues and negotiations diminished along with union presence and influence, they became increasingly responsible for the management of individual employment disputes. While operational managers may have had decision-making power, they were largely dependent on 'personnel' or 'HR' to manage disciplinary, grievance and other individual issues.

Nonetheless, it is easy to underestimate the important role played by many personnel and HR managers in maintaining and negotiating relationships with key organisational actors – managers and trade union representatives. These relationships underpinned more informal processes of discussion, mediation and resolution. HR practitioners were therefore involved in negotiating informal resolutions, investigating disputes, and ensuring the implementation of formal procedure. In some workplaces this was a complex and challenging role, often treading a very delicate line between building and maintaining trust with union representatives while providing support and advice to operational managers. In addition, they were often viewed as playing a neutral and impartial role, ensuring equity, consistency and fair treatment. In particular, they were often relied upon by trade union representatives as an honest broker in disputes.

More recently, two related developments have had a fundamental impact on the role played by HR practitioners within the management of conflict. First, the HR function has attempted to develop a more strategic focus, more closely aligned with 'business' goals and objectives. Second, as we discussed earlier in this book, responsibility for the day-to-day management of people, and particularly conflict, has been increasingly devolved to line and operational managers. In relation to conflict management this has seen HR practitioners attempt to adopt a more 'arm's length' advisory service, leaving managers with direct responsibility for handling difficult issues.

The extent to which HR practitioners have been successful in distancing themselves from the operational management of conflict varies greatly from organisation to organisation. In some cases, a lack of managerial confidence and competence has meant that there is still a significant degree of dependence on HR practitioners. Nonetheless, HR practitioners and employment relations specialists still play an important role (Hunter and Renwick, 2009) in developing, maintaining and ensuring the consistent application of workplace procedures. Moreover, they are routinely seen as a source of expert advice in relation to employment law. This has required the development of increased knowledge and expertise and, as Sisson and Purcell (2010: 90) argue, there is evidence of greater 'all-round competence' within the HR community. In addition, it would be mistaken to characterise HR practitioners as simply ensuring procedural and legal compliance. They can also play a key role in coaching and developing managers through conflict situations and (in unionised environments) acting as a link between managers and trade union representatives. For example, regular meetings between employment relations professionals and union representatives can help to identify potential areas of conflict, while informal 'off-the-record' discussions can explore potential resolutions (Saundry and Wibberley, 2014).

However, recent trends in the development of HR structures threaten to make this more difficult. Many organisations, in seeking to increase the efficiency of their HR function, have moved to centralise certain HR services. These shared service centre models have generally been employed to handle issues such as payroll and other HR administration. But in some cases, this has included employee relations advice, with operational managers at local level relying on online guidance and an employment relations specialist on the end of a telephone. This poses a number of possible challenges. First, we previously noted the importance of high-trust relationships in underpinning more informal channels of discussion, negotiation and resolution. This may be more difficult in remote settings – in fact, some remote employment relations advice services actively discourage managers from asking for specific individual advisers. Second, remotely located advisers may not have the contextual knowledge of the workplace and workforce that could lead to more nuanced and creative approaches to employment disputes. Finally, the centralisation and (in some cases) outsourcing of employee relations advice suggests that managing conflict is a transactional issue which does not require specialist knowledge or skill.

**?**   REFLECTIVE ACTIVITY 11.8

In organisations in which you have worked, what has been the role played by HR practitioners in handling workplace conflict? Have they helped to try to resolve issues informally? Or have they focused on ensuring that policy and procedure have been followed?

### 11.5.2 LINE MANAGERS AND CONFLICT – A QUESTION OF CONFIDENCE?

The ability of HR professionals to develop a more advisory 'arm's length' role depends on whether line and operational managers have the skills and the confidence to deal with their new responsibilities. Unfortunately, the signs are not encouraging – the Government has argued that 'it is clear that many more problems could be prevented from escalating into disputes if line managers were better able to manage conflict' (BIS, 2011: 17). At the same time, CIPD research found that 'conflict management' and 'managing difficult conversations' were the two skills that line managers found most difficult to put into practice (CIPD, 2013). In fact, this is consistent with a large amount of research evidence, which points to a lack of confidence among UK line managers (Hutchinson and Purcell, 2010; Teague and Roche, 2012).

Traditionally, operational managers have tended to prefer to manage conflict informally, relying on instincts and 'gut feeling' (Rollinson *et al*, 1996: 51) rather than having to abide by written rules and procedures. This could just reflect a reluctance to take on the administrative burden that inevitably accompanies disciplinary and grievance processes. However, line managers could argue that operational imperatives may need a more flexible approach to such issues. For example, they may be less strict in applying rules in order to maintain morale. Similarly, they may be more lenient in dealing with members of staff who they see as important to the team. Although this is perhaps understandable, one problem of giving managers discretion in this way is that it is open to favouritism, discrimination and potential breaches of organisational procedures that have legal implications.

More recent research has suggested that instead of dealing with conflict informally, managers increasingly appear to be taking shelter behind the rigid application of process and procedure (Saundry and Wibberley, 2014). This may reflect the lack of confidence and skill, particularly given the potential for litigation. However, line managers may also come under pressure from their managers to meet short-term operational objectives. Thus, they may not have the time and space to resolve issues through discussion and communication. Importantly, competences in relation to conflict management (and people management in general) rarely feature in the recruitment, development and promotion of managers.

**?**   REFLECTIVE ACTIVITY 11.9

What are the key challenges facing front-line managers in handling workplace conflict? What do you think organisations can do to overcome these problems?

### 11.5.3 EMPLOYEE REPRESENTATION AND VOICE – THE KEY TO EARLY RESOLUTION?

In the context of the changes outlined in the previous two sections, it has been argued that the growing 'representation gap' in British workplaces has in turn created a 'resolution gap' (Saundry and Wibberley, 2014). Employee representatives play a very important role in the management and outcomes of workplace conflict. For example, the decline of collective regulation in general, and trade union organisation in particular, has seen a dramatic reduction in collective industrial action but has also been influential in the growing number of employment tribunal applications.

As we noted above, there is a clear statistical relationship between falling trade union density and the rapid growth of employment tribunal applications during the 1990s and 2000s. At the same time, workplaces in which trade unions are recognised and union density is high tend to have lower rates of disciplinary sanctions and dismissals. Conversely, employee grievances are perhaps more likely to occur in unionised settings. Why is this? One explanation could be that stronger trade unions are more likely to challenge managerial decisions, deterring them from taking disciplinary action or supporting their members in bringing legal claims through the tribunal system.

However, research has shown that the role of employee representatives is much more complex and nuanced. Union representatives, for example, can play a crucial role in resolving disputes in a constructive way and helping to maintain and repair employment relations – they can help to manage the expectations of their members, make the potential implications of certain behaviours and conflict clear, and negotiate with managers to resolve issues or minimise sanctions (Saundry et al, 2008). In fact, managers in unionised environments tend to be very positive about the role played by representatives in identifying problems and exploring potential resolutions (Saundry and Wibberley, 2014). This also depends on the quality of employer–union relationships. Where these are negative, representatives may be more likely to adopt adversarial approaches in defending members – here, a grievance or a disciplinary issue may become something that is either 'won' or 'lost' rather than an issue that needs to be resolved. In contrast, high levels of trust give managers, HR and unions the confidence to discuss issues 'off the record' in order to try and find informal solutions to difficult workplace problems. Where there are positive relations, a virtuous circle can develop whereby high trust enables the parties to resolve an issue informally, which in turn further strengthens working relationships, facilitating constructive approaches in the future.

Therefore, the decline of employee representation potentially shuts down these informal channels of conflict management and resolution. Of course, this gap could potentially be filled by non-union employee representatives. However, while there is evidence of isolated attempts to develop roles for non-union employee representatives within discipline and grievance processes in companies such as Marks & Spencer PLC, there is little evidence as to their impact. Furthermore, while improved employee engagement may prevent or slow down the development of workplace conflict, it does not provide representational structures through which conflict can be discussed and resolved when it does occur.

---

**?    REFLECTIVE ACTIVITY 11.10**

What is your experience of the role played by employee representatives in disciplinary and grievance processes? Do you think they play a constructive role or make the process more adversarial? If you were facing disciplinary allegations, would you seek the support of a representative and, if so, what would you expect?

## 11.5.4 DEVELOPING A STRATEGIC APPROACH – FROM DISPUTE RESOLUTION TO CONFLICT MANAGEMENT

Growing concerns over the cost and impact of workplace conflict have seen increased attention being given to alternative approaches to dispute resolution and conflict management. Much of the innovation in this area has originated in the United States and revolves around the idea of integrated conflict management systems (ICMS). The essential idea behind ICMS is that organisations need to move away from using individual dispute resolution tools in a fragmented and isolated way. Instead, organisations need a combination of rights-based processes (such as disciplinary and grievance procedures) and interest-based processes (such as workplace mediation). Moreover, this needs to be developed as part of a strategic approach.

Importantly, this also involves a much broader change in the organisational 'mindset' with regards to workplace conflict and how it should be managed (Lipsky and Seeber, 2000: 23). Lynch (2001) argues that this involves a change in philosophy from dispute resolution where managers apply processes in an ad hoc manner to resolve specific disputes to conflict management, which aims to address underlying sources of discontent. In this way an environment is developed in which organisations do not simply wait for disputes to escalate before attempting to resolve them, but one in which managers are expected to prevent, manage, contain and resolve all conflict at the earliest time and lowest level possible. In this way, ICMS creates a 'conflict competent culture' where all conflict may be safely raised and where workers will feel confident that their concerns will be heard, respected and acted upon (Lynch, 2001: 212–213).

In relation to the design of ICMSs, Lynch points out the importance of an organisational champion to drive the development of conflict management. Furthermore, while integrated approaches may be triggered by 'crisis', the need for regulatory 'compliance' and a desire to reduce 'cost', they may also be developed in the pursuit of 'cultural transformation' in order to underpin their broader strategies and seek 'competitive advantage' (Lynch refers to these as the '5Cs').

In the US, Lipsky et al's (2012) study of Fortune 1000 companies suggests organisations are increasingly adopting more strategic and proactive approaches to managing conflict. Overall, one-third of the corporations in the sample had adopted features associated with conflict management systems. Furthermore, there was evidence of a wide range of practices, beyond mediation and arbitration, such as 'early case assessment' and 'peer review' (a process by which disputes are adjudicated by a panel of co-workers).

In contrast, in Great Britain and Ireland, there has been very little sign of this type of innovation being commonly used. Research conducted by Paul Teague and Liam Doherty from Queens University, Belfast, found that senior managers in a sample of non-unionised companies were extremely unwilling to concede that 'conflict' should be accepted as a part of organisational life. In fact, they found that managers were resistant to even talk about the issue of conflict let alone see it as an important strategic issue. This perhaps explains some of the pressures experienced by front-line managers – if the management of conflict is not seen as a strategic imperative, this will be reflected in the time that managers are able to devote to it, the extent to which they are trained and supported, and also whether it is seen as a core competency in the recruitment and promotion of managers.

Nonetheless, there are examples of organisations adopting more proactive and co-ordinated approaches. The case of Northumberland Healthcare Trust (outlined in the following case study) is particularly interesting.

MORE THAN JUST A MEDIATION SCHEME – THE CASE OF
NORTHUMBERLAND HEALTHCARE TRUST

Northumberland Healthcare Trust's approach to conflict management began with the development of an in-house mediation service in 2006. One of the main drivers for this was stress management standards by the Health and Safety Executive in 2005, which included the promotion of 'positive working to avoid conflict and dealing with unacceptable behaviour', and the need for organisations to:

- have systems in place to respond to individual concerns
- promote positive behaviours at work to avoid conflict and ensure fairness
- have agreed policies and procedures to prevent or resolve unacceptable behaviour
- have systems to enable and encourage managers to deal with unacceptable behaviour.

Consequently, the establishment of an internal mediation service was supported at a high level by senior management. Initially, a cohort of 12 staff were trained, drawn from a range of posts within the organisation including consultants, managers, nurses, HR staff and trade union representatives. This reflected a deliberate attempt to embed the service in different areas of the organisation. Subsequently, a further seven mediators were trained in 2011. The champion of the service was a consultant clinical psychologist in NHCT's occupational

health department, and there was also palpable commitment from senior management.

Crucially, this reflected an acceptance that managing conflict more effectively was central to the well-being and engagement of staff and also standards of patient care. As a result, conflict management was a specific strand of the organisation's HR strategy. Subsequently, existing 'rights-based' policies were rewritten to emphasise the role of mediation and the importance of conflict resolution. In addition, training for managers, in 'holding difficult conversations', was rolled out along with more specialised conflict-resolution training. Furthermore, people management attributes became a core competence under a new values-based system.

A broader approach to managing conflict and its consequences has been developed through a partnership between occupational health psychologists, trade unions, HR and senior management. A Health and Well-being Steering Group identifies conflict stress 'hotspots' within the organisation by analysing a range of key indicators. A range of interventions are then considered and deployed including individual mediation, targeted training, stress risk assessments, team facilitation and conflict coaching.

Source: Latreille and Saundry (2015)

The case of Northumberland Healthcare Trust highlights a number of principles that arguably underpin effective conflict management:

- The management of conflict needs to be seen as a strategic issue – critical in underpinning well-being, engagement and performance.
- Conflict resolution and people skills should be viewed as a core competence for front-line managers.
- Working in partnership with organisational stakeholders is crucial in facilitating early and informal resolution of conflict.

- Organisations need to combine traditional disciplinary and grievance procedures with a range of alternative dispute resolution (ADR) approaches and tools.
- Conflict management intervention needs to be flexible and based on systematic analysis of data.

## 11.6 SUMMARY

In this chapter we have provided an overview of the nature and pattern of workplace conflict and examined the key factors that shape the ability of organisations to manage it effectively. It is almost impossible to say whether there has been any reduction or increase in workplace conflict in recent years. However, the last 20 to 30 years have seen a fundamental shift in the channels through which workplace conflict is expressed. The decline of trade unions and the collective regulation of employment have seen a significant decline in the use of strike action and a relative increase in individual employment disputes. The most visible example of this has been employment tribunal claims, which increased rapidly during the 1990s and early 2000s.

Conventionally, the application of policy and procedure has been seen as central in managing conflict and avoiding unnecessary employment disputes. However, the Gibbons Review marked an important turning point, with the conclusion that formality could block early resolution of disputes and in some situations make litigation more likely. Gibbons saw mediation as one way to deal with this problem. However, while the use of mediation has become more prominent, government policy has instead primarily revolved around attempts to reduce the threat of litigation by minimising the risks faced by employers when terminating employment. Perhaps the most significant and far-reaching measure has been the introduction of tribunal fees, which has undoubtedly substantially curtailed the volume of employment claims.

However, there is a danger that lower levels of litigation will mask some of the underlying problems with conflict management 'competence' in UK workplaces. Barriers to early resolution are not simply made up of unduly formal procedures but by an inability or unwillingness within many organisations to recognise the inevitability of conflict and develop clear strategies to manage it.

In the following chapters we look at different processes through which conflict is managed and disputes resolved. First, we examine the management of workplace discipline. Second, we explore the nature and pattern of employee grievances and how these can be addressed and handled. Third, we focus on the management of redundancy and finally, we examine the theory and practice underpinning workplace mediation.

## KEY LEARNING POINTS

1   There has been a substantial and possibly permanent decline in the incidence of industrial action. This has largely been caused by the erosion of trade union organisation and the reduction of the bargaining power of labour, which in turn has blunted the potency of strike action.

2   These changes coincided with a rapid growth in employment tribunal volumes. However, it is questionable whether this represents an individualisation of conflict. Many of the main sources of tribunal claims are collective in character, and much of the growth was driven by multiple applications.

3   Recent government policy has revolved around employers' concerns over the burden of employment litigation in general and on the costs of litigation in particular. While there is little evidence that employer perceptions reflect the actual burdens of employment legislation, these perceptions have shaped the way that conflict has been managed and encouraged more formal approaches.

4    Legislative reform has focused on reducing the risk faced by employers in dismissing employees. In particular, the introduction of employment tribunal fees has substantially reduced the number of applications. Employers' organisations argue that this is due to individuals with weak claims being deterred from applying. Others suggest that it simply reflects a reduction in access to justice.

5    The capacity of organisations to manage conflict has been restricted by three related factors: the changing nature of the HR function; the erosion of workplace structures of employee representations; and a lack of confidence among front-line managers in handling difficult issues. Consequently, informal processes whereby conflict is resolved through discussion and negotiation have been increasingly replaced by rigid procedural adherence.

6    There is limited evidence of organisational innovation in conflict management in the UK. There has been some growth in interest in workplace mediation and there is evidence that this can have a range of benefits. However, it tends to be used as a last resort rather than as part of a strategic approach to the management of conflict.

## ? REVIEW QUESTIONS

1    What are the main reasons for the reduction in strike action in the UK over the past four decades? To what extent does this represent a permanent change in employment relations?

2    What were the main recommendations of the Gibbons Review? Evaluate the impact of these recommendations on UK policy and on organisational practice?

3    Did the introduction of employment tribunal fees represent a sensible rebalancing of workplace power or an unacceptable restriction on access to justice? Did these changes enhance or obstruct the development of innovative conflict resolution strategies?

4    What are the implications of the devolution of responsibility for people management from HR to the line for conflict management, and the ability of organisations to resolve difficult issues in an early and informal manner?

5    Does the organisation in which you work have a conflict management system? What are the main barriers to the adoption of strategic approaches to conflict management by UK organisations?

EXPLORE FURTHER

DIX, G., FORTH, J. and SISSON, K. (2009) Conflict at work: the changing pattern of disputes. In BROWN, W., BRYSON, A. and FORTH, J. (eds). *The evolution of the modern workplace.* Cambridge: Cambridge University Press.

JORDAN, E., THOMAS, A. and KITCHING, J. (2013) Employment regulation – part A: employer perceptions and the impact of employment regulation. *Employment Relations Research Series.* 123. Department for Business, Innovation and Skills.

SAUNDRY, R. and DIX, G. (2014) Conflict resolution in the UK. In ROCHE, W., TEAGUE, P. and COLVIN, A. (eds). *The Oxford handbook on conflict management.* Oxford: Oxford University Press Research and Policy Papers.

SAUNDRY, R., LATREILLE, P. and DICKENS, L. (2014) *Reframing resolution – managing conflict and resolving individual employment disputes in the contemporary workplace.* Acas policy series.

**Website links**

www.acas.gov.uk is the website for the Advisory, Conciliation and Arbitration Service.

# CHAPTER 12

# Managing Workplace Discipline

## OVERVIEW

In this chapter we explore the challenges faced by employment relations professionals when managing employee behaviour and performance. This includes the principles of discipline-handling, the characteristics of a fair and effective disciplinary procedure, the legal aspects of discipline and dismissal, and the monitoring and evaluation of disciplinary procedures. The chapter stresses the importance of focusing on improving or changing behaviour, rather than punishing employees who fall below expected norms and standards. It sets out the key elements of the Acas Code of Practice on Disciplinary and Grievance Procedures and explains in detail the steps that managers should follow in order to manage disciplinary issues in a fair, consistent and effective manner. The chapter ends with a discussion of issues that managers need to consider in responding to issues related to performance and absence.

## LEARNING OUTCOMES

When you have completed this chapter, you should be able to:

- explain and critically reflect on the purpose of disciplinary procedures
- understand the importance of, and draft, clear rules
- explain the importance of informal resolution and understand the roles played by managers, employment relations specialists and union representatives in this regard
- design, apply and give advice in regard to effective disciplinary procedure in accordance with the principle of natural justice
- understand and assess the particular issues facing managers in handling issues relating to performance and absence.

## 12.1 INTRODUCTION

In recent years, responsibility for many employment relations issues has been devolved from HR practitioners to line managers. Perhaps the most important of these is the management of workplace discipline. Front-line managers are now expected to: address issues of poor performance or behaviour; explore informal resolutions; enact and conduct disciplinary procedures; and take decisions over possible sanctions. As we have discussed in the previous chapter, many managers find this extremely daunting. Therefore, the employment relations professional in an organisation plays a critical role in providing advice at all stages of the process and often in coaching managers, who may lack confidence. Furthermore, they can help to ensure that disciplinary matters are handled fairly and consistently across the organisation.

## 12.2 DISCIPLINE – IMPROVING BEHAVIOUR?

Discipline is an emotive word in the context of employment. The dictionary offers several definitions of the word discipline, ranging from 'punishment or chastisement' to 'systematic training in obedience'. There is no doubt that discipline at work can be one of the most difficult issues with which a manager has to deal. It brings to the forefront matters relating to an individual's performance, capability and conduct. In the context of employment, the most appropriate definition to adopt might well be:

> 'to improve or attempt to improve the behaviour, orderliness, etc, by training, conditions or rules.' (Collins Concise Dictionary)

We argue that discipline should be used as an opportunity to improve the conduct and performance, rather than punish employees for failing to meet organisational norms and standards. The prime objective should always be to keep the employee in the organisation wherever possible and to seek to develop their potential. We have noted earlier in this book that changes to the framework of employment rights have reduced the risks associated with 'hiring and firing' staff. However, such an approach not only means that investment in recruitment and training is lost but also undermines perceptions of organisational justice, which, as John Purcell (2012) has argued, is one of the main pillars of employee engagement.

Therefore, it is important for managers, at all levels, to appreciate that organisational effectiveness can be damaged if issues relating to conduct, capability and performance are not addressed at the earliest possible point and handled professionally, fairly and consistently. It is important to understand that this does not just reflect a set of prescriptive rules and guidelines. Taking into account the context of the organisation and the circumstances of each situation is critical to the effective management of discipline.

Employment relations professionals should also be aware that many managers are reluctant to address problems with conduct and capability because they believe that disciplinary procedures are cumbersome and ineffective, and fear that any attempt to manage 'difficult issues' could result in legal challenge or internal criticism. Furthermore, managers often lack necessary training and sometimes the support of senior colleagues. This can then result in problems being ignored and/or procedures being implemented in a rigid and inflexible way. Providing sound and sensible advice and coaching inexperienced managers in handling disciplinary issues is therefore a critical aspect of the HR function.

## 12.3 DISCIPLINARY PROCEDURES

Having a written disciplinary procedure is essential for any organisation. It allows the organisation to establish clear standards and to provide a clear process through which all disciplinary issues can be managed. It helps to ensure consistency, particularly in large organisations, and to underpin fairness and equity. The starting point for any disciplinary procedure is the Acas Code of Practice on Disciplinary and Grievance Procedures. Not only does the Code provide a clear benchmark of 'good practice', but it is taken into account by employment tribunals when considering claims of unfair dismissal. While breach of the Code of Practice is in itself not unlawful, managers can be reassured that if they follow the terms of the Code and their own procedure, they will normally be seen to be acting fairly. Furthermore, tribunals are able to adjust any awards made in relevant cases by up to 25% if they consider that any party has unreasonably failed to follow the guidance set out in the Code. The Code is also supported by guidance entitled Discipline and Grievances at Work, which provides detailed advice for dealing with discipline and grievances in the workplace.

## 12.3.1 THE DISCIPLINARY PROCESS

For a number of years, disciplinary procedures commonly observed a specific sequence as follows:

● Oral warning
● Written warning if the required improvement was not forthcoming
● Final written warning if conduct or performance was still unsatisfactory
● Dismissal.

Under this type of procedure, employers routinely issued oral warnings that were anything but 'verbal'. More often than not, such warnings were followed up in writing and placed on an employee's personnel record – thus, in effect, making them a written warning in everything but name. The latest Acas guidance recognises this contradiction and suggests that cases of minor misconduct or unsatisfactory performance are dealt with informally. In the informal stage, which effectively replaces the oral warning, managers are seeking an agreement with the employee on how to ensure that the misconduct (perhaps in timekeeping) is not repeated or that steps are taken to overcome the performance issues. There is no reason why, if agreement is reached on the way forward, that it is not confirmed in writing. If managers do this, however, it is important to confirm that nothing that has been said, done or agreed that constitutes disciplinary action.

This also reflects an increased emphasis in Acas guidance on the importance of addressing issues at an early stage before they have escalated. By doing this, disciplinary sanctions can be avoided; the chances of improving behaviour and repairing the employment relationship are much greater if difficult issues are not left to fester. In doing this, good relationships between HR practitioners, line managers and also employee and union representatives can be extremely helpful. Research conducted by Saundry and Wibberley (2014) into the management of workplace conflict found that, in large organisations, regular meetings between HR practitioners and employee representatives were vital in identifying emerging problems and trying to find ways of 'nipping them in the bud' before there was a need to launch formal disciplinary proceedings. Managers, in particular, can be wary of having 'difficult conversations' with their staff and are also sometimes concerned that informal discussions will cause legal and other problems. However, this is where the HR practitioner can play a key role: by providing managers with the confidence to look for more creative solutions to problems and brokering relationships with trade union and other employee representatives.

It is only if the informal approach does not work, or matters are too serious for such an approach, that employers are recommended to move into the formal stage. The essential components of the formal stage, which could result in a written warning, final written warning or dismissal, are clearly set out in the Code of Practice. These are that you must:

● inform the employee of the problem in writing
● hold a meeting with the employee to discuss the problem
● allow the employee to be accompanied at the meeting
● decide on appropriate action
● provide the employee with an opportunity to appeal.

In addition to the key steps outlined above, the Acas Code also sets out a number of principles that should underpin effective disciplinary procedures. These are important in two respects: first, they reflect the key tenets of natural justice that tribunals will consider in deciding whether a procedure used in dismissing an employee is fair; second, they underpin procedural justice, which in turn is a key factor in generating high-trust employment relations.

DISCIPLINARY PROCEDURES – KEY PRINCIPLES

Disciplinary procedures should:

- be in writing
- not discriminate
- provide for matters to be dealt with without undue delay
- provide for proceedings, witness statements and records to be kept confidential
- clearly indicate the disciplinary actions that may be taken
- specify the levels of management that have the authority to take the various forms of disciplinary action
- provide for workers to be informed of the complaints against them and, where possible, to see all relevant evidence before any hearing
- give employees time to prepare the case before the hearing
- provide workers with an opportunity to state their case before decisions are reached
- provide workers with the right to be accompanied
- ensure that, except for gross misconduct, no worker is dismissed for a first breach of discipline
- ensure that disciplinary action is not taken until the case has been carefully investigated
- ensure that workers are given an explanation for any penalty imposed
- provide a right of appeal – normally to a more senior manager – and specify the procedure to be followed.

## 12.3.2 THE IMPORTANCE OF RULES

The basis of workplace discipline is the rules that define and make clear exactly what standards of behaviour are expected in the workplace. If these are not clear, it will be impossible to manage disciplinary issues in a fair and consistent way. Typically, rules cover the following areas:

- timekeeping
- absence
- health and safety
- misconduct
- use of company facilities
- confidentiality
- discrimination.

Normally, these will be contained in an employee handbook or a range of different policies. However, the most important consideration is that they are clear and not open to interpretation. In addition, as we note below, it is important that they distinguish between ordinary misconduct and gross misconduct. It is no good having a very clear procedure, laying down the type and number of warnings that an individual should receive, if the rules that are being applied are imprecise or do not reflect the attitudes and requirements of the particular business.

For example, vague statements about whether a breach of a specific rule 'may' be treated as gross misconduct can leave room for doubt and confusion. If an employee stole a large sum of money from the company, there is little doubt that they would be charged with gross misconduct and, if the allegation was proved, dismissed without notice. What, though, would happen if the alleged theft was of items of company stationery or spare parts for machinery? Employment relations professionals have to be aware of these potential contradictions when helping to frame rules that govern the employment relationship. Allowing different managers to take a different view about the seriousness of certain acts of theft brings inconsistency into the process. Therefore, a clear rule in relation to theft may be:

'stealing from a company, its suppliers or fellow employees is unacceptable – whatever the value or amount involved – and will be treated as gross misconduct.'

Using this style of wording should help to ensure that every employee in the organisation knows the consequences of any dishonest action on their part. Ensuring that managers apply the sanction consistently is another problem, and one that we will examine later in the chapter.

## ? REFLECTIVE ACTIVITY 12.1

How often are the rules in your organisation reviewed, and when were they last updated? Can you think of a rule that is vague and difficult to enforce? How could this be changed to make it more effective?

It is also important to make sure that rules reflect current industrial practice, as is illustrated by the case of *Denco* v *Joinson [1991] IRLR 63* (Case Study 12.1).

## 👁 STATING THE OBVIOUS?

**CASE STUDY 12.1**

*Denco v Joinson [1991] IRLR 63*

The applicant, who was a union representative, had been dismissed for gross misconduct for gaining unauthorised access to his employer's computer system. He had accessed a part of the system that would normally not be available to him by using another employee's password. In his defence, it was argued that 'he had only been playing around' with the system, and that there had been no intent to obtain information to which he was not entitled. Furthermore, although he might have been doing something wrong, it was not 'gross misconduct' and could have been covered by a disciplinary warning. In upholding the dismissal for gross misconduct, the Employment Appeal Tribunal (EAT) stated:

*'The industrial members are clear in their view that in this modern industrial world if an employee deliberately uses an unauthorised password in order to enter or to attempt to enter a computer known to contain information to which he is not entitled, then that of itself is gross misconduct, which prima facie will attract summary dismissal, although there may be some exceptional circumstances in which such a response might be held unreasonable.'*

In essence, the EAT were making the same point that had been made some years earlier in *C A Parsons & Co Ltd* v *McLaughlin (1978) IRLR 65*, that some things should be so obvious that it ought not to be necessary to have a rule forbidding it. However, for the avoidance of doubt, the EAT went on to say in the *Denco* case that:

'It is desirable, however, that management should make it abundantly clear to the workforce that interfering with computers will carry severe penalties. Rules concerning access to and use of computers should be reduced to writing and left near the computers for reference.'

While these comments may seem perfectly reasonable, it should be remembered that employers have an absolute duty to demonstrate that they have acted reasonably when they dismiss somebody. In *Denco*, the EAT acknowledged that there might be circumstances in which an employer's particular response might be 'unreasonable' even about something that is supposedly obvious. The message is very clear. If something is not allowed, say so – and spell out the consequences of breaching the rule. Because technology, or the ownership of businesses, can change, and what may have been acceptable once, may now be frowned on.

A classic contemporary example is the growth of the use of social media through sites such as Facebook, Twitter and Instagram. In some respects, the potential problem for employers is the use of social media for non-work purposes during working hours. However, in many occupations, workers are now encouraged to use social media for marketing, public relations and recruitment activities, which further complicates the development of clear policies and rules. Furthermore, social media can be a cause of conflict that spills over into the workplace. Research commissioned by Acas and conducted by the Institute of Employment Studies identified some of the key challenges facing employers and concluded that:

> 'A good and clear policy on what constitutes an unacceptable use of social media in a particular organisation will help both the employer and the employee to understand where the boundaries between acceptable and non-acceptable use lie.' (Broughton *et al*, 2010: 30)

Acas advises that policies should clearly define what is regarded as acceptable and unacceptable behaviour in the use of social media at work. In addition, an organisation should be clear about what employees can comment on in relation to work. Finally, it should make a clear distinction between using social media in relation to business and using it privately. This includes setting limits as to how social media can be used for private use while at work.

For example, the following is an extract from a policy used in an NHS trust setting out rules as to the private use of social media:

## DUTIES AND RESPONSIBILITIES – PRIVATE USE OF SOCIAL MEDIA

1   Staff and contractors of the Trust may use designated facilities provided by the Trust for their private social media purposes during their work breaks.

2   Staff should be aware that the Trust reserves the right to use legitimate means to scan the Web, including social networking sites for content that it finds inappropriate. The Trust also reserves the right to monitor staff usage of social networking sites in work time.

3   Staff are encouraged not to divulge who their employers are within their personal profile page. However, those that do divulge their employer should state that they are tweeting/blogging etc in a personal capacity.

4   Staff and contractors are ultimately responsible for their own online behaviour. Staff and contractors must take care to avoid online content or actions that are inaccurate, libelous, defamatory, harassing, threatening or may otherwise be illegal. It is possible for staff or contractors to be subject to civil proceedings or criminal prosecution.

5   Staff and contractors are not authorised to communicate by any means on behalf of the Trust unless this is an accepted normal part of their job, or through special arrangement that has been approved in advance by the Communications Team. No social media sites or pages

relating to the Trust should be set up by staff and/or contractors without prior approval from the Communications Team.

6    Staff and contractors who use social media must not disclose information of the Trust that is or may be sensitive or confidential, or that is subject to a non-disclosure contract or agreement. This applies to information about service users, other staff and contractors, other organisations, commercial suppliers and other information about the Trust and its business activities.

As we stated above, there are a number of variables – such as technological developments – in the drafting of company rules, and employment relations professionals should try to ensure that in his or her organisation they are the subject of regular monitoring and review so that they properly reflect the organisation's current values and requirements.

## 12.4 GROSS MISCONDUCT

As we noted previously, clear rules are most important when dealing with issues of potential gross misconduct. We have already pointed out that it can be fair to summarily dismiss an employee (without notice) if they have been found to have committed an act of gross misconduct. But what is 'gross misconduct'? Acas very helpfully provides a list of actions that would normally fall into this category.

### POTENTIAL ACTS OF GROSS MISCONDUCT

- Theft or fraud
- Physical violence or bullying
- Deliberate and serious damage to property
- Serious misuse of an organisation's property or name
- Deliberately accessing websites containing pornographic, offensive or obscene material
- Bringing the organisation into serious disrepute
- Serious incapability through alcohol or the influence of illegal drugs
- Causing loss, damage or injury through serious negligence
- A serious breach of health and safety rules
- Serious acts of insubordination
- Unlawful discrimination or harassment
- A serious breach of confidence

While that is quite an extensive list, a number of items are still open to interpretation. For example, what is an act of serious insubordination? Would it cover the refusal to carry out instructions received from a supervisor? What is serious negligence or serious incapability through alcohol? Although attitudes have changed and people tend not to socialise so much during their breaks, drinking at lunchtime still happens. How do you decide when a lunchtime drink crosses the threshold? One of the difficulties managers face in dealing with this type of disciplinary issue is ensuring that they do not impose their own moral standards on other people. Furthermore, the culture of the organisation is relevant to deciding whether a particular behaviour constitutes gross misconduct.

One way in which a distinction can be drawn is by reference to the relationship of trust that has to exist between employer and employee. We noted in Chapter 4 that it is implied in every contract that for an employment relationship to be maintained there has to be mutual trust and confidence between employer and employee. When issues of discipline arise, that relationship is damaged. One of the purposes of disciplinary action is to bring about a change in behaviour, and if, for instance, the offence is one of poor timekeeping, there is usually no question of a total breakdown of trust: the expected outcome of disciplinary action is improved timekeeping and a rebuilding of the relationship. Conversely, if the cause of the disciplinary action is a serious assault on another employee, perhaps a manager, a disciplinary sanction might bring about a change in behaviour or ensure that the offence is not repeated, but there is a high probability that the relationship of mutual trust and confidence might be damaged beyond repair, and it might be impossible for the employment relationship to be maintained.

Nonetheless, in matters of gross misconduct there will sometimes be a lack of clarity over when somebody has 'overstepped the mark'. The potential difficulties caused by this lack of clarity mean that whatever procedure you establish, it reflects the organisation's structure and culture – the norms and beliefs within which an organisation functions. This is why the writing of clear company rules is so important. Not only do they help to distinguish between ordinary and gross misconduct, but they provide employees with clear guidelines on what is acceptable in the workplace, in terms of both behaviour and performance.

### 12.4.1 USING WARNINGS TO IMPROVE BEHAVIOUR

Most disciplinary offences do not constitute gross misconduct and the use of warnings can be a way of helping employees to improve their behaviour of their performance and fulfil their potential in the organisation. The most important consideration is that when employees are issued with a warning, the nature of the problem and the expected improvement is made clear. Where appropriate, this may also be backed up by training, support, mentoring and ongoing review. However, it also crucial that the warning has a finite 'life', which indicates the length of time that a particular disciplinary sanction will stay on the record. 'Live' warnings can trigger more serious action. For example, if an employee receives a first warning for poor timekeeping, which lasts for a period of six months, a failure to improve within that period could legitimately lead to a final written warning. However, if the employee improves their timekeeping initially but then this deteriorates again after the six months has elapsed, the employer would normally have to return to the start of the procedure. Many organisations will have different timescales for different levels of warning. For example, a written warning might only be 'live' for six months, whereas a final written warning might be live for 12 months.

Although it is to be hoped that any disciplinary problems within an organisation can be resolved at the earliest opportunity, and without recourse to all levels of the procedure, the world of work is not so simple. Many managers complain that employees may initially respond to a warning by improving their behaviour or performance, only for the issue to resurface once the warning ceases to be 'live'. To avoid such a situation, two points must be considered. First, it is important that the life of the warning is appropriate. If it is for too short a time, you run the risk of only achieving short-term changes in behaviour. On the other hand, a sanction that remains on an employee's record for an excessive period of time relative to the original breach of discipline can act as a demotivating influence. Second, the Acas Code of Practice makes it clear that the procedure may be implemented at any stage. Therefore, it is permissible to take into account the past disciplinary record before deciding whether to issue a first or a final written warning.

A more contentious question is whether expired warnings can be taken into account when reaching a decision to dismiss. In the case of *Airbus* v *Webb (2008)*, Webb was one of five employees found watching television when they should have been working. While they were all disciplined, Webb was the only one to be sacked because he had had a previous warning, although expired, for a similar matter. The Court of Appeal ruled that although employers should not rely on expired warnings 'as a matter of course', they could be one factor to be taken into account in deciding whether the employer had acted reasonably or not. In broad terms this suggests that employers can take the wider personnel record of an employee into account in arriving at a decision. However, they should not use spent warnings as a reason for dismissal in themselves.

The purpose and scope of a disciplinary procedure should be very clear. It should allow all employees to understand what is expected of them in respect of conduct, attendance and job performance, and set out the rules by which such matters are governed. The aim is to ensure consistent and fair treatment for all.

> ## ?  REFLECTIVE ACTIVITY 12.2
>
> Is your organisation's disciplinary procedure clear? Does it set out the time for which individual warnings will remain 'live', and is it capable of ensuring consistent and fair treatment for all employees? Are there any ways in which your disciplinary procedure could be improved?

## 12.5 HANDLING DISCIPLINARY ISSUES

The way in which managers and employment relations professionals approach disciplinary issues will be subtly different, depending on the nature of the problem. Most organisations will have some form of disciplinary procedure, and probably some company rules as previously outlined, but the use and application of the procedure may vary from company to company and from manager to manager. In some organisations disciplinary action is very rarely taken, either because standards are clear and accepted by employees or because standards are vague and applied haphazardly. In others, standards are maintained by an overreliance on automatic procedures, which usually acts as a demotivating influence on the workforce.

The purpose of any disciplinary procedure should be to promote good employment relations and fairness and consistency in the treatment of individuals. It should also provide managers with a clear framework for handling disciplinary issues. However, in addition, it should allow for a sensible degree of flexibility so that managers are able to react and respond appropriately to the circumstances of each situation.

### 12.5.1 INFORMAL AND EARLY RESOLUTION

If managers are only concerned with legal compliance, they will not be as effective as those who are driven by the need to operate 'good practice'. The law on unfair dismissal is now so ingrained into the fabric of the workplace that only by maintaining such standards does it cease to become an issue. Good managers have nothing to fear from the laws relating to individual employment rights. Furthermore, reaching for the disciplinary procedure should be the last resort. Instead, managers and HR practitioners should always consider whether some other route would be more appropriate. Maintaining good standards of discipline within an organisation is not just about applying the rules or operating the procedure. It is about the ability to achieve standards of performance and behaviour without using the 'big stick'. One way this might be done, and avoid becoming embroiled in the disciplinary process, is through informal discussion between a manager and the worker, or sometimes a facilitated meeting involving an HR practitioner. This is sometimes referred to as 'counselling', but it is important for managers to be careful not to attempt to deal with serious emotional issues for which a qualified professional counsellor would be required.

However, managers and HR practitioners can help an individual, in a non-threatening way, to come to terms with a particular problem. The problem may be about performance, about timekeeping, about drug or alcohol abuse or about another employee – for example, an accusation of sexual harassment. In a situation, for example, involving potential drug or alcohol abuse, managers may not have the necessary skills to fully address such a sensitive issue, but even if they conclude that specialist assistance is required, they can still help to bring the problem out into the open. In other cases, provided the problem is approached in a systematic way, this type of intervention may avoid disciplinary action.

In addition, as we have pointed out earlier in this chapter, developing constructive relationships with trade union and employee representatives may be extremely useful in providing an environment in which early and informal resolution takes place. In many cases, representatives can act as an 'early warning system' of escalating conflict. Crucially, a worker or employee who is embroiled in a disciplinary issue is much more likely to confide in, and trust, their representative rather than their manager or an HR practitioner, and this can be invaluable in helping to find creative solutions to what may seem like intractable problems.

As we discussed at start of this chapter, the first question facing a manager in addressing a potential disciplinary issue is whether informal discussion and potential resolution is appropriate. Even cases of serious misconduct can often be complex and multifaceted. A sensitive and informal approach in the first instance may reveal underlying causes that can be resolved, helping the worker change their behaviour, retaining valuable skills and avoiding the costs involved in disciplinary action and potential dismissal. Accusations of bullying and harassment are one area in which early informal resolution can be effective. Of course, if this involves serious mistreatment, disciplinary action may be warranted. However, some complainants simply want the offending behaviour to cease. At the same time, the alleged harasser or bully often does not realise that their behaviour or actions are causing offence or fear. Sitting down with an individual and explaining to them that some of their words or actions are causing distress to another employee can often be very effective. However, it is important not to leave it there but to monitor the situation, ensure that the behavioural change is permanent, and see that the complainant is satisfied with the action taken and the eventual outcome. Moreover, as discussed in Chapter 14, techniques such as workplace mediation may also be invaluable if used at an early point in the process.

## ? REFLECTIVE ACTIVITY 12.3

Does your organisation's disciplinary code say anything about equal opportunities or discrimination? Is there, for example, a clear rule that says sexual harassment or racial discrimination will not be tolerated? Do you think there any circumstances when such informal resolution is suitable for such issues?

### 12.5.2 USING THE DISCIPLINARY PROCEDURE

If informal attempts to resolve the problem are not successful, it may be necessary to initiate the disciplinary procedure. However, starting down the disciplinary path can, ultimately, lead to a dismissal. Therefore, it is important to remember the requirement that in taking a decision to dismiss somebody, you should act reasonably and in accordance with natural justice.

## Investigation

In all cases of alleged misconduct it is vital that a proper investigation is carried out. Such an investigation should take place in a timely and sensitive fashion and must be seen to be fair and thorough. The manager selected to carry out the investigation has an obligation to explain to the individual being investigated that the process will involve an objective and non-judgemental inquiry into the facts of the alleged misconduct – that the purpose is not to build a case against the employee but to search for evidence that confirms or refutes the allegation.

As we note later, where possible and practicable the investigation should be undertaken by a person different from the one who might hear any consequent disciplinary case. As with all employee relations activities, it is advisable to keep clear notes of any interviews with witnesses and the accused employee. A thorough investigation should take account of any relevant work documents, policies and procedures and seek to establish whether any relevant training had been carried out.

## Accompaniment and Representation

One of the key principles outlined previously is that workers should have the opportunity to be accompanied at a disciplinary hearing by either a union representative or a work colleague. If an employer refuses to allow this, it is likely to render any subsequent dismissal unfair. In fact, under the Employment Relations Act (1999), all workers have a statutory right to be accompanied at disciplinary and grievance hearings by either a work colleague or a trade union representative. The right does not extend to family members, friends or legal representatives unless they happen to be a work colleague. It is important to note that the right to be accompanied applies to every individual, not just union members, and it is of no consequence whether the organisation recognises unions or not. The right applies where the worker is required or invited by his or her employer to attend a disciplinary hearing at which a sanction may be levied and when he or she makes a reasonable request to be accompanied. Importantly, the onus is on the worker to request accompaniment; however, it is good practice for employers to remind workers of this right.

Companions are able to provide advice and support to the worker and can address the hearing to put the case on their behalf of the employee, sum up the case and ask questions. They can also respond to any views expressed at the hearing. However, they are not permitted to answer questions on behalf of the worker, or address the hearing, if the worker does not want the companion to do so. They must also not prevent the employer from explaining his or her case or do anything that prevents any other person at the hearing from making his or her contribution to it. In reality, some employers may find it useful for companions to answer for workers who may find it difficult to express themselves, particularly in the stressful environment of a disciplinary hearing.

The right only applies to hearings or meetings that could result in a sanction being levied or confirmed. Therefore, it does not apply to an informal discussion, counselling session, facilitated meeting or investigatory interview. However, in some unionised organisations, it is common practice for workers to be offered representation during investigations. Whether this is advisable largely depends on the context of the organisation and the nature of relationships between management and unions. There is a danger that representation at an early stage can escalate matters unnecessarily. This said, research has shown that where relationships between representatives and managers are good, representatives can play an important role during the disciplinary process. Not only can they ensure that processes are implemented fairly, but they can help to manage the expectations of workers, uncover mitigating circumstances and act as a broker in negotiating potential resolutions.

Research conducted on behalf of Acas suggested that non-union companions, who are generally work colleagues with little experience or training, tend to play little role in disciplinary hearings apart from offering moral support (Saundry *et al*, 2008). In most cases, they have little idea of what they are able to do and therefore, we would suggest that managers, where possible, brief companions prior to the hearing. The same research also suggested that in most unionised organisations managers were very positive about the role played by union representatives during disciplinary hearings. Having representatives present helped to ensure that issues were explored and also that the process was fair. In addition, representatives were able to explain the implications of the process and manage the expectations of the worker, often reducing tensions and unnecessary confrontation. However, this was dependent on high-trust relationships between employers and unions. Where employee relations were poor or in non-unionised companies with little experience of unions, managers perceived union representatives to be adversarial and found their legal and procedural knowledge daunting. This suggests that good employment relations are very important in providing the basis for managing discipline in an effective and constructive manner.

### Preparing for the Disciplinary Hearing

If the outcome of any investigation is that the disciplinary procedure should be invoked, then – as with all management activities – the preparatory process is of particular importance. There are various steps that must be taken in preparing to conduct a disciplinary interview, and a number of points to consider, some of which are a statutory requirement:

1   Prepare carefully, and ensure that the person who is going to conduct the disciplinary hearing has all the facts and details of the investigation. In larger organisations, the person who will make the decision at a disciplinary hearing must not have been involved in the investigation. If the investigation and decision is not separated in this way, any decision to dismiss is likely to be unfair.

2   Ensure that the employee knows what the nature of the complaint is and what the potential outcome could be. In particular, if there is a possibility that the hearing could result in dismissal, the employee needs to be forewarned, normally in the invitation letter to the hearing. This again sounds straightforward but is often the point at which things begin to go wrong. For example, it would not be sufficient to tell an employee that they are to attend a disciplinary hearing in respect of their poor performance. They have to be provided with sufficient detail so that they can prepare an adequate defence and so that the employer can demonstrate that it has met the relevant statutory requirements. It is good practice to provide the employee with any evidence that could be relied on during the disciplinary hearing, including copies of witness statements.

3   Arrange a suitable time and place for the interview. There is a tendency for managers to arrange meetings within their own offices, where the potential for being interrupted is more pronounced or privacy less easily guaranteed.

4   Ensure that the employee knows the procedure to be followed. It is always wise to provide them with a new copy of the disciplinary procedure – not least because there may have been amendments since they received their version.

5   Advise the employee of their right to be accompanied. Where individuals work in a unionised environment, this tends to be automatic, with an invitation to attend the meeting sent directly to the appropriate union official. However, in non-unionised environments people are not always sure who would be an appropriate person to accompany them or whether they want to be accompanied at all. As a matter of good practice, it is wise to encourage somebody to be accompanied, but if they refuse, this should be respected.

6 Allow the employee time to prepare their case. The question here is how much time should be allowed. It is important that issues of discipline are dealt with speedily once an employee has been advised of the complaint against them, but it is important for the employee not to feel unfairly pressured in putting together any defence that they have.

7 Ensure that personnel records and other relevant documentation are available. This covers more than basic information about the individual and includes records relating to any previous disciplinary warnings, attendance and performance appraisals.

8 Where possible, be accompanied. It is very unwise for a manager to conduct a disciplinary interview alone because of the possible need at some future time to corroborate what was said. It also helps to rebut any allegations of bullying or intimidation that may be made by a disgruntled employee.

9 The Acas Code of Practice advises that employees should be given a reasonable opportunity to call relevant witnesses. Therefore, they should be asked if they wish to do this and, if so, who should be invited to the hearing. The employer may also request witnesses to attend. If so, it should be explained to them that the employee would have the opportunity to question them.

10 Consider the evidence and whether any further investigation is necessary. If there are any loose ends to the investigation or if it seems that there may be additional relevant information, the manager should follow this up. It is not uncommon for an employee to withhold information in relation to mitigating circumstances, particularly if this is of a personal nature. In such circumstances, good relationships with union and employee representatives can be vital. Employees may often confide in their representative and therefore an off-the-record discussion with that representative may reveal information that will help to ensure a fair decision, and potentially avoid dismissal.

## The Disciplinary Meeting

Good preparation underpins the effective management of the disciplinary meeting or hearing. There are a number of points to remember at this stage:

1 Introduce those present – not just on grounds of courtesy, but because an employee facing a possible sanction is entitled to know who is going to be involved in any decision. In a small workplace this may be unnecessary, but it can be important in larger establishments.

2 Explain the purpose of the meeting and how it will be conducted. This builds on the need to ensure that the employee fully understands the nature of the complaint against them and the procedure to be followed. As with any hearing, however informal, what it is for, what the possible outcomes are, and the method by which it is to be conducted are important prerequisites for demonstrating adherence to natural justice. If it is apparent that, for whatever reason, the employee does not fully understand the nature of the complaint against them, you must halt the proceedings until they are clear – even if this means postponing to another day.

3 If the employee is accompanied, it may be useful to define the role of the companion. This may not be necessary if the employee is accompanied by an experienced trade union representative. However, if they are accompanied by a work colleague, it should be explained to them that they are able to address the hearing, confer with the employee and ask any relevant questions, but they are not permitted to answer questions on behalf of the employee.

4   Set out precisely the nature of the complaint and outline the case by briefly going through the evidence. This may seem like overkill, but it is important to ensure that there are no misunderstandings. It is important to ensure that the employee and their representative or companion, if they have one, have been given copies of any witness statements and afforded a proper opportunity to read them.

5   Give the employee the right to reply. Put simply: no right of reply – no natural justice, and any decision to dismiss will almost certainly be unfair.

6   Allow time for general questioning. If witnesses have been called, it is important that you allow the employee and/or the representative time to question them. If this did not happen, it would be difficult to persuade a tribunal that the test of reasonableness had been achieved.

7   No matter how carefully you prepare, or how well you are conducting a disciplinary hearing, things might not always proceed smoothly. People can get upset or angry, and the whole process becomes very emotional. In such circumstances, it might be advisable to adjourn and reconvene at a later date. Again, the representative or companion can play a key role here. It is perfectly reasonable to use an adjournment to hold discussions with the companion with a view to ensuring a fair outcome or a possible resolution.

8   Sum up the key points and give the employee an opportunity to make any final representations.

9   Adjourn so that a properly considered decision can be made. If this is not done, no matter how clear the issues, it will suggest that the decision has been pre-judged, something that can render a dismissal unfair.

### Making the Decision

As outlined above, all disciplinary decisions need to be taken with care. All the evidence should be reviewed and alternative courses of action considered. The law is an important factor and providing advice in relation to this is a key function of the employment relations professional. However, the most important thing is to ensure that decisions are fair, consistent and, where appropriate, give employees an opportunity to improve their behaviour or performance. The following steps provide a useful guide:

1   Decide whether the accusation is proved. In some cases this will be straightforward – the employee may admit to misconduct or the evidence may be incontrovertible. Nevertheless, particularly where misconduct is involved, you may have to weigh up conflicting accounts. In doing this, the courts have provided some useful guidance. As we noted in Chapter 4, the 'Burchell test' relates to a case that was decided in 1978 involving an incident of alleged theft (*British Home Stores* v *Burchell [1978] IRLR 379*). This provides three conditions that employers must meet when considering whether an employee is guilty of alleged misconduct:

- The employer must have a genuine belief in the reason for dismissal.
- The belief that the employee committed the offence must be based on reasonable grounds – that is, that on the evidence before it, the employer was entitled to say that it was more probable that the employee did, in fact, commit the offence than that they did not.
- These grounds must be based on a reasonable investigation in the circumstances. If any one of these conditions is not met, a claim for unfair dismissal will normally succeed.

It is important to note that the standard of proof in employment cases is the 'balance of probabilities, ie, is it more likely than not that the employee committed the alleged misdemeanour(s)? This is weaker than in criminal prosecution, which is based on proof 'beyond a reasonable doubt'. This means that it is entirely possible for an employee to be fairly dismissed for an act of misconduct over which they have faced previous criminal investigation and been acquitted.

2   The next question is what type of sanction to impose. If this is likely to be short of dismissal, the main considerations should be whether the sanction will have the desired effect on the behaviour or performance of the individual and whether this is fair and consistent given the facts of the case and previous practice within the organisation. However, if dismissal is a possibility, a range of questions must be asked. First, are there any alternatives to dismissal? For example, would a final written warning or a demotion be more appropriate? Remember, dismissal should be a last resort. Second, what is the record of the employee concerned? Matters such as length of service, performance, previous disciplinary infractions and absence should be considered. Here, it may be appropriate to take a more lenient approach if the employee has an otherwise exemplary record. Third, are there any mitigating factors? If so, it may be important to explore whether these circumstances are likely to be ongoing and whether the support of the organisation could help the situation. If a claim for unfair dismissal is brought, the 'dismissing officer' will have to account for her/his reasoning behind the decision, so having considered each of the issues will be crucial in demonstrating 'reasonableness'.

3   Once the decision has been made, the meeting should be reconvened and the decision explained clearly to the employee. If the decision is to warn the employee, the period of the warning, the required improvements, and the consequences if improvements are not forthcoming should be clearly set out. If the decision is to dismiss, the reasons for this should be given. In either event, the employee should be offered the right to appeal and provided with details of the process. This should be confirmed in writing.

## Appeals

Every disciplinary procedure must contain an appeals process – otherwise, it is almost impossible to demonstrate that the organisation has acted reasonably within the law. In common with every other aspect of the disciplinary process, it is important to ensure fairness and consistency within an appeals procedure, which should provide for appeals to be dealt with as quickly as possible. An employee should be able to appeal at every stage of the disciplinary process, and common sense dictates that any appeal should be heard by a different manager – one who is senior to the person who has imposed the disciplinary sanction. However, this will not always be possible, particularly in smaller organisations.

The appeals procedure generally falls into two parts: action prior to the appeal and the actual hearing itself. Before any appeal hearing the employee should be told what the arrangements are and what their rights under the procedure are. It is also important, then, to obtain and read any relevant documentation. At the appeal hearing, the appellant should be told its purpose, how it will be conducted, and what decisions the person or persons hearing the appeal are able to make. Any new evidence must be considered and all relevant issues properly examined. Although appeals are not regarded as an opportunity to seek a more sympathetic assessment of the issue in question, it is equally true that appeals are not routinely dismissed. Overturning a bad or unjust decision is just as important as confirming a fair decision. It is an effective way of signalling to employees that all disciplinary issues will be dealt with consistently and objectively.

Many organisations fall into the trap of using their grievance procedure in place of a proper appeals process. This is to be avoided wherever possible. The grievance procedure should be reserved for resolving problems arising from employment that the employee has highlighted – this is covered in the next chapter. Finally, not only should appeals be dealt with in a timely fashion, but the procedure should specify time limits within which appeals should be lodged.

> **?    REFLECTIVE ACTIVITY 12.4**
>
> Imagine that your organisation had dismissed somebody for bad timekeeping and unauthorised absences, and the employee had challenged this in an employment tribunal. What evidence would you need to present in support of your organisation's action?

## 12.6 CAPABILITY, PERFORMANCE AND ABSENCE

Many HR and employment relations professionals find that conventional disciplinary procedures are more suited to the handling of issues of conduct rather than the capability of employees. Although capability is potentially a fair reason for dismissal; it is often more nuanced and complex than misconduct. For example, it could be questioned whether it is either appropriate or productive to use disciplinary sanctions to address problems with an employee's performance or sickness record. For this reason many organisations now have specialist procedures for dealing with capability related to performance and also for sickness absence.

### 12.6.1 POOR PERFORMANCE

Advising line managers who are dealing with poor performance is an increasingly important part of the HR practitioner's role. Very often, the initial step in this advisory role is to persuade the line manager not to take precipitative action. It is not unusual for the employment relations professional to be told by a manager that a particular employee is not 'up to the job' and that they need help to 'get rid of them'. Persuading a line manager not to launch into a formal process without considering what other options are open to him or her is very important. Earlier, we looked at the question of counselling and noted that in the event of an ultimate dismissal, an employment tribunal would want to satisfy itself that an employee knew what standards were expected of them, that they had been given an opportunity to achieve them and that all this had happened before any formal disciplinary procedures had begun. Another option might be the provision of alternative work, training or mentoring for the employee concerned, if they were having difficulties coping with their current tasks.

Whatever options are taken, the employee is entitled on grounds of fairness to be told exactly what is required of them, what standards are being set, and the timescale in which they are expected to achieve them. During the period of time that an individual is being given to reach the desired standards, a good manager ensures that they are kept informed of their progress. This process is made easier if there is a structured performance management process through which managers meet with employees on a reasonably regular basis to discuss their needs for training and development, and identify and discuss any areas in which they may need to improve.

If some form of formal action is required, the disciplinary procedure can be enacted. However, many managers feel that this can often seem inappropriate and have a negative and demotivating effect on the employee concerned, who has done nothing wrong but simply has performance issues that need to be addressed. Furthermore, unlike conduct, it is very difficult to devise clear and unambiguous rules and standards relating to performance. Consequently, many companies now include a section on capability within their disciplinary procedures (an example of which is provided in the box below) or have a separate and dedicated capability procedure.

---

## CAPABILITY

We recognise that during your employment with us your capability to carry out your duties may vary. This can be for a number of reasons, the most common ones being that either the job changes over a period of time and you have difficulty adapting to the changes, or you change (most commonly because of health reasons).

**Job changes**

a. If the nature of your job changes and we have concerns regarding your capability, we will make every effort to ensure that you understand the level of performance expected of you and that you receive adequate training and supervision. This will be done in an informal manner in the first instance and you will be given time to improve.

b. If your standard of performance is still not adequate, you will be warned, in writing, that a failure to improve and to maintain the performance required will lead to disciplinary action. If this were to happen, the principles set out in paragraph 2 above will apply. We will also consider a transfer to more suitable work, if possible.

c. If we cannot transfer you to more suitable work and there is still no improvement after you have received appropriate warnings, you will be issued with a final warning that you will be dismissed unless the required standard of performance is achieved and maintained.

**Personal circumstances**

a. Personal circumstances may arise in the future which do not prevent you from attending work but which prevent you from carrying out your normal duties (eg a lack of dexterity or general ill-health). If such a situation arises, we will normally need to have details of your medical diagnosis and prognosis so that we have the benefit of expert advice. Under normal circumstances this can be most easily obtained by asking your own doctor for a medical report. Your permission is needed before we can obtain such a report, and we will expect you to co-operate in this matter should the need arise. When we have obtained as much information as possible regarding your condition, and after consultation with you, a decision will be made as to whether any adjustments need to be made in order for you to continue in your current role or, where circumstances permit, a more suitable role should be found for you.

b. There may also be personal circumstances that prevent you from attending work, either for a prolonged period or periods or for frequent short periods. Under these circumstances we will need to know when we can expect your attendance record to reach an acceptable level, and again this can usually be most easily obtained by asking your own doctor for a medical report. When we have obtained as much information as possible regarding your condition, and after consultation with you, a decision will be made as to whether any adjustments need to be made in order for you to continue in your current role or, where circumstances permit, a more suitable role should be found for you.

---

## 12.6.2 MANAGING ABSENCE

This can be one of the most difficult issues that managers have to face, and must be handled with sensitivity. There is always scope for disputes to arise in this area, and it is important that the employment relations professional makes himself or herself aware of all the circumstances in which absences can occur and, where these involve legal rights, ensures that he or she understands the scope of such rights. Time off work for domestic emergencies is one example.

Absence from work can occur for a number of reasons. Some – such as holiday, bereavement or paternity leave – are normally arranged in advance and are underpinned by statutory rights, and often extended provision is made within organisational policies. The absences that cause disruption within any organisation are those that are unplanned. Cases of unauthorised absence, in which an employee simply fails to turn up for work with no notification or explanation, would normally be treated as misconduct and managed through the disciplinary procedure. Whether disciplinary action is taken will clearly rest on the facts of each individual case, but in any event action should follow the guidance given above for preparing and conducting a disciplinary interview, particularly in respect of mitigating circumstances and other explanations.

However, in the majority of establishments, the most widespread cause of absence from work is sickness; and while it would be wholly unreasonable to treat a case of genuine sickness as a disciplinary matter, incapacity for work on health grounds can be a fair reason for dismissing an employee. For this reason the way in which an employer deals with health-related absences is very important.

### 12.6.3 SICKNESS ABSENCE

The CIPD's 2014 absence survey estimated that the median cost of absence per employee was £609, the equivalent of over £18 billion across the UK workforce as a whole. In recent years, the pressure on organisations to reduce costs and increase efficiency has seen the spread of absence management processes. This often involves the use of set trigger points whereby a certain number of absences within a certain period will automatically result in a warning. Further absences will trigger a final warning and ultimately this can lead to dismissal if the attendance record of the individual concerned does not improve. For many organisations, this approach provides clarity and consistency. However, such processes can be rigid and some commentators have argued that such policies have been used simply as a way of driving down costs and intensifying work, particularly in the public sector.

The CIPD's own evidence suggests that sickness absence is falling. Each year, the CIPD produces a survey of absence management policy and practice (see the CIPD website www.cipd.co.uk), and the 2014 survey showed that the average level of employee absence was 6.6 days per employee. This was down from 7.6 days per employee in the previous year and showed a general downward trend. However, the report also suggested the growth of presenteeism, with a significant increase in employees coming to work despite being sick. In particular, the report suggested that employees find balancing work and domestic responsibilities increasingly difficult, often having caring responsibilities for both children and ageing relatives. Absence remains highest in the public sector at 7.9 days, although again this shows a significant reduction. The report also highlighted the increased impact of stress-related absence, with two-fifths of employers reporting that stress absence had increased in the last year.

This underlines the importance of developing clear and effective absence management policies in your organisation, or to benchmark those that you have. For managing absence effectively, the starting point has to be adequate record-keeping. Acas advises that 'records showing lateness and the duration of and reason for all spells of absence should be kept to help monitor absence levels'. Such records enable a manager to substantiate whether a problem of persistent absence is real or imagined. All too often the employment relations specialist who is asked for advice is expected to work with insufficient data. Managing absence is not just about applying rules or following procedure – it is about addressing problems of persistent absence quickly and acting consistently. This sends out a clear and unambiguous message to all employees that absence is regarded as a serious matter.

But how do you act rigorously and at the same time retain fairness and consistency? The most effective way is through the return-to-work interview. The CIPD survey shows this to be the 'most commonly used approach to managing short-term absence', with 83% of organisations using them. The return-to-work interview sends a clear message to employees that absence matters, that the employer has noticed their absence, and that they care. In its booklet 'Discipline and grievances at work – the Acas Guide', Acas provides comprehensive guidance on 'dealing with absence' and handling frequent and persistent short-term absences. It supports the principle of the return-to-work interview, which helps to ensure a consistency of approach. The following box highlights other factors that must be taken into account:

---

## MANAGING ABSENCE – KEY FACTORS

- Absences should be investigated promptly and the employee asked to give an explanation.
- Where there is no medical advice to support frequent self-certified absences, the employee should be asked to consult a doctor to establish whether medical treatment is necessary and whether the underlying reason for absence is work-related.
- If after investigation it appears that there were no good reasons for the absences, the matter should be dealt with under the disciplinary procedure. If the absence could be related to a disability, the employer should consider whether they could make reasonable adjustments to help the employee – this could, for example, involve making changes to working hours or equipment.
- Where absences arise from temporary domestic problems, the employer, in deciding appropriate action, should consider whether an improvement in attendance is likely. It is also important to consider whether any of the absences should, or could, have been covered by time off under the provisions of the Employment Rights Act 1996 relating to time off for dependants. Employers could also consider whether more flexible working arrangements may help the situation. Employees have the right to request flexible working and employers must have a good business reason for rejecting any application.
- In all cases the employee should be told what improvement is expected and warned of the likely consequences if it does not happen.
- If there is no improvement, the employee's age, length of service, performance, the likelihood of a change in attendance, the availability of suitable alternative work and the effect of past and future absences on the business should all be taken into account on deciding appropriate action.

Source: Acas (2015)

---

## 12.6.4 LONG-TERM ABSENCE

In some cases absences may be long term. These situations raise a specific set of considerations and issues. Acas suggest it is important that:

- the employee should be contacted periodically, and they [the employee] should maintain regular contact with the employer
- the employee should be advised if employment is at risk.
- the employee should be asked if they will consent to their own doctor being contacted, and should be clearly informed of the employee's right to refuse consent, to see the report and to request amendments to it (detailed guidance in relation to making such a request can be found in 'Discipline and grievances at work – the Acas Guide')
- the employee's doctor should be asked if the employee will be able to return to work, and the nature of the work they will be capable of carrying out

- on the basis of the report received, the employer should consider whether alternative work is available
- employers are not expected to create special jobs, nor are they expected to be medical experts; they should simply take action on the basis of the medical evidence
- as with other absences, the possibility of an independent medical examination should be considered
- where an employee refuses to co-operate in providing medical evidence, they should be told, in writing, that a decision will have to be taken on the basis of what information is available – and that the decision may result in dismissal
- where the employee's job can no longer be kept open and no suitable alternative is available, the employee should be informed of the likelihood of dismissal.

This last point can be very emotive. Where you are dealing with an employee who has long service, an exemplary work record, and is genuinely suffering from a serious illness which has left them unable to work, telling them that they are likely to lose their job can be very difficult – not only because the employer is genuinely concerned about the impact of such a decision, but because the employer is concerned about the possibility of legal action for unfair dismissal being taken against him or her. It is also important that managers are aware of, or take advice on, the implications of the Equality Act 2010 in cases where the employee's condition may constitute a disability as defined by the Act. This is discussed in greater detail in Chapter 4.

In cases where illness or injury is obvious and the medical prognosis reasonably clear, following the Acas guidelines will help to ensure that the decisions that are made will stand up to external scrutiny. However, long-term absences, particularly those related to workplace stress, may have their roots in other problems in the workplace. In dealing with these situations, partnerships between HR practitioners, employee representatives, managers and – in large organisations – occupational health professionals can be very important. In some organisations, workplace mediation has been used to resolve interpersonal disputes, which may be the cause of the problem.

## 12.7 SUMMARY

In this chapter, we have explained why managing discipline is such a key area for the employment relations professional and the line manager. For most practitioners in large organisations, and for most front-line managers, responding to issues that may have disciplinary implications is a regular part of the job. However, if issues related to conduct and performance can be dealt with at an early stage, the need for formal disciplinary action may often be averted. Employment relations professionals have an important role to play in giving line managers the skills to have difficult conversations with staff and the confidence to pursue more informal resolutions. Good relationships with trade union representatives can also be helpful in identifying problems and finding possible solutions.

If disciplinary action is inevitable, this chapter has set out the key steps that managers need to follow in order to ensure that matters are dealt with fairly and consistently. Although managers often complain that the procedure is cumbersome and inflexible, an effective process is simple and straightforward: employees must be provided with the details of the problem; they must be invited to a meeting to discuss the problem; and if a sanction is imposed, they must be given a right to appeal. Along with ensuring that matters are properly investigated, and that individuals are allowed to be accompanied to disciplinary hearings, these simple steps are the basis of natural justice. These principles are not only important in avoiding legal challenge but are a key ingredient in ensuring organisational justice and maintaining trust and commitment.

## KEY LEARNING POINTS

1 Managing discipline is about acting with just cause, using procedures correctly, acting consistently and following the rules of natural justice.

2 A fair and effective disciplinary procedure is one that concentrates on improving or changing behaviour, and not one that relies on the principle of punishment. It should allow all employees to understand what is expected of them in respect of conduct, attendance and job performance, and set out rules by which such matters will be governed.

3 It is important to discuss any emerging problems in relation to conduct or performance at the earliest possible point. In unionised workplaces, representatives can also be helpful in trying to resolve issues informally and avoid the need for formal action.

4 Employees are entitled to know the details of allegations against them and to be able to respond to these allegations at a disciplinary hearing. They have a right to accompaniment and must be offered the opportunity to appeal against any disciplinary sanction levied against them.

5 Managing absence should be a priority for any organisation and appropriate policies established for that purpose. It is important that employment relations professionals are able to understand and analyse the root causes of absence and develop effective strategies to deal with relevant issues.

## REVIEW QUESTIONS

1 Using research into the contemporary policy and practice of organisations, identify at least three factors that can affect the way discipline is handled in the workplace.

2 A senior manager wants you to brief supervisors about the different purposes of a disciplinary policy. The manager would like you to emphasise that discipline is not simply a matter of punishment. Using examples from your own organisation, outline what you would say, and add why.

3 You have been asked to investigate an allegation of cyber-bullying. What steps would you take to investigate this issue? If you find that the allegations have substance, how would you recommend that this be dealt with?

4 An employee is regularly late back from lunch – as often as three or four times a week. His line manager has mentioned several times to him that this is unacceptable, usually in passing or during a conversation about something else. Provide the line manager with advice on how to progress the matter.

5 A salesman in your organisation has submitted expenses for travelling and entertaining over a four-week period and they do not tally with his record of customer visits. His line manager says he is 'on the fiddle' and should be dismissed. You are responsible for advising line managers on how to deal with difficulties like this. Explain how you would handle this situation.

EXPLORE FURTHER

ACAS (2015) *Discipline and grievances at work: the Acas guide*. London: Acas.

ACAS (2009) *Disciplinary and grievance procedures: the Acas code of practice*. London: Acas.

BROUGHTON, A., HIGGINS, T. and HICKS, B. (2010) *Workplaces and social networking – the implications for employment relations*. Acas research papers, No 11/11. London: Acas.

CIPD (2014) *Absence management – annual survey report*. London: CIPD.

LEWIS, D. and SARGEANT, M. (2013) *Employment law: the essentials*. 12th ed. London: CIPD.

PURCELL, J. (2012) The management of employment rights. In DICKENS, L. (ed.) *Making employment rights effective: issues of enforcement and compliance*. Oxford: Hart Publishing.

SAUNDRY, R., ANTCLIFF, V. and JONES, C. (2008) *Accompaniment and representation in workplace discipline and grievance*. Acas research paper, No 06/08. London: Acas.

**Website links**

www.acas.org.uk/publications gives access to the Code of Practice on Discipline and Grievance Procedures.

www.bis.gov.uk is the website of the Department for Business, Innovation and Skills and gives access to the main pieces of legislation relevant to discipline.

www.cipd.co.uk gives access to the CIPD employment law service.

# CHAPTER 13

# Managing Employee Grievances

## OVERVIEW

This chapter explores the management of employee grievances. It begins by discussing how employees conceive of, and 'characterise', mistreatment, and the implications of managerial responses. We then provide an analysis of recent data to give an overview of the incidence of individual employee grievances in British workplaces and the development of process and procedure. The next part of the chapter sets out the business case for adopting a proactive approach to grievance management and outlines key aspects of informal processes of resolution. However, this is not always successful or appropriate. Consequently, we move on to explain in some detail the main elements of effective grievance procedures and the ways in which these processes can be managed fairly and consistently and with a view to negotiate outcomes that are acceptable to all parties. Finally, the chapter briefly examines the place of specialist procedures for dealing with specific types of employee grievances, such as complaints related to dignity at work.

## LEARNING OUTCOMES

When you have completed this chapter, you should be able to:

- explain and critically analyse the processes through which employee grievances escalate
- describe the nature and pattern of employee grievances in British workplaces and critically evaluate the development of workplace procedures
- understand and critically assess the business case for resolving grievances
- describe the key stages of informal and formal processes to manage and resolve grievances
- discuss and evaluate the main strategies and skills needed to implement a grievance procedure and negotiate fair and acceptable outcomes
- identify and critically assess the limitations of conventional grievance procedures and how these issues can be addressed through specialist processes.

## 13.1 INTRODUCTION

The Acas Code of Practice on Disciplinary and Grievance Procedures defines grievances as 'concerns, problems or complaints that employees raise with their employers'. For some commentators, a complaint is the informal expression of discontent to the line manager, whereas a grievance is the more formal manifestation. Furthermore, grievances can revolve around individual issues or those which are collective in nature (Dundon and Rollinson, 2011: 25). Irrespective of the definition we may use, finding quick and effective resolutions is vital. To the individual concerned, his or her grievance is of immediate importance. In addition, an organisation cannot ignore employee grievances since the mishandling of an individual's grievance could lead to an escalation of the dispute, which will have implications for the well-being and performance of the complainant but could also impact on the team or unit they work in. The objective of grievance management is to address grievances by:

- thoroughly investigating the situation
- identifying the cause of the employee's complaint
- taking appropriate action to resolve the complaint to the mutual satisfaction of the employee and the management
- resolving the grievance as quickly as possible.

A key aspect of fairness at work is the opportunity for the individual employee to complain about, and receive redress for, unfair treatment. The 2004 *Workplace Employment Relations Survey* reported that in 95% of workplaces, the responsibilities of employment relations professionals included providing line managers with advice in managing employee grievances. However, the subsequent 2011 survey revealed that operational managers are enjoying greater autonomy in dealing with grievance (van Wanrooy *et al*, 2013). Therefore, in this chapter, we explore the knowledge, skills and techniques that line and operational managers can employ to handle employee grievances fairly, consistently and effectively.

## ?    REFLECTIVE ACTIVITY 13.1

In your experience, what are the main reasons for a grievance being raised in your organisation? With this in mind, as you read through this chapter, critically reflect on: the different types of grievances; the ways in which managers in your organisation respond to complaints and grievances; and consider how grievance management in your organisation could be improved.

## 13.2 PERCEPTIONS OF MISTREATMENT AND THE ESCALATION OF GRIEVANCES

Before we discuss the nature and management of employee grievances in British workplaces, it is important to examine the dynamic processes through which grievances escalate. To do this, we draw on critical analysis of the causes and the consequences of unresolved grievances undertaken in the USA. This work highlights the need for employment relations practitioners to adopt a more nuanced, rather than merely procedural, approach when dealing with grievances in the workplace. Olson-Buchanan and Boswell (2008) present a model that focuses on the way in which employee perceptions of mistreatment and the managerial response can combine to produce specific outcomes. In particular, they explore how complainants: 'characterise' mistreatment; perceive the severity of that mistreatment; and the negative implications for the employment relationship if the individual feels that justice has not been fully served.

### 13.2.1 CHARACTERISATION OF MISTREATMENT

For Olson-Buchanan and Boswell, the nature or character of the mistreatment as perceived by the individual can affect how that individual may react, particularly in terms of the degree to which they may feel maligned. In earlier work, Boswell and Olson-Buchanan (2004) usefully make the distinction between whether the complainant feels that they have been mistreated due 'to an individual's discretionary actions ("personalized") as opposed to an organisational procedure or administration of a work policy ("policy related")'.

Significantly, for any assessment of the causes, consequences and, crucially, successful resolution of grievances, this study alerts us to the distinction that mistreatment related to enactment of organisational policy is less likely to be 'internalised' and thus not seen as a personal attack by the employee. In contrast, perceived 'personalized mistreatment' can have a far more negative impact on their emotions, which can lead to greater 'job withdrawal'. It is clear that these perceptions, founded or otherwise, have real implications for managers charged with addressing and trying to resolve grievances.

### 13.2.2 SEVERITY OF MISTREATMENT

A second key dimension of the grievance that they highlight is the degree of 'severity' or 'seriousness' the individual attributes to their perceived mistreatment. Todor and Owen also note that the severity of the dispute is *'perhaps the central factor in determining the responses of the parties involved'* (1991: 44). Conceptually, for Olson-Buchanan and Boswell (2008), these 'individual perceptions of injustice' can be located across a continuum of severity, from minor to severe, as perceived by the complainant. The harsher the employee feels the treatment to have been, the more likely there will be a higher level of negativity in response. This is also the case if the individual feels that the mistreatment was intentional in nature or due to some 'socially unacceptable reasons', which could include discrimination or harassment.

### 13.3 THE OUTCOMES

Finally, and arguably of most significance to the effective management of grievances, if the complaint is not seen to have been fairly dealt with or indeed there is a perception of ongoing mistreatment, this will have a negative impact on the long-term performance and attitude of the employee. In contrast, if they perceive that they have achieved a positive resolution to their complaint, the individual is more likely to feel greater allegiance to the organisation and feel better generally. For the individual, however, who does not feel that their grievance has been properly heard, the consequences for them and the organisation can be highly damaging. To illustrate this point, Olson-Buchanan and Boswell cite the example of an individual who experiences retaliation for voicing their grievance and may choose:

> 'To not pursue voicing the mistreatment further, and instead may withdraw from his or her job, ultimately lowering job performance. This lowered performance may be noticed by the supervisor, resulting in a lower performance evaluation, possibly triggering another perception of mistreatment.' (2008: 92)

This example of a potential vicious circle clearly highlights the need for all managers, supported by HR colleagues, to respond quickly and effectively to all perceptions of mistreatment.

---

**CASE STUDY 13.1**

### A PROBLEM WITH FACEBOOK 'FRIENDS'

You are the HR adviser at an SME employing around 170 staff, which operates in the financial services sector. One Monday morning, you receive an urgent email from a member of staff who claims that he is being 'picked on' by members of his team and he needs your help. He is part of the sales team based in a small call centre in the company's main office in town. The email goes on to outline that for the last three weeks, but particularly over the last weekend, he has experienced increasing criticism and insulting comments from other members of the team on Facebook. People who he had considered 'friends' are now openly 'attacking' his sales ability and say that 'he is not up to the job'. He explains that he has raised the issue with his line manager previously. However, she did not see it as an issue because it is happening outside of working hours.

You have agreed to speak to the member of staff but first need to establish what information you need for that discussion. The issue is not helped by the fact that your company has not, as yet, got a social media policy. However, different forms of social media are used quite extensively in the firm, none the least by sales staff when chasing up leads on potential clients.

In preparation for your first discussion with the member of staff who has raised the grievance, use the Olson-Buchanan and Boswell mode to establish the potential character, severity and outcomes of the grievance. Then, set out a plan of action for addressing and resolving this problem.

## 13.4 THE NATURE AND PATTERN OF EMPLOYEE GRIEVANCES

The following section examines key trends in the nature and extent of employee grievances. Until recently, there was little quantitative data that explored this important issue. However, WERS2011 measured, for the first time, the incidence of grievances. This has allowed us to paint a more detailed picture of the pattern and causes of grievances and the procedures that have been developed to manage these issues.

### 13.4.1 THE INCIDENCE OF FORMAL GRIEVANCES

As we have seen in earlier chapters, data from the WERS series offer us a valuable insight into trends in employment relations. In terms of grievances, the analysis of the 2011 survey data by van Wanrooy *et al* (2013) showed little overall change in the proportion of workplaces experiencing a formal grievance from the previous survey (see Table 13.1). They were more likely to be found in the public sector. In contrast, there were marked differences in the private sector, with a significant fall in the proportion of manufacturing workplaces reporting grievances compared with an overall increase in the private service sector.

Table 13.1 Grievances by ownership of sector and formality of incidence: comparison, 2004–11

| Sector | Any formal grievance |
|---|---|
| **Public sector** | |
| 2004 | 25 |
| 2011 | 23 |
| | |
| **Private manufacturing** | |
| 2004 | 21 |
| 2011 | 11 |
| | |
| **Private services** | |
| 2004 | 16 |
| 2011 | 20 |
| | |
| **All workplaces** | |
| 2004 | 18 |
| 2011 | 19 |

Source: van Wanrooy *et al* 2013

With respect to the overall number of formal grievances reported within and across sectors and size of organisation, there were 1.5 formal grievances per 100 employees in the 12 months prior to the 2011 survey. However, there were relatively few differences between workplaces of different size and between unionised and non-unionised sites (van Wanrooy *et al*, 2013: 152–3).

## 13.4.2 THE CAUSE OF INDIVIDUAL GRIEVANCES

Grievances from individual employees can centre on a wide range of issues. However, WERS2011 found that the most cited reason, by almost 40% of respondents, was an employee claiming 'unfair treatment' by their manager or supervisor – for instance, in relation to performance appraisals or perceived victimisation. Other key reasons for lodging a grievance were related to terms and conditions and pay (30%), and bullying and harassment by a colleague or manager (23%). There were also some differences between the public and private sector, with behavioural issues being more closely linked to public sector grievances. Specifically, grievances relating to unfair treatment stood at 52% in the public sector as opposed to 37% in the private sector. Similarly, 39% of grievances were raised with regard to bullying and harassment in the public sector in contrast to 20% in the private sector.

These statistics point to the growing importance of performance management, and bullying and harassment as sources of employee grievances. This is an example of the complexity of individual employment disputes whereby employee complaints of bullying may be linked to managerial action on capability or conduct. In cases where grievance and disciplinary cases overlap, Acas advises that it may be appropriate to deal with both issues concurrently. However, where an employee raises a grievance during the disciplinary process itself, it is good practice to address the complaint before proceeding, thereby temporarily suspending the disciplinary procedure while the grievance is addressed. Conversely, where the grievance and disciplinary cases are related it may be appropriate to deal with both issues concurrently.

## 13.4.3 THE EXTENT OF GRIEVANCE PROCEDURES

Turning to the role of formal procedures in resolving grievances, WERS2011 indicated that the number of workplaces that had procedures for handling employee grievances had increased since 2004, as had the percentage of workers covered by those procedures. The key findings are set out in Table 13.2. However, procedures were already almost universal in workplaces with more than 50 employees in 2004. By 2011, all workplaces with 50 or more employees now had a formal grievance procedure in place. Interestingly, the greatest rate of increase was in the smallest workplaces and those without union recognition. This reflects a gradual filling in of 'procedural gaps' in UK employing organisations. At the same time, Wood *et al* (2014) found that procedural adherence in relation to grievances lagged substantially behind that for disciplinary issues. This could reflect the greater scope for resolution within grievance processes or, alternatively, the added pressures of compliance when considering dismissals.

Table 13.2 Presence of procedures for handling grievances, 2004 and 2011

| Type of workplace | Presence of written grievance procedure (%) | |
|---|---|---|
| | 2004 | 2011 |
| All workplaces | 82 | 89 |
| Workplace size | | |
| 5–9 employees | 74 | 82 |
| 10–19 employees | 81 | 90 |

| Type of workplace | Presence of written grievance procedure (%) | |
|---|---|---|
| | 2004 | 2011 |
| 20–49 employees | 91 | 97 |
| 50–99 employees | 99 | 100 |
| 100–499 employees | 99 | 100 |
| 500 or more | 100 | 100 |
| Union recognition | | |
| No recognised union | 77 | 86 |
| Recognised union | 99 | 99 |

Source: van Wanrooy *et al* (2013)

### 13.4.4 COLLECTIVE GRIEVANCES

Employee grievances can also be collective in that a group of employees have a common complaint relating to their employment or an individual has a grievance that has collective implications. The main causes of grievances raised by a group of employees typically include:

- the interpretation and application of an existing agreement
- pay and bonus arrangements
- organisational change
- new working practices
- grading issues.

Traditionally, collective disputes have been handled through joint negotiation with recognised trade unions. The process used was often codified through a formal collective disputes procedure. However, such procedures are now not as widespread as individual grievance procedures. WERS2011 found that just over a third of workplaces had an internal procedure for handling collective disputes, compared with 40% in 2004 (van Wanrooy *et al*, 2013). In workplaces with no recognised union, only one-quarter had such arrangements compared with three-quarters of workplaces with recognised unions. Therefore, the contemporary reality is that most workplaces have no process, whether formal or informal, for handling collective grievances. As a consequence, where there are no channels for collective negotiation, it is likely that discontent that is collective in character will be expressed through individual disputes and/or through other manifestations, such as high staff turnover, absenteeism, low morale and reduced performance.

## ?    REFLECTIVE ACTIVITY 13.2

To what degree do collective grievances get raised in your organisation? Do you think that individual grievances reflect collective concerns and issues?

## 13.5 THE BENEFITS OF EFFECTIVE RESOLUTION

Employee grievances on a wide variety of issues (including discrimination, harassment and bullying) arise even in the best-managed organisations. If grievances are not dealt with or handled quickly, they are likely to fester and harm the employment relationship. A grievance may also be felt by a group as well as an individual and, if left unresolved, may develop into a major collective dispute. However, whether individual or collective, all employee grievances have the potential to damage the quality of an organisation's employment relations. Furthermore, unresolved grievances can result in:

- employee frustration
- deteriorating interpersonal relationships
- low morale
- poor performance, resulting in lower productivity and/or a poorer quality of output or service
- disciplinary problems, including poor performance by employees
- resignation and loss of good staff (increased labour turnover)
- increased employee absenteeism
- the withdrawal of employee goodwill
- resistance to change – if employees feel they have been treated badly, they are likely to oppose the introduction of change.

Clearly, this will also have a negative impact on organisational performance and efficiency. In addition, unresolved grievances can lead to employees feeling so strongly that their 'employment rights' have not been respected that they resign from their employment and may seek to make a claim for unfair constructive dismissal to an employment tribunal. A reputation for employee dissatisfaction also gives an organisation a negative image in the labour market. This image will accentuate the organisation's problems of recruiting and retaining the appropriate quantity and quality of labour services necessary to achieve its organisational objectives. As noted in Chapter 11, it can be argued that a sense of procedural justice underpins employee engagement – therefore good practice not only helps to ensure fairness and consistency, but it makes good business sense (Purcell, 2012).

## 13.6 HANDLING EMPLOYEE GRIEVANCES

As we noted earlier in this chapter, the way that managers respond to the concerns of their employees will have a significant effect on whether discontent escalates into a formal grievance and also on employees' perceptions of equity and justice. Ideally, skilled and confident managers will seek to address and resolve issues at the lowest possible point. However, in some cases it will be necessary to enact a grievance procedure, which needs to be applied and managed in a transparent, consistent and fair manner.

### 13.6.1 THE POTENTIAL OF EARLY RESOLUTION

Most employees' complaints over management behaviour do not reach the formal grievance procedure for many reasons. First, as noted previously, the employee may merely want to get their dissatisfaction 'off their chest'. Second, on reflection, the employee may feel that the issue is not serious enough to go through the potential stress of a formal process. Third, in times of high levels of unemployment, individuals are often reluctant to raise grievances formally, fearing that management may hold it against them and react by denying them promotion or access to training. Fourth, employees may, in some cases, see little point in raising their grievance since they have little faith in the process itself. Finally, some individuals are unwilling to express their dissatisfaction with management for fear of offending their immediate superior, who may see the complaint as a criticism of their competency.

This underlines the importance of managers developing an 'open culture' within their teams, providing clear channels for communication and consultation. In this way, problems and concerns can be voiced, discussed and settled as a matter of course. We would argue that whenever possible, managers should seek to resolve issues raised by employees informally. Sometimes an employee simply wishes to make their feelings or concerns known and for them to be properly recognised by the employer. Depending on the issue, good management practice is to discuss those concerns and genuinely commit to addressing them. The first step should always be to explore whether the issue can be resolved at an early stage without the need for the time, anxiety and potential for further conflict that formal grievance proceedings often involve. For issues between members of staff, as we will discuss in detail in Chapter 15, early referral to mediation can often offer an alternative route to resolution without the need to formalise the dispute.

However, as we saw in Chapter 11, many managers lack the confidence and the skills to manage issues in this way. In this context, training for managers is crucial. It is also important that this extends beyond the application of procedure but also covers how to manage 'difficult conversations' with staff. In discussing concerns with staff, managers should:

- always try to use face-to-face discussions
- listen carefully – and try to understand what is the underlying cause of the problem
- rephrase or reinterpret what's been said so that the individual concerned can see the issue from an alternative perspective
- try to move the focus of the individual on to their interests, not positions and personalities; in particular, try to adopt or encourage a 'future focus'.

After such discussions, it is important to keep a note of what was said in the event that the conflict escalates. It may also be appropriate to involve others. A more senior manager or HR practitioner may be useful in a facilitated discussion to try and provide an objective view of the particular problem. If a more structured approach is needed, mediation could be considered. This can be particularly effective if the issue involves the deterioration of a relationship between two colleagues. We look at this in greater detail in Chapter 15.

When the concerns raised by an individual are symptomatic of a wider problem within a team, it may be necessary to provide additional training, support and/or coaching to the manager. If it appears that the complaint suggests mistreatment or serious bullying, formal action may be the correct course of action to ensure that such behaviour is not allowed to continue and to clearly signal that it will not be tolerated by the organisation.

## ?    REFLECTIVE ACTIVITY 13.3

Has the grievance procedure in your organisation been activated in the last 12 months? If it has, what were the issues and groups of workers involved, and what was the outcome? Why weren't these issues resolved informally?

### 13.6.2 GRIEVANCE PROCEDURES

If attempts to resolve the issue through informal means are not successful or appropriate, a systematic grievance procedure should be followed. The purpose of a grievance procedure is to:

- ensure the fair and consistent treatment of employees
- reduce the risk of 'unpredictable' action
- clarify the manner in which grievances will be dealt with
- maintain a good employment relations environment
- help the employer to avoid disputes or costly legal action.

It can therefore be useful to define, in advance, the purpose of the policy. For example, the grievance procedure for the Freight Transport Association (FTA) in the UK starts with the following explanation of its purpose:

## PURPOSE OF THE POLICY

We seek to ensure that if you wish to raise a work-related grievance it will be treated in a fair and equitable manner. Every effort will be made to settle grievances to the satisfaction of all concerned, using the procedure set out in this policy. If you have a grievance relating to your working conditions, your pay and benefits, working hours, treatment at the hands of your fellow workers, or if you are concerned about your health and safety or a breach of your statutory employment rights or any other issue affecting your employment, you should first talk the matter over with your immediate team leader/manager. In some instances it may not be appropriate to approach your manager, in which case you should bring the matter to the attention of the Head of HR. This procedure complies with the Acas statutory Code of Practice on grievance.

Interestingly, as an initial alternative to a formal grievance, FTA offer counselling through their employee assistance programme. Meanwhile, at Manchester University the grievance policy and procedure states that:

## GENERAL PRINCIPLES

1   The provisions of this procedure are in accordance with arrangements relating to grievances as set out in Acas guidelines and the University's Statutes and Ordinances, which will prevail in the event of any conflict of provision.

2   It is the policy of the University to ensure that all employees have access to a procedure to help resolve any grievances relating to their employment fairly and without undue delay. This does not prevent parties from attempting to seek resolution to grievances informally outside this procedure. Grievances may be concerned with a wide range of issues, including the allocation of work, working environment or conditions, the opportunities that have been given for career development or the way in which staff have been managed.

3   This procedure applies to all employees regardless of length of service.

It is important to note that in different ways both introductions signal the importance of trying to resolve the issue informally as a first step. Significantly, at Manchester University the grievance policy and procedure also refers to mediation as a potential channel for dispute resolution.

## RESOLVING GRIEVANCES: MEDIATION

1   At any stage in this procedure any party may request that this matter be dealt with via referral to mediation. Mediation offers support to resolve interpersonal disputes between parties; it cannot mediate between an individual and the University.

2   Mediation is voluntary and will only take place if all parties agree. However, it is hoped that complainants will be amenable to any suggestion made by the University to refer grievances to the University Mediation Service, and it is hoped that complainants will co-operate with all efforts to resolve their complaint. The use of external mediators may be considered in exceptional cases.

### 13.6.3 UNDERLYING PRINCIPLES OF GRIEVANCE PROCEDURE

Importantly, all grievance procedures should reflect a number of principles – fairness, transparency, consistency, representation and promptness. More specifically, procedures should:

- prevent management from dismissing the employee's complaint out of hand on the grounds that it is trivial, too time-consuming and/or too costly
- ensure that there is a full investigation by an unbiased individual to establish the facts of the case
- provide the employee with adequate time to prepare their case and to question management witnesses
- allow for the case to be heard by individuals not directly involved in the complaint
- provide for the right of appeal to a higher level of management and, in some cases, to an independent external body.

A grievance procedure with a clearly demarcated number of stages and standards of behaviour at each stage provides consistency of treatment and reduces the influence of subjectivity. When a complaint is raised, the procedure should provide the individual with the right to be accompanied by a work colleague or trade union representative in accordance with the Employment Relations Act 1999 (as set out in the previous chapter). This legal right only extends to a formal grievance hearing. However, some organisations feel that it is reasonable to extend this. The promptness principle is achieved by the procedure having a small number of stages, each of which has time limits for their completion. This enables the grievance to be resolved as quickly and as simply as possible.

### 13.6.4 FORMS OF PROCEDURE

The form of grievance procedures varies immensely. In a small non-union establishment, the procedure is likely to be relatively short and is often written into the employee's contract of employment. In larger organisations, grievance procedures will often be more detailed and may have been negotiated with trade union representatives. The grievance procedure is likely to be available on the organisation's intranet, typically via the HRM pages on the site, and reproduced in the company handbook or made available as a separate document. However, irrespective of the size of the organisation, the Acas Code sets out three key principles that should be adhered to:

1   The employee sets out the nature of their complaint.

2   A meeting is held to discuss the complaint (at which the employee can be accompanied) and a decision is made.

3   The employee has the right to appeal against that decision.

A typical grievance procedure has a standard format of:

- a policy statement of the purpose of the procedure (see above)
- a statement of the scope of the procedure – who the procedure applies to
- a statement of the general principles to be applied in its application

- a number of stages – at each stage the aim is to identify action that stops the problem recurring or continuing; the number of stages in a procedure can range from two to five, but three stages are the most popular arrangement in practice
- a list of time limits by which each stage should be completed, so that a speedy resolution of the grievance can be secured
- a list of the individuals who are to be involved at each stage
- notification of the right to accompaniment
- notification of the monitoring and review arrangements.

In most organisations, procedures for managing employee complaints relating to health and safety provision, job grading (job evaluation scheme), bullying and harassment and dignity at work, and 'whistle-blowing' are normally separate from the general grievance procedure. These specific procedures are discussed in greater detail later in the chapter.

### 13.6.5 STAGES

There are a number of stages in a typical grievance procedure. At each stage, the procedure will normally:

- spell out the details of who hears the case (eg the departmental manager, the managing director) and the individuals to be present (eg the HR manager, the line manager and the employee concerned), including who may represent the employee (eg a colleague, a friend or a shop steward)
- explain the appeal mechanisms available to employees
- define the time limits by which the stage must be complete
- explain what will happen if the grievance is not resolved or remains unsettled.

---

## A BASIC THREE-STAGE GRIEVANCE PROCEDURE

**Stage 1**

If you wish to raise a formal grievance you should, in the first instance, raise it orally or in writing with your immediate supervisor or manager. The supervisor/manager will normally respond within five working days.

**Stage 2**

If the matter is not resolved at Stage 1 or within five working days, you may refer it in writing within three working days to the next level of management, who may also involve a representative of the Personnel Department. You should set out the grounds for the complaint and the reasons for your dissatisfaction with the Stage 1 response. A meeting will normally take place to consider the matter within seven working days of the request being made. You will have the right to be accompanied by a work colleague or trade union representative.

**Stage 3**

If the matter is not resolved at Stage 2 or within seven working days, you may refer it in writing within three working days to the next level of management, who may involve a representative of the Personnel Department. You should set out the grounds for the complaint and the reasons for your dissatisfaction with the Stage 2 response. A meeting will normally take place to consider the matter within ten working days of the request being made. You will have the right to be accompanied by a work colleague or trade union representative. The decision of the Divisional Executive is the final stage of the procedure and will be given in writing.

Although the aim of grievance procedures is to reach a resolution of the employee's complaint as quickly as possible, it cannot, however, be done with undue haste. Nonetheless, in managing grievances, the management's objective is to settle the complaint as near as possible to the point of its source. If employee complaints are permitted unnecessarily to progress to a higher level, this principle is undermined. A professional employment relations manager ensures that his or her managerial colleagues – but particularly line managers – understand the limits of their authority when operating within the parameters of the grievance procedure. The procedure is a problem-solving mechanism, and the significance of each of the different procedural stages is reinforced when grievances are settled as near as possible to the point of origin.

While defined stages are essential, there is no ideal number of stages. The number is a function of many factors, including the size of the organisation. However, natural justice principles would point to a minimum of two stages because this at least ensures one level of appeal from the first immediate decision. Nor should the procedure contain too many stages, since this makes the process unduly cumbersome and helps neither the complainant nor the organisation.

---

### ? REFLECTIVE ACTIVITY 13.4

Do you have a grievance procedure in your organisation? If not, why not? If you do, how effective do you think it is?

---

### 13.6.6 EMPLOYEE REPRESENTATION AND ACCOMPANIMENT

Fair and reasonable behaviour by an employer in managing employee grievances requires the employee to have the right to representation by an individual who can advocate their case. Representation assists the individual employee, who may lack confidence and the experience to deal with his or her line manager or senior manager. However, as we argued in the previous chapter with respect to managing discipline, representation can also be helpful to the employer in both managing grievances and finding resolutions. Offline discussions between representatives and managers can explore issues and potential solutions in an informal manner and in a way that may not be possible in the formal environment of a grievance hearing. In addition, the representative can help to manage employee expectations of the process. The Employment Relations Act (1999) gives workers a statutory right to be accompanied by a fellow worker or trade union official where they are required or invited by their employer to attend certain categories of grievance hearings and when they make a reasonable request to be so accompanied.

As is the case in disciplinary hearings, companions can address the hearing, ask questions and confer with the worker – but have no statutory right to answer questions on the worker's behalf. Analysis of WERS2011 undertaken by Wood *et al* (2014) found that almost all workplaces allowed employees to have a companion at formal meetings to discuss individual grievances. However, there was significant variation in how this was applied, with some employers moving beyond the statute. For example, around one in three workplaces allowed anyone chosen by the employee, and around one in ten were prepared to allow legal representatives to accompany employees. Furthermore, approximately one in five workplaces allowed accompaniment from friends or family members. While, in exceptional circumstances, it may be reasonable to allow friends or family members to accompany an employee, research and our own experience suggests that this should be generally avoided. Friends and family members may find it difficult to provide the objectivity and distance from the issue that marks effective representation.

Although the statutory right to accompaniment only applies to a grievance hearing, some organisations routinely provide access to representation at all stages of the process. Whether this is appropriate in a particular setting depends on the nature of employment relations. In some circumstances, offering representation at a very early stage may formalise the situation and make an early resolution more difficult. However, where there are good relationships between representatives and managers or HR practitioners, early discussions involving representatives may be what's needed to avoid formal proceedings. Our research has often found that in organisations with effective approaches to conflict resolution, it is routine to alert the trade union representative of any potential or actual grievances or for the representative to contact management if a member has first come to them with a complaint.

## ? REFLECTIVE ACTIVITY 13.5

What is the involvement of employee representatives in grievances in your organisation? Do they help to facilitate resolution? Do you think that representation is important in grievance processes, and if so, why?

### 13.6.7 THE ROLE OF THE EMPLOYMENT RELATIONS PROFESSIONAL

Grievance procedures are an integral part of the way in which an organisation is managed. They directly affect line management at all levels. As we have noted already in the book, recent years have seen the progressive devolution of responsibility for handling disciplinary and grievance issues from HR to the line. However, many line managers lack the confidence to manage grievances in a proactive and effective way. Consequently, the relationship between the employment relations professional and the line manager is crucial. While it is important that the employment relations professional does not take responsibility for managing grievances, they need to build trust and rapport with managers – guiding, advising and sometimes coaching them through the process.

Furthermore, the employment relations professional should:

- identify line management training and development needs with regard to managing grievances; it is important to train line managers both to listen to grievances properly and to deal with them in a consistent manner
- devise and implement a training and development programme so that line managers can acquire and develop the skills necessary to become effective managers of employee grievances
- ensure that line managers have a clear understanding of the way in which grievance procedures are intended to operate
- devise a grievance procedure that conforms with 'good practice' and spells out what has to happen at each stage, and why
- promote awareness among line managers of 'good practice' in managing grievances
- ensure that employees are aware of their rights under the procedure.

The HR practitioner also has an important role to play in monitoring and reviewing the operation of the grievance procedure, and in recommending revisions to its design or operation. Following the revisions to the Acas Code of Practice in 2009, many organisations sought to revise their procedures accordingly, placing a greater emphasis on informal resolution and possible alternative approaches such as mediation (Rahim et al, 2011). This also involves reviewing the outcomes of the grievance decisions and assessing whether these outcomes have been those intended and desired by the management – and if not, why not. For example, is it because line managers are not undertaking a thorough investigation of the complaint? This review and monitor function also requires the employment relations professional to analyse the subject matter of individual employee grievances, to consider why the outcomes have been what they have, and to check that the procedure has been applied in all cases fairly and consistently (ie that management have behaved reasonably in processing employee grievances).

### 13.6.8 THE ROLE OF THE LINE MANAGER

The front-line manager remains a key player in the operation of a grievance procedure. The filing of a grievance by an employee may be seen by front-line managers as reflecting badly on their managerial competence. If grievance procedures are to operate effectively, senior management must reassure front-line managers that their managerial competence may not be the main cause of the dispute. On the contrary, front-line managers should be encouraged by their own managers to hear and listen properly to grievances. The front-line manager has little executive authority, and this limits his or her ability (as well as confidence) to make decisions without reference to a more senior manager. If a front-line manager/team leader frequently refers a grievance up to a superior, the employee will realise that a possibly quicker way of having their problem resolved is to short-circuit the first-line manager and go directly to their superior. If this happens, the legitimate authority of the front-line manager becomes undermined. Moreover, this also removes the grievance from its source of origin, which can slow down the process, cause confusion and create bad feeling. To avoid this happening, the employment relations professional must ensure that:

- everyone knows, within the procedure, the limits of their own and others' authority
- the procedures are operated consistently by line managers
- front-line managers have the authority to settle grievances.

Furthermore, it is vital that senior managers try to provide line managers with space and time to resolve potential grievances at the earliest possible stage. Informal resolution can be time-consuming and is often not very visible, but it can provide significant long-term benefits to the organisation.

It is equally important that front-line management continues to be involved in the settling of grievances, even if the complaint proceeds beyond the stage at which they are formally involved. This can be achieved by their attendance at subsequent meetings or at the very least by being kept informed of the outcome as the grievance proceeds through subsequent stages of the procedure. In addition, it may be the case that the grievance is with the individual's direct manager, and in this case an alternative route through which the grievance can be made is useful. This is one reason why organisations have developed specialist procedures for dealing with complaints of bullying and harassment, which we explore at the end of this chapter.

### 13.6.9 KEEPING RECORDS

When a grievance progresses to a higher stage in the procedure, documentation of what happened at the previous stage is needed by those managers who now become involved for the first time and are not familiar with the issues involved. In practice, the extent to which records of grievances are kept varies widely. The Acas Code of Practice advises employers to keep a written record of any grievance cases with which they deal. Records should include the nature of the grievance, what was decided, the action taken, the reason for the action, whether an appeal was lodged, the outcome of the appeal, and any subsequent developments. Records have to be treated as confidential. Summaries or transcriptions of meetings should be given to the employee, including copies of any formal minutes that may have been taken.

Grievance records serve useful purposes for management. If there is a failure to agree at any stage, a written record clarifies the complaint and the arguments put forward about it by the individual employee and/or his or her representative. Such a record is also helpful to those managers involved in the next stage of the procedure. Grievance record forms assist the personnel/HRM function to keep in touch with the progress of unresolved grievances, and to analyse trends in the use and outcomes of the grievance procedure.

## ? REFLECTIVE ACTIVITY 13.6

Does your organisation keep grievance records? If not, why not? If it does, what information does the record contain, and why?

## 13.7 MANAGING THE GRIEVANCE PROCEDURE

As outlined previously, ideally, most grievances are resolved informally through discussion or mediation before formal proceedings are needed. However, inevitably some grievances will need to be managed through the procedure. Management must deal with all grievances in a competent and systematic manner, which involves a number of stages:

1  Management must hear the grievance.
2  Management prepares for the meeting with the employee and/or his or her representative.
3  Management meets with the employee and/or his or her representative.
4  Management confirms the common ground between the employee and the management.
5  Management resolves the grievance.
6  Management reports the outcome.

### 13.7.1 THE GRIEVANCE MEETING

The grievance meeting enables an individual to state his or her complaint, and for management to examine the issue, explore any potential resolution and come to a decision about what action to take. Good management practice in preparation for a grievance meeting is to check on the employee's employment record with the organisation and conduct any initial investigations that might shed light on the complaint. As suggested above, if the individual is to be represented at the meeting, an informal discussion with the representative in advance of the meeting may be useful.

In conducting the meeting itself, the focus should be on providing the employee with an opportunity to explain their complaint. The manager needs to use good watching, listening and questioning skills in order to gather information about the employee's grievance. Although the issues may be sensitive, it is important to ascertain the details of 'who, what, when and why' to ensure that a fair decision can be reached. Furthermore, the manager must explore what the employee wants the organisation to do if their grievance is found to have substance, as this will inform any potential resolution. On the basis of the information collected from the grievance interview, the manager then makes an assessment of the complaint/problem.

At the end of the interview, management may conclude that the grievance is unfounded. However, all grievances are important to the individual concerned – so, if management receives a complaint, which they judge to be without substance, it is not good practice to dismiss it in an arbitrary manner. They should find out why, and how, it happened and also explain clearly why it is a complaint that merits no action. This not only sets the record straight but also allows everyone to see that all complaints are handled seriously. It is important that the issue is handled in a way that avoids the individual feeling ignored or snubbed.

Even if the grievance is unfounded, there may be a need to put measures in place to repair relationships between the complainant and other colleagues. For example, an employee may feel that their manager is placing undue pressure on them and treating them unfairly. Even if as a result of the grievance meeting it is concluded that the complaint has not been substantiated, there is clearly an issue between the employee and their manager, which needs to be resolved, possibly through further discussion or even mediation.

On the other hand, the manager hearing the grievance may decide at the end of the grievance meeting that further investigation is needed before a decision can be made. For example, do any agreements cover the area of dispute and what do they say? What is company policy on the issue? Are there any witnesses or other people with relevant information who should also be interviewed? In such circumstances, management will make arrangements with the employee and their representative for a further meeting. Alternatively, following the meeting, management may decide that the employee's grievance is genuine. In this situation, management informs the employee of their decision but will also try to make arrangements for a further meeting with the employee and their representative to resolve the issue.

---

**CASE STUDY 13.2**

### ◉ LOSING PATIENCE...

You are the owner of a small firm. An employee has been complaining that she is being given too much work and cannot complete it on time. You have told the employee that her predecessor had no problem completing the same amount of work and that things got easier with experience. During this conversation, you lost you temper, raised your voice and as a result the employee became extremely upset. The employee is not happy and has put her grievance to you in writing.

You invite the employee to a meeting to discuss the grievance. The meeting reveals that the employee has been working on a computer that is different from the one used by her predecessor and also that the computer she has been using is slower, and uses an older version of the software required to carry out the work.

How should you deal with this grievance and what are the risks associated with the complaint?

---

### 13.7.2 RESOLVING THE GRIEVANCE

If the grievance is upheld, the key task for the manager is to decide how the issue can be resolved. In some situations, if the grievance involves serious misconduct by another member of staff, disciplinary proceedings may be initiated. However, many grievances are not clear-cut but have the potential to escalate into litigation or collective disputes. In these cases, the manager will need to meet the complainant and their representative again to try to negotiate a settlement to the individual's grievance. In essence, the techniques and skills used to negotiate a resolution in this context are similar to those needed in negotiating a pay claim or any other terms of employment.

There are normally three main stages to preparing for such a meeting:

- analysis (or the research stage)
- establishment of the aims as to how the grievance can be resolved while at the same time protecting management's interests
- planning the strategy and tactics to achieve the established aims.

### 13.7.3 ANALYSIS

The analysis stage involves the manager collecting and analysing relevant information to substantiate their proposals for resolving the individual employee's grievance. It also includes developing the argument(s) to be put to the employee and his or her representative to support the objective(s) that the manager is seeking to achieve. In managing grievances, the main sources of relevant information are the colleagues and employees who are regarded as likely to have factually useful information (for example, they witnessed the incident about which the employee is complaining) relevant to the issue that is the subject of the complaint.

The analysis stage also involves the managers checking whether the subject matter of the grievance has been complained of previously by employees, and if so, what the outcome was. Knowledge of such outcomes enables management to know whether any precedent exists for dealing with the employee's grievance. It is also important to explore whether there are any relevant company rules, custom and practice, personal contracts or collective agreements.

Any agreement on a resolution may be reached by the parties 'trading off' the details surrounding the issue but retaining certain principles. In making a decision about which 'details' to trade, management assess their value to the employee and anticipate which 'details' they will be prepared to trade in return.

For example, let us consider a complaint from a member of staff that their manager prevented them from accessing Facebook during work hours and in doing so insulted them in an abusive way. At the same time it was common practice for members of the team (including the manager) to access social media. The grievance meeting found that the complaint was based on fact but that this was related to concerns over the performance of the member of staff, which had not been addressed. In developing a potential resolution, the manager handling the grievance would need to consider what the organisation's social media policy stated. They would also need to think about whether disciplinary action of any sort or an apology from the manager was warranted and the potential implications of this on team dynamics. If appropriate, they may ask whether the parties would be prepared to agree to mediation. A fundamental question would be what the employee wanted and whether they were prepared to take further action if the issue was not resolved.

### 13.7.4 ESTABLISHING A STRATEGY

In order to achieve a satisfactory conclusion, it is important that clear management objectives are set prior to any meeting taking place. For example:

- How would they ideally like the grievance to be resolved?
- How do they think the grievance can realistically be resolved?
- What is the least for which management will settle (the fallback position)?

As part of the objective-setting process it might be appropriate to construct an aspiration grid. A possible aspiration grid for management is shown in Table 13.3. It shows that management would ideally like the issue to be resolved through an apology to the team member. However, management have assessed this as an unrealistic position, partly because the line manager concerned does not think she has done anything wrong and because the complainant has threatened that unless some formal action is taken against her she will resign and claim constructive dismissal. They have established a 'realistic' position of a compromise resolution centring on an informal reprimand for the manager and an agreement to resolve the issue through mediation. Their fallback position is to commence formal disciplinary action against the manager (with a likely outcome of a written warning), but they are concerned that this could lead the manager (who is generally well respected) to resign and have a negative impact on the team as a whole.

Figure 13.1 Aspiration grid

| Possible resolution to grievance | MANAGEMENT | | | EMPLOYEE | | |
|---|---|---|---|---|---|---|
| | Ideal | Real | Fallback | Fallback | Real | Ideal |
| Disciplinary action against manager | X | X | O | O | O | X |
| Informal reprimand against manager | X | O | O | O | X | X |
| Mediation | X | O | O | O | X | X |
| Apology | O | O | O | X | X | X |

Remember: **O** means prepared to trade; **X** means not prepared to trade

Using an aspiration grid can help identify if there is a basis for a resolution to the employee's complaint and can help when meeting with the individual employee and their representative. At this point you would expect to present a broad picture of your proposals for resolving the grievance subject to discussion and negotiation between the parties.

## 13.7.5 RESOLVING THE ISSUE

If a resolution to a grievance is found – but before finally accepting that the resolution has been agreed – management must:

- be convinced that the employee understands what has been agreed
- 'play back' to the employee what management understand the resolution of the grievance actually means to prevent any misunderstanding from arising
- agree to restart negotiations if this process reveals that the employee has indeed misunderstood what has been agreed, and that the misunderstanding cannot be cleared up in further discussion.

Once management has an oral agreement for the resolution of the employee's grievance, it should be written up. In many grievances, this will take the form of an internal memo/letter to another manager and to the employee recording what has been agreed. For example, if the complaint was one of denial of or access to a training opportunity, and it is upheld via the grievance-handling process, a manager will write to the personnel or the appropriate department reporting it has been agreed that the individual concerned should attend the next available appropriate training course. On the other hand, 'writing up' can, depending on the issue, take the form of a signed agreement by the manager concerned, the individual employee and his or her representative. The outcome is then reported to the appropriate interested parties. Clarity is important, and the manner in which what has been agreed is recorded should leave no room for doubt.

? **REFLECTIVE ACTIVITY 13.7**

Outline the skills required of managers in successfully handling grievances. Which do you consider to be the most important – and why?

### 13.7.6 THE APPEAL MEETING

Where an employee feels that his or her grievance has not been satisfactorily resolved (ie he or she is unhappy with the decision) at the grievance meeting, he or she has the right of appeal. The employee should inform the employer of the grounds for his or her appeal without unreasonable delay and in writing. Appeals should likewise be heard without unreasonable delay, and at a time and place that should be notified to the employee well in advance. The appeal has to be handled with impartiality and by a more senior manager than the one who dealt with the original grievance. This senior manager must not previously have been involved in the case. Employees have a statutory right to be accompanied at any such appeal hearing. The outcome of the appeal must be communicated without unreasonable delay.

In small organisations, even when there is no senior manager available, another manager should, if possible, hear the appeal. If this is not possible, consider whether the owner or, in the case of a charity, the board of trustees, should hear the appeal. Whoever hears the appeal should consider it as impartially as possible. As with the first meeting, the employer should write to the employee with a decision on his or her grievance as soon as possible. The employer should also tell the employee if the appeal meeting is the final stage of the grievance procedure. Some larger organisations do permit a further appeal to a higher level of management, such as a director.

## 13.8 SPECIALIST PROCEDURES

The grievance procedure deals with the broad range of complaints and problems. However, some areas of organisational life generate complaints and disputes that are particularly complex and require more specialised approaches. In this section, we examine two types of specific procedures that organisations are increasingly using to deal with issues related to job grading and evaluation and dignity at work.

**?** **REFLECTIVE ACTIVITY 13.8**

Does your organisation have specialist procedures to deal with complaints over certain issues? If it does, what issues do they cover? Why do these specific procedures exist?

### 13.8.1 JOB GRADING APPEAL PROCEDURES

Job evaluation helps determine the appropriate level of a job as measured against criteria such as decision-making, working conditions (for example, exposure to hazards, working in the open air as opposed to in an office, etc), contacts within and outside the organisation, the degree of supervision received, the complexity of the work (for example, gathering and inputting data as opposed to gathering and then manipulating data to produce a report with recommendations) within the organisation's structure. The appropriate level within the organisational structure influences the pay level and seniority associated with the job. A grievance that centres on such an issue arises mostly when an individual claims that his or her job has changed relative to when it was last evaluated because it now carries greater responsibility for:

- people (in terms of supervising and training them)
- financial resources (increased budget, financial control)
- physical resources (modern high-tech expensive equipment).

On the other hand, management may argue that the post has not changed in responsibility and that what has changed is an increase in the volume of tasks, at the same level of responsibility. It therefore makes sense in resolving such a dispute to have a procedure tailored to cover the specific circumstances of job grading, including access to specialist and expert individuals.

In a typical job evaluation appeals procedure, the first stage normally requires the individual employee to discuss the basis of the appeal with his or her immediate line manager/team leader. The second stage normally requires the individual to complete a 'formal appeal form', which then goes before a meeting of a job evaluation appeals panel. The complainant, accompanied by his or her representative, presents the case to the appeals panel, as does the employer. The appeals panel will decide either to upgrade the job or to reject the appeal. The decision is usually communicated to the individual through their line manager. If the appeal is upheld, the decision will be implemented from the date of the panel's decision.

If the job holder is dissatisfied with the decision of the appeals panel, he or she may request that the case goes to a third stage and be heard by an independent appeal body. At this stage the job holder (assisted by his or her representative) will present the basis of the appeal, a member of the appeals panel will present justification for its decision and the independent appeal body – which is usually chaired by an independent chairperson acceptable to both parties – will make a decision that is final and binding. In some organisations with job-evaluated grading structures, this means that individual grievances over job gradings are, at the end of the day, decided by arbitration.

A job evaluation procedure is relatively clear-cut and straightforward. It has the advantage over the standard grievance procedure of building in access to experts at each appeal stage and providing more specialist panels to hear the appeals.

## ?    REFLECTIVE ACTIVITY 13.9

Critically reflect on the processes you have in place for job grading in your organisation. What elements of that process could give rise to an employee raising a grievance? What strategies could you adopt to fairly address those concerns?

## 13.9 DIGNITY AT WORK

Harassment based on gender, race and disability, and bullying at work have received increasing attention in recent years as organisations and worker representative bodies have become more concerned about the dignity of individuals in the workplace. Many organisations have policies and procedures that link the complaints procedure on harassment and bullying with the existing grievance procedure, rather than establishing separate arrangements for such complaints. Others have treated it as a specific issue. Both approaches can work.

Harassment, in general terms, can be defined as:

unwanted conduct affecting the dignity of men and women in the workplace. It may be related to age, race, disability religion, nationality or any personal characteristics of the individual, and may be persistent or an isolated incident. The key is that the actions or comments are viewed as demeaning and unacceptable to the recipient.

Bullying may be characterised as:

offensive, intimidating, malicious or insulting behaviour, an abuse or misuse of power through means intended to undermine, humiliate, denigrate or injure the recipient.

Bullying or harassment may be what one individual does to another individual (perhaps by someone in a position of authority, such as a manager or front-line manager) or involve groups of people. It may be obvious or it may be insidious. Whatever form it takes, it is unwarranted and unwelcome to the recipient individual. Bullying and/or harassment include:

- spreading malicious rumours or insulting someone by word or behaviour
- sending or copying emails that are critical about someone to others who do not need to know
- ridiculing or demeaning someone – picking on him or her, or setting him or her up to fail
- unwelcome sexual advances – touching, standing too close, a display of offensive materials
- deliberately undermining a competent worker by overloading and constant criticism.

Bullying and/or harassment can make someone feel anxious and humiliated. Feelings of anger and frustration at being unable to cope may be triggered. Some employees may try to retaliate in some way. Others may become frightened and demotivated. Stress, loss of self-confidence and self-esteem caused by bullying and/or harassment can lead to job insecurity, illness, absence from work and even resignation. Almost always, job performance is affected and relations in the workplace suffer.

Employers are responsible for preventing bullying and harassing behaviour. It is in their interests to make it clear to everyone that such behaviour will not be tolerated. The costs to the organisation may include poor employment relations, low morale, lower productivity and efficiency, and potentially the resignation of staff. An organisational statement to all staff about the standards expected can make it easier for all individuals to be fully aware of their responsibilities to others.

In organisations where a bullying and harassment policy exists, it is normal for a dual system to operate. The initial action is usually confined to the specifics of the complaint within the procedure laid down for managing harassment and/or bullying. If the problem cannot be resolved within the limits of the policy and is proved to be an issue that merits disciplinary proceedings, the disciplinary procedure is triggered. In addition, specialist dignity at work policies make it possible for a complaint to be made to someone other than the line manager, as they are often the subject of many complaints of this type. In addition, complainants are commonly provided with sources of support and advice, in addition to union or employee representatives.

In dealing with allegations of harassment and/or bullying, the manager dealing with the complaint first conducts a thorough investigation to establish whether there is a prima facie case of harassment and/or bullying for the accused employee to answer. If the manager decides, on the basis of the investigation, that there is a case to answer, disciplinary proceedings may be instigated against the accused employee.

However, many cases are not clear-cut. The definition of 'bullying' in particular is inevitably subjective. In recent years, researchers have noted an increase in the numbers of bullying claims related to processes of performance management. In essence, employees believe that they are being bullied by their manager, while the manager believes that they are simply trying to 'manage' the employee. In some situations, therefore, complaints of bullying may reflect a breakdown of relationships between colleagues and particularly between employees and their line managers. Here, there may be significant scope for early and informal resolution. In fact, there tends to be a greater emphasis on the potential of workplace mediation in 'dignity at work' policies and procedures than in more generic grievance procedures.

This is reflected in Manchester University's well-respected 'Dignity at Work and Study Procedure'. For a harassment or bullying case, four options open to complainants are set out in the procedures:

---

### EXTRACT FROM MANCHESTER UNIVERSITY'S 'DIGNITY AT WORK AND STUDY PROCEDURE'

- Many complaints can be resolved informally and this approach is encouraged where possible.
- Mediation is also available at any stage of the procedure and offers a less adversarial method of dispute resolution.
- However, if complainants do not feel able to follow either the informal procedure or mediation, or if the incident is too serious for such approaches, they should proceed straight to the formal stage.
- As a general principle, the decision of whether to progress a complaint is up to the individual. However, the University has a duty to protect all staff and may pursue the matter independently if it considers it appropriate to do so.

---

However, where informal resolution mediation has not been successful or is not appropriate, the complainant has the right to activate the formal procedure. Importantly, this is not made to their line manager but to an HR manager who acknowledges receipt of the complaint and will refer the matter to an appropriate investigating officer. The university also provides harassment advisers to support employees. Different organisations define their acceptable standards of behaviour differently, particularly with respect to gross misconduct. In many organisations, harassment and/or bullying is regarded as gross misconduct, carrying the threat of summary dismissal if proved. If this is the case, this should be clearly spelled out to employees in the organisation's policy statement on sexual harassment and/or dignity at work.

There are, therefore, good reasons for dealing with harassment and/or bullying complaints outside of the general grievance procedure. First, there is a reasonable chance that the person who is the subject of the complaint is the line manager of the employee making the complaint. This can make it difficult to resolve the grievance as near to the point of its origin as possible. Second, there is a link between grievance, discipline and harassment. The role of the employment relations professional in harassment/bullying complaints is to act as a backup for line managers in managing the issue, by providing them with general expertise and support, advising them on the appropriate course of action and ensuring that they have access to training programmes to handle dignity at work issues.

CASE STUDY 13.3

**BRUSHING OFF BANTER**

A recent article in *People Management* highlighted one of HR's ten most expensive mistakes as 'brushing off banter'. As Jo Faragher reported:

'It can seem harsh to quash workplace chatter. But sometimes you have to. An employment tribunal in 2012 [*Nolan v CD Bramall Dealership Ltd t/a Evans Halshaw Motorhouse Worksop ET/2601000/12*] held that an engineering firm had demonstrated age discrimination against an employee who was close to retirement. Colleagues often referred to him as 'Yoda' and had changed his number plate from 'OAB' to 'OAP'. His manager had not seen a problem with it 'if everyone was getting on'.

Reflecting on our discussion in the chapter:

How would you deal with the case if the older worker had raised a grievance against the harassment they were receiving from work colleagues?

Who do you think is culpable in the harassment taking place?

What sort of guidance could you put in place to ensure that all managers in the organisation were clear that this sort of 'banter' was not appropriate in the workplace?

## 13.10 SUMMARY

This chapter began by examining the dynamic process through which grievances are formed and escalate. This discussion highlighted the critical importance of the way that managers respond to initial complaints of mistreatment. Perhaps, most importantly, it suggests that if managers deal with such concerns quickly and appropriately, trust can be rebuilt and commitment to the organisation strengthened. Unfortunately, many managers lack the confidence to do this and, as a result, grievances often become intractable and extremely damaging for the individual involved and the organisation.

Managers should ideally attempt to resolve grievances informally at an early stage and, as we saw in respect of disciplinary issues in the previous chapter, employment relations professionals have a key role to play in providing the support and advice that line managers need. In addition, good relationships with union and employee representatives are valuable in providing channels through which resolutions can be found.

Of course, not all grievances can be resolved in this way and, for more serious complaints, there is little alternative to invoking formal procedure. If this is the case, the chapter sets out sound advice as to how grievance procedures can be implemented in a fair and effective manner. Importantly, unlike disciplinary issues, grievance outcomes are not clear-cut and rest on the wishes of the complainant. Therefore, there is the potential to negotiate outcomes that are satisfactory to the employee and also serve to rebuild the employment relationship.

**KEY LEARNING POINTS**

1   The extent to which employee grievances escalate and their implications for the organisation are dependent on the adequacy of the managerial response. Recognition of the issue and prompt action to seek a resolution can rebuild the employment relationship and the complainant's commitment to the organisation, but a failure to address the complaint can deepen the seriousness of the grievance with damaging consequences.

2   Most employee complaints against management behaviour do not reach the formal grievance procedure. Often, this is due to the inadequacy of procedures or a lack of confidence in management's capacity to react reasonably.

3   The grievance procedure ensures that employees are treated in a fair and consistent manner, and they know where they stand and know what to expect. In managing employee complaints, management should be guided by a number of principles – fairness, transparency, consistency and promptness.

4   In managing grievances, management's objective is to settle the employee's complaint as near as possible to the point of its source. Early and informal resolution can be supported by effective employment relations and high-trust relationships with union and employee representatives.

5   Where a grievance is well founded, the manager must decide on the appropriate response. In some cases, this will be clear-cut and disciplinary proceedings will need to be started if there has been serious misconduct. Where the issues are more complex, a process of negotiation can be used to find a mutually acceptable outcome.

6   Organisations may need to design specialist procedures for dealing with certain types of grievances, such as job evaluation and grading, and bullying and harassment.

**REVIEW QUESTIONS**

1   Frank has been given the most unpopular job in his department for three weeks in a row. He thinks this is unfair and that the supervisor should be sharing it among all the employees in his department. You are the HR representative, and Frank has approached you and voiced his discontent. How should you deal with the situation?

2   You are responsible for conducting workshops for new line managers on employment relations techniques. One of the topics you have been asked to deal with is managing employee complaints in the workplace. Explain, and justify, the key areas of knowledge and skills that you would cover in your workshop.

3   Explain the principles that underpin a grievance procedure.

4   Explain, and justify, the criteria you would use to evaluate whether a grievance procedure was operating effectively.

5   An employee has approached you as her HR adviser. She feels that she is being bullied by her line manager and asks for your advice. She reports that the line manager constantly shouts at her in front of colleagues. She also alleges that he has made sexual innuendoes to her. What advice do you give the employee, and how will you deal with the situation?

EXPLORE FURTHER

ACAS (2009) *Code of practice on disciplinary and grievance procedures*. London: Acas.

ACAS (2014) *Bullying and harassment at work – a guide for managers and employers*. London: Acas.

ACAS (2014) *Discipline and grievance at work: the Acas guide*. London: Acas.

OLSON-BUCHANAN, J. and BOSWELL, W. (2008) An integrative model of experiencing and responding to mistreatment at work. *Academy of Management Review*. Vol 33, No 1: pp76–96.

VAN WANROOY, B., BEWLEY, H. and BRYSON, A. (2013) *Employment relations in the shadow of recession: findings from the 2011 Workplace Employment Relations Study*. Basingstoke: Palgrave Macmillan.

WOOD, S., LATREILLE, P. and SAUNDRY, R. (2014) *Analysis of nature, extent and impact of grievance and disciplinary procedures and workplace mediation using WERS2011*. Acas research papers, No 10/14. London: Acas.

**Website links**

www.acas.org.uk is the website of Acas and will give you access to the Acas *Code on grievance and disciplinary procedures* and other guidance for employers on employee grievance management.

www.gov.uk/handling-employee-grievance is the government website that gives advice to employers on how to manage grievances.

www.worksmart.org.uk is the website of the TUC, which will give you access to their guidance on understanding grievance procedures.

# CHAPTER 14

# Managing Redundancies

## OVERVIEW

The financial collapse of 2008 and the subsequent prolonged recession in the UK highlighted the central importance of redundancy and downsizing within the management of employment relations. The starting point of this chapter is to explore the organisational and personal impact of redundancy and the importance of looking for alternatives wherever possible. Of course, all redundancies have damaging effects, but these can be ameliorated, to some extent, where organisations handle the process in a sensitive and equitable manner. To this end, we examine the case for robust redundancy policies and procedures, and consider recent research into experiences of the managers who handle redundancies, which highlights the need for support and training to be provided to those who have to take on this difficult role. Consideration of alternatives is an important element of redundancy consultation, and we examine the legal obligations of employers relating to collective consultations and also the need for employers to consult with individuals to ensure that any redundancy dismissals are reasonable and fair. We then discuss the importance of adopting fair selection criteria when employers are forced to make compulsory redundancies, and we close the chapter by examining 'good employment practice' in maintaining the well-being of the employees who remain in employment after the redundancy. This covers issues such as counselling, outplacement and the problems of 'survivor syndrome'.

## LEARNING OUTCOMES

When you have completed this chapter, you should be able to:

- understand and critically evaluate the connection between redundancy and the management of change
- critically assess the roles played by managers tasked with making staff redundant
- explain how to produce a redundancy policy and associated procedures
- understand and provide advice on the legal framework in respect of redundancy, in particular the requirements on consultation
- evaluate the long-term implications of redundancy for organisational survivors and identify appropriate measures for managing this issue.

## 14.1 INTRODUCTION

The 2008/09 recession saw private sector businesses encounter highly volatile market conditions, while public sector organisations were forced to contend with the effects of significant reductions in government spending. Consequently, employers and employees throughout the UK were increasingly faced with the threat and the reality of restructuring and redundancy. The 2011 Workplace Employment Relations Survey (van Wanrooy *et al*, 2013) reported that 13% of the organisations surveyed had made redundancies in the previous year, with 47% citing the main reason as being less demand for their product or service. Other factors included the need to reorganise working methods, reduction in budgets, the need to cut costs or improve competiveness.

Whatever the reason, it highlights the point we made in Chapter 3 – namely, that the economic environment in which an organisation operates will have an influence on employment relations. Significantly, how we handle redundancy is crucial for long-term business and organisational success. A CIPD report in 2010 revealed that many employees were not satisfied with how redundancies had been dealt with in their organisation. Four years later, the CIPD (2014) highlighted this as a continuing issue, in that large numbers of employees remained discontented with senior management over how they were consulted 'about important issues' (such as downsizing). Therefore, in this chapter, we not only look at the legal obligations with which employers have to comply when considering redundancies but the ways in which organisations can try to ensure that the redundancy process is managed fairly and equitably.

## 14.2 RECESSION AND REDUNDANCY

The fluctuating nature of the economic cycle means that we become used to hearing the words 'downturn', 'slowdown', and 'downsize'. The impact of economic factors on the jobs market was reinforced during 2008 and 2009 because of what was, by common consent, the worst recession to hit the UK for over fifty years. The CIPD *Labour Market Outlook* survey in February 2010 found that just under a fifth of employees (19%) thought that it was likely or very likely that they could lose their job as a result of the recession. The survey also identified increased worries by public sector workers over their future job security. These worries were probably justified given the sharp decreases in public expenditure that were to take place over the subsequent years. Therefore, these external issues and their impact on the labour force mean that redundancy, or the possibility of redundancy, is always a central consideration for employment relations professionals.

---

**?    REFLECTIVE ACTIVITY 14.1**

Is redundancy the only option? Best practice, it is argued, is that making staff redundant is only one of the options open to an organisation considering downsizing. As you read through this chapter, reflect on the merits of this argument. Think about the alternatives that are available to the HR practitioner, and identify their advantages and their drawbacks.

---

## 14.3 DEFINING REDUNDANCY

Redundancy is defined in section 139 of the Employment Rights Act (1996) as follows:

1   The fact that [the] employer has ceased or intends to cease –

   to carry on the business for the purposes of which the employee was employed by him, or
   to carry on that business in the place where the employee was so employed, or

2   The fact that the requirements of that business –

   for employees to carry out work of a particular kind, or

for employees to carry out work of a particular kind in the place where the employee was employed by the employer, have ceased or diminished, or are expected to cease or diminish.

To put that in everyday language: redundancy occurs when the employer closes down completely, moves premises, requires fewer people for particular jobs or requires no people for particular jobs. Redundancy can also occur when an individual has been laid off or kept on short-time for a period. Assuming that the reason that an individual's employment comes to an end is within one of the statutory definitions, or that they have been laid off or kept on short-time, and assuming that they have a minimum period of qualifying employment, they are entitled to a statutory redundancy payment.

However, there are certain situations in which employees may perceive that they have been made redundant, but employers could argue that the definition of redundancy is not met. First, an employer might say that the events leading to an individual's leaving employment had nothing to do with redundancy but were simply the consequences of a legitimate and lawful business reorganisation.

---

## CASE STUDY 14.1

### LESNEY PRODUCTS V NOLAN (1977) IRLR 77

Nolan argued that the change from a long day shift with overtime to a double day shift was a diminution in the employer's requirements for work of a particular kind, and that the employee should have received a redundancy payment. The Court of Appeal held that such a change was a legitimate reorganisation, based on efficiency, and that therefore no payment was due.

---

Second, an employee may have a clause in her contract that provides for her to work at more than one site. If one site closes, the employer could argue that there is no redundancy. Therefore, it is important, when drawing up the employee's Statement of Terms and Particulars of Employment as required by the Employment Rights Act (1996), to identify whether 'the employee is required or permitted to work at various places' (section 1(4)(h)).

Third, even if an employee has no mobility clause in their contract, in a redundancy situation, they could be offered alternative employment at another location. If the employee refuses 'suitable alternative employment', there will be no redundancy and therefore they will not qualify for a redundancy payment. Whether the offer was suitable would depend on the distance of relocation and the ease of travelling to the new location. Location is not the only consideration. An employee could also argue that alternative employment that involves a substantial change in role, responsibility or terms and conditions is not 'suitable' and consequently that they retain their right to refuse the offer and be paid a redundancy payment. If an employee is unsure about the suitability of alternative employment, they can opt for a trial period of four weeks, after which time, if the job is not suitable, a redundancy payment is still payable.

## 14.4 REDUNDANCY AND THE MANAGEMENT OF CHANGE

In the context of redundancy, we need to look at what causes firms to initiate changes and ask whether job losses are inevitable. In many cases, organisations have no option but to declare redundancies – for example, for an urgent need to cut costs, or because of a failure to win an important contract. In a complex business world, we have to recognise that business change will continue to lead to reduced workforces because organisations are under continuous pressure to improve efficiency and increase profitability. But redundancies could sometimes have been avoided if organisations had invested more time in human resource planning, training or skills development.

---

**? REFLECTIVE ACTIVITY 14.2**

Have there been any redundancies where you work in the past two years? What was the reason for this and what impact did this have on the organisation and the remaining employees?

---

For many organisations in the UK, the response to change and uncertainty has been to downsize the organisation or to introduce flexible working practices. However, according to Sparrow and Marchington (1998), these responses:

'raise questions about the most appropriate organisational form ... Under the burden of economic and competitive pressure, a range of organisational strategies is aimed at competing not just on cost but on quality and speed of response.'

Remarkably, despite the forecast of huge job losses resulting from the 2008/09 recession, the outcome was less draconian than feared. This was due to many organisations, having learned the lessons from past downturns, seeking other ways to mitigate the impact of lost business and reduced revenues. Furthermore, staff and unions were prepared to a restriction in  pay and find new ways of working to avoid job losses. Throughout 2009 and subsequent years, there were many examples of innovative alternatives to redundancy implemented by firms that understood the need to hold on to their best people. These ranged from reducing working hours, reducing pay, wage freezes to sabbaticals. Furthermore, decisions on redundancy, because they are often made to address an immediate and short-term problem, can be counterproductive. They can engender a mood of disillusionment and cynicism that can destroy any of the short-term financial gains of a redundancy exercise, together with any hope of gaining employee commitment to the future.

Sparrow and Marchington (1998) make the point that in relation to downsizing and de-layering:

'immediate financial and performance measurements made today cannot assess the implications of correct or incorrect decision-making, as such decisions now tend to operate and be proved effective [only] over a longer time-span.'

Therefore, if employee commitment is to be obtained, together with high levels of motivation, employees have to feel secure in their employment, and not afraid for their future. As noted previously, the CIPD *Labour Market Outlook* surveys would suggest that the fear factor has not gone away. In a 1996 report the IPD stated that 'insecurity has damaged people's commitment, a state of affairs that if not remedied has the potential to damage competitive performance'. This is just as true today as it was in 1996, and there is continuing evidence that redundancy remains a spectre that can affect an individual's perception of his or her job security.

Insecurity is often generated by a failure on the part of senior management to recognise the need for prompt and accurate communication when people's livelihoods are at risk. Linked to this is the need to ensure that messages are communicated in a way that minimises distress to those affected. The potential for poor communication is exacerbated by the use, or misuse, of media – such as email, text messaging and social media. Sadly, there are a number of examples of organisations that have advised employees about impending redundancies by email or text message – not always with bad intentions, simply through lack of foresight.

One of the most common ways in which poor communication impacts on redundancy situations is during the course of a merger or an acquisition. Company A will often signal an intention to bid for, or merge with, company B, and as part of its strategy to win shareholder approval for its plans, will announce what savings may be expected if it is successful. These savings can often include a declared intention to downsize the workforce. The first the affected employees hear about it is through press announcements or email messages. A typical example is the successful bid by Kraft for Cadbury's in 2010. Initially, Kraft signalled an intention to reverse a previously announced factory closure made by Cadbury's – a promise Kraft subsequently reneged on. While the staff at the affected factory were no worse off than before the takeover, other staff were left wondering how secure jobs were.

There is no magic formula for achieving commitment. A CIPD Outlook survey in 2009 found that nearly three-quarters (70%) of employees felt that redundancies had damaged their morale; with 22% claiming that the way that redundancies had been handled had led them to look for new jobs in the future. Ranieri (2010), in an Acas discussion paper, argued that the way that redundancy is managed affects both those who lose their jobs and those that remain. However, regular communications and more meaningful consultation can help to improve trust and minimise the negative effects.

Pfeffer (1998) suggests that an employee's apprehension about his or her employment prospects will undermine the organisation's investment in innovative work practices, productivity improvements, and labour–management co-operative efforts. He argues that:

'laying employees off too readily constitutes a cost for firms that have done a good job selecting, training and developing their workforce ... Layoffs put important strategic assets on the street for the competition to employ.'

Virgin Airlines discovered this in the aftermath of the 11 September 2001 terrorist attacks. Speaking at the 2004 European HR Forum, Virgin's Director of Organisational Development, Moira Nagle, explained how, less than a week after the attack, the airline decided to lose 25% of its staff. But – and this is the key point – Virgin did not have any redundancy procedures. As a consequence, and as Nagle freely admitted, it lost some very skilled employees, many of whom have since been rehired:

'We thought getting people out of the door was the thing we needed to do [and] we probably lost some very skilled people we would have preferred not to lose.'

## ? REFLECTIVE ACTIVITY 14.3

Do you and your colleagues feel secure, or is there some concern about the future? If so, what could your employer do to remedy this?

## 14.5 MANAGING REDUNDANCY – THE ROLE OF THE 'ENVOY'

A critical role in managing redundancy is played by those managers and HR professionals tasked with 'delivering the news' to employees. Ashman (2013) conducted a study into what he termed downsizing 'envoys' for Acas in 2012. Crucially, the research identified the skills and experience those envoys need to do that job effectively. In an article published in *People Management* in July 2012, Ashman set out key considerations in the management of the redundancy process:

- The message must be communicated accurately and with sensitivity.
- A balance is needed between strategic intent, procedural fairness and humane treatment.
- People leaving the organisation do so with dignity (especially given the moral and PR implications).
- Workers being redeployed are transferred into roles for which they are suited.
- Survivors experience and witness a just process, and can feel comfortable in their task of taking the organisation forward.

The research also explored the experiences of envoys and the strategies that they used to cope with extremely challenging situations. Importantly, organisations often underestimate the difficulties facing envoys who are rarely trained or prepared for the role. Adjectives that envoys used to describe the emotional impact of the role included: 'traumatic', 'nerve-wracking', 'dreadful', 'very upsetting', 'hideous' and, ultimately, 'stressful'. Typical coping strategies ranged from emotional hardening and cognitive distancing (separating the 'downsizing me' from the 'real me') to using procedures as a psychological support that depersonalises individuals and events. Despite the heightened emotional burden, the envoys always felt it right and proper that they should take responsibility for delivering the news of downsizing to their subordinates and colleagues because they knew them best and wanted to provide support.

Significantly, the research highlighted the unique relationship between the line manager and the HR practitioner as joint envoys and raises a number of important issues for us to consider in any redundancy situation. For line managers, the role of envoy became additional to their normal role and therefore led to role overload. Also, they often felt isolated because they could not talk to other managers in a similar position. In contrast, HR envoys had access to others in their organisation and in the HR community to share their experiences, and were also able to incorporate the role into their normal workload.

As Ashman concludes, a responsibility therefore rests with the HR envoy to ensure that their line manager partner has the necessary support, without encroaching on their autonomy to manage that role. The ability of the envoy to manage that pressure effectively will come with more experience of the role. However, organisations need to do more to help envoys prepare. This could include: mentoring, role-playing in CPD training and greater understanding of the psychological and emotional impact of organisational change. Furthermore, depending on the scale, involving envoys in the strategic decisions and rationale for redundancies and offering them the chance to meet with other envoys were seen as highly effective elements of best practice. Similarly, ensuring that people 'buy into' rather than feel coerced into the role, and providing support to deal with the inevitable emotional stress they themselves will encounter, is essential. This is particularly the case when having to deal with colleagues with whom they have worked often for a long time.

## 14.6 REDUNDANCY POLICY AND PROCEDURES

For HR professionals, job security policies and the avoidance of redundancy are an increasingly important part of the employment relations framework. Organisational change leads to the inevitable weakening of employees' confidence in their employer's ability to maintain job security. If redundancy is unavoidable, 'good practice' dictates that organisations have policies and procedures in place which enable them to deal with a difficult situation with sensitivity and equity. Policies and procedures are important not only because the law implies certain requirements but also because there is a good business case for doing so.

A statement of policy on redundancy might in some ways be better classified as an organisation's statement of intent in respect of their commitment to maintaining employment (for example, see the following sample policy). Such a policy statement does not make any commitment to no compulsory redundancies, but it is an important first step in recognising people as an important asset and can be a key plank in building a partnership between management and workforce.

## ? REFLECTIVE ACTIVITY 14.4

Does your organisation have a redundancy policy? If it does, what does it say about job security? What other policies is it linked to and why?

Redundancy procedures should be written and designed to cater for the individuality of each organisation. Draft procedures can be obtained from professional bodies such as the CIPD or from commercial organisations, but they should always be treated as guidelines or templates and be amended to meet individual organisations' requirements. The following are some extracts from an actual redundancy policy, which indicate some of the steps that have to be taken when redundancies do arise.

## RREDUNDANCY POLICY

Philosophy

It is the aim of the Company to provide continuity of employment for staff consistent with the need for continuing efficiency and effectiveness in a changing business environment. The Company will constantly attempt to plan so that any required reductions in staffing levels can be accommodated through natural turnover or redeployment of employees. The Company recognises, however, that on occasions it may be necessary to undertake redundancies. If redundancies cannot be avoided (eg through redeployment), the Company will aim to treat all staff fairly and consistently.

Consultation

*Justification*

Justification for the redundancies must be thorough, robust and detailed.

*Communication*

Individual consultation/counselling to take place with affected people, who will be given the option to be accompanied by a work colleague or union representative.

The timing and method of communication of redundancies to be handled 'sensitively' wherever possible.

There may be occasional situations where the interests of the business do not allow for consultation prior to the selection of individuals for redundancy (eg for commercial reasons). Such situations should be exceptional.

*Voluntary redundancy*

A voluntary scheme to allow for volunteers to be identified from the affected area, before compulsory redundancy is applied (other than in the situation where a 'unique' role is identified as redundant).

To apply the rationale that volunteers will be allowed to leave on redundancy (subject to the numbers volunteering matching the numbers required), unless there is an overriding business reason (ie in respect of voluntary redundancy, the Company to reserve the right to be selective in sanctioning the redundancy, subject to an overriding business reason). The judgement about whether an individual is business-critical (and therefore cannot be released) will be made by the line manager, who will provide a supporting justification to the appropriate Director/HR Director.

- Any employee affected in this way will have the right to appeal against this decision.
- He/she must do so in writing, within seven calendar days of being advised that he/she cannot be released for voluntary redundancy.
- This appeal will be made to the appropriate Director and the HR Director, who will conduct an appeal hearing. If the decision of this hearing is still disputed by the individual, he/she must register a further appeal in writing to the MD without delay. The MD will conduct an appeal hearing with the individual. The MD's decision will be final.
- All appeal hearings will be completed within 14 calendar days of the employee's first registering his/her appeal.
- This appeal process will take precedence over the Company's grievance procedure.

Where the number of volunteers matches the number of redundancies, the business-critical reasoning outlined will apply.

The rest of the procedure goes on to set out provisions in relation to compulsory redundancy selection, redundancy payment terms and outplacement support. It also provides a mechanism for review of the procedure and a commitment that no individual made redundant will be employed within the next 12 months.

## 14.7 REDUNDANCY CONSULTATION

The first part of the redundancy procedure outlined above is the process for consultation. If there is a possibility that employees will be made redundant, employers need to consider their legal obligations regarding consultation.

### 14.7.1 COLLECTIVE CONSULTATIONS AND THE LAW

Currently, under section 188 of the Trade Union and Labour Relations (Consolidation) Act 1992, consultation on large-scale redundancies must start 'in good time' and must begin:

- at least 30 days before the first dismissal takes effect if 20 to 99 employees are to be made redundant at one establishment over a period of 90 days or less
- at least 45 days before the first dismissal takes effect if 100 or more employees are to be made redundant at one establishment over a period of 90 days or less.

This was the result of fundamental changes to the collective redundancy consultation requirements enacted by the Government in 2013. The minimum consultation period for an employer proposing 100 or more redundancies was reduced from 90 to 45 days. The same reduction was made to the period of notice employers must give to the Government.

The Government argued that consultations were often completed within the 90-day minimum period and that, consequently, important restructuring was delayed and workers faced delays in finding new work. However, others argued that the changes reduced protection for workers and encouraged employers to use redundancy rather than looking for alternative approaches (Renton and Macey, 2013: 14).

Some commentators have also expressed doubt about how the phrase 'proposing redundancies' should be interpreted, particularly as the Collective Redundancies Directive uses the phrase 'contemplating redundancies'. The broad consensus on this issue is that the duty to consult arises when the employer has developed a plan that is likely to result in redundancies, ie when the employer has proposals. In most cases, starting to consult after making a firm decision has been made to make redundancies will be unlawful.

Consultations should be conducted with 'appropriate representatives'. These appropriate representatives should be union representatives where there is a recognised union in the workplace. Where this is not the case, there is a duty to consult with elected employee representatives. Where employees decide that they want some form of collective representation in such circumstances, it is for the employer to arrange for the election of representatives. The number of representatives and their period of 'office' should be sufficient to represent all employees properly, for example by having representatives for different sections of the workforce. Representatives must themselves be affected by the proposed redundancy and all those affected should be given a vote. The ballot should be secret and each person may cast as many votes as there are representatives to be elected.

In addition, when considering redundancies on this scale, employers must notify the Redundancy Payments Service before any consultations staff start using the prescribed HR1 form, which can be downloaded here: www.gov.uk/government/publications/redundancy-payments-form-hr1-advance-notification-of-redundancies.

### 14.7.2 CONSULTATION AND EMPLOYMENT RELATIONS

Notwithstanding the legal considerations, it is still good employee relations practice to begin consultation as soon as possible if a satisfactory outcome is desired. Acas argue in their guide to handling large-scale redundancies (Acas, 2014) that good communication and consultation can: lead to better discussions; keep employees motivated and engaged; protect employee well-being; help the business survive and plan for the future; potentially minimise job losses; and ultimately provide costs savings for the organisation. At the same time, alarming speculation about redundancies can be extremely damaging for employees and the organisation, so taking great care in the way that employees and their representatives are informed about potential redundancies is crucial.

Good relationships with trade unions and employee representatives can also have a very positive impact. A prime example of this is the role played by employer and union learning partnerships in addressing some of the negative elements of a downsizing programme.

---

CASE STUDY 14.2

### LEARNING PARTNERSHIPS IN THE NHS

In one NHS trust, large-scale redundancies due to technological change were managed through the learning partnership between management and unions identifying retraining to redeploy those at risk and so avoiding compulsory redundancy. The local union branch secretary involved explained this as follows:

'A prime example of why it was necessary to work together in partnership ... Medical records were going to shut completely. There were about 50 people working in medical. Now, as a result of the technological change, all that was going to change, there'd be no need to store the record. It's all stored electronically. So, as a result of that, their jobs are going to disappear – what do you do with them? Luckily enough there was a lead-in time for this, and what it gave both the union and the employer time to do was to sit down and think how we were going to manage that situation. If we'd done nothing, that place would have closed and the staff would have been redundant. So we developed a plan ... and that was where retraining [to enable redeployment] was part of that.'

(Bennett, 2014: 27)

Findings from this research suggested that if downsizing is perceived to be handled fairly by staff, and the learning strategy is timely and effectively applied, it can help reduce the negative effects of survivor syndrome. Also, people who leave the organisation are more likely to feel that they have been fairly and well supported through the process.

### 14.7.3 INFORMATION REQUIRED BY EMPLOYEE REPRESENTATIVES

The timetable described can only start to run once employees or their representatives have been provided with certain information:

- the reasons for the employer's proposals
- the numbers and descriptions of the employees to be dismissed
- the method of selection the employer proposes for dismissal
- the method of carrying out the dismissals the employer proposes, having due regard to any procedural agreement that might be in existence
- the period of time over which the programme of redundancies is to be carried out
- the method the employer intends to use in calculating redundancy payments, unless the statutory formula is being applied.

Should an employer fail to provide any or all of the information required, or the information that is provided is insufficient, the consultation period will be deemed not to have started. In such circumstances, the employer faces the risk of a penalty being imposed. It is difficult to give precise guidance on what, and how much, detail must be provided, but vague and open-ended statements will not be acceptable. For the employment relations specialist, there has to be an acceptance that every case must be decided on its merits.

### 14.7.4 CONSULTATION MUST BE GENUINE

For consultation to be deemed genuine it has to be undertaken 'with a view to reaching agreement' with employee representatives. Ranieri (2010: 4), for instance, reported that complaints by employees regarding inadequate consultation rose during the last recession. We argue that three things have to happen. An examination has to take place on ways to avoid dismissals. If avoidance is impossible, ways to reduce the numbers to be dismissed should be looked at. Finally, ways should be found of mitigating the consequences of any dismissals. However, the employer is under no obligation to negotiate. Instead, they must approach the discussions with an open mind and, where possible, take account of any proposals put to them by the representatives.

### 14.7.5 ALTERNATIVES TO REDUNDANCY

One of the main purposes of consultation is to establish whether any potential job losses can be achieved by means other than compulsory redundancies. Factors that would normally be considered at this juncture include:

- a ban on recruitment (unless unavoidable)
- retraining of staff
- redeployment of staff
- restricted use of subcontracted labour, temporary and casual staff
- reduced amount of overtime working
- voluntary redundancy
- early retirement.

Depending on the nature of the business, other considerations – as we have seen previously – might include temporary lay-offs, short-time working, pay cuts/freezes or even job-sharing.

### 14.7.6 VOLUNTARY REDUNDANCY AND EARLY RETIREMENT

One of the first considerations for organisations when faced with the need for redundancies is to explore whether it is possible to avoid compulsory redundancies by asking for volunteers for either early retirement or voluntary redundancy. As Redman *et al* argue, 'this method has increasingly become most employers' preferred method of downsizing' (2013: 467). However, there are clear issues that must first be considered.

Any offer of voluntary redundancy must be subject to the company's need to retain a balanced workforce with the appropriate mix of skills and knowledge. There are obviously a number of advantages in adopting the voluntary approach. Firstly, it can help to avoid some of the demotivating effects that redundancy inevitably has on an organisation. Secondly, it can be cost-effective. While persuading people to go, rather than forcing them to leave, will probably require higher individual payments (possibly in pension costs), the financial benefits of a redundancy exercise can begin to impact much earlier if a costly and time-consuming consultation exercise can be avoided. However, there is a danger that if a voluntary approach is adopted, more people will want to opt out of work than was originally envisaged. This can have unbudgeted cost implications. For this reason it is important, before paying extra costs in this way, to carry out a comprehensive human resource planning exercise in order to assess future labour requirements.

Another factor that must be considered before making any announcements about voluntary redundancy is an assessment of who might volunteer. It is the authors' experience that individuals who have volunteered and then been refused display a serious lack of commitment to any reorganisation precipitated by the redundancy situation. Avoiding this requires a careful evaluation of which individuals would be allowed to go, if they volunteered – and again, it is the authors' experience that too many managers make assumptions about individuals within their teams. This is where the employment relations professional, in his or her role as objective adviser, can make a valuable contribution.

It may also be appropriate to ask for volunteers for early retirement. This is only an option if the business has its own regulated pension scheme, which allows for the payment of pensions early on grounds of redundancy. It is possible, however, that the employer might have to make a substantial payment into the pension fund – more than a redundancy payment, in many cases – to ensure that there is no detriment to the early-retired employee. Alternatively, the employer might have to provide a one-off lump sum that will take the employee up to an agreed date for receiving his or her pension.

It is important that these financial considerations are taken into account by employment relations professionals when they are asked, as they often are, to cost the available options for reducing the workforce. Furthermore, to allow early retirement on redundancy grounds or to enhance the value of an individual's pension, are not management decisions. They are trustee decisions. This means that the question of whether early retirement as an alternative to compulsory redundancy is an option must be carefully costed and researched.

### 14.7.7 PENALTIES FOR FAILING TO CONSULT

If there has been a failure to follow the proper consultation process, an application can be made to an employment tribunal for a declaration to this effect, and for a 'protective award' to be paid. This is an award requiring the employer to pay the employee remuneration for a protected period. The legislation relating to protective awards is quite complex, but some of the important elements are:

- the affected employee receives payment at the rate of one week's gross pay for each week of the 'protected period'
- unlike some compensatory awards, there are no statutory limits on a week's pay

- subject to certain maximums, the length of a protected period is at the employment tribunal's discretion; the test is 'what is just and equitable having regard to the seriousness of the employer's default'
- the maximum periods are 45 days when 45 days should have been the consultation period, and 30 days when 30 days should have been the consultation period; in any other case the maximum is 28 days.

As Lewis (1993) points out, the financial implications of protective awards can be quite significant because there are often substantial numbers of employees involved. It is unlikely that employers with well-established redundancy procedures will come into conflict with the law over a failure to consult. Notwithstanding this, the prudent employment relations specialist will keep the procedure under review in the light of any relevant tribunal decisions. The real problems arise for those organisations that do not have a procedure, or that try to put together a process in a hurried and casual manner when redundancies are imminent. Such organisations might find that the price they pay for a lack of preparedness is extremely high. Employment tribunals have shown an increasing tendency to take a very narrow view of any special pleading by employers that there was no time to consult.

## 14.7.8 INDIVIDUAL CONSULTATION

Irrespective of the duty to consult over collective redundancies, a failure to consult individually in any redundancy will leave an employer vulnerable to a claim of unfair dismissal. Many managers have fallen into the trap of assuming that when only one or two individuals are to be made redundant there is no obligation to consult or that consultation can be cursory. This is incorrect. The Employment Rights Act (1996) identifies redundancy as a fair reason for dismissal provided that the employer has acted 'reasonably'. This requirement opens the door for an employee to claim unfair dismissal on the grounds that the employer, by failing to consult, had not acted reasonably. Although not giving rise to an employment tribunal claim, an article in *People Management* (22 November 2001) provided a classic case study on 'How not to shed staff' (see Case Study 14.3).

---

**CASE STUDY 14.3**

### NICKY H AND REDUNDANCY

Nicky H worked for a publishing company as head of the central marketing team, which acted as an internal agency. The first inkling that anything was wrong came from a colleague who heard via an email that the team was to be disbanded in a reorganisation.

Nicky immediately tried to see her boss, but was told he was tied up in meetings all day. When they did meet, he was accompanied by a woman she had never seen before.

'He told me I was out of a job,' she says. 'Then he said: "But that's not the point. The point is that you are completely incompetent. The team can't stand you, you have no management skills, and I

don't know why we hired you – you can't even photocopy anything."'

'I was then told I would be escorted straight to the HR department and would not be allowed to speak to my team. When I got to HR, the manager said she had no idea what was going on and offered me a box of tissues.'

The incident came a few weeks after Nicky's three-month review, at which, she says, no criticisms were made of her competence. 'I have never felt like such a piece of trash in my life,' she says. 'I had bad dreams about that day for a year afterwards, and it killed my confidence. To be treated like that in front of a complete stranger was absolutely horrendous.'

She did manage to get a message to her team, however. They met her in the pub later and were sympathetic. But she could do nothing more, having been at the company for less than six months.

Shortly afterwards, she took a low-level job at a friend's firm to help rebuild her confidence, until that suffered cash-flow problems and had to shed some staff. She then joined a major management consultancy, but again found herself a victim of cutbacks.

This latest redundancy was a complete contrast to Nicky's earlier experience. She got three months' salary, outplacement support and backing from the company, which allowed her to send emails to contacts, kept in touch, and invited her back for social events.

What, for you, does this case tell us about how not to make a member of staff redundant? Reflecting on our discussion so far, how might it have been better handled and what would have been the more positive outcomes for both the employee and the organisation?

Most claims for unfair dismissal in respect of redundancy are usually in one of two areas: unfair selection, and lack of consultation. If the scenario reported at the beginning of the case study had concerned an employee with the required length of service to register a claim for unfair dismissal, it is inconceivable that the employer's actions would have been judged anything other than unreasonable. But, as noted in Chapter 11, 'good practice' demands that you operate reasonably and with just cause on every occasion, not just when you think an employee can make a claim against you.

Many employers have argued that because the redundancy only affected one or two individuals, consultation would not have made any difference. This defence has been virtually closed to employers since the decision of the House of Lords in *Polkey* v *A E Dayton Services Ltd (1987) IRLR 503*, but unwise and unprofessional employers still try to use it. In *Polkey*, the House of Lords did not say that consultation was an absolute requirement, but that the onus is on the employer to demonstrate that consultation would have been 'utterly useless'. In the majority of cases, it would be difficult to demonstrate the uselessness of something that had not been tried.

By far the best option for employers is to recognise that good employee relations would be best served by adopting a systematic approach to consultation whether the proposed redundancies are going to affect five people or 50 people. This means that you should always allow enough time for a proper consultation exercise, immaterial of the number of people who are to be made redundant. You should give very careful consideration to the possibilities of alternative employment, even lower-paid alternative employment. You must allow people time and an opportunity (normally through individual meetings) to:

- consider their options
- challenge the need for redundancy
- propose their own alternatives
- comment on selection criteria
- provide feedback on or challenge selection decisions.

The employer does not have to go along with any alternatives proposed, but must be able to demonstrate that they have been given careful and objective consideration. In one case in which we were involved, the employer was found to have unfairly dismissed an employee because the employer had made assumptions instead of properly consulting. In this particular case, the employer had assumed that the employee, who was a long-serving manager, would not be interested in a lower-ranked and lower-paid job, and so had not discussed it with him. At the tribunal hearing, the employee was asked by the chairman whether he would have taken such a job – and he answered in the affirmative. As the chairman explained to the employer, it was not about whether he should have been given the lower-paid job – that may not have been appropriate in the circumstances – but that it should have been discussed with him.

## ? REFLECTIVE ACTIVITY 14.5

What are the organisational benefits of consulting over redundancies? Design an action plan for a process of consultation for your own workplace that could be used in the event of redundancies.

## 14.8 COMPULSORY REDUNDANCY

If the voluntary option is not feasible, the next step would have to be compulsory redundancies. At this point in the procedure there should be an acknowledgement that the organisation would, as far in advance of any proposed termination date as possible, notify all those employees at risk of compulsory redundancy.

### 14.8.1 SELECTION CRITERIA FOR REDUNDANCY

The method of selection should be part of the consultation process and ideally agreed with representatives or, where statutory consultations are not required, with the affected individuals. Employers should be careful when choosing the criteria against which selections are made.

Particular care should be taken if using criteria that may be discriminatory – for example, using length of service would discriminate indirectly on the basis of both age and sex. This does not necessarily mean that length of service cannot be used but to do so, employers must show that the inclusion of the length of service criterion is a proportionate means of achieving a legitimate aim. For example, in the case of *Rolls Royce PLC* v *Unite the Union (2009) EWCA Civ 387*, it was found that the aim of rewarding loyalty was a legitimate aim. Nonetheless, it was only seen as proportionate because it was one of a large number of criteria and was not on its own a determining factor. Even if length of service is seen as reasonable criteria, over-reliance on this may mean that organisations will lose their youngest employees or those with the most up-to-date skills. For this reason, many organisations have adopted a selection system that is based on a number of criteria, such as attendance records, range of work experience, disciplinary records, etc. Such criteria, which need to be as objective as possible, and be based on a system of points scored, tend to be looked on very favourably by tribunals.

### 14.8.2 CREATING A POINTS SCORE

Once management has determined what criteria should be used, it is suggested that each employee should be scored by an appropriate number of points for each criterion (usually on a scale of ten). Using attendance as criteria must also be treated with some caution as this could be seen to discriminate on grounds of disability. Consequently, employers should generally ignore any periods of absence related to a condition defined as a disability under the Equality Act 2010. Clear guidance should be given to the managers who are asked to make the decision on the number of points each individual receives. Some thought should also be given to weighting each criterion by a factor that would take into account the importance of that factor to the employer. For example, you could decide which particular attribute or criterion is the most important and then multiply that score by a factor of, for example, five. The criterion that has the lowest importance might be multiplied by a factor of, for example, one.

It is important that great care is taken in setting scoring guidelines. There may be certain employees who are engaged in particular projects or have certain skills that are critical to the organisation. If that is the case, this should be reflected in the criteria. Alternatively, such individuals should be removed from the pool for selection. When all the scores have been calculated, those employees with the lowest scores will be the ones who should be selected for redundancy. While employers are sometimes dissatisfied with the results, as Judge, in an interview for *People Management* (22 November, 2001), made clear:

> The key to devising a selection process that is seen to be fair and can withstand scrutiny by trade unions and employment tribunals is to be clear about the skills and experience the company will need in the future. This is only possible if business objectives are clear to all employees.

In summary, therefore, an employer should make a note of those objective criteria which it considers appropriate, decide upon a scoring system, and then establish the weighting factor for each criterion (see the following specimen matrix and score sheet in Figure 14.1).

Figure 14.1 A specimen selection matrix and score sheet

## Matrix and score sheet

| Name: | Age: |
|---|---|
| Date of birth: | Years of service: |
| Department: | Job role: |

| Employee assessment | | | |
|---|---|---|---|
| Criteria | Score out of 10 | Weighting (maximum × 5) | Total |
| | | X | |
| Skills | | X | |
| Attendance | | X | |
| Flexibility | | X | |
| | | X | |
| | | X | |
| | | X | |
| Grand total | | | |
| Assessed by:. . . . . . . . . . . . . .<br>Checked by: . . . . . . . . . . . . . . | | | |

As noted, it is important to give individuals selected for redundancy the opportunity to receive details of the scoring and the opportunity to provide feedback to the employer, and, if necessary, challenge the scoring decisions made. This can be done through individual meetings or providing an appeal process. The failure to do this may render any subsequent dismissal on grounds of redundancy unfair.

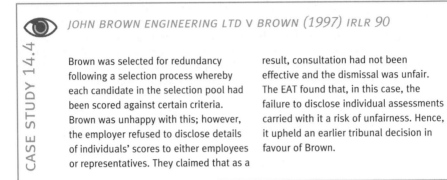

**CASE STUDY 14.4**

**JOHN BROWN ENGINEERING LTD V BROWN (1997) IRLR 90**

Brown was selected for redundancy following a selection process whereby each candidate in the selection pool had been scored against certain criteria. Brown was unhappy with this; however, the employer refused to disclose details of individuals' scores to either employees or representatives. They claimed that as a result, consultation had not been effective and the dismissal was unfair. The EAT found that, in this case, the failure to disclose individual assessments carried with it a risk of unfairness. Hence, it upheld an earlier tribunal decision in favour of Brown.

### 14.8.3 ASSISTANCE FOR REDUNDANT EMPLOYEES

Once the selection of individuals has been confirmed, it is important that the employer makes reasonable efforts to look for alternative employment. The individual consultation process can be used here to discuss with the individual other roles that they would be prepared to consider. Of course, alternative employment is not always possible, nor is it always desired by those to be made redundant. Nevertheless, it is incumbent on the employer to make every effort to look for alternatives and, where they exist, to consider redundant employees for suitable vacancies.

Nevertheless, the procedure needs to set out the basis on which employees will be interviewed for any vacancies and the terms and conditions on which alternative jobs will be offered. Terms and conditions may be the standard terms for the job in question. They may be the terms previously enjoyed by the individual concerned or there may be some form of transition. These are all issues that the employee relations specialist needs to consider. Naturally, the procedure needs to say something about trial periods.

**CASE STUDY 14.5**

**REDUNDANCY**

Northtown College is a large college of further education based in the north-east of England. It employs a total of 250 staff (of which 160 are teaching/lecturing staff) across four locations within a 20-mile radius of the city of Gateley. It recognises UCU and UNISON for collective bargaining purposes.

In recent years, universities have been lowering their admission requirements. This has had a significant impact on the college and student admissions have fallen significantly. This has had a knock-on effect on the finances of the college. About 12 months ago, the senior management of the college decided that redundancies were inevitable; however

they have been waiting for the right time to announce them in order to minimise bad publicity and opposition from staff. However, it has now been decided by university management to announce that 58 lecturing staff and 42 support and administrative staff will be made redundant, with the first of these taking effect in one month's time. The redundancies are spread equally across the four sites. Redundancy notices have been drawn up and are to be sent out just as the redundancies are to be announced.

Staff have been selected on the basis of a number of factors: contractual status (whether full-time or part-time); length of service; absence record; qualifications and skill; disciplinary record; performance. Heads of department were asked to score each member of staff out of ten on each criteria and come up with a total score. These were then compared across the whole college with the lowest scores selected for redundancy. These were done about three months ago in utmost secrecy – as management didn't want to cause staff any unnecessary worry.

You are an HR practitioner who has been asked to comment on the college's plans. What advice would you give?

It would be normal practice for a redundancy procedure to set out what steps the organisation proposed to take in assisting the redundant employee who could not be found alternative employment within the business. Such steps should include provisions for paid time off to attend interviews, to seek retraining opportunities or to attend counselling sessions. This latter point will be dealt with in more detail later in the chapter.

### 14.8.4 STATUTORY RULES ON PAYMENT

All those employees with a minimum of two years' service will (with certain exceptions) qualify for a statutory redundancy payment. The key rules on the nature of redundancy payment are covered in depth on the government website (www.gov.uk) and through Acas guidance. However, payments are calculated as follows:

For each complete year of service up to a maximum of 20, employees are entitled to:

- for each year of service under 22 – half a week's pay
- for each year of service at age 22 but under 41 – one week's pay
- for each year of service at age 41 or over – one and a half weeks' pay.

There is a maximum statutory limit (for current rates see www.acas.org.uk/redundancy payments) on the amount of a week's pay that may be reckoned. This figure is reviewed annually and employers may also pay in excess of the statutory minimum (www.gov.uk). Importantly, redundancy payments are generally not taxable up to a maximum of £30,000.

### 14.8.5 NOTICE OF REDUNDANCY

It is important that employers do no not issue notices terminating employment on grounds of redundancy until collective and individual consultation has been completed. If this is done, a tribunal is likely to conclude that the consultation has been a 'sham' and therefore in breach of legal requirements. Notices can only be given before the end of the minimum period, if the consultation is genuinely complete. In this case, it is important to note that the dismissal itself cannot take effect until the minimum period of consultation has expired and individual notice periods have been observed. The date on which a dismissal 'takes effect' is the date on which the notice expires, not the date on which it is given. However, employment can be terminated before the end of the notice period where an employee has agreed to take a payment in lieu of notice. The employer must give at least the minimum statutory notice period. This is:

- one week's notice if the employee has been employed by the employer continuously for one month or more, but for less than two years; or
- one week's notice for each year employed if the employee has been employed by the employer continuously for two years or more, up to a maximum of 12 weeks.

For example, if an employee has worked for five years, they are entitled to five weeks' notice.

## 14.9 TRANSFER OF UNDERTAKINGS

When the ownership of a business transfers, there is always the possibility that redundancies will be one of the results that flows from such an action. Under the Transfer of Undertakings Protection of Employment (TUPE) Regulations 2006, all employees who are covered by employment protection legislation receive additional protection in respect of job security if the identity of their employer changes. This does not mean that an employer who acquires a new business is obliged to retain all the inherited employees irrespective of the commercial realities, but if an employee is dismissed either before or after a transfer and the sole or principal reason for the dismissal is the transfer, it will be automatically unfair.

Should employers find that, on the transfer of a business, there is a redundancy situation, then the existing law regarding redundancy applies. This means if any employees are made redundant and they have the requisite period of service with their old employer to qualify for a redundancy payment, the new employer cannot avoid making a redundancy payment to them. In the context of consultation, all the issues of representation and the right to information that we have discussed previously, with respect to collective redundancies, apply equally to transfers of undertakings.

## 14.10 THE AFTERMATH OF REDUNDANCY

The rise in unemployment in recent years has meant that more attention is now paid to the needs of redundant employees. In this section, we look at the growth in both counselling and outplacement services and, in addition, the position of those employees who remain in employment and who may consequently suffer the so-called 'survivor syndrome'. Crucially, as Redman *et al* report, 'there is considerable evidence to suggest that such help can have a very positive impact on the management of redundancy at a relatively low cost' (2013: 473).

### 14.10.1 COUNSELLING

Although redundancy has become part of everyday life, the loss of one's job usually comes as a tremendous personal blow. Even when 'the writing is on the wall' and the prospect of job losses in the organisation is inevitable, individuals still hope that they will be unaffected. There can be a tendency for employers to want a redundancy exercise to be forgotten as quickly as possible. This can appear uncaring. The employment relations specialist should be reminding managerial colleagues that they have a continuing responsibility for their redundant employees and, as the CIPD guide on redundancy authored by Fowler states, must provide displaced employees with access to a counselling service. Redundant employees can feel anger, resentment and even guilt – emotions which, if not carefully managed, can inhibit an employee from moving forward to the next phase of their career – and this is where effective counselling becomes crucial. However, it is important to proceed cautiously. As we stressed earlier in this book, in another reference to counselling, there is a need for proper training. Where for Fowler (1993):

> Handling the first stage of redundancy counselling requires considerable skill, and should not be attempted by anyone who does not, as a minimum, understand the general principles of all forms of counselling.

Not every redundant employee will agree to or want counselling, but nevertheless it is important to understand its key purpose. If you talk to redundant employees, as we have done, you are struck by the intense mood swings that can occur during the initial post-redundancy phase. Depending on the personality of the individual concerned, the mood can swing from pessimism about the future to unfounded optimism, from anger at the former employer to a feeling that they have been given an opportunity to do something different. The objective of counselling is to bring all these emotions out into the open and to help individuals to make decisions about their future. It is not a panacea – it will not stop people being angry or feeling betrayed – but it might help them to view their future constructively.

---

**CASE STUDY 14.6**

### THE ROYAL MAIL

Having made a loss after tax of £940 million in 2001/02, the Royal Mail announced one of the biggest restructures in British corporate history. In 2002, around 30,000 redundancies were announced, and more have been made since then.

Andrew Kinder was formerly principal welfare co-ordinator and chartered occupational psychologist for the Royal Mail, and now provides the same services for the agency SchlumbergerSema. Describing the impact of such large-scale change on Royal Mail staff, he says: 'Many individuals find it hard to cope – some feeling that they have to work harder to secure their futures, others feeling deep concerns about why they kept their jobs. Royal Mail is committed to addressing these issues not only because they could have a negative effect on productivity but also because the organisation takes its legal duty of care to individuals very seriously. Reorganisations like this happen, and we as humans can't control change, but we can control how we respond to it.

Counselling is one of the key aspects of the firm's efforts to empower employees to cope with change.'

Pauline Leech, head of information services in the Royal Mail's property division, has taken advantage of Kinder's counselling services. 'The team in which I work has been going through so much change that we felt it would be useful to bring in a counsellor,' she says. 'Andrew ran a session helping us develop a number of coping strategies. We talked about our feelings and behaviour, completed a questionnaire and discussed responses to situations. A drama triangle – involving three people playing the role of victim, persecutor and rescuer – was very interesting and gave an insight into different approaches to the same situation. It gave us a good insight into the pressure felt by colleagues. For me, it helped to know that the firm cared enough to offer this support.'

Source: PICKARD, J. (2001) When push comes to shove. *People Management*. Vol 7, No 23. 22 November. pp30–35.

---

Because redundancies are often cost-cutting exercises, many organisations are reluctant to hire counsellors to help with the aftermath. But a study in 2003 by Professor John McLeod of the School of Social and Health Sciences at the University of Aberdeen suggests that it might be an investment worth making (Blyth, 2003).

The findings of more than 80 studies on workplace counselling show that 90% of employees are highly satisfied with the process and outcome. Evidence suggests that counselling helps to relieve work-related stress and reduces sickness absence rates by up to half. Case Study 14.6 indicates the potential effectiveness of such an approach.

### 14.10.2 OUTPLACEMENT

Outplacement is a process in which individuals who have been made redundant by their employer are given support and counselling to assist them in achieving the next stage of their career. There are a large number of organisations that offer outplacement services, but the range and quality of their services vary greatly and the employment relations specialist must carefully research prospective suppliers if a decision to use outplacement is taken. Broadly, outplacement consultancies offer services on a group or individual basis, which fall into the following general categories:

- CV preparation
- researching the job market
- communication techniques
- interview presentation
- managing the job search.

Each organisation operates differently, but in the best organisations the process would probably start with a personal session with a trained counsellor. Once this has been carried out, the next step would be the preparation of the CV. This involves identifying key skills and past achievements so that the job-hunter can market himself or herself from a position of strength. Step three would be to make decisions about job search methods (cold-contact, advertisement, recruitment consultants, etc) and contact development – for example, networking. Step four would be to ensure that the key communication skills of letter writing, telephone techniques and interview presentation were of a sufficiently high standard to enhance the job search. Where skills have to be improved, the better consultancies provide the necessary training at no extra cost.

---

### CASE STUDY 14.7

### ROLLS-ROYCE

When aero-engine company Rolls-Royce had to axe 4,800 jobs worldwide in the wake of the 11 September attacks on targets in the USA, it was well placed to deal with the crisis. Here in Britain, the company had set up six resource centres in early 2000 to handle an anticipated downturn in the market.

The centres, one at each of the company's main UK sites, provide a three-day career transition training programme and continuing, open-ended support and advice. The centres take CIPD good practice as a model. Each is staffed with a manager, a counsellor, several other dedicated Rolls-Royce personnel, and a flexible team from the company's two external outplacement providers, Capita Grosvenor and Winchester Consulting. The providers give access to national jobs databases with online search facilities.

Since the centres opened, hundreds of employees affected by cutbacks have used them for careers guidance, advice on writing CVs, training and so on. Eighty-five per cent have found new employment, typically after some weeks.

'One of the challenges was the reputation that resource centres have in other organisations,' says John McKell, Rolls-Royce head of employment policy. 'They are renowned for providing minimal provision to lower-paid workers in pokey surroundings, while managers get executive packages. But at Rolls-Royce, the service is gold-plated for everyone.'

The company has involved employees and unions from the start. In response to a proposal from union officers, it set up a resourcing committee by means of which employee and union representatives could review redundancy support. Several improvements, such as better communications, have resulted.

Source: BLYTH, A. (2003) Art of survival. *People Management*. Vol 9, No 9. 1 May. pp38–40.

---

The final step is managing the actual job search, setting personal targets, keeping records of letters and phone calls, maintaining notes of interviews, and carrying out a regular job search evaluation. Running alongside these basic services are a range of support services, such as secretarial help, free telephone and office space, and financial planning advice. What an individual gets will depend on the particular package that the former employer purchases on his or her behalf.

Of course, not every employer will be able to afford the cost of outplacement, particularly if large numbers of employees are affected by the redundancies. In such circumstances, organisations must consider what they can do to help from within their own resources, or by using a mixture of internal and external resources. The TUC has also recognised the value of good advice being made available to workers facing redundancy. It has produced a guide on how employees can make the best use of the Government's Rapid Response Service (RRS). RRS was established in 2003 and aims to help workers affected by major redundancies. Operated through local Job Centre Plus centres, it aims to help people into new jobs before they lose their current ones by providing specialist advice services.

## ? REFLECTIVE ACTIVITY 14.6

Does your organisation have any sort of policy on counselling and outplacement? Having considered the arguments in the previous sections, what sort of proposals could you put in place to improve the experiences of staff involved in downsizing?

### 14.10.3 SURVIVOR SYNDROME

When people are forced to leave employment because of redundancy, those that are left behind can be affected just as much as those that have left. Anecdotal evidence we have gathered from the finance sector and local UK government organisations indicates that disenchantment, pessimism and stress are the likely result of even a small-scale redundancy exercise. Survivor syndrome, as it is called, can be minimised if those who are to be made redundant are treated fairly and equitably, and there is a decision made to invest in an effective post-redundancy programme. Further research by one of the authors suggests that if the conflict – both for individuals and collective group – which arises out of redundancy is properly managed through fair and transparent consultation processes, this negative element of redundancy can be minimised (Bennett, 2014). This usually means a time commitment from senior managers and a good communications process. The impact can be significant, as the findings from a survey conducted by Industrial Relations Services in 2009 (Murphy, 2009) with respect to survivor syndrome reveals (Table 14.1).

Table 14.1 The impact of redundancy on 'survivors'

| Impact | Percentage |
|---|---|
| Low morale and commitment | 67 |
| Increased stress | 65 |
| Reduced motivation | 53 |
| Breakdown of trust in management | 50 |
| Lower productivity | 19 |
| Increased absence | 17 |
| Staff retention problems | 17 |

| Impact | Percentage |
|---|---|
| Poorer performance | 16 |
| Greater risk avoidance | 15 |

Source: IRS (2009)

The feelings referred to above are the result of two factors. The first is that the remaining employees are often asked to 'pick up' the work of their former colleagues, either directly or indirectly. In one local authority, individuals had to reapply for their own jobs three times in three years, following a series of redundancies and reorganisations. The second factor concerns communication. Anecdotal evidence suggests that in many organisations the remaining employees are not always communicated with effectively, thus providing the opportunity for rumour and disenchantment to thrive. Getting the message across about why redundancies were necessary and what happens next is vitally important, and yet most people we have spoken to identify poor communication as one of the principal causes of their dissatisfaction.

## 14.11 SUMMARY

Redundancy is one of the most emotive issues that any manager can be called upon to deal with. Calling an individual into your office and informing them that they no longer have a job is never easy. For the employment relations specialist who is at the beginning of his or her career, managing a redundancy exercise can be extremely challenging. No matter how experienced you are, managing redundancy is never straightforward, but in this chapter we have attempted to set the process into some sort of organised framework. Most redundancies occur because organisations need to change, and although we have recognised this, we nevertheless felt it important that employment relations specialists recognise that there should be alternatives to reducing an organisation's headcount. In particular, we stressed that in an era of constant change, businesses need to retain their competitive advantage. This is unlikely to happen if their employees are constantly looking over their shoulders, fearing for their jobs.

One of the challenges that all managers, whether or not they are personnel practitioners, face in the twenty-first century is how to reconcile the need for organisational change with the individual's need for contentment and security at work. Not only does the employment relations specialist have to understand the need for organisations to change, but he or she must understand that this has to be accommodated within a well-developed legal framework that directs and constrains his or her actions. Importantly, the obligation to consult provides opportunities to avoid or minimise the impact of redundancy and to deal equitably with those employees who are directly affected.

Finally, as we discussed in the closing section of the chapter, redundancy leaves 'survivors' in its wake, and these individuals have to receive the highest levels of communication and consideration. They often experience a psychological state that is not unlike bereavement, and they inevitably suffer a loss of trust in their organisation or even in their immediate manager. Crucially, as we further highlighted, effective training and support for the envoys in the organisation who must deliver that message is also key in limiting the emotional impact of redundancy on both those leaving and those remaining in the organisation.

KEY LEARNING POINTS

1   The definition of when redundancy occurs is important because it determines an individual's right to consultation, compensation, etc.

2   Redundancy should always be a 'last resort', and it is therefore important to have effective policies and procedures for dealing with a redundancy situation.

3   Selection in redundancy situations must be objective and capable of standing up to external scrutiny.

4   Employers must ensure that they fulfil their statutory obligation to consult collectively if proposing to dismiss 20 or more employees. This consultation must be meaningful with a view to reaching an agreement. In all cases of redundancy, the employer must also consult with any individual worker they are proposing to dismiss – a failure to do this is likely to result in a claim for unfair dismissal.

5   People do not forget how a redundancy exercise was handled, and the professional HR practitioner will take care to ensure that any redundancy exercise considers the needs of all individuals as well as those of the organisation.

6   When redundancy is unavoidable, 'good practice' dictates that the organisation has in place policies and procedures that enable it to deal with a difficult situation with sensitivity and equity. In addition, the managers tasked with 'delivering the news' need proper support and training.

7   The employment relations professional has a key role to play in this process in advising management colleagues on the scope and extent of any policy, and in advising them on how to manage the redundancy process.

8   An important element in the management of a redundancy situation is the need to provide effective counselling and support for the redundant employee, as well as giving support in terms of job security and outplacement. Of equal importance is the need to ensure that those who come to remain in employment and may be fearful for their future are not ignored. Ignoring the 'survivors' is likely to produce a demotivated workforce that is prone to conflict with management.

REVIEW QUESTIONS

1   Your organisation needs to reduce the workforce by 20%. Your chief executive officer, who is fully aware of the statutory need to consult with the workforce, wants, in achieving this, to act in a fair, reasonable and consistent way. You have been asked to advise her on how the required redundancies can be achieved with the business. Drawing on evidence-based research and policy and practice, justify what you would give as your advice.

2   You are employed as head of human resources (HR) at an organisation employing some 750 staff who will now have to be cut back drastically. It will mean a 50% reduction in the size of the present workforce. You have been asked to produce a position paper for the senior management team explaining how the workforce reduction might be achieved while minimising any adverse impact on morale. Drawing on contemporary research and policy and practice, justify what you would include in your position paper.

3    You are the human resource (HR) adviser for a retail chain of 34 shops. The area manager has asked your advice on a possible redundancy situation. He has identified one shop that will probably have to close sometime in the next few months. The shop in question has 27 people. The organisation is non-unionised, but there is an employee consultation forum. He does not know how to initiate the process and has asked your advice about what he should do, and why. How would you respond?

4    Your human resource director is concerned that with a sudden downturn in the economy, the company needs to review its redundancy policy. She would like you to brief her on the things that a redundancy policy should include as a minimum, and what else could be considered good employment practice. Prepare an outline of the briefing you will give her, justifying what you will include.

**EXPLORING FURTHER**

ACAS (2014) *Handling large-scale redundancies*. London: Acas.

ASHMAN, I. (2012) *Downsizing envoys: a public/private sector comparison*. Acas research paper. 11/12. London: Acas.

BLYTH, A. (2003) The art of survival. *People Management*. Vol 9, No 9. pp39–40.

FOWLER, A. (1993) *Redundancy*. London: CIPD.

PFEFFER, J. (1998) *The human equation: building profits by putting people first*. Boston: Harvard Business School Press.

RANIERI, N. (2010) *Collective consultation on redundancies*. Acas discussion paper. London: Acas.

REDMAN, T., WILKINSON, A. and PANDEY, A. (2013) Downsizing. In WILKINSON, A. and REDMAN, T. (eds) *Contemporary human resource management*. 4th ed. Harlow: Pearson Education.

**Website links**

www.bis.gov.uk is the website of the Department for Business, Innovation and Skills, and gives access to the law on redundancy.

www.acas.org.uk is the website of Acas, and gives access to Acas publications, including guides and information on redundancy management.

www.cipd.co.uk is the website of the CIPD, and gives access to the CIPD's wide range of publications and information on redundancy, including its *Labour Market Outlook* survey.

# CHAPTER 15

# The Role of Mediation in Conflict Resolution

## OVERVIEW

The chapter is structured in two parts. Part one begins by defining workplace mediation in contrast to other alternative dispute resolution processes. The key benefits of workplace mediation are then discussed, followed by a critical review of the extant literature and current research on the topic. The chapter then turns to discuss workplace mediation as an alternative to more formal and conventional methods of resolving employment disputes, such as grievance and discipline procedures. Like any other method of resolving disputes, it is argued that mediation is not a panacea for all disputes. Rather, when the process is better understood by all parties, and depending on the issue and the outcomes sought by the disputants, mediation can help to rebuild employment relationships that have become fractured. Furthermore, in terms of the exercise of power and control in the management of workplace conflict, we ask whether mediation offers greater equality of access to justice.

Part two of the chapter focuses on the practice of mediation, by examining the nature of the process and the role played by HR practitioners and employment relations specialists. This is followed by a more detailed discussion of the stages of mediation, from referral to resolution, and an exploration of the knowledge, skills and attitude needed to be an effective mediator. The chapter closes by reflecting on the future prospects for workplace mediation.

## LEARNING OUTCOMES

When you have completed this chapter, you should be able to:

- understand and describe the term 'workplace mediation' and its main functions
- critically assess the key benefits that mediation can bring to an organisation
- identify and critically analyse the limitations of mediation and barriers to its use
- understand and critically evaluate the key theoretical concepts developed in the study of workplace mediation
- provide an analytical account of mediation's relationship with more formal dispute resolution practices
- explain and evaluate the role of the key players in the process
- identify, describe and explain the process of initiating, managing and concluding a mediation case.

## 15.1 INTRODUCTION

As we identified in Chapter 11, there has been a growing trend to consider alternative approaches to resolving disputes instead of the more traditional channels of grievance, discipline and performance management (Latreille, 2011). However, as subsequent discussions in Chapters 12 and 13 demonstrate, 'rights-based' procedures remain the main way in which workplace disputes are handled. Nevertheless, there is growing evidence to support the argument that, for certain types of disputes, organisations are increasingly turning to different methods of resolution. The focus of this chapter is on one increasingly popular alternative method for resolving disputes between individuals – workplace mediation. Mediation is not a new concept. It has its origins in the resolution of family and community disputes, and has been used successfully for many years in the United States, particularly in addressing employment disputes in the public sector (Mareschal, 2003). Its long-standing use and success within the US Postal Service is a particularly impressive example of a large-scale industrial strategy for the resolution of individual employment disputes in a key sector (Bingham and Pitts, 2002).

Mediation is argued by its advocates to be a model of dispute resolution, which lends itself particularly well to situations where the parties have become entrenched in their positions (Acas/CIPD, 2013). From a practical perspective, it is a method of resolving workplace disputes that seeks to avoid a more formal and often more confrontational route, such as grievance and discipline procedures; rather than attributing blame, it looks to rebuild damaged relationships for the future.

In the UK, the publication of the Gibbons Review in 2007 marked the start of government support for mediation as a dispute resolution strategy to reduce 'the burden' on the employment tribunal system (Gibbons, 2007). Further evidence of continued government interest in the strategic role of workplace mediation was provided in its consultation on workplace dispute resolution policy and practice (BIS, 2011: 19–20).

However, evidence of the use of mediation in the UK is mixed. Requests for structured mediation on individual issues doubled between 2004/05 and 2010/11 (Acas, 2005; 2011), while surveys conducted by the CIPD reported that mediation use by its members had increased from 43% in 2008 to 57% in 2011 (CIPD, 2008; 2011). An analysis of WERS2011 data found that 17% of workplaces that had experienced a dispute in the previous 12 months had used mediation (Wood *et al*, 2011), while a more recent representative survey of employers found that 24% had used internal mediators to resolve a dispute in the last year, and a further 9% had contracted external mediators (CIPD, 2015). In contrast evidence suggests that the use of mediation tends to be greater in larger organisations and in the public sector (Saundry *et al*, 2014; Wood *et al*, 2014). Having considered its context, let us turn to the questions of: what is mediation? What are said to be its potential benefits? How does it work in practice?

## 15.2 WHAT IS WORKPLACE MEDIATION?

Mediation is one of a number of dispute relation processes that have been developed in recent times as alternatives to the more traditional processes for resolving disputes in the workplace. Alternative dispute resolution (ADR) can be defined as 'the use of any form of mediation or arbitration as a substitute for the public judicial or administrative process available to resolve a dispute' (Lipsky and Seeber, 2000: 37). In the US, in particular, ADR mechanisms have been increasingly integrated into newly developed conflict management systems.

In some ways, in order to understand the potential role of mediation, it is useful to first define it in terms of how it differs from other ADR processes. For instance, it is not the same as conciliation; which is, rather, 'a process whereby a third party, such as Acas, will *guide* the parties in dispute to try and reach a compromise that suits both parties' (Ridley-Duff and Bennett, 2011: 109 – our emphasis). Similarly, it is unlike arbitration, which, as Aubrey-Johnson and Curtis explain, involves 'an independent and impartial expert determining the outcome of the problem. Arbitration differs from conciliation and mediation because the arbitrator acts like a judge – making a firm decision on a case' (2012: 315). In contrast:

'Mediation is where an impartial third party, the mediator, helps two or more people in dispute to attempt to reach an agreement. Any agreement comes from those in dispute, not from the mediator. The mediator is not there to judge, to say one person is right and the other wrong, or to tell those involved in the mediation what they should do. The mediator is in charge of the process of seeking to resolve the problem but not the outcome.' (Acas/CIPD, 2013: 8)

The decision as to which of these different resolution processes are used often turns on the type of dispute, the stage of the dispute and, crucially, what type of resolution is being sought. For example, if a dispute has escalated to the stage where an employee submits a claim against their employer to an employment tribunal, as we have discussed in Chapters 4 and 11, the employee must first notify Acas to give it an opportunity to conciliate between the parties to settle that dispute before it proceeds to the ET. If the parties wish to avoid the time demands and stress of going through litigation, and the employment relationship is so far compromised as to be beyond 'repair', then an independent arbitrator can be assigned to the case under the Acas Arbitration Scheme. It is of note, however, that this option is very seldom exercised. Conversely, if the relationship is felt by all parties as worth rebuilding, for instance if the dispute turns largely on personality issues, then mediation could be the most appropriate route to resolution.

Nevertheless, the choice of mediation does not preclude other channels. The mediation process is confidential and does not, therefore, prejudice any subsequent decision to turn to other means of resolution if mediation is not successful (Acas/CIPD, 2013). Mediation can and is used at any point in the course of resolving a dispute. However, it can be at its most effective when the mediation begins at the earliest stage in the dispute, as discussed further below.

## ? REFLECTIVE ACTIVITY 15.1

Thinking about disputes in which you have been involved at work, would mediation have been an appropriate course of action? If your answer is yes, why would mediation have been useful?

Facilitative mediation is the most common model utilised in the UK. The facilitative method is based on an approach of avoiding 'positions', looking beyond parties' legal entitlements to a negotiated settlement that reflects their underlying needs and interests. Essentially it is a process of joint problem-solving, where the disputants identify, evaluate and agree suitable solutions to the problems they face. A key facet of facilitative mediation is to promote communication between the parties, so that they can candidly 'air their differences' but at the same time identify shared interests and look for common ground that may lead to a settlement. Because in facilitative mediation the mediator is neutral, they can assist the disputants to communicate with each other in a way that would not be possible through other dispute resolution channels. It is, therefore, a model that lends itself to situations where the parties have become entrenched in their positions. The following box outlines the key principles of facilitative mediation.

---

## FACILITATIVE MEDIATION

1   Mediation is a confidential and voluntary process in which a neutral person helps people in dispute to explore and understand their differences so that they can find their own solution.

2   Mediation is based upon the principles of it being voluntary, impartial, confidential and binding in honour.

3   The key skills and qualities of a successful mediator are: fairness, being non-judgemental, empathy, building rapport and facilitating agreements through questioning, active listening, summarising but not leading, and adhering to practice standards.

4   The mediation process is normally made up of:

- a separate first contact meeting with each client
- a subsequent joint meeting with the parties in dispute in order to set the scene; explore the issues; build agreement; reach closure and agree follow up.

5   Mediation is about being clear and honest with disputants with respect to:

- what can and cannot be achieved
- how the process works
- what is expected of each person in terms of setting ground rules for behaviour; respecting the other party; commitment to the process; commitment to seeking and agreeing a joint solution
- the facilitative role of the mediator
- looking for ways to maintain an ongoing and future relationship rather than apportioning blame for actions in the past.

Source: Ridley-Duff and Bennett, 2011

---

Workplace mediation in the UK is generally accessed in two ways. First, organisations can employ an 'external' mediator from one of a number of specialist mediation and conflict management providers. Second, larger organisations may want to invest in 'in-house' mediation capacity. This can range from training one or two HR specialists to the development of an in-house mediation service, in which a number of employees are trained as mediators. They are then allocated cases by a mediation co-ordinator who has overall responsibility for administering the service. The key advantages and disadvantages of internal and external mediation are discussed later.

Interestingly, to date, other than Acas's (2013) yearly survey of the commissioners of their mediation service and the participants in those mediations, little is known about the experiences and perception of the key player in the process – the disputant. Saundry *et al*'s (2013) cross-sectoral report, however, gives some initial insight into this important issue. Their findings are summarised in the following box.

---

## DISPUTANT RESEARCH – WHAT DO THE DISPUTANTS ACTUALLY THINK?

- Many of the disputes within the sample were complex – for example, approximately half the cases involved allegations by one party of bullying or unfair treatment following attempts by the other party to manage performance or raise performance concerns. Therefore, issues tended to involve both potential grievances and discipline issues.

- The initial trigger for mediation mostly came from either senior managers or HR practitioners. Problematically, it tended to be used as a last resort for particularly difficult issues.
- Attitudes to taking part in mediation were mixed. While some respondents welcomed the opportunity to voice concerns within a safe environment, managers were more sceptical, particularly where the mediation involved a challenge to their decisions or attempts to address performance.
- Respondents were generally very positive about the role played by mediators.
- Most respondents felt that they had benefited from taking part in mediation, but they also found the process extremely challenging.
- In the majority of cases, mediations resulted in agreement. However, this often did not lead to any fundamental change in behaviour and/or attitude, and, in around half of cases within the sample, were not ultimately sustained.
- Perceptions of 'success' were nuanced – in some cases, even where there was no significant change in attitude and behaviour, mediation paved the way for a degree of pragmatism, allowing the parties to continue to work together in some form. Moreover, for employees who had complained of unfair treatment, the opportunity to air their views could be cathartic and empowering, even if mediation did not deliver the justice that they sought.
- Crucially, almost all respondents would either recommend mediation to others or consider taking part again in the right circumstances.

## ?   REFLECTIVE ACTIVITY 15.2

If you were considering introducing an internal mediation service into your organisation, what lessons would you draw from the research findings outlined in the box?

## 15.3 A THEORETICAL APPROACH TO WORKPLACE MEDIATION

To further understand workplace mediation, it is useful to consider Ridley-Duff and Bennett's (2011) conceptual model of dispute resolution. This explores whether mediation offers an alternative and more equitable means of dispute resolution than conventional procedural approaches (see the Figure 15.1). They argue that most organisations handle conflict by imposing and enforcing consistent standards of 'fairness', which revolve around the culpability of individuals. An alternative perspective is that workplace conflict and individual employment disputes stem from relationship and communication issues, not personality characteristics or failings. Thus, through mediation, the object of investigation is the relationship between two people, and the goal is increasing the capacity of disputants to maintain and develop that relationship. Thinking back to Fox's (1974) frames of reference discussed in Chapter 2, it is argued that:

> 'Mediation errs not just towards pluralism, but towards the Marxian perspective on emancipation and transformation. Traditional discipline and grievance practices operate within a framework of line management and a unitary ideology. While they may permit discussion of an issue or person, they prevent discussion about the nature of the relationship, or the legitimacy of hierarchical power.' (Ridley-Duff and Bennett, 2011: 115)

Both in theory and in practice, there are fundamental differences that underpin disciplinary procedures, arbitration, conciliation and the various forms of mediation potentially available to disputants. If we recognise these differences, mediation begins to challenge the process-driven approaches of discipline and grievance. From this perspective, they posit that mediation can empower employees and allow them to challenge managerial authority.

Ridley-Duff and Bennett (2011) argue further that traditional disciplinary and grievance procedures are underpinned by managerial and organisational notions of appropriate behaviour. Mediation, on the other hand, does not accept this framework in an uncritical way. It gives that authority to the disputants to best decide how their dispute is resolved. Moreover, they suggest that mediation is a dispute resolution mechanism based on direct, rather than representative, democracy, which seeks solutions that best suit the disputants but that cannot necessarily be fully shared within the public domain. Critics may see this as a weakness. However, it is argued that, conceptually and practically, direct representation, free of public expectations to follow set procedures and fully disclosing outcomes, allows the realisation of solutions that better maintain long-term relationships and give a greater sense of equity than more traditional approaches. It is this that makes it a more radical alternative.

Figure 15.1 A theoretical framework for understanding dispute resolution (Ridley-Duff and Bennett, 2011)

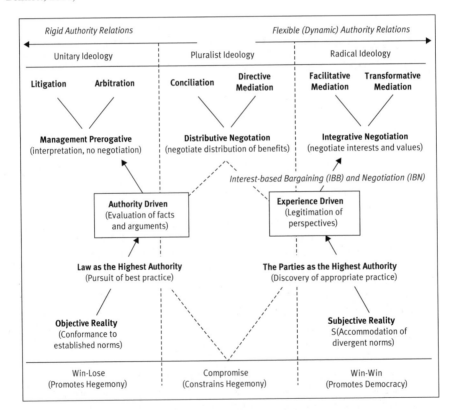

In contrast, other commentators have argued that, rather than empowering employees, mediation can offer a means of controlling dissent and asserting control (Colling, 2004; Latreille and Saundry, 2014). By using mediation in certain cases, the responsibility for unfair treatment could be shifted to the employee and the employer could evade the responsibility for changing practices and holding managers to account. Keashly and

Nowell (2011) point out that because mediation focuses on the future, it has no means of addressing or 'punishing' past behaviour. Therefore, some writers have questioned whether mediation is appropriate in addressing sensitive and power-based disputes over bullying and harassment.

## ? REFLECTIVE ACTIVITY 15.3

Critically reflect on the appropriateness of referring bullying and harassment cases to mediation. What are the advantages and disadvantages of using mediation for these types of cases?

The utilisation of mediation can also vary among and within sectors depending on the context. Organisational and managerial drivers will also impact, to some degree, on the mediation process. The issue of sectoral differences is illustrated by Bennett's (2014b) research into the use of mediation in higher education. Importantly, this study revealed that mediators saw a key strength of mediation as being its ability to address inequality and 'power imbalance' between disputants. The key findings from this study are outlined in Case Study 15.1.

## CASE STUDY 15.1

### 'MANAGING ACADEMICS IS LIKE HERDING CATS': THE USE OF MEDIATION IN HIGHER EDUCATION

The study of a cross-section of universities in the north of England uncovered a number of interesting findings in terms of how conflict and its management are predicated on specific elements of the context, culture and type of workers in that sector.

Watson's (2006) observation that 'managing people was like herding cats' was echoed by a number of HR managers as a metaphor for the challenges presented to them and line managers in managing professional workers such as academics, and the sources of conflict that could arise.

The unique nature of the academic role, the need to be critical and challenge, the competitive nature of academia and the largely unchallenged sanctity of academic freedom were all reported causes of conflict and barriers to its resolution.

The 'reluctant' academic manager, rewarded through promotion but with no real desire to manage others, could be an equal cause of conflict that HE mediators were called to address.

For many respondents to the research, the very ethos of the HE sector – in terms of developing academic but also life skills in students and staff, and also framed in a culture of mutual respect – lent itself well to this type of dispute resolution process. Although for many critics, in reality, disputes occurred more often because of poor management skills or inappropriate 'Taylorist' approaches to managing staff.

Many of the universities were part of a mediation network between HE institutions in the region.

A number of universities extended their service to their client group and their students, with a high measure of success.

What are your thoughts about the 'herding cats' metaphor that the university HR managers used in relation to academics in the case study? University lecturers are not unique among professional workers in 'jealously guarding' their independence. What other occupations might fall into the same category? What challenges for managing conflict might that raise for you as an HR practitioner?

## 15.4 THE DIRECT BENEFITS OF MEDIATION

Advocates of mediation highlight a number of important benefits. First, it is an opportunity to intervene early and resolve specific disputes, thereby avoiding grievance and disciplinary procedures, the long-term absence of those involved, and, in some cases, employment tribunal proceedings. Furthermore, it provides an opportunity to repair and restore the employment relationship. Therefore, for employers, mediation offers significant financial savings compared with other, more conventional routes. Second, it could be argued that disputants find mediation a more acceptable approach to resolving their differences and, are more likely to commit to any final agreement. Research also suggests that mediation provides an opportunity for individuals to approach a complaint or grievance in a less confrontational manner than is possible through conventional processes. Consequently, staff who would otherwise leave are able to make their concerns known while remaining with their employer. Third, mediation allows employees to have 'their day in court', where they can express their views and emotions, but without the procedural limitations of organisational grievance and disciplinary processes.

Through the mediator, the disputants also consider what they can get from a possible solution by focusing on common ground, not their differences. Because the process is facilitated by a neutral mediator to create a non-threatening environment, people are more likely to listen to the other person's viewpoint and experiences, and to understand how their behaviour is affecting the other person. The aim of mediation is to change that behaviour.

It is also argued that people are more likely to commit to a solution if they have been a party to finding that solution. So, if the disputants feel that it has not been imposed upon them, it can be argued that there is a feeling of a greater ownership of the outcome. The confidential nature of mediation is another important benefit of the process. The parties are reassured that anything that they say will not be put on record or be used later should the mediation process prove unsuccessful.

## 15.5 MEDIATION – INCREASING CONFLICT COMPETENCE?

While most organisations turn to mediation to find resolutions to specific disputes, there is some evidence that it can also have a positive impact on the way that organisations manage conflict more generally. For example, Gibbons saw mediation as one element in developing 'culture change, so that parties to employment disputes think in terms of finding ways to achieve an early outcome for them, rather than in terms of fighting their case at a tribunal' (2007: 38). Moreover, the Government argued in 2011 that mediation could lead to improved 'employer-employee relationships, the development of organisational culture and the development of "high-trust" relationships' (BIS, 2011: 3).

There is certainly evidence that managers, employees and mediators who are involved with mediation feel that they gain additional skills and often a new perspective on handling conflict. Perhaps not surprisingly, mediation training is seen to have a very positive impact on conflict-handling skills and enhances 'creative problem-solving' (Kressell, 2006: 747). Some have claimed that this can be 'transformational'. A study of the introduction of mediation into an NHS organisation, carried out by Saundry, McArdle and Thomas, cited the case of the self-styled 'grievance king', a union representative who had developed a very adversarial approach to workplace conflict. For this individual, taking part in mediation training significantly changed his approach and attitude towards his members' problems and convinced him of the need to look for informal resolutions rather than reverting to formal procedure.

---

**CASE STUDY 15.2**

### THE 'GRIEVANCE KING'

An Acas-commissioned case study of East Lancashire Primary Care Trust (ELPCT) highlighted the potential of the introduction of internal mediation capacity to have a broader effect on employment relations.

Prior to the introduction of a mediation service at ELPCT, employment relations had become highly adversarial – in a climate of rapid and substantial change, trust between managers and union representatives had been substantially eroded. As a result, employee grievances had become a battleground. The unions encouraged formal grievances as a way of highlighting wider issues, while management reacted defensively. Cases became mired in complex and time-consuming procedures. At the centre of this was a senior shop steward who was referred to as the 'Grievance King'.

In setting up an internal mediation scheme, an acting HR director persuaded the 'Grievance King' to train as a mediator: he was not convinced but agreed to attend the training to sabotage the whole process:

'I thought they were looking to convince me. I went in with the attitude ... I thought if anything I'll come in and I'll kibosh it. I will get my voice heard that there is no other better way than a grievance procedure.'

In fact, the experience had a profound effect. Managers, HR professionals and union representatives were trained together and gained a new understanding of each other's perspectives. Subsequently, the 'Grievance King' became one of the mediation scheme co-ordinators. Union support for the scheme was based on a belief that the outcomes for their members were, in most cases, much better than those possible through formal grievance procedures. Furthermore, working together in the mediation scheme rebuilt trust between union representatives and management, which, in turn, underpinned informal routes to conflict resolution.

Source: Saundry et al, 2013

---

Of course, not all staff can be trained in mediation, but research has also suggested that participating in mediation can develop communication and conflict-management skills (Bush and Folger, 2005). Recent research in the UK has also found that managers who go through the mediation process are encouraged to reflect on their own behaviours and practice, encouraging them to address issues at an earlier stage (Saundry and Wibberley, 2014). The most significant evidence of the transformative impact of mediation comes from analysis of the REDRESS programme introduced by the US Postal Service. This found that supervisors who underwent mediation training and/or mediation 'listen more, are more open to expressing emotion, and take a less hierarchical top-down approach to managing conflict' (Blomgren Bingham et al, 2009: 43).

?

**REFLECTIVE ACTIVITY 15.5**

You have been tasked by your manager to produce a short presentation to the HR team comprising a critical review of the merits of mediation in the workplace. What key aspects of the process would you include and why? What sources would you use to support your arguments?

## 15.6 BARRIERS TO WORKPLACE MEDIATION

Despite its potential benefits, recent research in the UK (Latreille, 2011; Saundry and Wibberley, 2014) has pointed to a number of barriers to the use of mediation and the development of internal mediation services. For smaller organisations with no in-house mediation capacity, an important deterrent is cost – bringing in an external mediator normally costs between £2,000 and £2,500. Although there is convincing evidence that this can represent good value for money in the longterm, compared with the costs of formal disciplinary and grievance procedures and litigation, this is sometimes not immediately apparent. Smaller organisations can also be resistant to bringing in an 'outsider' to 'wash their dirty laundry'.

In larger organisations, the main opposition has come from line and operational managers, who find their authority threatened by the ability of employees to ask for mediation. This is particularly acute in cases involving performance management, where managers felt that attempts to manage performance could be effectively challenged through employees referring issues to mediation. Managers are also reluctant to refer cases to mediation as they are concerned that this could be seen within the organisation as an admittance of failure. With in-house schemes, this appears to be exacerbated when the provision of the mediation service is located within the HR function, as managers might be reluctant to signal that they are incapable of handling a specific problem. In addition, where only HR professionals are trained as mediators, the diffusion of skills is inevitably limited.

---

**'A FEAR OF FAILURE' – MEDIATION IN THE PRIVATE SECTOR**

CASE STUDY 15.3

Saundry and Wibberley's (2012) case study of Qualco, a large private sector organisation, highlighted a number of the key benefits of mediation but also some of the barriers to it becoming embedded within managerial practice.

The researchers found that the success rate of mediations was high and that those that had used mediation were highly satisfied. Mediation had been used to resolve a wide range of disputes, including employment tribunal claims. This was seen to have retained staff and resuscitated employment relationships that had seemed irretrievably broken.

There was also evidence that managers who had been through the mediation process had reflected on, and subsequently changed, their approach to conflict.

However, at the time of the research, awareness of the service was limited and managers were also reluctant to refer cases to mediation. In particular, bringing in help from outside their workplace, in the form of a trained mediator, was seen as an admittance of failure. This was made more acute by the fact that the mediation service was located in the HR department and the mediators were mostly senior HR professionals. Therefore, there was a concern in individual units that referring cases could invite scrutiny and possible criticism from 'head office'. According to one manager:

'...there's a bit of a barrier around admitting that there is an issue and we try and resolve things in-house because sometimes we don't want other [parts of the business] to know there is a problem' (Operational manager).

In their eyes, a referral to the mediation scheme had become a formal 'last resort' to be considered only when all other procedures had been exhausted.

A problem facing internal mediation services is sustainability – mediators often find it hard to find time to combine mediation with normal duties. Consequently, there can be a high turnover of mediators. The viability of mediation can therefore become dependent on a small number of key individuals. This fragility means that the understanding and support of senior managers is crucial.

There can also be resistance from employees and their representatives. For employees, mediation is often perceived as a relatively formal process, and sitting in a room without representation, challenging their manager or another work colleague, can be extremely daunting. This illustrates concerns that power inequalities in the workplace are inevitably felt within the mediation process. Keashly and Nowell (2011) question whether mediation participants can actually negotiate on equal terms. In contrast, research into the views of disputants in the UK by Saundry et al (2013) found that it was managers who felt most uncomfortable in being challenged by their subordinates.

Mediation has also been viewed with suspicion by trade union representatives who have concerns that it may be a way of restricting their traditional role and their ability to contest decisions made by the employer – importantly, employee representation is not normally permitted within the mediation 'room'. Even where trade union representatives can see the potential benefits of mediation for their members, they are sometimes reluctant to become actively involved as, for example, mediators because of concerns that this could lead to a conflict of interest.

Finally, and crucially, there is the key question of the sustainability of any agreement arising from a mediated dispute. This turns initially on the original decision to refer a dispute for mediation. The HR manager, line manager and, where there is an internal mediation service, the co-ordinator need to be sure that mediation is appropriate for the outcomes expected by the disputants. If they want, for instance, a finding that will be made public, the dispute should be referred to another route. Furthermore, it is crucial for all parties to realise that they are committing to an ongoing process. It is not a 'one-off meeting'. Rather, it is a process that begins with individual meetings with the disputants to understand their concerns and expectations. It then progresses to a joint meeting, or meetings, to seek to resolve those differences. Fundamentally, if successful, it culminates in an agreement to put the solutions identified into practice on an ongoing basis. If this is not realistic, then again the 'commissioner' of mediation, the disputants or the mediator should, on reflection, look to alternative, more formal, means of resolution open to them within the organisation's conflict management systems and structures.

For instance, as Saundry et al (2013) discovered in their research, agreements were often short-lived. This was because the parties were not fully committed to the process or that the agreed outcomes were not really achievable. Typically, this is due to underlying problems being outside the gift of the disputants to resolve (ie the reality is that workplace mediation takes place within the context and therefore the constraints of the dominant management style and the strategy of the organisation).

**?    REFLECTIVE ACTIVITY 15.6**

What barriers do you think you would encounter if you suggested that your organisation should make use of mediation? What arguments would you use to persuade sceptics that mediation could make a positive contribution?

## 15.7 MEDIATION IN PRACTICE

Having critically reflected on the context of workplace mediation, and the key theoretical and conceptual considerations that its study and practice have raised, this part of the chapter will focus on the practical aspects of mediation in terms of the process, its objectives and the role of the mediator.

### 15.7.1 DEVELOPING AN INTERNAL MEDIATION SERVICE

For larger organisations, which may have to deal with complex conflict on a fairly regular basis, it may be worthwhile to consider in investing in their own internal mediation service. Typically, this will involve training a number of staff as accredited mediators who can be deployed to mediate cases as part of their normal duties. Establishing an internal mediation service can be costly and requires a significant commitment from the organisation. However, it has a number of important advantages:

1  In the long term, it is much more cost-effective than engaging external mediators and, if cases are resolved, it is both cheaper and faster than using conventional disciplinary and grievance procedures.

2  Internal mediators may be much better placed to understand the specific organisational context, which may help participants to find a sustainable resolution.

3  Training a cohort of mediators can be one way of diffusing key conflict-handling skills and changing the culture of conflict management, particularly if mediators are selected strategically.

4  Trained mediators can be deployed flexibly to a wide range of conflict management situations – for example, in facilitated meetings, team discussions, training provision and as conflict coaches.

Even if an organisation has its own internal mediation service, if senior and well-known figures in the organisation are in dispute, it may be necessary to look to an external provider in order to ensure impartiality. Another alternative is to develop a network or sharing agreement between a number of organisations, whereby mediators can be deployed on a reciprocal basis.

In developing and designing an internal mediation service, research has pointed to a number of key considerations:

*Organisational support and commitment* – the backing of senior management is vital if internal mediation is going to be sustainable. This does not just mean approving the initial start-up costs of training, but also ensuring that mediators are given time and encouragement in undertaking their role and developing their skills. It is also crucial that the scheme has a champion, or champions, who occupy an influential position within the organisation.

*Locating the scheme* – as suggested, try to avoid locating the service within the HR department. Good relationships between HR and any internal mediation service are vital, but if mediation is seen as a department of HR, managers may be more reluctant to use it.

There are interesting examples of this in the NHS – in East Lancashire Primary Care Trust, joint co-ordinators were appointed. The involvement of the union provided the service with a greater degree of legitimacy and increased take-up by union members (Saundry *et al*, 2013).

*Selecting your mediators* – it may be tempting to simply select HR practitioners as mediators, but evidence suggests that when mediators are drawn from different parts of the organisation, it is more likely that support for, and awareness of, the service will increase and that an emphasis on early resolution will be encouraged. This will particularly be the case if influential individuals are trained – this may include senior managers, trade union representatives or simply members of staff who come into contact with large numbers of other colleagues through their normal role.

*Review your procedures* – examine your existing disciplinary, grievance and dignity at work procedures and see whether mediation can be built into the early stages. Furthermore, placing a greater emphasis on the importance of conflict resolution more generally may increase the use of mediation.

*Use your mediators flexibly* – think about different ways in which trained mediators can be used in addition to conventional mediations. For example, they could be used to train managers, assist in facilitated meetings and also to coach managers in teams where there is a particular problem.

*Evaluate the results* – try to make sure that resources are in place to evaluate mediations but also to follow this up at a later point to see whether the solution has been sustained. Evaluations will also help to establish the value of the service.

## 15.7.2 CO-ORDINATING MEDIATION

Internal mediation services normally have a dedicated co-ordinator, whose job it is to manage the overall mediation service for the organisation. All referrals are channelled in the first instance to the co-ordinator. She or he then 'triages' each case, usually through an informal conversation with each party in dispute, to establish if mediation is the best route to resolving their dispute. If this is felt to be the case, then, depending on whether the service is provided externally or internally, the external provider is contacted or one of the team of internal mediators is allocated to the case.

The basis for that choice varies across organisations but is typically based, of course, on availability or having no direct knowledge of the disputants (in a university this would mean, for instance, allocating a mediator from another school or faculty). Biographical variables, such as one's position or gender, in our experiences can occasionally be a factor for the disputants; in which case the mediator may seek to accommodate this request. Interestingly in the HE sector, some universities are able to draw on a network of mediators based in other institutions to mediate in disputes where an internal mediator may not be suitable.

In organisations without in-house capacity, engaging external mediators is normally the responsibility of the HR professional or manager dealing with that case. It is critical that someone liaises between the external mediator and the participants. Recent research in the UK found that in some circumstances, once the external mediator was employed, the organisations provided very little support to those involved, and in more than one case left it to the participants to organise the mediation itself (Saundry *et al*, 2013).

## 15.7.3 THE ROLE OF HR PRACTITIONERS, LINE MANAGERS AND REPRESENTATIVES

Unsurprisingly, the role of the line managers is very different in mediation than in grievance or disciplinary procedures. She or he could actually be one of the disputants. If not, then they may have referred a dispute to the mediation service or advised members of their team to go to mediation. In any case, this is where their involvement ends in the process until they are advised by HR that the dispute has been resolved or not. Only with the full agreement of the disputants will the nature of the resolution be shared with the line manager.

This is also the case with the HR team. HR advisers and business partners are one of a number of channels of referral of disputes. In organisations with internal mediation schemes, HR advisers and business partners will normally be fully briefed on the mediation process and are able to signpost cases they think are appropriate. Furthermore, some of the HR team may be part of the mediation team. Research has indicated that this varies among organisations (Saundry, 2012; Bennett, 2013). It can be of significant benefit as involvement in the scheme can encourage buy-in from senior HR practitioners. However, as noted above, if mediation is seen as being a function of HR, there is a danger that this could deter referrals.

In general, the involvement of employee and union representatives is crucial in winning support for mediation and in developing a culture of early and informal dispute resolution. However, in the UK, representation within the mediation room itself is not generally permitted or encouraged. As the basis of mediation is that the participants develop their own solutions, many mediators feel that representation would disturb this balance. Of course, that does not mean that representatives cannot play a vital role in supporting and advising employees both before and after the mediation takes place.

---

### ?  REFLECTIVE ACTIVITY 15.7

Your organisation has chosen to establish an internal mediation service. The head of HR has asked for a short report outlining both the merits and drawbacks of the HR department co-ordinating the service and encouraging business partners to train to be internal mediators. What would be your conclusions?

---

### 15.7.4 IS MEDIATION THE RIGHT CHOICE?

A critical question is whether mediation is the right response to a particular issue or dispute. Typically, mediation is seen as appropriate where there are breakdowns in relationships, poor management and communication problems (CIPD, 2011; Bennett, 2013). Mediation is also more likely to be employed to resolve grievances brought by employees. However, issues around which conflict can occur present complex and difficult choices for those considering mediation.

Mediation is often employed to resolve complaints that emerge from attempts by managers to manage performance. Therefore, a manager may seek to address a problem with performance, behaviour or attendance. But, the employee may argue that this and/or the approach used by the manager could constitute bullying or harassment. In such cases, mediation is a relatively common response, and reference to mediation can increasingly be found in bullying and harassment and dignity at work policies.

Nonetheless, both managers and employees can have reservations about the use of mediation in such cases. Managers argue that, while mediation can resolve relationship issues, it does nothing to address the underlying performance issue. Conversely, for some employees, as discussed previously, mediation can be perceived as an inadequate response to mistreatment and effectively denying them access to 'justice'.

In some respects, generalised rules are not particularly helpful and each case should be treated on its merits. Crucially, mediation is most likely to be appropriate where a central element of the dispute involves a breakdown in the relationship between two (or sometimes more) people and critically where both parties are prepared to attempt to rebuild and maintain that relationship. In contrast, mediation may not be the best way forward:

- if either (or both) party (parties) is/are unwilling to engage in the process
- when either party is incapable of taking part or can't keep an agreement
- if it is not in the interests of one party to settle
- if the dispute needs a public judgment (Liebmann, 2000).

In such cases, the utilisation of formal procedures may be necessary or inevitable. Furthermore, if an employee has 'broken the rules', such as committing an act of gross misconduct, then disciplinary action will often be more appropriate. This could include accusations of mistreatment and serious bullying and harassment. Here, organisations may also wish to adopt a formal response to make clear that such behaviour is not acceptable. Furthermore, as noted above, mediation cannot resolve underlying performance problems, so ultimately, disciplinary or capability procedures may need to be enacted.

### 15.7.5 SINGLE OR DUAL MEDIATION

Whether to use single or dual mediation (using two mediators) is also a key consideration for organisations to consider in providing a mediation service. In Bennett's (2014) research in higher education, a number of the universities studied utilised dual mediation as a matter of best practice, as had been prescribed by their original training provider. In other institutions, it was felt that it was harder to effectively manage dual mediation, because of the difficulties of securing time off for mediators or on the basis of costs. Ultimately, however, for many co-ordinators in this sector – given the fairly limited number of cases they were managing, as the service initially marketed itself within the organisation – dual mediation was seen as a useful way to offer their mediators ongoing opportunities to practise.

## 15.8 THE FIVE STAGES OF THE MEDIATION PROCESS

Having considered the role of the main players in workplace mediation and the key issues in designing an internal scheme, this section explains the mediation process in detail.

### 15.8.1 STAGE 1: SEPARATE MEETINGS WITH THE PARTIES

In the pre-stage of the process, the mediator contacts the parties separately and, having gained their agreement to take part, arranges a separate meeting with each disputant. This is the first time the mediator will meet each party in person. The mediator and disputant will introduce themselves, and the mediator will explain their role and outline the process and objectives of mediation. In particular, they will stress their neutral position, their non-judgemental approach and that all conversations are in total confidence. At this stage, the mediator seeks through questions and listening to understand the situation; the context of the dispute; and the perceptions of each party as to the causes and consequences of the dispute. The mediator will also explain the potential outcomes of mediation. This is the first opportunity for the mediator to build a rapport with each of the parties and gain their trust. Each party is encouraged to talk about themselves, their job role and their relationship with others, including the other disputant. Through this process of openness and empathy to the concerns and feelings of each party, the mediator seeks to get the agreement of each party to continue the process and crucially to move to the next stage, which is the joint meeting.

### 15.8.2 STAGE 2: HEARING THE ISSUES

The second stage in the process is about setting the scene for the mediation and hearing the issues with both the parties present. The joint meeting opens with a welcome from the mediator and an introduction to the parties. This takes the form of the mediator outlining the process, the purpose of the joint meeting and how the meeting is to be conducted. A key aspect of this part of the meeting is the need to establish ground rules for the meeting and the rest of the process. For example, the mediator will stress the need to respect the other's point of view, to use appropriate language and not to interrupt the other party whilst they are giving their account of the dispute. Each party then gets the opportunity to 'tell their side of things', to put their case, and for the other party to reflect on the feelings of, and impact on, the other person. When both sides have put their case, the mediator summarises the points raised by both parties and suggests an agenda for discussion. If this agenda is agreed by both parties, the process moves to the third stage.

### 15.8.3 STAGE 3: EXPLORING THE ISSUES

This is the stage that gives an opportunity for both parties to express in more detail how they feel about the issues causing the conflict and the impact that it is having on them in the workplace. The mediator will direct questions to each party to check their understanding of issues. Crucially, this stage in the process offers participants the chance to acknowledge their differences, accept different perspectives on issues and seek to move on from those differences. Throughout stage 3, the mediator's role is to maintain the agenda or, if new issues arise, to negotiate with the parties to table these for further discussion. A key aspect of the mediation process, particularly when utilising the facilitative model, is to change the focus of the relationship between the two disputants from the past to the future. The mediator manages this through getting the parties to express their feelings about past events, articulate 'the history' of their relationship, but then to emphasise the positive aspects of looking to a settlement, which can seek to repair or restore their relationship in the future. When the mediator decides that discussion has progressed sufficiently, they will summarise the areas of consensus and disagreement between the two parties. This allows the mediator to demonstrate the progress that has been made and then allows a focus on the issues that remain to be addressed.

### 15.8.4 STAGE 4: BUILDING AND WRITING AGREEMENTS

In this stage of the process, the mediator helps the parties to suggest options for resolving the issues that lie between them. They then assess which options may be most acceptable or practical. At this juncture, the process of negotiation may start in earnest as the mediator encourages the parties to offer a concession on an issue in return for an offer from the other. A key aim at this point is to get the two parties to prioritise their resolution and to jointly look for a settlement. The role of the mediator here is to highlight gestures of conciliation made by the parties. This stage closes by the mediator summarising the actions that have been agreed between the two parties, including issues that may still need to be discussed or where differences have been conceded. The mediator then records the agreement made between the two parties. Finally, the mediator writes up the agreement for the parties.

### 15.8.5 STAGE 5: CLOSURE AND FOLLOW-UP

This is the final stage in the process and the point at which the mediator congratulates the parties on the progress they have made and to reiterate what has been achieved through the mediation process. This statement acts as a summary but also aims to reconfirm the two parties' commitment to the agreement and their relationship. Closure is then achieved through the parties' signing the agreement and taking their copies. The mediator at this point will also ask the parties if they want a follow-up or review meeting before formally leaving. With the exception of signing an agreement, the mediator would close similarly when no agreement had been reached, summarising what alternative action the parties have agreed to take.

## 15.8.6 THE SKILLS AND KNOWLEDGE NEEDED FOR EFFECTIVE MEDIATION

There are a number of key skills, qualities and knowledge required to be an effective mediator in the workplace. For a more detailed discussion, Crawley's (2012) practical guide to workplace mediation is helpful where, in particular, he advocates skills such as 'being a good listener', having 'empathy' and being 'self-aware' and 'reflective' as crucial for effective mediation. Table 15.1 sets out the key skills, qualities and knowledge needed for effective mediation.

Table 15.1 Effective mediation – key skills, qualities and knowledge

| Skills | Qualities | Knowledge |
|---|---|---|
| Active listening | Empathy | Theory of conflict |
| Good written and | Approachability | resolution |
| communication skills | Impartiality and fairness | Causes and consequences |
| Questioning | Ability to be non- | of conflict |
| Observing | judgemental | Dispute resolution |
| Understanding of body | Professionalism | techniques |
| language and people's | Honesty and integrity | The mediation process |
| behaviour | Credibility, creativity and | Principles and practice |
| Effective summarising and | flexibility | standards |
| being able to review and | | Legal context of mediation |
| evaluate | | Equal opportunities and |
| Ability to reflect and be | | diversity issues |
| self-aware | | Dynamics of power and |
| Influencing skills | | conflict |
| Ability to build rapport | | Context of the particular |
| Assertiveness | | dispute |
| Facilitation | | |
| Analysis of information | | |
| and problem-solving | | |
| Planning and time | | |
| management | | |
| Negotiation skills | | |

## 15.8.7 THE ATTITUDE AND APPROACH NEEDED TO BE AN EFFECTIVE MEDIATOR

The mediator makes a priority of building rapport with the client, establishing empathy and demonstrating their impartiality. All of these actions are fundamental aspects of what a mediator does. In addition, there are a number of other approaches that the mediator undertakes in any intervention.

The mediator should always aim to be fair and non-judgemental. They need to be patient to ensure that participants are able to fully make their case. Communication skills, including picking up on non-verbal cues, are crucial, as is the ability to time-manage the process, allowing sufficient space for both parties to feel that they are being fully heard but judging when to summarise a discussion and move on to the next issue or issues. The mediator must clearly introduce the parties to the process and establish the issues. She or he must set ground rules for all meetings, summarise when appropriate and look to gain agreement when the parties are disposed to do so. The mediator must be able to encourage the parties to agree solutions when judged to be in their best interests and felt by the mediator to genuinely offer a potential resolution to their conflict.

In encouraging people to participate in mediation, the mediator can adopt a particular strategy to engage with the disputants. The mediator stresses that there is no compulsion to participate and that mediation does not preclude them from raising a grievance or taking further action should the mediation not succeed. By stressing the neutrality of the process and setting clear ground rules, the mediator hopes to allay any fears that participants may have. The skilled mediator will discuss the alternatives and balance their potential efficacy against that of mediation in terms of time, costs, loss of control and chances of success.

The mediator remains realistic with the two parties as to what is possible and emphasises that success is dependent on all parties being committed to the process. In this respect, there are a number of things that a mediator cannot do. These must be made clear to the two parties to avoid misunderstandings and misconceptions. It is not the role of the mediator to judge clients or the case that they make. Neither is it their role to offer advice to the parties, offer solutions or take sides. The mediator's role is to facilitate discussion between the clients, which will allow them to make informed choices between possible solutions generated through their own discourse. Even if they see merit in an argument or the case of one party, it is the role of the mediator to assist the disputants to weigh up the merits of their cases and seek solutions through dialogue and informed negotiation. It is not the task of the mediator to apportion blame. Rather it is their role to move the parties away from the past and blaming one another to seek a solution that will hold for the future. Finally, the mediator must never break the confidentiality of either party unless there has been agreement to do so.

## ?    REFLECTIVE ACTIVITY 15.8

What sort of managing conflict training do you have in your organisation for line managers? Would managers in your organisation benefit from a workshop on basic mediation skills? If the answer is yes, what would the main advantages be?

## 15.9 DEVELOPING A MODEL OF GOOD PRACTICE

Having reviewed both the process and some of the key findings from current research on mediation, the main generic elements of workplace mediation are mapped out in Figure 15.2. This allows us to consider how a model for mediation can be applied in practice.

First, there are key variables that will inform the successful implementation of the initiative, such as a champion at the senior level, the culture of the organisation and the key partners to be involved in the process. Second, in terms of managing the system, evidence suggests that developing clear and multiple channels of referrals, managed by a single co-ordinator, is the most effective approach. This also helps in making decisions over the appropriateness of dispute for mediation and whether the mediation should be conducted by an internal or external mediator. Third, as in any HRM process, evaluation is a key element captured in the model. This allows appropriate feedback to senior management to demonstrate its effectiveness and, crucially, for action to be taken to address any limitations in the service. This can then feed into a broader reappraisal of the strategic objectives of the initiative.

## 15.10 SUMMARY

There has been a growing interest within the field of HRM, and in terms of government strategy and policy, in the process of mediation. However, to date, the take-up is still relatively small in comparison with more conventional dispute relation methods. Nonetheless, as our critical review of the existing literature has shown, it is an increasingly significant area of conflict resolution that we, as students and practitioners of employment relations, need to consider. This said, we do not suggest that mediation is a panacea for all disputes. Rather, depending on the reasons for the dispute and the outcomes expected by the disputants, mediation can offer the potential to rebuild and maintain an employment relationship that

Figure 15.2 A practical model of workplace mediation

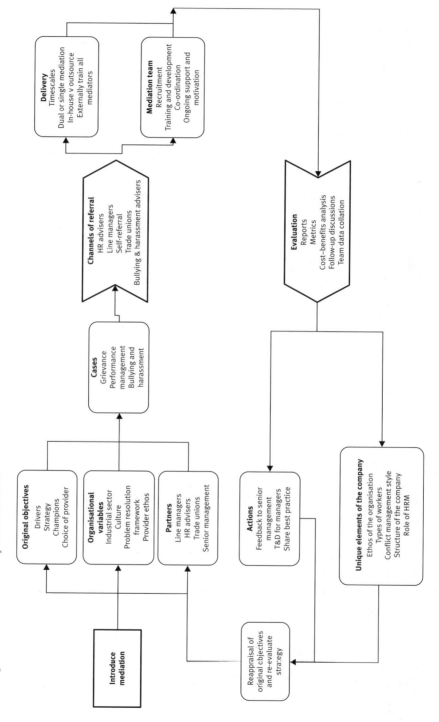

has become compromised without resort to more formal means of resolution. Mediation can also empower employees, allowing them an opportunity to challenge managerial prerogative in a way that is not possible through conventional dispute resolution procedures. Furthermore, given the problems faced by line managers in addressing and resolving 'difficult issues', the skills and techniques used in workplace mediation have the potential to provide the basis for the development of much needed conflict resolution skills.

## KEY LEARNING POINTS

1 Unlike more formal routes for resolving disputes, mediation is confidential, and the process and outcome are determined by the disputants. The mediator acts only to facilitate the overall process.

2 Mediation is an alternative dispute resolution process. However, unlike conciliation, the disputants are not 'guided' torough the process towards a solution. Equally, it is not like arbitration where the arbitrator acts as a judge and finds in favour of one party or the other. The mediator at all times remains neutral.

3 Mediation is not a panacea for all disputes. However, where this involves a breakdown in the relationship between two or more parties, it can provide an effective means of rebuilding and restoring relations to allow them to continue to work effectively.

4 The knowledge, skills and the approach used in mediation can also potentially inform and enhance the more general practice of managers and HR professionals in managing conflict.

5 Dispute resolution is more likely to be successful if the mediation takes place at an early stage in the conflict.

6 The introduction of in-house mediation capacity can have a positive impact on the way that organisations manage conflict more broadly. However, for this to occur, mediation should be seen as a central element of HR strategy.

## REVIEW QUESTIONS

1 In what type of situations, where workplace conflict has occurred, do you feel that mediation may be most appropriate and why?

2 Why do you think that the take-up of workplace mediation in the UK is relatively low? What could be done by policymakers and practitioners to extend its use?

3 To what extent does mediation allow organisations to evade responsibility for workplace mistreatment?

4 What do you feel are the key issues to be taken into account if you are considering the introduction of an internal mediation service in your organisation?

5 As an HR practitioner, what sort of role do you think you might take up in such a service?

6 To what degree do you think that mediation genuinely offers a more equitable approach for workers in dispute than more conventional methods of resolution?

EXPLORING FURTHER

ACAS/CIPD (2013) *Mediation: An approach to resolving workplace issues*. London: Acas.

BENNETT, T. (2013) Workplace mediation and the empowerment of disputants: rhetoric or reality? *Industrial Relations Journal*. Vol 44, No 2. pp189–209.

BENNETT, T. (2014) The role of workplace mediation: a critical assessment. *Personnel Review*. Vol 43, No 5. pp764–779.

CRAWLEY, J. (2012) *From argument to agreement: Resolving disputes through mediation*. London: John Crawley Mediation.

LATREILLE, P. and SAUNDRY, R. (2014) Mediation. In ROCHE, W., TEAGUE, P. and COLVIN, A. (eds). *The Oxford handbook on conflict management*. Oxford: Oxford University Press.

SAUNDRY, R., BENNETT, T. and WIBBERLEY, G. (2013) *Workplace mediation: the participant experience*. Acas research paper, No 2/13. London: Acas.

SAUNDRY, R. and WIBBERLEY, G. (2014) *Workplace dispute resolution and the management of individual conflict – a thematic analysis of five case studies*. Acas research paper, No 06/14. London: Acas.

TUC/ACAS (2010) *Mediation: a guide for trade union representatives*. London: TUC/Acas.

WOOD, S., SAUNDRY, R. and LATREILLE, P. (2014) *Analysis of the nature, extent and impact of grievance and disciplinary procedures and workplace mediation using WERS2011*. Acas research paper, No 10/14, London: Acas.

**Website links**

www.acas.org.uk gives access to guides and research reports on conflict management and workplace mediation. This is a really valuable source of both current research and practical guides to how mediation works in practice.

www.cipd.co.uk gives access to CIPD guides and reports on conflict management and workplace mediation. It is a very useful source for reports on CIPD members and their experiences of mediation, through reports and survey results. It is an excellent source of practical guides on the subject.

www.uclan.ac.uk/research/explore/groups/institute_research_organisations_work_employment_irowe.php gives access to a range of research findings on conflict management in the workplace from Lancashire Business School's Institute for Research on Organisations, Work and Employment (IROWE).

# CHAPTER 16

# Conclusion: Thoughts for the Future

As we have stressed throughout this book, the employment relations approach adopted by any organisation is strongly influenced by the philosophy of the government of the day and its views on affairs of the workplace. Consequently, the macro-economic policies of the new Conservative Government, elected in 2015, and particularly its attitude to issues such as employment rights and trade unions will shape the conduct of employment relations until 2020.

Nonetheless, government policy is not the only factor that determines the context of employment relations. We also live in a world that is increasingly interconnected, both through information technology and global trade – so that changes in the value of stocks in China, increases in the supply of oil from the Far East, and the interest rate policies of the US Government's Federal Reserve will be felt in British workplaces.

Therefore, practitioners must be acutely aware of identifying and addressing environmental issues that impact on employment relations strategy and practice. At the time of writing this short concluding chapter for the sixth edition of *Managing Employment Relations*, we cannot be certain of the consequences of these dynamic forces for employment relations; however, in the rest of this section, we identify six themes which we believe will be critical for employment relations practitioners over the next five years.

## 16.1 GLOBALISATION AND THE FUTURE OF EUROPE

We considered in Chapter 5 how the global market and our membership of the EU have significantly impacted on employment relations in the UK in recent years. As we go to print, it is clear that the UK Government is fully committed to the UK's role within the global market. Indeed, the need to protect and create jobs in the face of increasingly intense international competition was the main justification for the Coalition Government's weakening of individual employment protection and reforms to the employment tribunal system.

This philosophy is also reflected in the current proposals for a referendum on EU membership due to be held in 2016. Although employment regulation is just one part of the argument for reform of the UK's relationship and/or withdrawal, the view that EU membership and the influence of EU social legislation is a constraint on free trade is a central argument of those critical of the status quo.

We are now very familiar with the reality that employment relations is not a neutral activity, either ideologically or practically. When different political parties take office, their overall world view has a driving influence on policies that affect the law governing employment rights and regulations, and how those aspects of the employment relationship are played out in the workplace. The debate on EU membership in many ways captures these ideological differences, but only up to a point. Neo-liberal, pro-market Conservatives and UKIP, we are led to understand, see membership as an economic, political and social constraint on the rights of the UK to determine its own destiny. In particular, EU regulations designed to protect employees are seen as an obstacle to economic growth and free trade.

In contrast, the social democrat majority in the Labour Party, along with, it can be argued, most centrist members of the Conservative, the SNP and Liberal Democratic parties, favour retaining membership, but with varying views of how and to what degree EU employment regulations should apply in the UK. Intriguingly, the traditional left and more members of the labour movement in general (King, 2015) also question the value of membership of an increasingly market-oriented system whose leadership seem intent on weakening the social constraints it had typically until fairly recently used to balance the power of the market and recognise the rights of the employee.

What does this mean in practice? Significantly, the UK Government, as part of its demands for concessions on membership to put before the voting public at the referendum, have stated that an opt-out from the Social Chapter might be part of those concessions (Wintour, 2015). As we noted earlier in the book, this was an ideological totem for the Conservative Party, only brought down when the New Labour Government of Tony Blair signed up to the Chapter in 1997. This led to an extension of individual employment protection, which was seen by many in business as an unwelcome burden and stimulated calls within the Conservative Party to return to a relationship with Europe based solely on free trade.

Irrespective of the outcome of the UK Government's renegotiation efforts and the subsequent referendum, the influence of increasing global competition is likely to define the context for employment relations, both in the UK and beyond. The prevailing pressure both within the UK and European Union is towards a weakening of employment regulation. For example, there has been growing debate about the plan to establish a Transatlantic Treaty Investment Partnership (TTIP) with the US. For its supporters, this is a logical next step in the globalisation process to open up the European markets to US companies, and the US markets to their European counterparts. In contrast, for critics of TTIP, this represents the next step in a neo-liberal project to privatise public services such as the NHS and education. These potential outcomes of the TTIP could have profound ramifications for HR professionals working in those and other sectors of the UK economy.

## 16.2 THE ROLE OF THE COLLECTIVE IN THE MODERN WORKPLACE

That the globalisation of production and competition has also contributed to the erosion of collective regulation has been a defining feature of employment relations in the UK over the past four decades. As we have discussed in this book, while the pace of the decline of trade union membership and the scale and scope of collective bargaining may have slowed, it has nevertheless continued (van Wanrooy et al, 2013). The crucial questions for us are: can trade unions recover lost influence and rebuild organisation? What are the implications of this for wider employment relations?

There is no doubt that the role of unions has changed in recent years. There is greater emphasis on representing and supporting individual members who have problems with their employers. Furthermore, the union agenda has widened, as illustrated by their championing of learning and skills for both life and work for all workers and citizens, as part of learning agreements and partnerships with employers (Stuart et al, 2013; Bennett, 2014). Similarly, the unions have and continue to carry out important work in the field of equality and diversity, through, for example, the development of specialist equality representatives.

At the same time, unions have devoted much greater time and resources into trying to rebuild grass-roots organisation and recruit new members. However, as we discussed in Chapter 9, while there have been some successes, there is little evidence of any sustained strengthening of union influence (Simms et al, 2013). This is not to say that these efforts have been for nothing – but, at best, unions have been able to consolidate rather than extend organisation. Critically, unions have found it particularly difficult to recruit among the new generation of workers, often employed in insecure and low-paid jobs.

Perhaps the most hopeful development here has been the success of community organising. The campaign to force large corporations and organisations to pay the 'Living Wage' to their workers in London was conducted by London Citizens – a coalition of religious and faith groups, student organisations, union branches, voluntary agencies and residents' associations. Its impact is illustrated not only by the fact that around 800 employers now are committed to paying the Living Wage, but that it has shaped national policy, with the Conservative Government committed to substantial increases in the National Minimum Wage. The record of union involvement in such alliances to date has been mixed, but this is perhaps one way in which they can extend their reach and influence in the future.

The future of trade unions is not simply an academic or political matter but has fundamental implications for business and employing organisations. For example, a 2014 OECD working paper argued that income inequality limits productivity and economic growth (Cingano, 2014). At the same time, it has long been argued that collective bargaining between employers and the unions will result in a more equitable distribution of economic rewards of economic endeavour and particularly reduce the persistent wage gap between men and women (Hayes and Novitz, 2013). There is also substantial evidence that high-trust relations between employers and trade unions are critical in supporting informal processes of conflict resolution (Saundry and Wibberley, 2014) and in underpinning channels of employee voice that in turn provide the basis of employee engagement (Purcell, 2012).

Despite evidence of the damaging impact of the UK's 'representation gap' and little sign that this is being effectively occupied by non-union mechanisms, the current Conservative administration is seeking to limit bargaining power through new measures designed to restrict industrial action. Under the Government's Trade Union Bill 2015:

- Industrial action will only have a legal mandate if a minimum 50% ballot turnout is achieved.
- Unions representing key services, such as health, education, fire, transport, border security and energy sectors, will require at least 40% of all members eligible to take part in the ballot to vote in favour.
- Rules on the legitimacy of large picket lines have been tightened and the ban on using agency workers to break strikes will be lifted.

The Bill also seeks to limit 'facility time' for trade union representatives within the public sector. However, research conducted by Kim Hoque and Nick Bacon (2015) based on an analysis of WERS2011 data shows that reducing facility time will in fact have a detrimental effect on productivity, certainly in the public sector. This is based on findings which reveal that workers in the sector perform better with an on-site union representative. Given that the strike restriction elements of the proposed bill come at a time when industrial action is at a historically low level (see Chapter 11), it is difficult to avoid the conclusion that these changes are driven by ideology as opposed to employment relations' considerations.

## 16.3 EMPLOYEE ENGAGEMENT

For many practitioners, employee engagement has come to define contemporary employment relations and in particular fill the space left by the erosion of collective bargaining and regulation. As Purcell (2014) has highlighted, the engagement 'industry' continues to thrive – staff engagement surveys are ubiquitous in large organisations and employee engagement is a key priority for HR practitioners. In 'Engage for Success', it has its own 'movement' supported by most major employers and senior HR professionals. However, most studies that attempt to assess levels of engagement show that only a minority of employees are fully engaged and a significant minority are actively disengaged.

As we saw in Chapter 7, even if one looks at the apparently positive figures for organisational engagement in the latest Workplace Employment Relations Survey, this masks a less rosy picture, which is revealed when the data is disaggregated between managers and employees.

It could be argued that this is a message that many employers are reluctant to hear. The design of staff engagement surveys is heavily influenced by positive psychology and few pose negative questions or questions designed to explore the dark side of engagement, such as work intensification, burnout and stress. In some senses, those who choose to 'disagree' with positive statements about their work or organisation are characterised as dissident voices.

Some writers have argued that the concept of employee engagement is essentially redundant (for example Guest, 2014) in that it adds nothing to existing notions of commitment, involvement and employee voice. Purcell disagrees, arguing that it focuses on 'employees, their beliefs, values, behaviours and experiences at work in a way not seen before in mainstream HRM or employee relations' (Purcell, 2014: 251). If, as we suggest is likely, the enthusiasm among practitioners in HRM and employment relations on 'employee engagement' persists, the key questions are why are so many employees disengaged and what can organisations do to remedy this?

One problem is implicit in the term disengagement – as Purcell argues, active disengagement is simply evidence of conflict in the workplace. However, as we discussed in Chapter 11, employers seem unwilling to admit that conflict is an inevitable feature of the employment relationship and therefore unable to respond to it. Purcell also argues that the four pillars of engagement outlined by MacLeod and Clarke (see Chapter 7) have been somewhat forgotten in the way that organisations have sought to develop engagement strategies. There has been an emphasis on leadership, which in turn has led to a top–down approach to engaging employees. However, the other three pillars have been neglected. As we note in this book, there is little evidence that organisations have invested sufficiently in 'engaging managers', while 'integrity' and 'voice' have been largely ignored. In particular, little attention has been given to the role of representative voice and the implications for engagement of trade union decline. At the same time, notions of fairness and organisational justice are taken for granted by most organisations. In some respects, this points to a need for employment relations to reclaim the engagement agenda and make the case for the processes, structures and institutions that provide employees with real participation in decision-making, deliver organisational justice and help to build high-trust workplace relations.

## 16.4 THE CHALLENGE OF FRONT-LINE MANAGEMENT

A key theme running throughout this book is the changing role of front-line managers. While HR practitioners are seen as the employment relations' experts in many larger organisations, it is the line manager who now has the main responsibility for dealing with employment relations issues. Not only do they have to respond to the operational demands of their role, but they also have to manage performance and absence, deal with disciplinary and grievance issues, communicate with and seek to engage members of their team. However, our examination of the evidence has shown that there are substantial doubts over the support that managers are given to enable them to cope with this increasingly complex range of tasks.

It is clear that the lack of managerial confidence and capability in managing employment relations is a critical factor that constrains not only the ability of organisations to handle and resolve difficult issues but also has a negative impact on employee engagement and organisational performance. We would argue that this deficit has three main causes. First, for example, many excellent sales people, engineers or academics have been rewarded for their professional achievements by promotion into a managerial role. However, organisations very often neglect to factor in whether that person really has the skills, knowledge and attitude to undertake the role of people management. Similarly, key employment relations competencies are often not seen as essential attributes when recruiting for new posts with managerial responsibilities. Second, once in post, time spent in managing employment relations is rarely acknowledged or rewarded – for instance, a front-line manager in a retail environment will have a range of key performance indicators, but these will be driven by operational considerations and are unlikely to reflect 'people' issues. Third, there is a danger that senior management, preoccupied with short-term operational targets and objectives, will see time spent on employment relations issues as wasted. Inevitably, therefore, employment relations will fall to the bottom of the agenda of many front-line managers.

One solution to this is training – certainly there is a skills deficit. Chair of Acas, Brendan Barber (2014), writing in *Personnel Today* in 2014, argued that there was a 'confidence gap' among line managers, and that training managers in handling difficult conversations with staff was beneficial. However, he also suggested that there needed to be a strategic commitment from senior management in organisations to see people management as a core competence.

## 16.5 FROM DISPUTE RESOLUTION TO THE MANAGEMENT OF CONFLICT

A feature of the landscape that we have surveyed in this book, and in particular the erosion of collective employment relations processes of negotiation, has been the increased emphasis on individual problems and disputes. Thirty years ago, the main preoccupations of employment relations specialists, both in management and unions, would be negotiating over collective issues and resolving collective disputes. Today, their time is much more likely to be occupied with individual cases revolving around capability, conduct, absence and accusations of bullying and harassment. Furthermore, dealing with disciplinary and grievance issues takes up an average of 18 and 14.4 days of management time respectively (CIPD, 2011); while workplace conflict, if left unresolved, can have devastating consequences for the individuals involved and undermine employee engagement and performance.

However, the conventional policies and procedures that organisations have developed to manage such issues often fail to deliver either procedural or distributive justice. Employees and managers alike find them time-consuming, stressful and ultimately unsatisfactory. Perhaps, more fundamentally, it has been argued that a 'resolution gap' has opened up in British workplaces. Saundry and Wibberley (2014) argue that this is a function of three factors discussed previously, and which run through the analysis of this book: the decline of employee representation and trade union organisation; the centralisation and consequent removal from the workplace of the human resource function; and the lack of confidence of line managers to whom responsibility for managing conflict has been devolved.

In this context, alternative processes of dispute resolution, and in particular workplace mediation, have become increasingly popular. This was helped by the active promotion of mediation in the 2007 Gibbons Report and its subsequent inclusion (for the first time) in the revised 2009 Acas Code of Practice on Discipline and Grievance, albeit only in the foreword. However, while mediation has become a tool for conflict resolution in a significant proportion of workplaces (Wood *et al*, 2014), this has tended to be limited to larger organisations, and there is some evidence that its use has begun to plateau. Furthermore, mediation is too often used as a 'last resort' to try and deal with problems that have not been addressed until they have escalated.

We would argue that mediation itself is not a panacea – organisations need to develop more systematic approaches to conflict management, accepting instead that conflict is an inevitable feature of organisational life and that the capacity to resolve it is an essential organisational function. In the USA, researchers have noted the development of integrated conflict management systems (ICMS) in which mediation is one part of a wider approach (Lipsky *et al*, 2012). These systems focus not only on resolving disputes but on equipping organisational stakeholders with the skills, capacity and processes to identify and resolve conflict at the earliest stage.

There is relatively little evidence that UK organisations are moving toward such strategic approaches. One notable exception is the case of Northumbria Healthcare Trust, which we highlighted in Chapter 11. One barrier to the adoption of greater innovation in conflict management may be the changes to employment regulation introduced by the Coalition Government. The introduction of employment tribunal fees has radically reduced the threat of employment litigation facing employers, but at the same time may also have reduced the incentives for employers to take conflict management and resolution more seriously.

## 16.6 THE ROLE OF SOCIAL MEDIA AND TECHNOLOGICAL CHANGE

Since the last edition of this book was published, the use of social media and the Internet both inside and outside the workplace has exploded. Much of the initial focus was on developing policies to respond to the potential for inappropriate use of such technologies while at work. This could typically include viewing offensive material, using the Internet for personal purposes during working hours or sending and circulating distasteful emails. In relation to such issues, much progress has been made – detailed guidance is now available from Acas and employers' associations and policies regulating the use of such technologies have been widely adopted.

More recently, however, matters have been complicated by the extent to which many employees are encouraged to use social media for professional purposes. Academics, for example, commonly use Twitter to promote their research and also use a range of social media to communicate with students. In such situations, the dividing lines between work and non-work can become increasingly blurred, and this poses particular problems for employment relations professionals. In particular, where professional and personal issues become intertwined, there is a significant potential for conflict (see Broughton *et al.*, 2010).

In recent research undertaken by one of the authors, social media was highlighted as a growing source of workplace conflict in two main respects: the first type of issue generally involved members of staff discussing work or making derogatory comments about their organisation or customers on social media platforms and were then disciplined for bringing the organisation into disrepute; disputes were also caused by existing problems at work escalating on social media or, alternatively, arguments and conflicts on social media then leading to a deterioration of relationships at work.

One of the main challenges that employment relations professionals face in dealing with such disputes is that social media provides a space where complex conflicts can be created and can escalate extremely quickly. Furthermore, they can exert very little control over the situation – a minor issue that emerges during work can have mushroomed by the time staff return the following day, and by which time any resolution will be extremely difficult.

This also relates to the wider impact of the use of electronic media in day-to-day workplace interactions. The prevalence of email also provides a forum in which bullying and abusive behaviours can flourish. Email (and other forms of social media) arguably depersonalises communication, making individuals feel able to say things that they would not be able to in person. In addition, email lacks any context so that messages can be easily misconstrued, leading to conflict between colleagues. However, at a more basic level, the use of technology arguably reduces the need for social interaction, leading to a formalisation of communication, and also provides a way in which managers who lack confidence can avoid talking directly to their staff.

In our view, this has major implications for employment relations. We have seen throughout this book that key features of effective managerial practice are: good communication; participation in decision-making; the facilitation of employee voice; the development of high-trust relations; and early identification of, and action on, problems. All these require managers to be able to talk to their staff, which in turn suggests a much broader appreciation of how email, social media and other Internet technologies are used by all members of the organisation.

In conclusion, we hope that you have found the new and updated version of our book of value, and that it has given you greater insight into both the theory and practice of employment relations. As the renowned management writer, Karl Lewin (1945), once said, 'nothing is as practical as a good theory'. We have been guided by this adage in the design of our book. In this summary chapter we have sought to highlight and concisely review what for us are likely to be the key issues and change drivers that will face practitioners tasked with the management of employment relations in the coming years.

For us, the employment relationship remains the key building block of the organisation. Therefore, its effective management is paramount to achieving the overall aims of that organisation. As Sisson argues, 'employment relations matter ... [because] it makes the employment relationship and its "governance" the central focus' (2010: vi). We would argue that this is more important than ever today given the challenges outlined previously. Managing the employment relationship is ultimately a political activity, in the sense that power is exercised by one set of parties and contested by others. A key theme of the book is that conflict is an inevitable part of the employment relationship. However, recognising this does not reflect organisational weakness or failure – instead, it underlines the necessity of developing structures and processes through which the interests of employees can be voiced and represented, and equips managers with the capability to reconcile these interests with the aims and objectives of the organisation.

# References

ABC (2015) *Protests, strikes on the rise in China*. Available at: http://www.abc.net.au/news/2015–04–15/china-workers-protest-outside-ibm-factory-reutersjpg/6394454 [Accessed 8 October 2015].

ACAS (1997) *Guide for small firms: dealing with grievances.* London: Acas.

ACAS (2005) *Evaluation of the Acas pilot of mediation, appeals and employment law visit services to small firms.* London: Acas.

ACAS (2009) *Code of practice on disciplinary and grievance procedures.* London: Acas.

ACAS (2009) *Managing conflict at work.* London: Acas.

ACAS (2011) *Annual report and accounts, 2010–2011.* London: Acas.

ACAS (2011) *Mediation explained.* London: Acas.

ACAS (2013) *Individual mediation: feedback from participants and commissioners.* Acas Research Paper, No 7/13. London: Acas.

ACAS (2014) *Bullying and harassment at work.* London: Acas.

ACAS (2014) *Discipline and grievance at work: the Acas guide.* London: Acas.

ACAS (2014) *Employee communications and consultation.* London: Acas.

ACAS (2014) *Front-line managers' booklet.* London: Acas.

ACAS (2014) *Handling large-scale redundancies.* London: Acas.

ACAS (2014) *The people factor – engage your employees for business success.* London: Acas.

ACAS (2015) *Code of practice on discipline and grievance procedures.* London: Acas.

ACAS (2015) *Discipline and grievances at work: the Acas guide.* London: Acas.

ACAS /CIPD (2013) *Mediation: an approach to resolving workplace issues.* London: Acas.

ACAS and Infogroup/ORC International (2010) *Evaluation of the first year of Acas' pre-claim conciliation service.* Acas Research Paper, No 08/10. London: Acas.

ADAM, D., PURCELL, J. and HALL, M. (2014) *Joint consultative committees under the Information and Consultation of Employees Regulations: a WERS analysis.* Acas Research Paper, No 04/14. London: Acas.

ADDISON, J.T. and SIEBERT, W.S. (1991) The social charter of the European Community: evolution and controversies. *ILR Review.* Vol 44, No 4. pp597–625.

ALFES, K., TRUSS, C. and SOANE, E. (2010) *Creating an engaged workforce: findings from the Kingston Employee Engagement Consortium project.* London: CIPD.

ANDERSON, V. (2013) *Research methods in human resource management: investigating a business issue.* London: CIPD.

ANSOFF, H.I. (1991) Critique of Henry Mintzberg's 'The design school': reconsidering the basic premises of strategic management. *Strategic Management Journal.* Vol 12, No 6. pp449–461.

ANTCLIFF, V. and SAUNDRY, R. (2009) Accompaniment, workplace representation and disciplinary outcomes in British workplaces – just a formality? *British Journal of Industrial Relations.* Vol 47, No 1. pp100–121.

ASHMAN, I. (2012) *Downsizing envoys: a public/private sector comparison.* Acas Research Paper, No 11/12. London: Acas.

ASHMAN, I. (2013) The face-to-face delivery of downsizing decisions in UK public sector organizations: the envoy role. *Public Management Review,* published first online in March, DOI: 10.1080/14719037.2013.785583.

ASTON CENTRE FOR HUMAN RESOURCES (2008) *Strategic human resources management: building research-based practice.* London: CIPD.

AUBREY-JOHNSON, K. and CURTIS, H. (2012) *Making mediation work for you: a practical handbook.* London: Legal Action Group.

BACCHETTA, M., ERNST, E. and JUANA, P. (2009) *Globalisation and informal jobs in developing countries.* Geneva: WTO Publications.

BACH, S. (2010) Public sector employment relations: the challenge of modernisation. In COLLING, T. and TERRY, M. (eds). *Industrial relations: theory and practice.* 3rd ed. Oxford: Wiley.

BACH, S., GIVAN, R. and FORTH, J. (2009) The public sector in transition. In BROWN, W., BRYSON, A. and FORTH, J. (eds). *The evolution of the modern workplace.* Cambridge: Cambridge University Press.

BACON, N. (2013) Industrial relations. In WILKINSON, A. and REDMAN, T. (eds). *Contemporary human resource management: text and cases.* 4th ed. Harlow: Pearson Education.

BALOGUN, J., HAILEY V. and STUART, R. (2014) *Landing transformational change.* London: CIPD.

BARBER, B. (2014) Do organisations expect too much of line managers? *Personnel Today.* 3 June.

BARRIENTOS, S. and SMITH, S. (2007) Do workers benefit from ethical trade? Assessing codes of labour practice in global production systems. *Third World Quarterly.* Vol 28, No 4. pp713–729.

BEAUMONT, P.B. and HUNTER, L.C. (2003) *Information and consultation: from compliance to performance.* London: CIPD.

BECKETT, F. and HENCKE, D. (2009) *Marching to the fault line: the miners' strike and the battle for industrial Britain.* London: Constable.

BEHREND, H. (1957) The effort bargain. *Industrial and Labour Relations Review.* Vol 10, No 4. pp503–515.

BENNETT, T. (2010) Employee voice initiatives in the public sector: views from the workplace. *International Journal of Public Sector Management.* Vol 23, No 5. pp444–455.

BENNETT, T. (2013) Workplace mediation and the empowerment of disputants: rhetoric or reality? *Industrial Relations Journal.* Vol 44, No 2. pp189–209.

BENNETT, T. (2014a) Do union–management learning partnerships reduce workplace conflict? *Employee Relations.* Vol 36, No 1. pp17–32.

BENNETT, T. (2014b) The role of workplace mediation: a critical assessment. *Personnel Review.* Vol 43, No 5. pp764–779.

BERCUSSON, B. (1996) *European labour law.* London: Butterworths.

BINDMAN, G. (2012) *White male judges: the Supreme Court and judicial diversity.* Available at: https://www.opendemocracy.net/ourkingdom/geoffrey-bindman/white-male-judges-supreme-court-and-judicial-diversity [Accessed 5 October 2015].

BINGHAM, L. and PITTS, D. (2002) Highlight of mediation at work: studies of the National REDRESS Evaluation Project. *Negotiation Journal.* Vol 18, No 2. pp135–146.

BIS (2011) *Resolving workplace disputes: government response to the consultation.* London: Department for Business, Innovation and Skills.

BIS (2015) Trade union membership 2014. *Statistical Bulletin.* June. London: BIS.

BLANDEN, J. and MACHIN, S. (2003) Cross-generation correlations of union status for young people in Britain. *British Journal of Industrial Relations.* Vol 41, No 3. pp391–415.

BLOMGREN BINGHAM, L., HALLBERLIN, C., WALKER, D. and CHUNG, W. (2009) Dispute system design and justice in employment dispute resolution: mediation at the workplace. *Harvard Negotiation Law Review.* Vol 14, No 1. pp1–50.

BLYTH, A. (2003) The art of survival. *People Management.* Vol 9, No 9. pp38–40.

BLYTON, P. and TURNBULL, P. (2004) *The dynamics of employee relations.* 3rd ed. Basingstoke: Palgrave Macmillan.

BOOTH, A. (1989) What do unions do now? *Discussion Papers in Economics.* No. 8903. Brunel University.

BOSWELL, W.R. and OLSON-BUCHANAN, J.B. (2004) Experiencing mistreatment at work: the role of grievance-filing, nature of mistreatment and employee withdrawal. *Academy of Management Journal.* Vol 47. pp129–139.

BOXALL, P. and PURCELL, J. (2011) *Strategy and human resource management.* 3rd ed. Basingstoke: Palgrave Macmillan.

BRATTON, J. and GOLD, J. (2015) Towards critical human resource management education (CHRME): a sociological imagination approach. *Work, Employment and Society.* Vol 29, No 3. pp496–507.

BRAVERMAN, H. (1974) *Labor and monopoly capital: the degradation of work in the twentieth century.* New York: Monthly Review Press.

BRITISH CHAMBERS OF COMMERCE (2011) *The workforce survey – small businesses.* October. London: British Chambers of Commerce.

BROUGHTON, A. (2011) *Workplaces and social networking – the implications for employment relations.* Acas Research Paper, No 11/11. London: Acas.

BROUGHTON, A., HIGGINS, T. and HICKS, B. (2010) *Workplaces and social networking – the implications for employment relations.* Acas Research Paper, No 11/11. London: Acas.

BROWN, A. (1995) *Organisational culture.* London: Pitman Publishing.

BROWN, W., BRYSON, A. and FORTH, J. (2008) Competition and the retreat from collective bargaining. *NIESR Discussion Paper*, No 318, August.

BRYSON, A. and GOMEZ, R. (2003) Why have workers stopped joining unions? *CEP Discussion Papers.* Centre for Economic Performance, LSE.

BUDD, J. and BHAVE, D. (2008) Values, ideologies, and frames of reference in industrial relations. In: BLYTON, P., HEERY, E. and BACON, N. (eds) *SAGE handbook of industrial relations.* London: SAGE.

BURGESS, S., PROPPER, C. and WILSON, D. (2000) Explaining the growth in the number of applications to industrial tribunals 1972–1997. *Employment Relations Research Series.* No 10. London: Department of Trade and Industry.

BURKE, T. (2015) *A new deal at work – the ICE regulations 10 years on.* Available at: http://www.ipa-involve.com/news/ [Accessed 6 July 2015].

BURNES, B. (1996) *Managing change: a strategic approach to organisational dynamics.* London: Pitman.

BUSCHA, F., URWIN, P. and LATREILLE, P. (2012) *Representation in employment tribunals: analysis of 2003 and 2008 SETA.* Acas Research Paper, No 06/12, London: Acas.

BUSH, R. and FOLGER J. (2005) *The promise of mediation: responding to conflict through empowerment and recognition.* San Francisco: Jossey Bass.

CASEBOURNE, J., REGAN, J. and NEATHEY, F. (2006) Employment rights at work – survey of employees. *Employment Relations Research Series.* No 51. London: DTI.

CASSELL, C. (2013) Managing diversity. In REDMAN, T. and WILKINSON, A. (eds). *Contemporary human resource management.* 4th ed. London: Pearson Education Ltd.

CAULKIN, S. (2001) The time is now. *People Management.* Vol 7, No 17. August.

CBI (2013) *On the up – CBI Accenture employment trends survey, 2013.* London: CBI.

CBI (2015) *What do we do?* Available at: News.cbi.org.uk/about/ [Accessed 25 June 2015].

CEBR and PINSENT MASONS (2014) *China invests West – can Chinese investment be a game-changer for UK infrastructure? A Pinsent Masons global infrastructure sector strategic insight report.* London: Pinsent Masons.

CERTIFICATION OFFICE FOR TRADE UNIONS AND EMPLOYERS' ASSOCIATIONS (2015) *Annual report of the Certification Officer 2014–2015.* Available at: https://www.gov.uk/government/uploads/system/uploads/attachment_data/file/449387/CO_Annual_Report__2014-2015_.pdf [Accessed 29 September 2015].

CHARLWOOD, A. and ANGRAVE, D. (2014) *Worker representation in Great Britain 2004–2011: an analysis based on the Workplace Employment Relations Study.* Acas Research Paper, No 3/14. London: Acas.

CHARLWOOD, A. and FORTH, J. (2009) Employee representation. In BROWN, W., BRYSON, A. and FORTH, J. (eds). *The evolution of the modern workplace.* Cambridge: Cambridge University Press.

CHARLWOOD, A. and TERRY, M. (2007) 21st-century models of employee representation: structures, processes and outcomes. *Industrial Relations Journal.* Vol 38, No 4. pp320–337.CHINA LABOUR BULLETIN (2015) *Worker unrest in China's factories reaches new heights in third quarter.* Available at: http://www.clb.org.hk/en/content/worker-unrest-china%E2%80%99s-factories-reaches-new-heights-third-quarter [Accessed 8 October 2015].

CINGANO, F. (2014) Trends in income inequality and its impact on economic growth. *OECD Social, Employment and Migration Working Papers,* No 163. Paris: OECD Publishing. Available at: http://dx.doi.org/10.1787/5jxrjncwxv6j-en# [Accessed 14 September 2015].

CIPD[AP1] (2008) *Workplace mediation: how employers do it.* London: CIPD.

CIPD (2010) *Employee outlook: year review* London: CIPD.

CIPD (2011) *Conflict management – survey report.* London: CIPD.

CIPD (2011) *Workplace mediation: how employers do it.* London: CIPD.

CIPD (2013) *Employee engagement.* Factsheet. London: CIPD.

CIPD (2013) *Organising HR for partnering success.* London: CIPD.

CIPD (2013) *Real-life leaders – closing the knowing–doing gap.* London: CIPD.

CIPD (2014) *Absence management.* Annual survey report. London: CIPD.

CIPD (2014) *The CIPD profession map: our professional standards v2.4.* London: CIPD.

CIPD (2014) *Employee outlook: spring review.* London: CIPD.

CIPD (2014*) Employee outlook: autumn 2014.* London: CIPD.

CIPD (2014) *Industrial strategy and the future of skills policy – the high road to sustainable growth.* Research insight. London: CIPD.

CIPD (2015) *Conflict management: a shift in direction?* Research report. London: CIPD.

CLARK, B. (2013) Mediation and employment disputes. In BUSBY, N., MCDERMONT, M. and ROSE, E. (eds). *Access to justice in employment disputes: surveying the terrain.* Liverpool: Institute of Employment Rights.

CLEGG, H. (1975) Pluralism in industrial relations. *British Journal of Industrial Relations.* Vol 13, No 3. pp309–316.

CLEGG, H.A. (1976) *The system of industrial relations in Great Britain.* Southampton: Camelot Press Ltd.

COLLING, T. (2004) No claim, no pain? The privatization of dispute resolution in Britain. *Economic and Industrial Democracy.* Vol 25, No 4. pp555–579.

COLLINS[AP2] , H. (2000) Recent case. Note. Finding the right direction for the 'industrial jury'. *Haddon* v *Van den Bergh Foods Ltd/Midland Bank plc* v *Madden*. *Industrial Law Journal*. Vol 29, No 3. pp288–296.

COX, A., MARCHINGTON, M. and SUTER, J. (2007) Embedding the provision of information and consultation in the workplace: a longitudinal analysis of employee outcomes in 1998 and 2004. *Employment Relations Series*. No 72. London: DTI.

COX, A., ZAGELMEYER, S. and MARCHINGTON, M. (2006) Embedding employee involvement and participation (EIP) at work. *Human Resource Management Journal*. Vol 16, No 3. pp250–267.CRAWLEY, J. (2012) *From argument to agreement: resolving disputes through mediation*. John Crawley Mediation.

CRIBB, J., EMMERSON, C. and SIBIETA, L. (2014) Public sector pay in the UK. *IFS Report R97*. London: Institute of Fiscal Studies.

CROUCH, C. (2010) British industrial relations: between security and flexibility. In COLLING, T. and TERRY, M. (eds). *Industrial relations: theory and practice*. 3rd ed. Chichester: John Wiley.

DANIELS, K. (2016) *Introduction to Employment Law: Fundamentals for HR and Business Students*. 4th ed. London: CIPD.

DARLINGTON, R. (2009) Leadership and union militancy: the case of the RMT. *Capital & Class*. Vol 33, No 99. pp3–32.

DAVIES, P. and FREEDLAND, M. (2007) *Towards a flexible labour market: labour legislation and regulation since the 1990s*. Oxford: Oxford University Press.

DEAKIN, S. and MORRIS, G. (2005) *Labour law*. Oxford: Oxford University Press.

DICKENS, L. (1994) The business case for equal opportunities: is the carrot better than the stick? *Employee Relations*. Vol 16, No 8. pp5–18.

DICKENS, L. (1999) Beyond the business case: a three-pronged approach to equality action. *Human Resource Management Journal*. Vol 9, No 1. pp9–19.DICKENS, L. (2007) The road is long: thirty years of equality legislation in Britain. *British Journal of Industrial Relations*. Vol 45, No 3. pp463–494.

DICKENS, L. (ed.) (2012) *Making employment rights effective: issues of enforcement and compliance*. Oxford: Hart Publishing.

DICKENS, L. (2012) Employment tribunals and ADR. In DICKENS. L. (ed.) *Making employment rights effective: issues of enforcement and compliance*. Oxford: Hart Publishing.

DICKENS, L. and HALL, M. (2010) The changing legal framework of employment relations. In COLLING, D. and TERRY, M. (eds). *Industrial relations: theory and practice*. Oxford: Wiley-Blackwell.

DIX, G., FORTH, J. and SISSON, K. (2009) Conflict at work: the changing pattern of disputes. In BROWN, W., BRYSON, A. and FORTH, J. (eds). *The evolution of the modern workplace*. Cambridge: Cambridge University Press.

DRIFFIELD, N., LOVE, J. and LANCHEROS, S. (2013) *How attractive is the UK for future manufacturing foreign direct investment?* London: BIS.

DROMEY, J. (2014) *MacLeod and Clarke's concept of employee engagement: an analysis based on the Workplace Employment Relations Study.* Acas Research Paper, No 8/14. London: Acas.

DROMEY, J. and BROADBELT, G. (2012) *Releasing voice for sustainable business success.* London: IPA and Tomorrow's Company.DTI (1996) *The Social Chapter – the British and continental approaches.* London: DTI.

DTI (2002) *High performance workplaces: the role of employee involvement in a modern economy.* London: DTI.

DTI (2003) *High performance workplaces: informing and consulting employees.* London: DTI.

DUNDON, T. and ROLLINSON, D. (2011) *Understanding employment relations.* 2nd ed. London: McGraw-Hill Higher Education.

DUNDON, T. and WILKINSON, A. (2013) Employee participation. In WILKINSON, A. and REDMAN, T. (eds). *Contemporary human resource management: text and cases.* 4th ed. Harlow: Pearson Education Ltd.

DUNDON, T., DOBBINS, T. and CULLINANCE, N. (2014) Employer occupation of regulatory space of the Employee Information and Consultation (I&C) Directive in liberal market economies. *Work, Employment and Society.* Vol 28, No 1. pp21–39.

DUNDON, T., WILKINSON, A. and MARCHINGTON, M. (2004) The meanings and purpose of employee voice. *International Journal of HRM.* Vol 15, No 6. pp1149–1170.

DUNLOP, J.T. (1958) *Industrial relations systems.* New York: Holt.

EATON, J. (2000) *Comparative employment relations.* Cambridge: Polity.

EDWARDS, P. (1986) *Conflict at work.* Oxford: Blackwell.

EDWARDS, P. (1994) Discipline and the creation of order. In SISSON, K. (ed.). *Personnel management: a comprehensive guide to theory and practice in Britain.* Oxford: Blackwell.

EDWARDS, P. (1995) Strikes and industrial conflict. In EDWARDS, P. (ed.). *Industrial relations: theory and practice in Britain.* Oxford: Blackwell.

EDWARDS, P. (2000) Discipline: towards trust and self-discipline? In BACH, S. and SISSON, K. (eds). *Personnel management: a comprehensive guide to theory and practice in Britain.* 3rd ed. Oxford: Blackwell.

EDWARDS, P. (2003) The employment relationship and the field of industrial relations. In EDWARDS, P. (ed.). *Industrial relations.* 2nd ed. Oxford: Blackwell.

EDWARDS, T. and WALSH, J. (2009) Foreign ownership and industrial relations in the UK. In BROWN, W., BRYSON, A. and FORTH, J. (eds) *The evolution of the modern workplace.* Cambridge: Cambridge University Press.

EEF (2014) *Backing Britain: a manufacturing base for the future.* London: EEF.

ETUI (2015) *Collective bargaining: the framework.* Available at: www.worker-participation.eu/National-Industrial-Relations/Countries/UK/Collectivebargaining [Accessed 25 June 2015].

EUROPEAN ECONOMIC COMMISSION (1993) *White paper on growth, competitiveness and employment*. Brussels: EC.

EWING, K. (1989) *Britain and the ILO*. London: Institute of Employment Rights.

EWING, K. and HENDY, J. (2012) Unfair dismissal law changes – unfair? *Industrial Law Journal*. Vol 41, No 1. pp115–121.

FARNHAM, D. (2010) *Human resource management in context: strategy, insights and solutions*. 3rd ed. London: CIPD.

FAWCETT SOCIETY (2105) *The gender pay gap*. Available at: http://www.fawcettsociety. org.uk/our-work/campaigns/gender-pay-gap/ [Accessed 4 October 15].

FAYOL, H. (1990) General principles of management. In PUGH, D.S. (ed.). *Organization theory*. 3rd ed. London: Penguin Group.

FLANDERS, A. (1970) *Management and unions: the theory and reform of industrial relations*. London: Faber.

FORTH, J., BEWLEY, H. and BRYSON, A. (2006) *Small and medium-sized enterprises: findings from the Workplace Employment Relations Survey 2004*. London: Routledge.

FOWLER, A. (1993) *Redundancy*. London: Institute of Personnel and Development.

FOX, A. (1974) *Beyond contract: work, power and trust relations*. London: Faber.

FOX, A. (1985) *Man mismanagement*. 2nd ed. London: Hutchinson & Co. Ltd.

FREDMAN, S. (2011) The public sector equality duty. *Industrial Law Journal*. Vol 40, No 4. pp405–427.

FREEMAN, R. and PELLETIER, J. (1990) The impact of industrial relations legislation on British union density. *British Journal of Industrial Relations*. Vol 28, No 2. pp141–164.

FROBEL, F., HEINRICHS, J. and KREYE, O. (1980) *The new international division of labour*. Cambridge: Cambridge University Press.

GALL, G. (2007) Trade union recognition in Britain: an emerging crisis for trade unions? *Economic and Industrial Democracy*. Vol 28, No 1. pp97–109.

GALLIE, D., FELSTEAD, A. and GREEN, F. (2013). *Fear at work in Britain – first findings from the Skills and Employment Survey, 2012*. Available at: http://www.cardiff.ac. uk/socsi/ses2012/[hidden]resources/4.%20Fear%20at%20Work%20Minireport.pdf [Accessed 13 November 2015].

GAPPER, J. (1990) At the end of the honeymoon. *Financial Times*. 10 January.

GEARY, J. (1994) Task participation: employees' participation enabled or constrained? In SISSONS, K. (ed.). *Personnel management*. 2nd ed. Oxford: Blackwell.

GENNARD, J. (2008) The Vaxholm/Laval case: its implications for trade unions. *Employee Relations*. Vol 30, No 5. pp473–478.

GENNARD, J. (2009) Is social Europe dead? *Employee Relations*. Vol 30, No 6. pp589–593.

GENNARD, J. (2009) The financial crisis and employee relations. *Employee Relations.* Vol 31, No 5. pp451–454.

GIBBONS, M. (2007) *A review of employment dispute resolution in Great Britain.* London: DTI.

GILMAN, M. (2013) Reward management. In WILKINSON, A. and REDMAN, T. (eds). *Contemporary human resource management: text and cases.* 4th ed. London: Pearson Education Ltd.

GOURLAY, S., ALFES, K. and BUL, E. (2012) *Emotional or transactional engagement – does it matter?* Research insight. London: CIPD.

GREER, I. and HAUPTMEIER, M. (2015) Management whipsawing: the staging of labor competition under globalisation. *Industrial and Labor Relations Review*, accepted December 2014.

GRINT, K. (2005) *Leadership: limits and possibilities.* Houndmills: Palgrave Macmillan.

GUEST, D. (2004) The psychology of the employment relationship: an analysis based on the psychological contract. *Applied Psychology.* Vol 53, No 4. pp541–555.

GUEST, D. (2014) Employee engagement: fashionable fad or long-term fixture? In TRUSS, C., DELBRIDGE, R. and ALFES, K. (eds). *Employee engagement in theory and practice.* Abingdon: Routledge.

HALL, M. (1994) Industrial relations and the social dimension of European integration. In HYMAN, R. and FERNER, A. (eds). *New frontiers in European industrial relations.* Oxford: Blackwell.

HALL, M. and TERRY, M. (2004) The emerging system of statutory worker representation. In HEALY, G., HEERY, E. and TAYLOR, P. (eds). *The future of worker representation.* Basingstoke: Palgrave Macmillan.

HALL, M., HUTCHINSON, S. and PARKER, J. (2007) Implementing information and consultation: early experience under ICE regulations. *Employment Relations Research Series*, No 88. September. London: BERR.

HALL, M., HUTCHINSON, S. and PARKER, J. (2010) Information and consultation under the ICE regulations: evidence from longitudinal case studies. *Employment Relations Research Series*, No 117. London: BIS.

HALL, M., PURCELL, J. and HUTCHINSON, S. (2011) Promoting effective consultation? Assessing the impact of the ICE regulations. *British Journal of Industrial Relations.* Vol 51, No 2. pp355–381.

HALL, P. and SOSKICE, D. (2001) Introduction. In HALL, P. and SOSKICE, D. (eds). *Varieties of capitalism: the institutional foundations of comparative advantage.* Oxford: Oxford University Press.

HARLEY, B., HYMAN, J. and THOMPSON, P. (2005) *Participation and democracy at work.* Basingstoke: Palgrave Macmillan.

HATCH, M.J. (2012) *Organization theory: modern, symbolic and postmodern perspectives.* Oxford: Oxford University Press.

HAYES, L. and NOVITZ, T. (2013) *Trade unions and economic inequality.* Liverpool: Institute for Employment Rights.

HEERY, E. (2002) Partnership versus organising: alternative futures for British trade unionism. *Industrial Relations Journal.* Vol 33, No 1. pp20–35.

HEERY, E., HEALY, G. and TAYLOR, P. (2004) Representation at work: themes and issues. In HEALY, G., HEERY, E. and TAYLOR, P. (eds). *The future of worker representation.* Basingstoke: Palgrave Macmillan.

HEPPLE, B. (2005) *Labour laws and global trade.* Oxford: Blackwell.

HEPPLE, B. (2013) Back to the future: employment law under the coalition government. *Industrial Law Journal.* Vol 42, No 3. pp203–223.

HEPPLE, B. and MORRIS, G. (2002) The Employment Act 2002 and the crisis of individual employment rights. *Industrial Law Journal.* Vol 30, No 1. pp245–269.

HIRSCH, B. (2004) What do unions do for economic performance? *Journal of Labor Research.* Vol 25, No 3. pp415–455.

HM GOVERNMENT (2012) *Consultation on modern workplaces – the Parental Leave (EU Directive) Regulations 2013 – impact assessment.* November 2012.

HOFFMAN, R. and MERMET, E. (2001) European trade union strategies on Europeanisation of collective bargaining. In SCHULTEN, T. and BISPINCK, R. (eds). *Collective bargaining under the Euro.* Brussels: European Trade Union Institute.

HOLMES, C. and MAYHEW, K. (2012) *The changing shape of the UK job market and its implications for the bottom half of earners.* London: Resolution Foundation.

HOQUE, K. and BACON, N. (2015) Workplace union representation in the British public sector: evidence from the 2011 Workplace Employment Relations Survey. *Warwick Papers in Industrial Relations.* No 101. August.

HOWELL, C. (2000) From New Labour to no labour? The industrial relations project of the Blair government. *New Political Science.* Vol 22, No 2. pp201–229.

HUNTER, W. and RENWICK, D. (2009) Involving British line managers in HRM in a small non-profit organization. *Employee Relations.* Vol 31, No 4. pp398–411.

HURD, R. (2004) *The rise and fall of the organising model in the U.S.* Available at: http://digitalcommons.ilr.cornell.edu/articles/301/ [Accessed 19 October 2015].

HUTCHINSON, S. and PURCELL, J. (2010) Managing ward managers for roles in HRM in the NHS: overworked and under-resourced. *Human Resource Management Journal.* Vol 20, No 4. pp357–374.

HYMAN, R. (1975) *Industrial relations: a Marxist introduction.* Basingstoke: Macmillan.

HYMAN, R. (1984) *Strikes.* 3rd ed. London: Fontana Press.

HYMAN, R. (1987) Strategy or structure? Capital, labour and control. *Work, Employment and Society.* Vol 1, No 1. pp25–55.

HYMAN, R. (2010) British industrial relations: the European dimension. In COLLING, T. and TERRY, M. (eds). *Industrial relations: theory and practice.* 3rd ed. Chichester: John Wiley.

HYMAN, J. and MASON, B. (1995) *Managing employee involvement and participation*. London: Sage Publications.

INDUSTRIAL RELATIONS SERVICE (various dates) *Employment review: policy, practice and law in the workplace*.

INSTITUTE FOR FISCAL STUDIES (2015) *This government has delivered substantial spending cuts; big differences in parties' plans for next parliament*. Available at: http://election2015.ifs.org.uk/public-spending [Accessed 4 October 2015].

INSTITUTE OF PERSONNEL AND DEVELOPMENT (1997) *Employment relations into the twenty-first century: an IPD position paper*. London: IPD.

INSTITUTE OF PERSONNEL AND DEVELOPMENT (1997) *The impact of people management practices on business performance*. London: IPD.

INTERNATIONAL LABOUR ORGANIZATION (2013) *Bangladesh – seeking better employment conditions for better socioeconomic outcomes*. Available at: http://www.ilo.org/wcmsp5/groups/public/—dgreports/—dcomm/documents/publication/wcms_229105.pdf [Accessed 8 October 15].

IPA (2003) *Informing and consulting your workforce: B&Q – listening to the grass roots*. Case study No 3, Series 4. London: IPA.

IPA (2004) *Informing and consulting your workforce: United Welsh Housing Association*. Case study No 8, Series 4. London: Involvement and Participation Association.

IPA (2015) *Diverse voices – Northern Gas Networks*. June. London: IPA.

JAUMOTTE, F. and OSORIO BUITRON, C. (2015) Power from the people. *Finance & Development*. International Monetary Fund: 29–31.

JENKINS, M. and AMBROSINI, V. (2002) *Strategic management: a multi-perspective approach*. Basingstoke: Palgrave Macmillan.

JOHNSON, G., SCHOLES, K. and WHITTINGTON, R. *(2008) Exploring corporate strategy*. 8th ed. London: Prentice Hall.

JORDAN, E., THOMAS, A. and KITCHING, J. (2013) Employment regulation – part A: employer perceptions and the impact of employment regulation. *Employment Relations Research Series*. No 123. London: Department for Business, Innovation and Skills.

JUDGE, G. (2001) The judge who has to sit in judgment. *People Management*. Vol 7, No 23. p32.

KAHN-FREUND, O. (1972) *Labour and the law*. London: Stevens, for the Hamlyn Trust.

KARAMBAYYA, R., BRETT, J. and LYTLE, J. (1992) Effects of formal authority and experience on third-party roles, outcomes, and perceptions of fairness. *Academy of Management Journal*. Vol 35, No 2. pp426–438.

KAUFMAN, R. (ed). (2004) *Theoretical perspectives on work and employment relationships*. Ithaca: Cornell University Press.

KAY, J. (1993) *Foundations of corporate success*. Oxford: Oxford University Press.

KEASHLY, L. and NOWELL, B. (2011) Conflict, conflict resolution and bullying. In EINARSEN, S., HOEL, H. and ZAPF, D. (eds). *Bullying and harassment in the workplace:*

*development in theory, research and practice.* 2nd ed. Boca Raton, Florida: CRC Press, Taylor and Francis Group.

KELLER, B. (2003) Social dialogue – the state of the art after Maastricht. *Industrial Relations Journal.* Vol 34, No 5. pp411–429.

KELLER, B. (2005) Europeanisation at sectoral level: empirical results and missing perspectives. *Transfer: European Review of Labour and Research.* Vol 11, No 3. pp397–408.

KELLY, J. (1998) *Rethinking industrial relations: mobilization, collectivism and long waves.* London: Routledge.

KELLY, J. (2004) Social partnership agreements in Britain: labor co-operation and compliance. *Industrial Relations: A Journal of Economy and Society.* Vol 43. pp267–292.

KERR, C., DUNLOP, J. and HARBISON, F. (1960) *Industrialism and industrial man.* Cambridge: Harvard University Press.

KERSLEY, B., ALPIN, C. and FORTH, J. (2006) *Inside the workplace: findings from the 2004 Workplace Employment Relations Survey.* London: Routledge.

KING, J. (2015) The left-wing case for leaving the EU. *New Statesman.* 11 June. Available at: http://www.newstatesman.com/politics/2015/06/john-king-left-wing-case-leaving-eu – [Accessed 16 November 2015].

KINNIE, N., HUTCHINSON, S. and PURCELL, J. (2005) Satisfaction with HR practices and commitment to the organisation – why one size does not fit all. *Human Resource Management.* Vol 15, No 4. pp9–20.

KIRTON, G. and GREENE, A. (2005) *The dynamics of managing diversity.* 2nd ed. Oxford: Elsevier Butterworth Heinemann.

KIRTON, G. and HEALY, G. (2013) Commitment and collective identity of long-term union participation: the case of women union leaders in the UK and USA. *Work, Employment and Society.* Vol 27, No 2. pp195–21.

KNIGHT, K. and LATREILLE, P. (2000) Discipline, dismissals and complaints to employment tribunals. *British Journal of Industrial Relations.* Vol 38, No 4. pp533–555.

KRESSEL, K. (2006) Mediation revisited. In DEUTSCH, M. and COLEMAN, P. (eds). *The handbook of constructive conflict resolution: theory and practice.* San Francisco: Jossey Bass.

KULAR, S., GATENBY, M. and REES, C. (2008) Employee engagement: a literature review. *Kingston Business School Kingston University working paper series.* No 19.

KURUVILLA, S. and VERMA, A. (2006) International labor standards, soft regulation and national government roles. *Journal of Industrial Relations.* Vol 48, No 1. pp41–58.

LATREILLE, P. (2011) *Mediation: a thematic review of Acas/CIPD evidence.* Acas Research Paper, No 13/11. London: Acas.

LATREILLE, P. and SAUNDRY, R. (2014) Mediation. In ROCHE, W., TEAGUE, P. and COLVIN, A. (eds). *The Oxford handbook on conflict management.* Oxford: Oxford University Press.

LATREILLE, P. and SAUNDRY, R. (2015) *Towards a system of conflict management?* Acas Research Paper, No 03/15. London: Acas.

LATREILLE, P., BUSCHA, F. and CONTE, A. (2012) Are you experienced? SME use of and attitude towards workplace mediation. *International Journal of Human Resource Management*. Vol 23, No 3. pp590–606.LEAT, M. (2006) *Exploring employee relations – an international approach.* Oxford: Butterworth Heinemann.

LEGGE, K. (2005) *Human resource management: rhetorics and realities.* London: Palgrave.

LEWIN, K. (1945) The research center for group dynamics at Massachusetts Institute of Technology. *Sociometry.* Vol 8. pp126–135.LEWIS, G. (2015) *Academics warn union crackdown could harm workplace productivity.* Available at: www.cipd.co.uk/pm/peoplemanagement/b/weblog/archive/2015/07/21/ [Accessed 10 October 2015].

LEWIS, G. (2015) Is this the end of strikes? *People Management.* August. Available at: http://www.cipd.co.uk/pm/peoplemanagement/b/weblog/archive/2015/07/23/is-this-the-end-of-strikes.aspx [Accessed 5 October 2015].

LEWIS, P. (1993) *The successful management of redundancy.* Oxford: Blackwell.

LEWIS, D. and SARGEANT, M. (2009) *Essentials of employment law.* 10th ed. London: CIPD.

LEWIS, D. and SARGEANT, M. (2013) *Employment law: the essentials.* 12th ed. London: CIPD.

LEWIS, R., DONALDSON-FIEDLER, E. and THARA, T. (2012) *Managing for sustainable employee engagement – developing a behavioural framework.* London: CIPD.

LIEBMANN, M. (2000) History and overview of mediation in the UK. In LIEBMANN, M. (ed.). *Mediation in context.* London: Jessica Kingsley Publishers.

LIPSKY, D. (2007) Conflict resolution and the transformation of the social contract. *Labor and Employment Relations Association Series Proceedings of the 59th Annual Meeting.* 5–7 January. Chicago, Illinois.

LIPSKY, D.B. and SEEBER, R.L. (2000) Resolving workplace disputes in the United States: the growth of alternative dispute resolution in employment relations. *Alternative Dispute Resolution in Employment.* Vol 2. pp37–49.

LIPSKY, D.B., AVGAR, A.C. and LAMARE, J.R. (2012) *The antecedents of workplace conflict management systems in U.S. corporations: evidence from a new survey of Fortune 1000 companies.* Mimeo.

LOON, M. and STUART, R. (2014) *LD: new challenges and new approaches.* Research report. London: CIPD.

LUCY, D. and BROUGHTON, A. (2011) Understanding the behaviour and decision-making of employees in conflicts and disputes at work. *Employment Relations Research Series.* No 119.

LYNCH, J.F. (2001) Beyond ADR: a systems approach to conflict management. *Negotiation Journal.* Vol 17, No 3. pp207–216.

MACHIN, S. (2000) Union decline in Britain. *British Journal of Industrial Relations.* Vol 38, No 4. pp631–645.

MACLEOD, D. and CLARKE, N. (2009) *Engaging for success: enhancing performance through employee engagement: a report to government.* London: Department for Business, Innovation and Skills.

MARCHINGTON, M. (2005) Employee involvement patterns and explanations. In HARLEY, B., HYMAN, J. and THOMPSON, P. (eds). *Participation and democracy at work – essays in honour of Harvie Ramsay.* Basingstoke: Palgrave Macmillan.

MARCHINGTON, M. (2015) Analysing the forces shaping employee involvement and participation (EIP) at organisation level in liberal market economies (LMEs). *Human Resource Management Journal.* Vol 25, No 1. pp1–18.

MARCHINGTON, M. and WILKINSON, A. (2005) Direct participation and involvement. In BACH, S. (ed.). *Managing human resources: personnel management in transition.* Oxford: Blackwell Publishing Ltd.

MARCHINGTON, M. and WILKINSON, A. (2012) *Human resource management at work.* 5th ed. London: CIPD.

MARCHINGTON, M., COX, A. and SUTER, J. (2007) *Embedding the provision of information and consultation in the workplace.* London: DTI.

MARCHINGTON, M., GOODMAN, J. and WILKINSON, A. (1992) *New developments in employee involvement.* Employment Department Research Series, Employment Department Publication, No 2.

MARCHINGTON, M., WILKINSON, A. and ACKERS, P. (1993) Waving or drowning in participation? *Personnel Management.* March. pp46–50.

MARCHINGTON, M., WILKINSON, A. and ACKERS, P. (2001) *Management choice and employee voice.* London: CIPD.MARESCHAL, P. (2003) Solving problems and transforming relationships: the bifocal approach to mediation. *American Review of Public Administration.* Vol 33. pp423–448.

MARGINSON, P. and MEARDI, G. (2010) Multinational companies: transforming national industrial relations. In COLLING, T. and TERRY, M. (eds). *Industrial relations – theory and practice.* 3rd ed. Chichester: John Wiley.

MARGINSON, P. and SISSON, K. (2002) European integration and industrial relations: a case of convergence and divergence. *Journal of Common Market Studies.* Vol 40, No 4. pp671–692.

MARGINSON, P. and SISSON, K. (2004) *European integration and industrial relations.* Basingstoke: Palgrave Macmillan.

MARSDEN, R. (1982) Industrial relations: a critique of empiricism. *Sociology.* Vol 16, No 2. pp232–250.

MARSH, A. and GILLIES, J.G. (1983) *The involvement of line and staff managers in industrial relations in industrial relations and management strategy.* THURLEY, K. and WOOD, S. (eds). Cambridge: Cambridge University Press.

MARTIN, J. (2001) *Organizational culture: mapping the terrain.* London: Sage Publications.

MASLOW, A.H. (1943) A theory of human motivation. *Psychological Review.* Vol 50, No 4. pp370–396.

McBRIDE, J. and GREENWOOD, I. (2009) *Community unionism: a comparative analysis of concepts and contexts.* Basingstoke: Palgrave Macmillan.

McLOUGHLIN, I. and GOURLAY, S. (1994) *Enterprise without unions: industrial relations in the non-union firm.* Buckinghamshire: Oxford University Press.

MELTZ, N.M. (1991) Sectoral realignment in Canada: shifting patterns of output and employment and the consequences for labour-management relations. In WILLIS, E.B. (ed.). *Industrial restructuring and industrial relations in Canada and the United States.* Kingston: Industrial Relations Centre, Queen's University.

METCALF, D. (2005) Trade unions: resurgence or perdition? An economic analysis. In FERNIE, S. and METCALF, D. (eds). *Trade unions: resurgence or demise.* London: Routledge. pp83–117.

MILLER, J. (2012) *Achieving sustainable organisation performance through HR in SMEs.* London: CIPD.

MILLWARD, N., BRYSON, A. and FORTH, J. (2000) *All change at work.* London: Routledge.

MILLWARD, N., STEVENS, M. and SMART, D. (1992) *Workplace industrial relations in transition.* Aldershot: Dartmouth.

MINISTRY OF JUSTICE (2011) *Employment tribunals and EAT statistics, 2010–11.* London: Ministry of Justice.

MINTZBERG, H. (1987) Crafting strategy. *Harvard Business Review.* July–August. pp66–75.

MINTZBERG, H. (1990) The manager's job: folklore and fact. In PUGH, D.S. (ed.). *Organization theory.* London: Penguin Group.

MINTZBERG, H. (1994) Rethinking strategic planning part 1: pitfall and fallacies. *Long-Range Planning.* Vol 27. pp312–321.

MOORE, S., TASIRAN, A. and JEFFERYS, S. (2008) The impact of employee representation upon workplace industrial relations outcomes. *Employment Relations Research Series.* No 87. London: BERR.

MORRIS, G. (2012) The development of statutory employment rights in Britain and enforcement mechanisms. In DICKENS, L. (ed.). *Making employment rights effective: issues of enforcement and compliance.* Oxford: Hart Publishing.

MULLER, F. and PURCELL, J. (1992) The Europeanization of manufacturing and the decentralization of bargaining: multinational management strategies in the European automobile industry. *International Journal of Human Resource Management.* Vol 3, No 1. pp15–24.

MULLER-JENTSCH, W. (2004) Theoretical approaches to industrial relations. In KAUFMAN, R. (ed.). *Theoretical perspectives on work and employment relationships.* Ithaca: Cornell University Press.

MULLINS, L.J. (2010) *Management and organizational behavior.* 9th ed. Harlow: FT, Prentice Hall.

MURPHY, N. (2009) Managing the survivor syndrome during and after redundancies. *IRS Employment Review*. London: Industrial Relations Services.

NGAI, P. (2005) Global production, company codes of conduct, and labour conditions in China: case study of two factories. *The China Journal*. Vol 54. pp101–113.

NOLAN, P. and WALSH, J. (1995) The structure of the economy and labour market. In EDWARDS, P. (ed.). *Industrial relations: theory and practice in Britain*. Oxford: Blackwell.

O'DEMPSEY, D., ALLEN, A. and BELGRAVE, S. (2001) *Employment law and the human rights act*. Bristol: Jordan Publishing.

OECD (2013) *FDI in figures*, April 2013. Available at: http://www.oecd.org/daf/inv/FDI%20in%20figures.pdf [Accessed 8 May 2015].

OFFICE FOR NATIONAL STATISTICS (2015) *Labour disputes annual article, 2014*. London: ONS.

OLSON-BUCHANAN, J. and BOSWELL, W. (2008) An integrative model of experiencing and responding to mistreatment at work. *Academy of Management Review*. Vol 33, No 1. pp76–96.

O'REILLY, J., SMITH, M. and DEAKIN, S. (2015) Equal pay as a moving target: international perspectives on forty years of addressing the gender pay gap. *Cambridge Journal of Economics*. Vol 39, No 2. pp299–317.

OXENBRIDGE, S. and BROWN, W. (2004) Achieving a new equilibrium? The stability of co-operative employer–union relationships. *Industrial Relations Journal*. Vol 35, No 5. pp388–402.

OXFAM INTERNATIONAL (2010) Better jobs in better supply chains. *Briefings for Business*. No 5. Available at: https://www.oxfam.org/sites/www.oxfam.org/files/b4b-better-jobs-better-supply-chains.pdf [Accessed 16 October 2015].

OXFAM INTERNATIONAL (2013) *The cost of inequality: how wealth and income extremes hurt us all*.

Oxfam Media Briefing. 18 January. Available at: https://www.oxfam.org/sites/www.oxfam.org/files/cost-of-inequality-oxfam-mb180113.pdf [Accessed 13 November 2015].

PETERS, M., SEEDS, K. and HARDING, C. (2010) Findings from the Survey of Employment Tribunal Applications 2008. *Employment Relations Research Series*. No 107. London: Department of Business, Innovation and Skills.

PFEFFER, J. (1998) *The human equation: building profits by putting people first*. Boston: Harvard Business School Press.

PICKARD, J. (2001) When push comes to shove. *People Management*. Vol 7, No 23. 22 November. pp30–35.

PODRO, S. and SUFF, R. (2009). *The alchemy of dispute resolution – the role of collective conciliation*. Acas Policy Discussion Papers. London: Acas.

POLLERT, A. and CHARLWOOD, A. (2009) The vulnerable worker in Britain and problems at work. *Work, Employment and Society*. Vol 23, No 2. pp343–362.

POOLE, M. (1986) *Industrial relations: origins and patterns of national diversity*. New York: Routledge and Kegan Paul.

PORTER, M. (1985) *Competitive advantage: creating and sustaining superior performance*. New York: Free Press.

PURCELL, J. (1987) Mapping management styles in employee relations. *Journal of Management Studies*. Vol 24, No 5. pp533–548.

PURCELL, J. (2010) *Building employee engagement*. Policy Discussion Paper, January. London: Acas.

PURCELL, J. (2012) The limits and possibilities of employee engagement. *Warwick Papers in Industrial Relations*. No 96. April. Industrial Relations Research Unit, University of Warwick.

PURCELL, J. (2012) The management of employment rights. In DICKENS, L. (ed.). *Making employment rights effective: issues of enforcement and compliance*. Oxford: Hart Publishing. PURCELL, J. (2014) Disengaging from engagement. *Human Resource Management Journal*. Vol 24, No 3. pp241–254.

PURCELL, J. and HALL, M. (2012) *Voice and participation in the modern workplace: challenges and prospects*. London: Acas.

PURCELL, J. and HUTCHINSON, S. (2007) Front-line managers as agents in the HRM–performance causal chain: theory, analysis and evidence. *Human Resource Management Journal*. Vol 17, No 1. pp3–20.

PURCELL, J. and KINNIE, N. (2007) HRM and business performance. In BOXALL, P., PURCELL, J. and WRIGHT, P. (eds). *The Oxford handbook of human resource management*. Oxford: Oxford University Press.

PURCELL, J. and SISSON, K. (1983) Strategies and practice in the management of industrial relations. In BAIN, G. (ed.). *Industrial relations in Britain*. London: Blackwell.

PURCELL, J., KINNIE, N. and HUTCHINSON, S. (2003) *Understanding the people and performance link: unlocking the black box*. London: CIPD.

PURCELL, J., KINNIE, N. and SWART, J. (2009) *People management and performance*. London: Routledge.

RAHIM, N., BROWN, A. and GRAHAM, J. (2011) *Evaluation of the Acas code of practice on disciplinary and grievance procedures*. Acas Research Paper, No 06/11. London: Acas.

RAINBIRD, H. and STUART, M. (2011) The state and the union learning agenda in Britain. *Work, Employment and Society*. Vol 25, No 2. pp202–217.

RAINNIE, A. (1989) *Industrial relations in small firms*. London: Routledge.

RAM, M., EDWARDS, P. and GILMAN, M. (2001) The dynamics of informality: employment relations in small firms and the effects of regulatory change. *Work, Employment and Society*. Vol 15, No 4. pp856–861.

RAMSAY, H. (1977) Cycles of control: worker participation on sociological and historical perspectives. *Sociology*. Vol 11, No 3. pp481–586.

RAMSAY, H. (1980) Phantom participation: patterns of power and conflict. *Industrial Relations Journal*. Vol 11, No 3. pp46–59.

RAMSAY, H. (1996) Involvement, empowerment and commitment. In TOWERS, B. (ed.). *The handbook of human resource management*. 2nd ed. Oxford: Blackwell.

RAMSAY, H., SCHOLARIOS, D. and HARLEY, B. (2000) Employees and high-performance work systems: testing inside the black box. *British Journal of Industrial Relations*. Vol 38, No 4. pp501–531.

RANIERI, N. (2010) *Collective consultation on redundancies*. Acas Discussion Paper. London: Acas.

RAYTON, B., DODGE, T. and D'ANALEZE, G. (2012) *The evidence: employee engagement task force 'nailing the evidence' workgroup*. Available at: http://www.engageforsuccess.org/ideas-tools/employee-engagementthe-evidence/ [Accessed 12 August 2015].

REDMAN, T., WILKINSON, A. and PANDEY, A. (2013) Downsizing. In WILKINSON, A. and REDMAN, T. (eds). *Contemporary human resource management*. 4th ed. Harlow: Pearson Education Ltd.

RENTON, D. and MACEY, A. (2013) *Justice deferred: a critical guide to the Coalition's employment tribunal reforms*. Liverpool: Institute of Employment Rights.

RENWICK, D. (2003) Line managers' involvement in HRM: an inside view. *Employee Relations*. Vol 25, No 3. pp262–280.

RENWICK, D. (2013) Line managers and HRM. In WILKINSON, A. and REDMAN, T. (eds). *Contemporary human resource management: text and cases*. 4th ed. Harlow: Pearson Publishing Ltd.

RHODES, C. and SEAR, D. (2015) The motor industry: statistics and policy. *House of Commons Library Briefing Paper,* No 00611, August.

RICKARDS, T. and CLARK, M. (2006) *Dilemmas of leadership*. Abingdon: Routledge.

RIDLEY-DUFF, R. and BENNETT, T. (2011) Mediation: developing a theoretical framework for understanding alternative dispute resolution. *Industrial Relations Journal*. Vol 42, No 2. pp106–123.

ROBINSON, D. and HAYDAY, S. (2009) *Engaging managers*. London: Institute of Employment Studies.

ROCHE, W. and TEAGUE, P. (2012) The growing importance of workplace ADR. *International Journal of Human Resource Management*. Vol 23, No 3. pp447–458.

ROLLINSON, D., HOOK, C. and FOOT, M. (1996) Supervisor and manager styles in handling discipline and grievance. Part two – approaches to handling discipline and grievance. *Personnel Review*. Vol 25, No 4. pp38–55.

ROUSSEAU, D. (1995) *Psychological contracts in organisations: understanding written and unwritten agreements*. Thousand Oaks: Sage.

SAKS, A. (2006) Antecedents and consequences of engagement. *Journal of Managerial Psychology*. Vol 21, No 7. pp600–619.

SALAMON, M. (2001) *Industrial relations: theory and practice*. London: Pearson Education Ltd.

SANDERS, D. (2012) *Placing trust in employee engagement*. London: Acas.

SAPIR, A. (2006) Globalization and the reform of European social models. *Journal of Common Market Studies*. Vol 44, No 2. pp369–390.

SARIDAKIS, G., SEN-GUPTA, S. and EDWARDS, P. (2008) The impact of enterprise size on employment tribunal incidence and outcomes: evidence from Britain. *British Journal of Industrial Relations*. Vol 46, No 3. pp469–499.

SAUNDRY, R. (2012) *Conflict resolution and mediation at Bradford MDC: a case study*. Acas Research Paper, No 08/12. London: Acas.

SAUNDRY, R. and DIX, G. (2014) Conflict resolution in the UK. In ROCHE, W., TEAGUE, P. and COLVIN, A. (eds). *The Oxford handbook on conflict management*. Oxford: Oxford University Press.

SAUNDRY, R. and WIBBERLEY, G. (2012) *Mediation and early resolution: a case study in conflict management*. Acas Research Paper, No 12/12. London: Acas.

SAUNDRY, R. and WIBBERLEY, G. (2014) *Workplace dispute resolution and the management of individual conflict – a thematic analysis of five case studies*. Acas Research Paper, No 06/14. London: Acas.

SAUNDRY, R., ADAM, D. and ASHMAN, I. (2016) *Managing individual conflict in the workplace – the role of Acas advice and guidance*. Acas Research Paper (forthcoming).

SAUNDRY, R., ANTCLIFF, V. and JONES, C. (2008) *Accompaniment and representation in workplace discipline and grievance*. Acas Research Paper, No 06/08. London: Acas.

SAUNDRY, R., BENNETT, T. and WIBBERLEY, G. (2013) *Workplace mediation: the participant experience*. Acas Research Paper, No 2/13. London: Acas.

SAUNDRY, R., JONES, C. and ANTCLIFF, V. (2011) Discipline, representation and dispute resolution – exploring the role of trade unions and employee companions in workplace discipline. *Industrial Relations Journal*. Vol 42, No 2. pp195–211.

SAUNDRY, R., LATREILLE, P., and DICKENS, L. (2014) *Reframing resolution – managing conflict and resolving individual employment disputes in the contemporary workplace*. Acas Policy Series. London: Acas.

SAUNDRY, R., MCCARDLE, L. and THOMAS, P. (2011) *Transforming conflict management in the public sector: mediation, trade unions and partnership in a PCT*. Acas Research Paper, No 1/11. London: Acas.

SAUNDRY, R., MCARDLE, L. and THOMAS, P. (2013) Reframing workplace relations? Conflict resolution and mediation in a primary care trust. *Work, Employment and Society*. Vol 27, No 2. pp213–231.

SCHEIN, E. (1978) *Career dynamics*. Reading, Mass: Addison Wesley.

SCHEIN, E.H. (1985) *Organizational culture and leadership*. New York: Jossey Bass.

SILVERMAN, M., BAKHSHALIAN, E. and HILLMAN, L. (2013) *Social media and employee voice: the current landscape*. London: CIPD.

SIMMS, M. and HOLGATE, J. (2010) Organising for what? Where is the debate on the politics of organising? *Work, Employment and Society*. Vol 24, No 1. pp157–168.

SIMMS, M., HOLGATE, J. and HEERY, E. (2013) *Union voices – tactics and tensions in UK organizing*. Ithaca, NY: ILR Press.

SISSON, K. (2010) *Employment relations matters*. Available at: www2.warwick.ac.uk/fac/soc/wbs/research/irru/ [Accessed 19 October 2015].

SISSON, K. and PURCELL, J. (2010) Management: caught between competing views of the organisation. In COLLING, T. and TERRY, M. (eds). *Industrial relations – theory and practice*. 3rd ed. Chichester: John Wiley.

SMITH, R. (1983) Work control and management prerogatives in industrial relations. In THURLEY, K. and WOOD, S. (eds). *Industrial relations and management strategy*. Cambridge: Cambridge University Press.

SPARROW, P. (1998) New organisational forms, processes, jobs and psychological contracts. In SPARROW, P. and MARCHINGTON, M. (eds). *Human resource management: the new agenda*. London: Pitman/Financial Times.

SPARROW, P. and MARCHINGTON, M. (1998) *Human resource management: the new agenda*. London: Pitman/Financial Times.

STANDING, G. (2011) *The precariat: the new dangerous class*. London: Bloomsbury Academic.

STEPHENS, C. (2015) Are HR business partners a dying breed? *People Management*. February. p36.

STREDWICK, J. and ELLIS, S. (1998) *Flexible working practices: techniques and innovations*. London: IPD.

STREECK, W. (1997) Industrial citizenship under regime competition: the case of the European works' councils. *Journal of European Public Policy*. Vol 4, No 4. pp643–664.

STREECK, W. (1991) On the institutional conditions of diversified quality production. In MATZNER, E. and STREECK, W. (eds). *Beyond Keynesianism: socioeconomics of production and full employment*. Aldershot: Edward Elgar.

STUART, M. and MARTINEZ LUCIO, M. (eds). (2005) *Partnership and modernisation in employment relations*. London: Routledge.

STUART, M., CUTTER, J. and COOK. H. (2013) Who stands to gain from union-led learning in Britain? Evidence from surveys of learners, union officers and employers. *Economic and Industrial Democracy*. Vol 34, No 2. pp227–246.

TAILBY, S. and WINCHESTER, D. (2000) Management and trade unions: towards social partnership? In BACH, S. and SISSON, K. (eds). *Personnel management – a comprehensive guide to theory and practice*. 3rd ed. Oxford: Blackwell.

TAYLOR, P. and BAIN, P. (1999) An assembly line in the dead – work and employee relations in the call centre. *Industrial Relations Journal*. Vol 30, No 2. pp101–117.

TAYLOR, S. and EMIR, A. (2006) *Employment law: an introduction*. Oxford: Oxford University Press.

TEAGUE, P. and DOHERTY, L. (2011) Conflict management systems in non-union multinationals in the Republic of Ireland. *International Journal of Human Resource Management.* Vol 21, No 1. pp57–71.

TEAGUE, P. and ROCHE, W. (2012) Line managers and the management of workplace conflict: evidence from Ireland. *Human Resource Management Journal.* Vol 22, No 3. pp235–251.

TERRY, M. (2010) Employee representation. In COLLING, T. and TERRY, M. (eds). *Industrial relations – theory and practice.* Oxford: Wiley.

THOMPSON, P. and McHUGH, D. (2009) *Work organisations: a critical approach.* 3rd ed. Basingstoke: Palgrave Macmillan.

TILLY, C. (1978) *From mobilization to revolution.* Reading: Addison-Wesley.

TODOR, W.D. and OWEN, C.L. (1991) Deriving benefits from conflict resolution: a macrojustice approach. *Employee Responsibilities and Rights Journal.* Vol 4, No 1. pp37–49.

TOWERS, B. (1997) *The representation gap: change and reform in the British and American workplace.* Oxford: Oxford University Press.

TRUSS, C., SHANTZ, A. and SOANE, E. (2013) Employee engagement, organisational performance and individual well-being: exploring the evidence, developing the theory. *International Journal of Human Resource Management.* Vol 24, No 14. pp2657–2669.

TRUSS, C., SOANE, E. and EDWARDS, C. (2006) *Working life: employee attitudes and engagement.* London: CIPD.

TUC (2002) *Partnership works.* London: Trades Union Congress.

TUC (2015) *Burnout Britain.* Available at: https://www.tuc.org.uk/international-issues/ europe/workplace-issues/work-life-balance/15-cent-increase-people-working-more? utm_source=dlvr.it&utm_medium=twitter [Accessed 7 October 2015].

TUC/ACAS (2010) *Mediation: a guide for trade union representatives.* London: TUC/ Acas.

TURNER, L. and WINDMULLER, J.P. (1998) Convergence and diversity in international and comparative industrial relations. In NEUFELD, M.F. and McKELVEY, J.T. (eds). *Industrial relations at the dawn of the new millennium.* Ithaca: Cornell University Press.

TYLER, R. (2006) Victims of our history? Barbara Castle and In Place of Strife. *Contemporary British History.* Vol 20, No 3. pp461–476.

UKTI (2014) *Inward investment report 2013/14.* London: UKTI.

ULRICH, D. (1997) Human resource champion: the next agenda for adding value and delivering results. *Harvard Business Review.* Vol 76, No 1. pp124–134.

ULRICH, D. (2015) The new HR operating model is all about relationships, not partners. *People Management.* April. Available at: http://www.cipd.co.uk/pm/peoplemanagement/b/ weblog/archive/2015/03/24/the-future-of-hr-is-about-relationships.aspx [Accessed 23 July 2015].

ULRICH, D. and BROCKBANK, W. (2005) *The HR value proposition.* Boston: Harvard Business School Press.

UNDY, R. (2008) *Trade union merger strategies: purpose, process and performance.* Oxford: Oxford University Press.

VAN WANROOY, B., BEWLEY H. and BRYSON, A. (2013) *Employment relations in the shadow of recession: findings from the 2011 Workplace Employment Relations Study.* London: Palgrave Macmillan.

WADDINGTON, J. and WHISTON, C. (1997) Why do people join unions in a period of membership decline? *British Journal of Industrial Relations.* Vol 35, No 4. pp515–546.

WAJCMAN, J. (2000) Feminism facing industrial relations in Britain. *British Journal of Industrial Relations.* Vol 38, No 2. pp183–201.

WALTON, R.E. (1985) From control to commitment in the workplace. *Harvard Business Review.* March–April. pp77–84.

WARD, D.A. and BECK, W.L. (1990) Gender and dishonesty. *Journal of Social Psychology.* Vol 130, No 3. pp333–339.

WATSON, S., MAXWELL, G. and FARQUHARSON, L. (2006) Line managers' views on adopting human resource roles: the case of Hilton (UK) Hotels. *Employee Relations.* Vol 29, No 1. pp30–49.

WATSON, T. (1995) *Sociology, work and industry.* 3rd ed. London: Routledge.

WATSON, T. (2006) *Organising and managing work.* 2nd ed. London: FT, Prentice Hall.

WEDDERBURN, LORD (1995) *Labour law and freedom.* London: Lawrence and Wishart.

WEDDERBURN, LORD (1997) Consultation and collective bargaining in Europe. *Industrial Law Journal.* Vol 26, No 1. pp339–53.

WELBOURNE, T. (2011). Engaged in what? So what? A role-based perspective for the future of employee engagement. In WILKINSON, A. and TOWNSEND, K. (eds). *The future of employment relations: new paradigms, new developments.* Basingstoke: Palgrave Macmillan.

WELLS, K. (2003) The impact of the framework employment directive on UK disability discrimination law. *Industrial Law Journal.* Vol 32, No 4. pp253–273.

WHITE, M., HILL, S. and MILLS, C. (eds) (2004) *Managing to change? British workplaces and the future of work.* Basingstoke: Palgrave Macmillan.

WHITTAKER, S. and MARCHINGTON, M. (2003) Devolving HR responsibility to the line: threat, opportunity or partnership. *Employee Relations.* Vol 23, No 3. pp245–261.

WILKINSON, A. (2001) Employment. In REDMAN, T. and WILKINSON, A. (eds). *Contemporary human resource management: text and cases.* London: FT, Prentice Hall.

WILLIAMS, S. (2014) *Introducing employment relations – a critical approach.* 3rd ed. Oxford: Oxford University Press.

WILLIAMS, S. and ADAM-SMITH, D. (2010) *Contemporary employment relations: a critical introduction.* Oxford: Oxford University Press.

WILLS, J. (2004) Trade unionism and partnership in practice: evidence from the Barclays-Unifi agreement. *Industrial Relations Journal.* Vol 35, No 4. pp329–343.

WILLS, J. and SIMMS, M. (2004) Building reciprocal community unionism in the UK. *Capital & Class.* Vol 82. pp59–84.

WINTOUR, P. (2015) Cameron to include employment law opt-out in EU membership negotiations. *Guardian.* 11 July.

WOOD, S., SAUNDRY, R. and LATREILLE, P. (2014) *Analysis of the nature, extent and impact of grievance and disciplinary procedures and workplace mediation using WERS2011.* Acas Research Paper, No 10/14. London: Acas.

YARLAGADDA, R., DROMEY, J. and FANSHAWE, S. (2015) *Diverse voices – engaging employees in an increasingly diverse workforce.* London: IPA/Astar-Fanshawe.

YU, X. (2008) Impacts of corporate code of conduct on labor standards: a case study of Reebok's athletic footwear supplier factory in China. *Journal of Business Ethics.* Vol 81. pp513–529.

ZEITLIN, M. (1989) *The large corporation and contemporary classes.* Oxford: Polity Press.

ZHELTOUKHOVA, K. (2014) *Leadership: easier said than done.* London: CIPD.

# Index